The Amateur Naturalist: A Monthly Magazine For All Nature Students, Volumes 1-3

Anonymous

ON THE AROOSTOOK RIVER, NEAR CARIBOU, MAINE.

SEE PAGE 9.

The Amateur Naturalist.

"To him who in the love of Nature holds communion with her visible forms, she speaks a various language."

VOLUME 1.   BINGHAMTON, NEW YORK, JANUARY, 1904.   NUMBER 1.

EXTERMINATED BY MAN.

BY CHARLES D. PENDELL.

MAN, in the exercise of his divine perogative to "Subdue the earth and have dominion over it," has in some instances exceeded even his own anticipations and ere he was aware has succeeded in completely exterminating entire species of both birds and mammals. In some instances this may be accounted for by the limited habitat of the species or, in the case of carnivorous beasts, as a matter of defense from their rapacious habits; but these reasons will not hold in all cases. Among the birds which have been thus exterminated by man may be mentioned a species of starling, a crested parrot, an owl, small but of very peculiar appearance, and a species of dove; all that now remains to tell the story of their existence being a few widely scattered but almost priceless stuffed specimens in European museums: their voices stilled, their wings motionless,—the last representatives of their kind.

In the early part of the nineteenth century a pied duck of a species allied to the eider was very common in the New England states and was also found in large numbers along the St. Lawrence river. But today not a single specimen exists alive, the last known bird of its kind having been killed at Halifax, in 1852. Little did the sportsman who fired that gun realize that with his shot an entire species then ceased to exist.

There is abundant evidence that the Giant Auk was at one time very numerous and widely disseminated, fragments of its remains having been found in so remote a place as the ancient "kitchen middens" of Denmark. But within historical times it has been an occasional visitor to the British Isles, St. Kilda and the Orkneys. Its proper home, however, was in Iceland, the Faroes and Newfoundland, though it was by no means an infrequent visitor to our own New England coast, and in the days of Audobon was quite frequently seen here. The giant auk was a bird of noble appearance, standing about three feet high, of a dark color on its back and wings, being of a white or grayish color on its breast, and having a black bill of four or five inches in length. It laid but a single white egg, about three inches across by five in length, which was white in color and was deposited without any attempt at a nest on the bare rock near the sea-shore. Its wings were small and of no use whatever in flying and on land it was the personification of stupidity, suffering the sailors to approach and kill it without any attempt at escape: thus in Iceland, in 1574, it was taken by the boatload to replenish the larder of a whaling vessel. But in water it was quite another creature. Here its wings served to aid its short legs and powerful webbed feet in swimming. An attempt to capture one in 1821 by the crew of a six-oard boat has been recorded by Dr. Flemming who witnessed the event. The chase lasted several hours, the bird eluding every attepmt at capture and at times making a speed while under water exceeding the rate of a mile and one-half a minute. But the giant auk, too, is now numbered among the extinct birds, the last known survivors having been shot on the coast of Maine in 1844. Forty specimens are all that are now known to science, of which American museums possess but four.

But turning to the antipodes we are startled by the strange and grotesque forms presented, as well as at the titanic proportions attained by some of the recent but now extinct forms of ornithological life presented. First may be mentioned the Dodo. Of this nothing was positively known, not even its existence, until 1598 when the Dutch discovered the island of Mauritius. But in less than one hundred years from that time not one was left. In 1681 Benjamin Harry, an English sailor, made record in his journal of having seen one; but since that time it has never been seen. Fancy for an instant a pigeon somewhat larger than the largest swan, and of similar shape, but having a large black bill several inches in length, the upper mandible curved down over the lower, great scally legs, no wings or but a rudimentary developement, covered with dark gray feathers and another bunch on the tail, the rest of the body being covered with a soft yellowish down like that of a gosling, and you have a very fair idea of the appearance of the dodo. Before the advent of man its limited intelligence was sufficient to enable it to thrive where it had comparatively no enemies and could feed undisturbed on the luxuriant herbage of the tropical woods. But with the advent of man and with his dogs, the poor dodo stood but little chance and its awkward, if not imbecile stupidity, hastened the extermination of this clumsy flightless bird; and in just eighty-two years from the date of its discovery it had ceased to be numbered among living species. Only one stuffed specimen had been saved and this had been allowed to decay, so that in 1755 the curator of the museum in which it was preserved (Ashmoleum, Oxford, England) ordered it destroyed, a fact much to be regretted. They little imagined that this was the last specimen in existence and that the portions escaping their sentence were to become objects of the highest interest to the whole scientific world. The head and foot of this specimen and three other fragments in as many different museums were all that remained except a few pictorial drawings which had been made by early travelers, until 1866, when Mr. George Clark discovered in the peat of a pool in the island quite a number of bones of this now extinct bird. Coexistent with it was the Aphanapteryx imperialis, a bird resembling in shape and size the cassowary but whose exquisite red silky plumage might vie with the handsome birds of the present era.

About three hundred miles east of Mauritius is the small island of Rodriguez, about fifteen miles long and six miles wide, which until 1691 was uninhabited. Peculiar to this semi-tropical island was the Solitaire, a genus in some slight respects resembling the dodo, but having a smaller bill and longer legs. The only species that represented this genus has become extinct in very recent times, as it was very abundant at the beginning of the eighteenth century. Its weight was about 45 pounds and in height it was somewhat taller than a turkey, and its neck, longer in proportion, was carried proudly erect. Its wings were useless for flight, but were probably capable of being used as weapons of defense, the bone at its extremity being large, round and hard. Its tail was an odd freak of nature, it being a mere wad or ball of feathers, placed at the caudal extremity seemingly for no other reason than that there was no where else to put them.

When the fossil footprints of certain biped were found in great numbers in the red sandstone formations in Connecticut which exceeded anything previously seen, scientists hesitated to admit that such enormous birds could have existed, even in those remote geological ages. But more recent research proves beyond a doubt that birds of even larger proportions have been coexistent with modern man.

The Dinornis, or Moa as it was called by the Maoris, who were the inhabitants of New Zealand at the time of its discovery by Tasman in 1642, existed in comparatively recent times; so recent at least that many traditions have been preserved in regard to this gigantic bird, and there is abundant evidence of its former existence. The moa was probably in general appearance similar to the emu of Australia or the cassowary of South America, but in size vastly exceeded them, the average specimen being twelve feet high, or twice the size of an ostrich; but specimens greatly exceeding this size have been found, the skeleton of the one in the College of Surgeons, in London, attaining the remarkable height of eighteen feet, while others of nearly as great size are to be found in other large museums. This height is the more notable when we take into consideration that it far exceeds that of any existing mammal with one exception—the giraffe. We can scarcely conceive of a bird attaining such a height, yet the undisputable evidence is furnished by their numerous skeletons, hundreds of which have been found. Not only tall but massive were these ornithological giants. The bone of a man's leg is only a spindle compared with those of this colossal bird. The bones of the toes (of which it had but three on each foot, the fourth or back toe being entirely lacking,) rival those of the elephant itself, and tracks made by this extraordinary pedel extremity have been found to measure twenty-two inches in length—larger even than the tracks aluded to which were found in the Connecticut sandstone. The dinornis may have lived as recently as the 17th century, though none have been seen alive since that time. The Maoris' traditions tell of great hunting expeditions in which the people turned out en masse to hunt the moa, and in many places the hillsides are strewn with its bones—the remains of the great feasts of the hunters. They have also been found in ancient cooking ovens, in some instances with fleshy ligaments still adhering and pieces of skin with feathers still attached. Eggs have also been found with the bones of the nearly hatched embryo within. In one instance an egg which measured 10 by 7 inches was taken from a grave where it rested in the hands of a human skeleton, hunting implements and weapons of war being also found.

With the dinornis one think the limits of size in bird life had been reached, but Madagascar comes forward with one which may have been even larger. This, however, must have been exterminated at a much earlier period, as but few of its bones have as yet been found, and the natives seem to have no record of it in their traditions. But to the comparative anatomist the few bones found sufficiently indicate a bird equal in height to the dinornis, and of a larger frame. This was the Epiornis and the remarkably large eggs which have outlived the skeleton of the bird that laid them attest the titanic dimensions of the parent. One of these eggs, now in the National Museum at Paris, measures 12¼ inches in length by 9½ in in width and the shell is ¾ of an inch thick. How great must have been the strength of the young "chick" to break its way into the world without! Another egg has been found somewhat larger than the foregoing, measuring 13½ inches in length—seven times as large as an ostrich's egg, and equal in bulk to 1,000 dozen eggs of the humming bird, which like a jewel bedecked sunbeam flits from flower to flower over our summer landscape.

When we consider that these birds have had an actual existence, and that, too, within so comparatively recent a period, the story of the roc in the tale of Sinbad the Sailor does not seem so incredible after all; and though these described were mostly deprived of the power of flight, may not the traditional knowledge of their existence have given birth to the thought embodied in the tale of fiction? But not alone is their very existence a cause of wonder, but also in the fact that instead of being found on continents, or even large islands, they inhabited small and isolated islands in the midst of a boundless tropical ocean. Perchance these are the remaining portions of the primeval continent on which the progenitors of these birds wandered at will o'er vast regions, while these few have survived through the countless ages on the peaks of that engulfed continent, antedating man's advent on earth by many cycles, back to the Fourth Day of creation, and since then undisturbed 'mid the rise and fall of continents and islands about them until exterminated by man.

The largest of flight birds is the California vulture or condor, measuring from tip to tip nine and a half to ten feet, exceeding considerably in size the true condor of South America. The bird lays but one egg each season—large, oval, ashy green in color, and deeply pitted—so distinctive in appearance that it cannot be confounded with any other. It is rapidly nearing extinction.

THE BOOKS OF NATURE.

BY A. BERGEN BROWE, D. D.

SOME of us from early childhood have been hearing about the book of nature, and happy indeed the child or youth whose attention is so called to the beauties of the world about them that a life-clinging impression is made. Personally I feel continuously grateful to dear parents who thus early directed my thoughts, for I am sure that I love God the more because of loving Nature as I do; but in passing moments of these later years I have come to look upon Nature as a library of illustrated volumes rather than a single book divided into departments, and I have also come to think that perchance the books of God to be opened in eternity, other than the one designated by its particular title, "The Book of Life," will be these ponderous volumes with their entrancing yet marvelous mysteries of which we as yet know so little, while so much remains unknown. It may be that a part of the employments of Heaven will be to look into this great library, and learn there that of which we never conceived, and each fresh item of knowledge gained will cause a fresh burst of song which will give glory and praise to the great Creator. The most eminent naturalists in the world, while indeed far beyond those who have never made any study of any special book of nature, are yet not so very far beyond the rudiments, and none are more aware of it than themselves; for in the study of nature the saying is particularly true that "the more one knows, the less he thinks he knows." Only the ignorant are conspicuously conceited. The forced warfare which the dabblers in science claimed between science and the Bible is no more. The conflict so loudly proclaimed half a century ago, but which never existed except in the minds and pronunciamentoes of those who understood but little of either, is unheard of now except it may be in some dying echo of the past. The great book of Geology which was especially supposed to demolish the truth and authenticity of the Bible, has proven to be most valuable in establishing its truth beyond a doubt, for none can gainsay the writing on the rocks and the imprints in clay and sand which corroborate the Written Word. It is of this one book that I especially write at this time—perhaps the least known and most recently opened of all the books. Of its utility to man in material things and its full value in leading the creature to adore the Creator when as a science it has had the years of study given to it that astronomy has, who will dare to tell? The latter needed to be enriched by the observation of many centuries and make its progress slowly through the way of unthinking prejudice before it came to be of real and acknowledged value to the race. The book of Geology has been opened but a brief time and yet what marvels it has unfolded and what wealth it has brought to the great household of humanity.

It is said that the time and money squandered in Great Britain alone, searching for coal in sections of the kingdom where the geologist could have informed the searchers that it was not, would pay twice over the entire cost of all the geological research of the world. Already the material value to man of geology exceeds that of astronomy, for its treasures are more surely within reach. It is much easier for us to dig than to fly, and the geologist informs us where to dig for success, not infallibly, but quite surely.

Educationally it is a wonderful book. Its testimony as to the beginning of things is not only deeply interesting but grandly marvelous. Through it we trace species and groups to their beginning, view their culminations and in some instances read in the records of rock and earth of their extinction. All animals and plants of the present had quite a recent beginning in geologic time, for as we turn the pages of the book with pick and spade and learn of the extinction of some previously existing forms we soon come to the print of the few forms of life of the Lower Cambrian strata and then the very next page below is the solitary barrenness of the Eozoon and we are now at the biblical second day of creation, learning that nothing known to geology is self creative, self-existent and eternal. The Book says there is a beginning, What is it? Where is it? Who is it? These are questions clamoring in the mind for a reply, for the geologist must think, and thinking will question and this is the basis of all real education.

If desired I will again contribute to the pages of this magazine, which has my best wishes and a hearty God-speed, for I believe it has a distinct and helpful mission in casting additional light on the beautiful books of God's great library. As a matter of further study allow me to suggest the progress from Eozoic time to present date.

ᘒ ᖫ

A thousand miles of mighty wood,
Where thunder-storms stride fire-shod;
A thousand plants at every rod,
A stately tree at every rood;
Ten thousand leaves to every tree,
And each a miracle to me,—
Yet there be men who doubt of God!

—*Joaquin Miller.*

ᘒ ᖫ

THE PURSUIT OF BOTANY.

BY WILLARD N. CLUTE.

THE terms flower gatherer, botanizer and botanist may stand for three distinct types of people interested in the vegetable kingdom. In youth we are all flower gathers, even the man whose sole interest in life, now-a-days, is the pursuit of the almighty dollar, was once a gatherer of wild-flowers, you may depend upon it, and it is possibly not to his credit that he has since lost his interest in so harmless and pleasant a pastime. In some cases he has not only lost his interest in such things but he has even come to look upon flower gathering as an employment befitting only women and children. Alas for him! He shall miss many pleasures in consequence. But to the man—or woman, either—who knows and is still interested in plants, shall be given extra powers of enjoyment. He shall take a greater zest in travel, whether to the next town or to a far country; he shall find friends and pleasant acquaintances among strangers; and he shall not be lonely in new places nor idle when work is done.

Flower-gathering, therefore, may be recommended to all—if it needs recommendation—for it is from the ranks of the flower-gatherers that the true botanists and botanizers come. This is an intimation that the flower-gatherer is not a botanist. Indeed, one may know the names of every showy flower in his vicinity and still have a very slender claim to the title. A knowledge of plant names is a very small and comparatively insignificant part of the science. It may be considered the first course in a series, that, completed, will make one a real botanist. To begin as a flower-gatherer, then, one can get no better book for his purpose than Mrs. Danas "How to Know the Wild-flowers." Miss Lounsberry's "Guide to the Wild-flowers" would probably come second.

There are many who gather flowers without ever trying to find out their names. But it is difficult to understand how anyone really alive can do so. No one should rest until he knows all the plants in his locality. This means not only the showy flowers, but also the weeds as those plants with inconspicuous flowers are called. In vain will the novice turn to his popular handbook for information on weeds. For this he must consult a botanical manual. Such books, however, are not pre-digested and he who consults such volumes must needs be familiar with technical terms—the language of the science. He must know the parts of the flower, the fruit, seed, leaf, branch, root and stem, their relationships and the terms that describe them and he must know how to use a "key" to the genera and species. Wood's "Class-book of Botany" is excellent for this purpose since it contains a full account of the plant as well as descriptions of the species in the Northeastern States. The beginner, working alone, can master this part of the science by its aid. Gray's "Manual" is the standard, but Wood's book is certainly best for the novice.

Thus far we have considered only the flowering plants. A botanist, however, should have at least a speaking acquaintance with that great group of flowerless plants represented by the ferns, mosses, hepatics, lichens, fungi, etc. It requires much special knowledge if one would go far in this direction and no single book attempts to deal with the entire list of plants, except in the most cursory way. In fact, so little known are many of the species that it is not easy to find literature concerning them.

After the botanist has become familiar with the appearance of the plants, he will, of course, wish to know how they are constructed. Until he does so he never can fully understand his subject, for function and structure are dependent upon each other and form upon both. For such information he will consult books like Atkinson's "Elementary Botany" or Goodalis "Physiological Botany." Since this part of the subject deals with life processes, it may be said in passing that the student should perform for himself the experiments outlined, if he would obtain the most good from his study.

And the botanizer? Well, strictly speaking, a botanizer is one who botanizes, and in view of the wide range of botanical studies the term may mean almost anything. Generally speaking, however, a botanizer is one of those contemplative individuals interested in plants as living things. Not every botanist can be a botanizer for it requires not only wisdom to perceive, but penetration to observe, energy to undertake, patience to carry out, exactness to guide and reason to judge. The subjects in the botanizer's category are those that have recently been assembled under the title of ecology—the relation of the plant in its surroundings—and when the botanist takes this turn, a new and unfamiliar field is opened to him in the midst of his own well-known locality. He begins to ask himself why plants are armed and why they possess perfumes or disagreeable odors; he is interested in the reason for every line and spot of color in the flower and in the cause that determined each curve or angle in the floral parts. He is interested in every device that plants have made use of in the struggle for existence, and along every roadside and in every field or wood finds something worth seeing. And so he becomes a flower-gatherer again, but one who gathers flowers with full understanding of their significance, and thus, like the youthful flower-gatherers, lives cheerfully and envies none.

ↄ ↄ

THE MANUSCRIPTS OF GOD.

BY HATTIE WASHBURN.

And Nature, the old nurse, took
The child upon her knee,
Saying, "Here is a story book
Thy Father has written for thee."

"Come, wander with me," she said,
"Into regions yet untrod;
And read what is still unread
In the manuscripts of God."—[*Longfellow.*

What has the author's pen portrayed that is not the faint echo of that which may be read from Nature, who holds the manuscripts of God where every blossom is a poem, an anthem, or a song which the wild bird carols from the waving bough beside the murmuring stream or on the grassy plain? What bard has written a sweeter song of love than the thrush trills in the soft hush of evening, while the well concealed and faithfully guarded nest tells of love of home and parental solicitude and fledglings with untried wings reveal their own simple tale of helpless innocence.

The rising sun with its burst of glory tells of the renewal of hope and endeavor; noon, of achievement and unremitting toil; and gentle evening, of peace and rest, when the sinking sun tints the western sky and paints the fleecy clouds with gold or crimson; the silent night, when from the dark azure vault of heaven, set with myriad shining orbs, looks down the radiant moon and gilds all things with silver, where may we read of greater mystery?

The roll of thunder, the vivid lightning's flash, the rush and roar of wind and rain portray the din and strife of battle. The quiet lake softly laving the reedy shore whispers of quietude.

In the moaning winds of Autumn with falling leaves and dying flowers is heard a dirge of inexpressable sadness. The winter landscape framed in skies of gray—innumberable are the thoughts we read from that vast unblotted page of snow. The gladsome spring when the tender buds unfold and the earth teems with life and joy renewed, is but a promise that the dead shall live again. The ripening fruit and ungarnered grain of summer time tell how the maker provides ever for his children.

All this and more I read from the manuscripts of God, writings as old as time but ever interesting, fresh and new.

ఆ ఌ

MAINE'S WOODS.

FEW persons realize the vast extent of the great woods of Maine, covering as they do one-half of the 29,895 square miles of the State, and exceeding seven times over the celebrated "Black Forest" of Germany. Probably no other locality of similar extent on the globe presents an equal area of forest, lake and river. The scenery is wild and beautiful. "Summer fills every nook with bright flowers and winter scatters everywhere fantastic creations of frost and snow." In these vast woods are more than 1,800 lakes of all sizes, their pure, pellucid waters teeming with fish, while the woods abound in game. In these lakes nearly 6,000 rivers and smaller streams take their rise, and combined with the lakes give a total of 3,200 square miles of water area. Mr. Charles Lenman writing a generation ago thus pleasingly describes this wilderness:

"The continuousness of the Maine woods * * * is one of the most impressive features; but behold with what exquisite taste aud skill nature interposes her relief! She plants old Moosehead near the center of the great forest, and scatters a thousand smaller gems of purest water on every side; bids a few mountain peaks rise up as watch-towers against the northern sky; sends the most beautiful rivers like flashes of light in every direction singing to the sea; and in a few localities spreads out those most wonderful fields which have been denominated 'oceans of moss,' sometimes several feet in thickness, and in one instance covering a space of many miles."

Around the lakes and along the water courses are a great variety of the more delicate and graceful trees, with shrubs and vines innumerable.

The Amateur Naturalist.

A Journal for those who Study Nature from a love of it.

ISSUED BI-MONTHLY.

SUBSCRIPTION, 50 CENTS PER YEAR.   SINGLE COPIES, 10 CENTS.

ADVERTISING RATES ON APPLICATION.

————EDITED AND PUBLISHED BY——— ——————

CHARLES D. PENDELL,

65 COURT STREET, - - - - BINGHAMTON, N. Y.

THE AMATEUR NATURALIST in making its salutatory bow should perhaps premise its entrance to the journalistic world with a few words as to the whyfore of its appearance and the purpose of its existence. It can hardly be called a new purpose as it has been an idea latent in the mind of its publisher for perhaps twenty years—ever since he left the study of the "three r's" in boyhood days and began his first collection of minerals—pebbles from a neighboring gravel bank. This was but the beginning of a study which developed with its continuation and the story of its progress will be left for further amplification in future issues of this magazine. But with the study of nature, thus begun, came a desire for literature on the subject—not too technical, but enough so to be useful to the amateur, collector and nature student. Such periodicals as were found embodied but partially the desired information and were mostly ephemeral in their existence.

Further experience and acquaintance has also convinced the publisher that most people are interested in the study of nature in some form or other, but are permeated with the idea that a real knowledge of the subject is beyond their reach—that it involves a laborious study of uninteresting data and long names, and yet a publication, interesting in its contents, accurate in information given, and within their scope of apprehension, devoted to natural history in its various branches would be welcomed by them. It is therefore to satisfy a desire which we have good reason to believe exists, and formerly at least personally shared, that this publication is issued. Judging by the many subscriptions received from our mere announcement of the intended publication of this journal, we have good reason to feel confident that we opined the situation rightly.

We shall not make any spread-eagle promises as to what we shall do, preferring to let each number be its own spokesman. The existence of THE AMATEUR NATURALIST does not depend upon the ordinary conditions in every respect. While we desire subscribers and no doubt shall make this desire known through our columns, it is no evidence of an impending suspension. This publication, though not published as a form of health tonic, is not wholly dependent for its continuation upon the number of subscriptions it receives; yet on the other hand its growth and development is.

Contributions are solicited. We do not promise to use all that may be sent, but will give all a careful reading and if in accord with our idea and purpose we shall gladly give them place. Otherwise Ms. will be returned when stamps are sent for that purpose. Articles that state facts interestingly will be given precedence over essays on generalities. Much of the current items in the daily and weekly press of the county is of itself interesting, and in some instances in our last pages we have culled and revamped some such articles worthy of a more permanent place of record than where we found them.

It was our intention originally to publish THE AMATEUR NATURALIST monthly. This intention has not been abandoned, but several unexpected circumstances have arisen which make it not impossible, but rather, unadvisable at the present time. We shall eventually assume the more dignified rank of a monthly, but for the present this journal will be issued as a bimonthly. That those who subscribed in advance may not feel that their confidence was misplaced we shall enter their subscription for two years; thus if during that time we change to the monthly publication (as is more than probable) they will be the recipients of the extra numbers, and in any event will receive the full twelve numbers. We trust this arrangement will be satisfactory, but if not the matter can easily be adjudicated by correspondence.

The ATLANTIC SLOPE NATURALIST in a recent number contains a descriptive list of the venomous and non-venomous snakes found in Pennsylvania and New Jersey, most if not all of which are found in New York State also. The list included twenty-three species, only two of which, the copperhead and the rattle-snake are venomous. It may be also of interest to add that the two listed as venomous produce their young alive while the others we believe without exception are oviparous.

THE AMATEUR NATURALIST is naturally anxious to build up a good subscription list—a desire for which many reasons might be adduced. However, as an inducement to those who would like to help us to attain that end we make this offer: Send us two subscriptions at fifty cents each—just a one dollar bill—and we will send you the magazine a year gratis for your effort. In other words we will send three subscriptions, if sent in at one time, for $1.

"The Making of an Herbarium," by Mr. Willard N. Clute, editor of *The American Botanist* and the *Fern Bulletin*, and author of a number of standard botanical works, is well under way, and we have no doubt but that by the time of our next issue it will have been completed, at which time full announcement will be made.

It may not be especially interesting to the general public, though to the editor it seems worthy of mention "as a matter of historical record," to note here that the first dollar received for subscription was from Dr. H. Beattie Brown, of Yonkers, N. Y.

Gems of the United States.

BY G. D. STORY.

IT is a remarkable circumstance that although this country is so rich in its mineral resources, and that the world draws from us a great part of its supply of the precious metals, we have so far discovered here only an insignificent quantity of precious stones.

Diamonds, it seems, have been found in various parts of the country but chiefly in California and North Carolina, though the largest diamond yet discovered here was dug up by a laborer, thirty or more years ago, in Manchester, Va. This stone, not at first recognized, originally weighed 23¾ carats, and when reduced by cutting, 11 11-16 carats, and it was deemed so valuable that at one time $6,000 was loaned on it, though because of its imperfections and undesirable color it is not worth more than a twentieth part of that sum. The California diamonds, found in fifteen or twenty different places, the most prolific being the Cherokee Flats, Butte County, are of all the colors known in the stone— white, yellow, straw and rose—but they are generally very small, ranging in value from $10 to $50 each.

Diamonds are always found in North Carolina in association with the flexible sandstone, called itacolumite, which is peculiar to that state, where, too, sapphires of notable brilliancy have appeared. A sapphire found at Jenk's mine, in Franklin County, is one of the finest known specimens of the emerald-green variety and because of its great rarity is probably worth $1,000. Fine specimens of chrysoberyl, a stone which sometimes is almost equal in appearance to the yellow diamond, and is principally obtained in Brazil and Ceylon, have been found in different parts of New England, New York and the Southern states, and the spinel, a beautiful gem which is often sold for oriental ruby, is distributed in the same way. The best crystals of topaz come from the Platte Mountains in Colorado, one of these, weighing 125 carats, being an extraordinarily fine gem. Only insignificant quantities of emeralds and beryls have been found within our boundaries, but garnets, which, although smaller, are equal to the best of Africa and Ceylon, are discovered on the Colorado River plateau. The amethyst is quite common in New England, and appears in several places in the Southern states. One specimen, found near Cheshire, in Connecticut, rivals in color the best amethyst of Siberia.

There are also many beautiful examples of less valuable stones which are in demand for cabinet collections.

The Mineral Hunters' Paradise.

From a few stray pages of an old magazine we glean the following in regard to Pescadero beach in California. We have no means of ascertaining the date of the magazine but probably similar conditions prevail at the present time.

Nearly all the varieties of quartz, chalcedony and opal are found on the Pescadero shore, except the iridescent, precious opal. Among the innumerable variety are seen the reddish brown jasper opal and a clear green stone—quite rare—erroneously termed "emerald." What is there called topaz, is probably a valuable yellow opal known as the false topaz, Chalcedony affords the beautiful red and pink carnelians that deepen in color with exposure to the sun, and also the moss agates found principally on Agate beach. Onyx, sardonyx and banded agates display their dark tones of gray, black and dull red, among the high lights of pearly moon stones, sparkling water crystals and the brilliant, fiery luster of the chatoyant opals. Stones closely resembling smoky quartz—very beautiful in their clear, deep tint —and others resembling rose quartz are sometimes found.

In addition to the gems mentioned, there is an infinite number of unclassified pebbles of every color, tint and shape. A curious and beautiful stone recently found on Pebble beach was of a clear bright yellow, half an inch long and shaped exactly like an acorn in the cup. Most of the stones are perfect in their natural state and well repay setting. The deposite varies with the tide. Where to-day lies a glinting bank of stones, to-morrow shines a clear stretch of sand, swept by the waves bare as a polished floor. First one beach and then another absorbs the attention of the collector, amateur and professional, who finds here an earthly paradise with its floor paved with gems. No other locality, perhaps, affords such unique facilities for the collection of these prized minerals, and in such abundance.

The Discoverer of Radium.

Mme. Sklodowsko Curie, whose remarkable work and discoveries in the radio active elements has created so much interest in the scientific as well as the nonscientific world, was born in Warsaw in 1867 and obtained her education in the college of that city. She subsequently studied in Paris, where she obtained a master's degree in both physics and mathematics. She married Professor Pierre Curie in 1895, since which time she has collaborated with him in his researches in physics and chemistry. She is not, however, merely a reflection of her husband, but has achieved great distinction along independent lines and has already made herself a name as one of the foremost of living scientists.

In 1900 Mme. Curie was appointed professor of physics in the State Normal school at Sevres. She has published two or three works on physical subjects. The Paris University conferred upon her the doctor's degree, the highest degree given in France.

One hundred and fourteen years ago the metal uranium was discovered. It was found in considerable quantity in the mineral pitchblende in Bohemia. In 1896 Professor Henri Becquerel discovered that salts of uranium emitted an "invisible radiation"—that is to say, possessed what chemists call radio activity. This is the property of constantly throwing off streams of infinitesimal particles that travel with inconceivable velocity. There was no doubt of the existence of these rays, for they went through metals and other solid bodies and produced images upon a photographic plate.

Mme. Curie was naturally interested in the radio activity of the salts of uranium and made experiments on her own account. She took pitchblende and separated its various chemical components. She found that some of these compounds exhibited radio activity in a more marked degree than even the extracted salts of uranium did.

She began a series of experiments on the refuse or slag of pitchblende after the uranium salts had been extracted, so as to make sure of what seemed to her a probability. Day after day in the off spells of housekeeping and looking after her little daughter she wrought with solvent and crucible. At last, enraptured, she found a new element which gave off the wonderful rays. Because of her native land — Poland — she named it polonium. And still the slag or by-produce of pitchblende, after the uranium and polonium had been extracted, gave off other chemical rays. There must still be some other substance, Mme. Curie concluded. Yet other experiments and radium itself, that marvelous thing, was discovered by Mme. Curie.

Secret of Roman Cement Re-discovered

Houses built of sand, but as substantial and durable as granite, have been made possible by a process just perfected in England by Mr. L. P. Ford, of Gresford, says the *American Inventor*.

A bed of clean sand and ground quicklime are all the materials needed for the new artificial rock. The ingredients are mixed in proper proportions mechanically and forced by a screw into a mold formed of a very strong steel cylinder. After the mold is filled it is placed in a box and the air it contains is sucked out by an air pump. Hot water is then admitted. The water rushes into every minute space and sets the particles of lime to slacking. The lime swells and causes a great pressure in the mold, while at the same time an intense heat is produced. Under the influence of the heat and pressure the sand and lime are molded into a rock which has sixty per cent. as much strength as the hardest granite. It is ready for use in eight hours.

The rock is of the same composition as the old Roman cement, the most durable of building materials. The secret of making this Roman cement has been lost for ages. The new building stone costs but 22 cents a cubic foot.

The Sources of Colors.

An interesting enumeration has been published in a technical trade journal of sources of color. From this it appears that the cochineal insects furnish the gorgeous carmine, crimson, scarlet-carmine and purple-lakes; the cuttle-fish gives sepia, that is, the inky fluid which the fish discharges in order to render the water opaque when attacked; the Indian yellow comes from the camel; ivory chips produce the ivory black and bone black; the exquisite Prussian blue comes from fusing horse hoofs and other refuse animal matter with impure potassium carbonate; various lakes are derived from roots, barks and gums; blue-black comes from the charcoal of the vine stock; Turkey red is made from the madder plant, which grows in Hindoostan; the yellow cap of a Siamese tree produces gamboge; raw sienna is the natural earth from the neighborhood of Siena, Italy; raw umber is an earth found near Umbria; India ink is made from burned camphor; mastic is made from the gum of the mastic tree, which grows in the Grecian archipelago; bister is the soot of wood ashes; very little real ultramarine, obtained from the precious lapis lazuli, is found in the market.

A Touch of Nature.

The old proverb. that "one touch of nature makes the whole world kin," was recently illustrated at the Zoological Garden in Lincoln Park, Chicago.

A gentleman gathered an armful of fresh, green catnip, and asked permission of the keeper to try the green stuff on the feline members of his family. The effect was marvelous. Before they reached the cage of the African leopard, he bounded from the shelf whereon he lay, apparently asleep, and stood expectant and alert, with brightened eyes, at the bars of the cage. When a handful of the catnip was passed through to the. door of the den the big cat pounced on it as though leaping on its prey. He ate a mouthful of the catnip, and then lay flat on his back and wriggle his sinnuous length through the green mass until his yellow, black-spotted hide was permeated with the odor of the plant from shoulders to

tail-tip. The big Indian tigers purred and mewed, and rolled about in the catnip like six-weeks-old kittens; while even the big lion ate it with dignified pleasure.

The Sea of Azov Disappearing.

The Sea of Azov is an inland lake, in the south of Russia, connected with the Black Sea by the long and narrow Strait of Kaffa. It has an area of about 14,000 square miles. Although sometimes regarded as an arm of the Black Sea, its water is nearly fresh. According to Associated Press dispatches, under date of December 16, 1903, the Sea of Azov is rapidly disappearing. The dispatch says: The Sea of Azov is disappearing and remarkable scenes are in course of enaction. At Tagandog the waters have receded to such an extent during the past five days that the bed of the sea is visible for a distance of several versts. (A verst is 3,500 feet.) High winds hurled clouds of sand shoreward covering the town. Vessels are lying high and dry and the greatest confusion prevails in the harbor. Work in the factories had to be reduced to a minimum, owing to lack of water.

Japan's Area.

The empire of Japan is composed of four large and three thousand small islands, forming an arc of a large circle extending from the northeast within a few miles of Kamchatka, southwest about 2,000 miles, and, with Formosa nearly 3,000 miles, from an arctic climate to one of perpetual spring and everlasting summer.

The Sensitive Plant.

BY LYMAN J. PENDELL.

THE sensitive plant is a name commonly given to a very delicate species of the *Mimosa* on account of the peculiar phenomena which is exhibited in their pinnæ or leaves and stalk when touched or shaken. All species of the *Mimosa* possess this singular property to a greater or less degree, but is more particularly noticeable in the half-shrubby, herbaceous plants, indigenous to our western prairies and also to the llanos of Brazil, where the stems are prickly, and some of the species possess small heads of beautiful rose-colored flowers. This plant is one of the most peculiar plants found in nature, and upon being approached in its wild state, lifts its head, seems to look at you very appealingly, and then drops suddenly, shrinking back in great alarm, its leaves and stem appearing to wilt under your raptured gaze. After you have passed on, the earth having ceased its vibration, the plant raises its head, quivering and trembling, as if not fully recovered from its shock, and in a few moments is all right again.

Beginnings of Plant Life.

The island of Krakatoa, on which all plant life was destroyed by the great volcanic eruption of 1883, is isolated from Java and Sumatra by twenty miles of water, and has given botanists a much prized opportunity for studying the birth of a new vegetation. The first observations were made by Dr. Treub after about three years. Microscopic algæ, which had covered the surface with a slimy layer, were decomposing the pumice stone, lava and ash into a suitable substratum for other plants, and about a dozen species of ferns were already abundant, while there were a few individuals of fifteen flowering plants. The reports of other German botanists who visited the island in 1897 have just been published. Very strangely, no more species of ferns were noted; but in all, sixty-two species of vascular plants were observed, including fifty flowering plants representing twenty-one natural orders. There were eight compositæ, six grasses and four orchids. A belt near the water was richest in species, while beyond were dense thickets of reeds and sugar cane, and the more thinly covered interior contained chiefly ferns. It is almost certain that sixty per cent. of the flowering plants were introduced by the sea, while thirty-two per cent. were probably borne by the wind, the others having been possibly carried by birds.

A Singular Siberian Tree.

Mr. George Kennan in his book Tent Life in Siberia tells of a curious tree or bush known to the Russians as "Kedrevnik," which translated into English, is equivelant to trailing pine. It is one of the most singular productions of Siberia, partaking more or less the characteristics of tree, bush and vine yet looking but very little like any of them. It resembles as much as anything a dwarf pine tree, with a remarkably gnarled, crooked and contorted trunk, growing horizontally like a neglected vine along the ground, and sending up perpendicular branches through the snow. It has the needles and cones of the common white pine, but it never stands erect like a tree, and grows in great patches from a few yards to several acres in extent. A man might walk over a dense growth of it in winter and yet see nothing but a few bunches of sharp green needles sticking up here and there through the snow. It is found on the most desolate steppes and upon the rockiest mountain sides from the Okhotsk Sea to the Arctic Ocean, and seems to grow most luxuriantly where the soil is most barren and the storms most severe. On great ocean-like plains, destitute of all other vegetation, this trailing cedar or pine lurks beneath the snow, and covers the ground in places with a perfect network of gnarled, twisted and interlocking trunks and branches. For some reason it always seems to die when a certain age has been attained and wherever its green spiney foliage is found will also be found dry white trunks, as inflammable as tinder. It furnishes almost the only fuel of the wandering native tribes and without it many parts of northeastern Siberia would be uninhabited by man.

The Thirsty Eucalyptus.

A curious root formation of the eucalyptus was recently found on a farm in Almeda County, California. It was taken from the bottom of a well, about sixteen feet below the surface. The trees to which the roots belonged stand fifty feet from the well. Two shoots pierced through the brick wall of the well, and sending off millions of fibers formed a dense mat that completely covered the bottom of the well. Most of these fibres are no larger than threads and are so woven and intertwisted as to form a mat as impenetrable and strong as though regularly woven in a loom. The mat when first taken out of the well was water soaked and covered with mud, and nearly all a man could lift, but when dry it was nearly as soft to touch as wool, and weighed only a few pounds. This is a good illustration of how the eucalyptus absorbs moisture, its roots going so far as to find water, pushing themselves through a brick wall, and then developing enormously after the water is reached.

Transplanting by Night.

A gentleman, anxious to ascertain the effect of transplanting by night instead of by day, made an experiment with the following result: He transplanted ten cherry trees while in bloom, commencing at four o'clock in the afternoon. Those transplanted during the daylight shed their blossoms, producing little or no fruit, while those transplanted in the dark maintained their condition fully. He did the same with ten dwarf trees after the fruit was one-third grown. Those transplanted during the day shed their fruit; those transplanted during the night perfected the crop and showed no injury from having been removed. With each of these trees he removed some earth with the roots. The incident is fully vouched for; and if a few similar experiments produce a like result, it will be a strong argument to horticulturists, etc., to do much work at night.

Forests of the Philippines.

In many places the great forests of the Philippines, which are estimated to cover at least 20,000,000 and perhaps 40,000,000 acres, and at present wholly unexplored, are practically inaccessible through lack of roads. In these forests more than six hundred species of trees have already been enumerated. Some of the trees attain a height of 150 feet. They produce gum, rubber, dyes, oils, tanbark, texile substances, medicines and timber.

Race of Dwarfs in Luzon.

Since the American occupation of the island of Luzon in the Philippines, one of the recognized races of dwarf men, the Aetas, has been brought to more prominent notice. Their average height is only four feet eight inches or four feet nine inches. They dwell among the mountains in the interior of the island, and are allied to the Andamanese, inhabiting islands in the Bay of Bengal. It is remarked by a recent writer that all of the dwarf races survive only in the most inaccessible parts of the continents or islands to which they belong. This has been shown to be especially true of the dwarf races of Africa.

Almost one-half of the species of insects are beetles. Lepidoptera comprises about 25,000 species.

The Plan of a Flower.

A flower is simply a modified branch and all the floral organs are transformed leaves, or more properly, are produced from what might otherwise have been leaves. This at first seems rather difficult to believe, but Nature, herself, has given us many hints in the matter. Thus in certain geraniums the central part of the flower, which we may regard as the end of the branch, continues to grow and to produce a new flower or even a truss of flowers rising out of the old ones. Apples and pears have been found with a leafy shoot growing out of the "blossom end" showing very clearly that the parts of the flower are in the nature of modified leaves. That singular object, the green rose, is like other roses in the bud, but when it opens, it shows that all its petals have reverted to small green leaves.

Upon examining some simple flower such as that of the stone-crop we find it consists of four kinds of organs. Beginning on the side next the stem there is a circle of five green leaf-like objects, the *sepals* and collectively called the *calyx*. Next is a circle of five colored leaflets, the *petals* which form the *corolla*. Then comes a circle of thread-like organs with little knobs on the ends, the *stamens;* and last, in the very center of the flower, certain bottle-shaped bodies, the *pistils*. These organs always have the same relative position. The pistils are always in the center of the flower, the sepals on the outside and the petals and stamens between.—*The American Botanist.*

Problems of Modern Astronomy.

Although astronomy generally speaking deals in distances the imensity of which the human mind can only grasp in the abstract, or by comparisons almost equally difficult to grasp, yet this science depends, too, on absolute accuracy in the seemingly minor problems. Chas. A. Young, writing for *Success*, makes the following observation:

The leading problems of what may be called "terrestrial astronomy" are, at present, a more accurate determination of the earth's form and density, and of the irregularities of its rotation. The former is not neglected; but just now special attaches to study of the slight "wabbling" of the earth's axis, and the strongly suspected variations in the length of the day. These phenomena lie at the very boundary of position, since its "wabble" was first detected, fourteen years ago, has been less than forty feet. It is studied only indirectly, through the infinitesimal changes in the latitudes of different observations. But the motion, slight as is it, is now beyond question; and the investigations of Dr. Chandler have shown that, although apparently extremely irregular, it is, in the main, really governed by law, and amenable to calculation. The theory, however, is still imperfect, and in order to obtain the necessary data a chain of astronomical stations encircling the earth has been established by different governments. There are six of these stations, all on or near the parallel of thirty-nine degrees ten minutes, where continuous observations of the latitudes are to be kept up for at least fourteen years.

Using a Watch for a Compass.

Few of the many persons who carry watches are aware of the fact that they are always provided with a compass, with which, when the sun is shining, they can determine a north and south line. All one has to do is to point the hour hand to the sun, and south is exactly half way between the hour hand and the figure 12 on the watch. Suppose it is 9 o'clock in the morning: Follow the rule given above, and we find the south as is indicated below. Prolong this line along the face of the watch, and you have a north and south line, and from this any point of the compass may be determined.

This may seem strange, but the reason is plain. While the sun is passing over 180 degrees (from east to west) the hour hand of the watch passes over 360 degrees (from 6 o'clock to 6 o'clock). Consequently the angular movement of the sun in one hour corresponds to the angular movement of the hour hand in half an hour; hence, if holding the watch horizontal, we point the hour hand toward the sun, the line from the pivot of the hands to the point midway between the hour hand and 12 o'clock will point to the south.

The earth has three motions: around its axis, around the sun, and with the sun and solar system. Its velocity in its motion around the sun is 68,305 miles an hour, over 1,000 miles a minute, or nineteen miles a second.

RANDOM NOTES.

There are over seven hundred species of the cactus family, all of them being indigenous only to North America.

Of the world's rainfall, three-fourths, it is estimated, is supplied by vapor from the Pacific and Indian Oceans.

Many comets will be seen during the twentieth century. The most interesting is Halley's—last seen in 1835. It is due in 1910 or 1911.

Cocoons of well fed silk worms often reel 1,000 yards, and reliable accounts are given of a cocoon yielding 1,295 yards, or a fibre three-fourths of a mile in length.

Persia has the most famous turquoise mines in the world, which have been worked no less than eight centuries. These pretty stones, however, are to be found in many other parts of the world.

A French naturalist asserts that if the world should become birdless, man could not inhabit it after nine years' time in spite of all the sprays and poisons that could be manufactured for the destruction of insects. The insects and slugs would simply eat all the orchards and crops; yet it is reliably estimated that 3,000,000 song birds were killed last year for the purpose of adorning women's hats with their plumage.

How deep is the ice of a glacier? A hole through a glacier has been bored at last by Profs. Blumcke and Hess, Bavarian students of these ice rivers. With a hand-boring machine and a special arrangement for washing out ice fragments, the Hinterris glacier in the Otzthal Alps was found to have a thickness of 502 feet. The glaciers of Greenland are said to exceed 1,000 feet in thickness.

By way of experiment a large spider was placed on a floating chip in a pool of water. After making a thorough survey of its floating island, the spider began to cast a web for the shore, throwing it into the air as far as possible with the wind. When the web finally caught on some grass the spider turned about, and, hauling on the line, drew the raft to the short. Remarkable ingenuity, to say the least.

The strongest telescopes bring the moon to an apparent distance of 100 miles.

There are no less than 3,262 species of fish inhabiting the waters of North America.

There are seventy thousand cochineal insects to a pound of dried cochineal; yet the world's crop of cochineal is from 300 to 500 tons annually.

Three Ceylonese deer have been imported into this country. They are the exact counter-part of the fallow deer so common to England, but are midgets. Although they are full grown, they are only 14 inches high.

The following are said by a Swiss hunter to have been found near the nest of an eagle he recently discovered in the Alps: A hare, 27 chamois' feet, 4 pigeons' feet, 30 pheasants' feet, 11 heads of fowls, 18 heads of grouse and the remains of a number of rabbits, marmots and squirrels.

Nearly one hundred years ago the Jesuits were banished from Mexico. It was known that they had immense hoards of gold, but feared to tempt cupidity by taking it all with them. What they did with the bulk of their savings has just been revealed by Pierre Guirre, who says that treasure to the value of over $20,000,000 was buried beneath the old cathedral in the little town of Typozottan, and is believed to be there yet.

Statistics show that 860 different languages are used in the world now and that these are subvided into about 5,000 dialects. Europe has 89 languages; Africa, 114; Asia, 123, and America, 417. The remaining 117 belong to the large and small islands of the world, particularly of the south seas. Many of those islands have their own distinctive language, although they are close to others in many instances.

To one not conversant with ornithology the statement that the eggs and nests of some well-known birds remain yet to be discovered must appear surprising. The eggs of a species of sandpiper were first discovered last July on an island at the mouth of the Siberian River, Yenisei. There are a few other birds which make their nests in remote regions, although living part of their lives among civilized men, whose eggs have not yet been found.

The Amateur Naturalist.

"To him who in the love of Nature holds communion with her visible forms, she speaks a various language."

VOLUME 1.   BINGHAMTON, NEW YORK, MARCH, 1904.   NUMBER 2.

FLOWERS THAT ARE NOT FLOWERS.

BY WILLARD N. CLUTE.

THERE is a great deal of difference between the botanist's definition of a flower and the definition that holds with the general public. The former, of course, is correct because his definition is exact, but the great army of florists, gardeners and flower-loving housewives persist in clinging to their own ideas of what constitutes a flower. Indeed, there is no reason why a word should not have two definitions, and the majority may, after all, be right in its opinion. For the sake of a little diversion, however, let us examine some of the cases in which botanist and flower grower do not agree.

We may start with the structures which are called flowers by scientist and gardener, alike. Without going much into details we will agree that a flower usually has sepals, petals, stamens and pistils, and name as examples buttercups, violets, orchids and such. The botanist is willing to forego the petals and sepals, and still maintain that he has a flower. The cultivator, however, will scarcely agree to this unless pistils and stamens are brightly colored, or otherwise conspicuous. But he often goes to the other extreme, and includes with the flower many parts that do not belong to it and in this sense we speak of his blossoms as flowers that are not flowers.

One of the most familiar of these masquerading flowers is borne by the dandelion. The golden hemisphere at the top of the dandelion's hollow stem is really a cluster of many flowers each one with five petals, one pistil and five stamens, all of which are easily recognized. The petals are joined side by side making a strap-shaped corolla; but one who has any doubts as to their nature may examine the center of a daisy or sunflower where he will find five similar petals arranged in a regular tubular corolla. Even the sepals are not missing from the dandelion blossom, but they are so disguised that we do not notice them until expanded into the feathery pappus by means of which each seed at the appointed time sails down the wind. "Flowers" like those of the dandelion and sunflower are typical of the great race of composites but as may now be seen, they are really not single flowers but clusters of flowers.

The blossom of the dogwood (*Cornus florida*) is another familiar example of a flower cluster. The four great white petal-like structures that give all the beauty to the dogwood flower—that gives the very name of flowering dogwood to the plant; as if other species did not flower—are not petals but bracts and more nearly allied to leaves than flowers. In fact, they do duty as bud scales all winter long. Perhaps their flower-like hue later is in payment for work well done. The small affairs that the great bracts have guarded so well are usually mistaken for the stamens and pistils, but are really separate flowers.

Something of a similar nature is found in the skunk's cabbage, Jack-in-the-pulpit, wild calla, greendragon and, in fact, the whole arum family where the most noticeable part of the flower is in the nature of an enfolding bract. To find the true flowers of skunk's cabbage examine the round head in the middle of the shell-like spathe; to find those of wild calla, search the cylindric object which the spathe tries to enfold.

The members of the great spurge family (*Euphorbia*) are worse off in the matter of flowers than most plants, for the male flowers consist of single stamens. The female flowers are somewhat more conspicuous but they are round little bodies at the top of a short stalk and are certainly not flowers in the popular sense. But when several male flowers are grouped about a female flower and surrounded by a calyx-like involucre it has not a little resemblance to a simple flower. Some species also add embellishments in the way of colored glands and bracts. In the plant known to florists as *Poinsettia* the bracts near the flowering parts are bright scarlet and by many are assumed to be petals. The tropics afford many more wonderful instances of flowers that are not flowers, but our own fields have many that are not here mentioned.

Binghamton, N. Y.

NOTES ON WINTER BIRDS IN MAINE.

BY J. MERTON SWAIN.

THE winter of 1903–4 in Maine has been one of the most severe that has been known for many years, the months of January and February being very cold and remaining so every day in those months, the thermometer running very low, ranging from 5° below to 20°, 30°, and even 40° below zero, and very windy and rough. But in spite of this fact, the winter birds have been very common throughout the state. Pine grosbeaks came early in November and many flocks of them have been seen gleaning in the orchards and by the road-sides for food; oftentimes not seeming to mind the extreme cold weather. Very large flocks of snow-flakes have been frequently seen, in fact, some of the largest flocks that we have ever seen in the state.

It was reported that there would be another flight of snowy owls this winter, but after seeing a few, no more have been reported. But three have come under my notice thus far.

Several flocks of gold-finches and siskins have been seen feeding beside the highways and several small flocks of redpolls were seen and others reported in the state. An occasional pileated wood-pecker has been seen and the usual winter residents, such as chickadee, white-breasted nuthatch, etc., have been seen in usual numbers.

Editor Brownson, of Portland, has reported a small flock of myrtle warblers wintering on Cape Elizabeth, just out from Portland. Mr. Norton, of Westbrook, has reported a meadow lark staying there very late. Robins have been frequently reported but on investigation all reports that have come to my notice have proven to be grosbeaks. Several winter chipping sparrows have been seen feeding upon the weed stocks beside the highways in a very monotonous and cheerless way. Along the coast the sea ducks and the usual water fowl have been observed feeding unusually near inland, many of their usual feeding places having been completely frozen over.

On February 5th, when on my usual route up in Franklin County, at Wilton, I was told of a duck that was frequently seen earlier about the open places in the lake and later when these places became frozen over, it was seen daily in the open water in the river, the outlet of the lake and in the canal, running through the village. Upon calling upon one of my customers, his clerk told me he had gone to the canal, in the rear of the woolen mill, to see the duck that was seen there. I at once went to the place and found him watching a duck that they were unable to name. It proved to be a solitary American golded-eye (*Glaucionetta clangula Americana,*—Bonap.) feeding leisurely, occasionally diving to the bottom for food. So accustomed had it become to being watched by passers-by that it would allow us to walk up on the ice to within four feet of it, not seeming to mind us more than would a domestic duck. It was probably a young bird, whose wing quills had not developed strong enough to carry the bird with the throng to the coast waters, thus it was left to brave the severe weather alone.

The severe weather is probably nearly over and in a few days a thaw will bring the prairie horned larks to the interior, then soon the crow will appear and immediately the spring birds will slowly follow. One solitary crow has been seen nearly every trip I've made along the electric line in Somerset County from Madison to Skowhegan. He must have passed a cold, lonesome winter, but soon his comrades will return north and life will then be worth the living to him.

Fairfield, Maine.

இ ௱

Next to sight, the principal sense of most, if not all, insects is probably the sense of touch, and the tactile organ is usually the tongue or antennæ. A familiar example of the use of the tongue in this manner is seen in the common house fly—a perfect marvel in its complexity—and which, viewed under the microscope reveals an instrument of most perfect construction on a most minute scale. It is this instrument that a fly uses when he samples the various articles of food upon the table, calmly sips from your tea-cup or as he alights on your face and pauses to smile into your countenance.

SOME GIANTS AMONG SMALL THINGS.

BY CHARLES D. PENDELL.

ALTHOUGH the minute organisms of nature, animate or inanimate, possess features as interesting as those of their larger prototypes, their very minuteness precludes their study by most persons. And again, anything which is familiar and of what might be aptly termed of a recognized standard of size, possesses a new and peculiar interest when it assumes dimensions greatly smaller or larger than those of this recognized standard. Every branch of nature possesses their individual giants or pygmies, and it is the purpose of this article to group together some of the giants among small things.

Were we to write of the geological predecessors of the existing species, volumes would be required to produce anything like an adequate description. Two examples from the past, however, will be better than none and may induce the reader to delve more deeply into the mysteries of that fascinating science, Geology.

The lobster of the present era, as commonly seen, does not exceed five pounds in weight and is oftener less; though when arrived at full maturity their weight is about ten pounds. But going back countless ages to the early Devonian era, we behold what may truly be termed a prince of lobsters. This giant crustacean, which is called Pterygotus, attained the length of six feet and was two feet in breadth. Its antennæ were armed with powerful claws, and in many ways did it possess double advantages over its modern congener. It possessed two pairs of eyes—a large pair on the front of its head and a smaller pair on the top. For perfect mastication it was provided with four pair of great serrated jaws. (Surely, it never became extinct through dispepsia!) On each side was a powerful paddle enabling it to swiftly pursue its prey; while if attacked by any predaceous superior, it could, by striking the water with its broad tail, retreat with the rapidity of an arrow.

The Triassic period furnishes another example in a species of frog, which sometimes attained a size fully equal to an ox. No complete remains of the Labyrinthodon, as it is called, have been found; but enough to fully establish its character. The mouth was furnished with numerous rows of small but closely set teeth, and from this fact it derives its name.

Conchology is not supposed to be replete with gigantic specimens, but in the archipelago of the Molucca Islands, such specimens are by no means rare. Here the *Tridacna*, sometimes weighing five hundred pounds, fasten themselves to the rocks and can only be cut loose with an axe. Their thick shells, five feet long, are used by the natives as bath tubs, ready cut and polished by nature.

Another mollusc of prodigious size is the cuttle-fish. One seen near the Canary Islands had a spread of arms of twenty feet and weighed over four thousand pounds.

A variety of sponge, known as Neptune's Cup, grows on the submarine rocks from three to six feet high. Their small stock and wide top, symmetrically hollowed out, is an almost exact representation of a colossal drinking goblet.

The marvelous delicacy of organization and still more marvelous intelligence of insects has always been a cause of wonder and a source of admiration; and in this class also, we find extremes of strength and size. One species, the Goliath of Drury, is much larger than many kinds of our more common birds, which it would pitilessly strangle and devour, were it in his power to capture them. This entomological monster is, from the extremity of the abdomen to that of the mandible, four inches long and is one half as broad, and, armed with its strong bony coat of mail, it well deserves its name. The Mormolyce, though measuring three and one-fourth inches in length, is not a powerful insect and its source of protection lies in the resemblance of its green wings to the leaf of the plants among which it lives. The antennæ are nearly three inches long, making its extreme length about six inches.

A species of butterfly exists in South America, the body of which is as large as that of a robin and its velvet wings, ornamented with the most gaudy coloring, extend a foot across.

Many spiders of the tropical world have a body three inches long and the circle of their legs six inches in diameter; and one species on the Amazon is five inches long. Some of these giant spiders are extremely active and will attack small birds and strangle them in their nests. One species, quite numerous in Columbia, sometimes fastens on the neck of chickens and pigeons, seizing them by the throat and killing them instantly. Others of these spiders obtain their prey by weaving webs so strong that large butterflies and small birds, even, become helpless victims. Though in the temperate zone spiders are of repulsive appearance, numbers of those of the tropical world are radiant with the sheen and metallic lustre of many and varied colors.

In the botanical world the leaves and flowers of plants generally attract us by their symmetry and regularity of outline, or the beauty and harmony of their color and their delicate but pleasant perfume. But if we transport ourselves again to the Amazon we find there the leaves of the *Victoria regia*, which display themselves on the surface like immense plains of verdure. These leaves are nearly circular and from eighteen to twenty-five feet in circumference. The upper surface is of a uniform and beautiful green; thus, when seen from a distance, presenting the appearance of floating tables covered with velvet. The frame work of these leaves is so strong that a child can float on them; and they are nightly used as a cool resting place by the many aquatic birds of that region.

The leaf of the great taliput palm which grows in India is so large that under its vast cover forty persons can shelter themselves. The leaf of this tree is sometimes fixed to the ceiling of museums of natural history, one leaf covering it completely.

The flower of the remarkable *Victoria regia*, the leaf of which has been referred to, was long considered the largest in the world. These brilliant rose and white blossoms often measure a yard in circuit and emanate a pleasant fragrance.

But the flower of the gigantic *Rafflesia Arnoldi* is a perfect monster of vegetation and leaves all others far behind. On account of its mammoth proportions, botanists for a long time refused to believe the existence of such a flower, and it was not until a specimen was sent to London and there examined that all doubts were dissipated. The flower is composed of a fleshy mass weighing from twelve to fifteen pounds. "Its border, the circuit of which is not less than ten feet, shows four lobes, forming a gaping excavation capable of holding a dozen pints." Its odor is unpleasant, having a carion-like smell. In Sumatra and Java where it is found, the natives almost make a divinity of it and clothe it with a supernatural power.

But while the ignorant savage of the mighty works of nature creates a divinity, the naturalist recognizes in them the manifestation of an omnipotent Creator, whose works and wonders are everywhere displayed to the observing mind.

THE SEASONS AND THE BIRDS.

BY NORMAN O. FOERSTER.

THE seasons and the birds—do we not naturally link the two? Winter—the very word recalls the tree sparrows, juncos, nuthatches and titmice. Spring—the gradual arrival of the early migrants, crowned by the dainty tribe of warblers. Summer—the appearance of the young, the general quietness preceeding the molting period, and August, when there is

"But silence, and a stirless breath."

Autumn—first, and simultaneously the gathering of the birds and the massing of the flowers, then the passing of the former and the fading of the latter. Thus, meditating on the seasons, we naturally get a comprehensive view of the whole of Nature's army, and meditating on certain birds, we naturally conjure up pictures of the seasons wherein they are prominent; and perchance a certain day.

I. THE PROGNOSTIC OF SPRING.

January 27 dawned cold and foggy. The trees were bare, the ground of the hills was like granite, and well-covered with the snow that crunches under foot like pulverized quartz, while the swamps were but alternate patches of brittle ice and pasty mud. Stern winter had long held sway; zero weather, heavy snowfalls and blizzards had followed one another in dreary succession. I walked along the road without a thought of spring—it seemed so very far off—when I was suddenly aroused by a song—that of a blue-bird! A thousand recollections rushed to my mind; I thought of sialis' harmonious part in the heydey of bird-life—spring; of the hot, mid-summer days when so few birds were about; of their last plantive notes in the fall, as sadly expressive of the fading year as the clatter of dead leaves blown over a frozen meadow. My whole heart went out to the blue-coated songster so gloriously singing, as it seemed to me, "Spring is here, spring is here."

II. A MIDSUMMER REVERY.

The hot, quivering air of a July day vanishes before the cool breath of evening. A feeling of quiet and peacefulness steals over the fields and hill-sides, voiced by the vesper sparrow's tuneful song, the field sparrow's plain-tive chant, the song sparrow's exuberant delight, the robin's uncertain but plaintive and inspiring melody, the meadow-lark's clearly enunciated lyrical music and the flicker's merry laugh. A Maryland yellow throat calls from the roadside shrubbery "O, peacefulness, peacefulness, peacefulness," but departing from the meaning of his text, strives for ascendancy over his musical relative. And he, with all the others, triumphs over one little voice —the humble, wiry strain of a grasshopper sparrow. But though insignifi-cant in the bird choir he might well be choir master of another, the vast orchestra of leg and back scrapers. "Bzwi, t't't, bzwi" in shrill stridulation is answered by a black cricket's regular "thrupp up, up, thrupp up, up, up" and other voices, humble, but so manifold that the very air quivers with the vibration. They sing not in tree-tops and bushes but in the blue and yellow meadow; among the confusedly mingled vervain, pentstemon, sundrops, black-eyed Susan, parsnip, golden-rod and St. John's-wort.

But wherefore all this vespertine celebration? Pure health, happiness and good spirits, no doubt. But the tired farmer driving homeward, alter-nately whistles and meditates for another reason. In the west is such a sunset as might thrill the most prosaic heart; slate-blue clouds, halt-trans-parent and half-translucent, radiate from the intense silver of the setting sun. Such an elysian sight is rare, for the atmosphere is seldom sufficiently clear, giving us only those saffron, amber, pink or light brown effects, beau-tiful in their way but polluted with terrene misty atmosphere, far inferior to the immaculate silver.

Gradually the silvery light fades, covered by opaque slatish clouds. With simultaneous graduality the fields and hillsides lose their detail, the orange fire of black-eyed Susan becomes indistinguishable from the paler yellow of sundrops.

In keeping with this relaxation is the dying out of the song-birds. The vesper sparrow's song loses its prominence, coming at longer and longer intervals; the field sparrows are soon silenced completely; a song sparrow sings now and then but with less vigor and joy; the meadow-lark's melody, prominent only in its absence, has deserted the field to the robin's soft but carrying notes; the flickers have had their fun and busily work for a last larvæ, signaling success by a loud, triumphant "kee yer," and the pert little Maryland yellowthroat? Alas, he has disappeared and is forgotten, despite his efforts.

After all other voices are hushed, when the light has quite faded from the slaty west, the grasshopper sparrow's insect-like "pit-tuk, z-ee-e-e-e-e" comes through the still air. His crepuscular rivals are the nasal-voiced night-hawk, gyrating overhead, swooping, sailing, swinging aloft, careering as fancy dictates, and the dark, silent whip-poor-will, winging his way over the meadows and, lastly, the herald of night, the ominous screech owl, whose tremulous whine is so suggestive of the transmigratory wanderings of a lost soul.

III. AN AUTUMNAL DAY-DREAM.

"Bob-white!" and "bob-white!" in a major key. Then after an interval an answering "bob-white!" in the minor. It is hard to be altogether self-satisfied when we hear that dear whistle. It savors so of the autumn sportsman, breaking the happy coveys to evince his marksmanship and tickle his barbarian pallet.

Indian summer—how, at any other season, we love to ponder over those dreamy, misty, mellow days! What a ravishing longing once more to recline on the prostrate leaves and look out over the rich, autumnal landscape! Despite this yearning for the impossible, Nature is never monotonous: wearied of winter's immaculacy, the eye loves to dwell on the gay light greens of spring; wearied of these, the sombreness of summer is readily acceptable; when this has held its long sway, nothing could be better appreciated than autumn's blaze of color.

Which color predominates, red, yellow, brown or blue? It is difficult to decide: the oaks and beeches and many other trees are brown; the tulips and maples golden yellow, and the shrub-like sumacs, with their intense scarlet, set all the roadsides ablaze; in the fields and wood borders the purplish-blue of the asters and gentians strives for dominion over the yellow of banked sunflowers and golden-rod.

The harmonious whole of these, with the balmy air, and the intense cool blue of the sky, and the comparative silence of Nature, creates an irresistable desire—ennui that we cannot withstand—to recline and ponder. Our thoughts are portentous rather than otherwise. How soon all this will be changed! "The next gale that sweeps from the north" tears the loose sere leaves from the branches and carpets the ground. Brilliant colors fade to browns and natural tints. Finally, a fitful breeze whirls down the road, accompanied by a regiment of noisy leaves, halts, wheels and colliding with the clattering crowd, whirls them round and round with ever increasing force until they ascend spirally. This gyration over, they descend rapidly and are at rest—for the time being—many feet from where they started. Helpless creatures of circumstance! And these October winds show no mercy.

Some of our trees are almost bare. But many leaves retain their grip as if reluctant to leave the sharer of their joys and sorrows and face the unknown world; contented to rest beside some thankful Christmas fern, but horrified by the chance of a half-mile undignified clatter along the dry road, terminating in a trampling-out-of-existence. Who says the leaves have no life?

Once again the scene is changed. The trees are bare, and the noisy—not merry—crackling of leaves trampled under foot disturbs the solitude of the deserted wood. The first snow of the year is falling—great, soft flakes that leave no impression on the warm earth and are seen only during their passage through the air. They fall thicker and faster until a cold November wind suddenly rushes through the trees and drives the flurry aslant, wrathful that the earth should thus receive her flaky heralds.

"Bob-white!" the clear, bold whistle, whose source is so mysterious, breaks in upon these unpleasant thoughts. Philosophically, we resolve to enjoy these superb days, regardless of those that will follow.

IV. A BOREAL REALITY.

Extract from my journal:

January 9. About 24°. The wind strong and penetrating on the upland meadows but seemingly absent in many valleys. Passed the exposed hillside near deserted farmhouse about 1 P. M. in the midst of a blizzardous wind that empurpled my ears and flecked my coat with thick clusters of the immaculate crystals that seemed to want to sift gradually but were hurried mercilessly by the cold blasts. The sky became so dark that I wondered whether the flakes would not turn to a similar shade. This snowstorm was a fitting climax to the continual but moderate precipitation of the morning. Immediately after the last flakes had joined their myriad congeners on the earth, the yellow sun pushed aside the dark clouds and sent his warm glow over the spotless landscape. Then the cyanean sky gradually gained territory. And what a blue!—deep and warm, in marked contrast to the frigidity here below. Simultaneously with this clearing of the sky the atmosphere became fascinatingly transparent, exposing with startling but eye-satisfying distinctness, the detail on distant hills. Transparency of atmosphere is rare after a rain or snow fall, but when it comes is amazing in its beauty. What a contrast to the uncertain color of the sky before; when the zenith was a leaden gray-white and the sky over distant woods a leaden pinkish-lavender.

Contrast is very capable of producing color illusions: the sere goldenrod fields behind Deserted Farmhouse glowed a live orange, such as we would have, could we imagine the solidity of the orange milkweed clusters made transparent; dark hedges lining snowdrifts were purplish-black or lemon-colored; the distant hills along the Allegheny looked light purple.

What shall I say of the rustle of sere oak leaves—heard so often to-day ? Is their noisy clatter ghostly, as some one has suggested ? Nay, to my ears it is a pleasant sound, suggestive of approaching June thunder-showers and wind-tossed grain fields, and yet, when I bethink myself of the season— stern winter—it seems but a grim smile, a mere reminder of what used to be but is not now.

Today the creek was completely snowed—and iced—over, save where some farmer had broken it for his cattle, showing the cool blue of a half-foot layer and the dark rushing waters underneath.

As to the roads—they were good where travelled much, but miserable otherwise. For several miles I plodded along an almost disused road. Only one person had broken the crust this morning, and his steps, coming the wrong way, were hard to follow. Once, when diagonally crossing a field I found myself in knee-deep drifts where only mice and squirrels had dared to venture.

My bird-list shows 12 species and 145 individuals. The first birds seen were four tufted titmice and a song sparrow. Then I heard the vigorous but seldom-repeated tattoo of a hairy woodpecker. A half-mile on was a chickadee, calling "day, day, day, day," and occasionally giving his silvery twist, best described I think, by two capital letters, S and Q. Next I heard the "chimps" of a song sparrow, the "tsits" of two juncos and the steely "peek" of a downy woodpecker. The subsequent quarter of an hour brought two tufted titmice, a song sparrow, another downy and a party of fifteen tree sparrows.

Beyond Iron Bridge were six juncos, eleven tufted titmice, a song spar- row, two chickadees, two drab-colored goldfinches and fifty tree sparrows in a scattered flock.

Next came a song sparrow and two downy woodpeckers.

Not another bird for a half-hour, though I passed through a valley con- taining the sempiternal green conifers. But beyond Deserted Farmhouse I heard the "caws" of several garrulous crows, and looking up saw two of them chasing a barred owl! The owl, with long, strong beats of his broad wings swung ahead easily, even taking time to defy his pursuers by sailing. After the crows desisted—i. e. had driven their mortal enemy from their domains—he gradually descended into some dense, shrubby bushes.

Pittsburg, Pa.

ᑫ ᑫ

The Mexican maguey tree furnishes a needle and thread all ready for use. At the tip of each dark green leaf is a slender thorn needle that must be carefully drawn from its sheath; at the same time it slowly unwinds the thread, a strong, smooth fibre attached to the needle and capable of being drawn out to a great length.

A VISIT TO THE BIG TREES.

*BY GEORGE G. PENDELL.

A COUPLE of weeks ago I went out to see some of California's "big trees," in the Santa Cruz grove. These are not the largest trees, nor the largest variety, in California. The largest are the *Sequoia gigantea*, to be found in the Mariposa groves. The trees that I saw are the *Sequoia semper virens*—ever living. That is, the trees spring up from the roots of the parent trees and continue the process through the centuries. The largest group that I saw has 22 trees. Nearby is the group called the "Twelve Apostles," there being just twelve trees in the group. "The Giant" measures (I think) 71 feet in circumference at the base and was formerly 380 feet high; but the top has broken off and it is now but 306 feet high. The largest trees are nearly all hollow; that is the way they die —beginning to hollow out at the roots and the hollow growing up through the trunk of the tree. Their roots reach out, covering a large area, but have very little depth. Some of them are estimated to be from 1000 to 5000 years old.

Great as these trees are—and they are truly great—they are wonderfully suggestive of a still greater past. These giants seem to grow in a circle, indicating that the trees of the present are but offshoots from the roots of a former era. Indeed some traces of the old parent trees are still visible. The circle is invariably broken at some point indicating the direction in which the parent tree fell, carrying down with it any smaller growth in that part of the circle. These circles show the former trees to have been—some of them—thirty or forty feet in diameter; to which the present giants are but pigmies. If the giants of the present are 1000 years old—and there can be no question as to that—to what age did the giants of long ago attain!

And speaking of big trees, a friend some time ago showed to me photographs of some of the *Sequoia gigantea*. One of them was taken with 26 men standing side by side in front of the tree, and still the front was not quite entirely covered. There was one tree more than *fifty feet in diameter*. He told me that he had counted the rings on a freshly cut stump about twenty-two feet across and that there were more than *twenty-nine hundred rings*. How old, then, think you, is that fifty-foot tree?

I am told that there is still a third variety of the *Sequoia* or redwood tree; but I do not know its specific name. I have seen considerable beautiful scenery, but the wildest scenic part of my trip is about to follow. I have left Oakland and started north. I shall "Sunday" in Sacramento. Two weeks from now I expect to be in Oregon and return east by the Northern Pacific Railway, stopping off en route to visit places of interest, at such times as my business will permit.

Vallejo, California.

*Excerpt from personal letter to the editor.

The Amateur Naturalist.

A Journal for those who Study Nature from a love of it.
ISSUED BI-MONTHLY.

SUBSCRIPTION, 50 CENTS PER YEAR.   SINGLE COPIES, 10 CENTS.
ADVERTISING RATES ON APPLICATION.

EDITED AND PUBLISHED BY
CHARLES D. PENDELL,
85-87 STATE STREET,   -   -   -   BINGHAMTON, N. Y.

It has long been our idea that a magazine along the line of nature study in a popular, understandable form, interesting yet reliable and accurate, would be cordially welcomed. The reception accorded the first number of THE AMATEUR NATURALIST has been very gratifying and the welcome on the part of friends and contemporary journals is truly appreciated. Some of the latter, in addition to the courtesy of exchange, have given us their editorial commendation. The financial returns have also been greater than the warnings of experienced friends had led us to expect, and we simply wish to renew our salutatory statement: THE AMATEUR NATURALIST has come to stay. The editor is proprietor of a well-equipped job printing plant and in publishing this journal is simply carrying out the plans that have been years in maturing; and now once started the publisher has no intention of receding from them.

Except for the apology due our subscribers we would not in our own columns advertise our tardiness with this issue. But the fact is we have moved. Our old quarters were hardly large enough for our printing business, and with the expansion and growth of that with the addition of this publication they were too small altogether. After the confusion incident to moving was over we had to wait a week for the electricians to wire our motor—and then another wait for the power company to connect power— but we are all right now and in better shape for business than ever before.

We note that *The Plant World* has increased its subscription price to $1.50 per year. As a matter of fact it is worth it, and how a magazine so well illustrated and containing so much in the way of original research could be published for less is a difficult problem to solve. It is now in its seventh year and is one of the few existing botanical journals that have made a success during that time.

In the January issue of THE AMATEUR NATURALIST mention was made of the California vulture, the largest existing bird that flies. The January number of *The Condor*, published at Palo Alto, California, contains a full-page halftone of this unique bird, besides much else that is of interest to ornithologists.

The Russo-Japanese war naturally has developed an interest in matters pertaining to the conflicting countries. That Russia seeks a more southern and open seaport for Siberia is well known. A traveller describing the advent of spring in this country in latitude about 60° writes as follows:— "The rapidity of the transition from winter to summer in the Arctic region is astonishing. In the early part of June it is possible to travel over the snow upon dog-sledges; by the last of the same month the trees are all in full leaf, primroses, cowslips, buttercups, valerian, cinque-foil and Labrador tea blossom everywhere upon the higher plains and river banks and the thermometer frequently registers 70° Fahrenheit in the shade. There is no spring in the usual acceptation of the word at all. The disappearance of snow and the appearance of vegetation are almost simultaneous. In less than a month after the disappearance of the snow more than sixty species of flowers have been collected in an area of not more than five acres."

On March 21st an earthquake shock was reported which extended over all the New England coast. An associated press dispatch ten days later states that "where old Bald Mountain has stood for centuries, now only exists a new born lake. Bald Mountain, celebrated for its inacessible steep sides, was situated in the Tiboque valley, a few miles from the New Brunswick line. At the base were boiling springs. Nearby is a hill called Plaster Rock, which furnishes plaster so good it is used for building purposes. It is now believed that Bald Mountain was the cone of a volcano which, when it sank March 21st, caused what all New England called an earthquake." If the foregoing is true an interesting field for investigation has opened to the naturalists of northern Maine.

With the coming of spring and the awakening of plant life a more or less transitory wish, not always expressed, comes to most persons, that they really knew more about botany. In "Botany for Beginners," being published serially in *The American Botanist*, Mr. Willard N. Clute has presented the subject of botany in a manner not only interesting, but absorbingly so. The usual plan of botanical text books is discarded and the subject at once entered into with the idea that the reader wants to know plants rather than scientific names. Whenever a technical term is introduced it is explained, easily, naturally, and the reader or student has mastered the lesson without conscious effort. Illustrations are used where necessary.

A peculiar example of the habit of some birds of returning to the same place to nest year after year was witnessed some years ago. The upper part of a balsam tree was forked, the two limbs being but a few inches apart for several feet. Here some robins, presumably the same pair, built their nest year after year, and when last seen by the editor five such nests had been built, one above the other.

WHERE RED-WINGS BUILD.

BY HATTIE WASHBURN.

I know a mystic cradle
That hangs above the wave,
Rocked by the passing breezes,
Lulled by the water's lave.

Swung from the nodding rushes
Where rank the grasses grow
And prove a trusty cable
Though fierce the wild winds blow.

Decked with red-like bursts of flame,
There sable forms are seen
Where the red-wings rear their young,
'Mid grasses rank and green.

Hushed in their hair lined cradle
By a strange lullaby;
The frog's melodeous tone
And the black tern's shrill cry;

The bobolink's burst of song
Shook from his little throat;
The wild duck among the reeds,
And the lone bittern's note.

There the salamander's voice
Is heard throughout the night,
The grasshopper's cheery song,
The beetle's drooning flight.

No hoof beat or stealthy tread
May ever wander there,
By all creatures it is shunned,
Save of the deep and air.

There the throb of life is heard,
Though man may never roam
Through marsh grasses rank and green
Where red-wings build their home.

Goodwin, S. D.

Quartz and Quartz Crystals.

BY EDMUND E. HOBBS.

QUARTZ is a siliceous rock, found in nearly every locality and indeed, comprising one-half of the crust of the earth. Its forms and varieties are so numerous and varied that the beginner may after having formed quite a respectable collection of minerals be surprised to learn that he has hardly stepped outside of the quartz family. It is the principal constituent of granite, syenite and most kinds of sandstone. When pure it is quite colorless but owing to the presence of impurities its colors are varied, and many minerals consisting chiefly of quartz have little to distinguish them but their color. Thus, rock crystal, rose quartz, topaz, chalcedony, carnelian, agate, amethyst, chryophrase, jasper, etc., are varieties of quartz.

It is in quartz rock that gold is far more frequently found than any other matrix. Quartz is found both massive and crystalized. The crystals usually being six-sided prisms terminated by six-sided pyramids, and sometimes in dodecahedrons; i. e., two six-sided pyramides base to base. These are called quartzoids. The pure quartz crystals are usually small and are found both singly and in clusters. Perhaps the most notable examples of crystals is a cluster in Dartmouth College cabinet weighing 147 pounds and the famous single crystal at Milan (Italy) 3 feet 3 inches long by 5½ feet in circumference, said to weigh 870 pounds.

In my personal collecting I have found crystals of the smoky quartz in Niagara County, N. Y., and in Herkimer County have found rose and milky quartz, besides the well known rock crystals, locally called "diamonds." These are best found on a bright sunny day soon after a rain and may readily be discovered in well cultivated ground—onion beds, for instance. These crystals are usually eighteen-sided; that is, a six-sided prism terminated by a six-sided pyramid on each end. They are sometimes found in the bed of the

West Canada Creek and most of them from this locality have a drop of water in the interior, and of course on freezing will break the crystal. Large and beautiful crystals of quartz are found in St. Lawrence County and others, smaller, in the Thousand Islands.

Quartz has no regular cleavage and when broken the fragments will be of all shapes and sizes, like glass. Thus one who is unacquainted with this fact may accidently ruin a splendid specimen.

Its hardness is 7 or 8 and it will readily scratch glass. It is insoluable in any acid but hydrofluoric.

An Albino Deer.

An albino deer, with a coat as white as the drifting snows, eyes a delicate pink, and with a tread as soft and discreet as an elk fawn, was killed in the Canyon Mountains of southern Oregon recently, says the *Scientific American*. It was one of the very few albino deer ever seen in the mountains of the west. Old hunters tell of seeing them, usually separate from the main herds, and at various times during the early days, but they were too shy and discreet to be approached near enough for a shot.

The deer which was killed in the Canyon Mountains, was with four other deer at the time it was found, and had not this been true, the hunters would not have taken it for a deer. Its white coat made it far more conspicuous than the remainder of the herd, and it is perhaps for this reason only albino deer are shunned by their mates.

The albino deer bears exactly the same relation to the deer family that the albino of the African race does to human kind. Aside from its white coat and pink eyes, it is like all other deer; possibly its fur is softer and more silky.

The specimen found in the pine forests of the Canyon Mountains will be made a part of the exhibit of albino mammals at the Smithsonian Institution.

An albino deer was shot a number of years ago in Warren County, N. Y., and is preserved in the State Museum at Albany where the editor of the AMATEUR NATURALIST has several times seen it.

Comets of the Past Century.

During the nineteenth century 235 new comets were discovered as against 62 in the eighteenth century. The nineteenth century also beheld a greater number of large and brilliant comets than did its predecessor. The finest of these were the comets of 1811, 1843, 1858, 1881 and 1882. In the year 1800 only one periodical comet was known, Halley's. Now many are known, of which at least 17 have been seen at more than one return to perihelion.

The Highest Waterfall.

What is considered the highest waterfall in the world bears the Indian name of Bassaseachic, and is located about 190 miles west of the city of Chihuahua, near the summit of the Sierra Madre Mountains in Mexico. The elevation of the mountain is 6,500 feet above sea level. The cascade falls 978 feet.

Deep Sea Fish.

Great forests of seaweeds cover the bottom of the ocean and reach from the greatest depths to the surface. In these forests there is life more diversified than in the primeval forests of the tropics. Spiders and wormlike animals of enormous size, infusoriæ, crabs, sea urchins, shells, crustaceans, starfish, turtles and millions of other living things of all kinds find their food in the equally varied plant life of the deep sea. A curious circumstance connected with deep sea fish is that none of these has ever been brought up alive. This is, of course, owing to the being subjected quickly to new and unnatural conditions, fish that swim at a depth of 100 fathoms being subject to a pressure of 259 pounds to the square inch. The atmospheric pressure at sea level is only 15 pounds to the square inch.

Recent deep sea explorations reveal the fact that the ocean still contains immeasurable treasures which await development and utilization by human inventiveness. The most fertile acre of cultivated land is a sterile desert compared with one acre of the surface of the deep sea bottom.

Curious Trees.

Among the most singular specimens of vegetable life are the bottle-trees of Australia. As the name implies, they are bottle-shaped, increasing in girth for several feet from the ground, and then tapering toward the top, where they are divided into two or more huge branches bearing foliage composed of narrow, lance-shaped leaves from four to seven inches long. The bark is rugged, and the foliage is the same in the old and young trees. The bottle-tree sometimes grows to a height of sixty feet, and measures thirty-five feet around the trunk. Many of these trees are supposed to be thousands of years old.

The angry-tree is also a native of Australia. It reaches the height of eighty feet after a rapid growth, and in outward appearance somewhat resembles a gigantic century-plant. If the shoots are handled, the leaves rustle and move uneasily for a time. If this queer plant is moved from one spot to another it seems angry, and the leaves stand out in all directions, like the quills on a porcupine. A most pungent and sickening odor, said to resemble that given off by rattle-snakes when annoyed, fills the air, and it is only after an hour or so that the leaves fold in the natural way.

The Victoria Falls.

The Victoria Falls of the Zambesi River, in Rhodesia, South Africa, are said to be as much ahead of Niagara in size and available energy as the latter is above most other water powers in the world. The Niagara River is half a mile wide at the falls, and these are 165 feet in height. The Zambesi at the Victoria Falls is one and one-quarter miles in width, and the water drops 400 feet. On the north of the falls are enormous deposits of rich copper ore, and a few miles south are the Wankie coal fields, which yield the best coal in South Africa.

White Waxworms.

On the banks of the river Anning, in China, there grows a tree—known as the *Ligustrum lucidum*—which in the spring becomes covered with little excrescences about the size of a pea. If we cut one of the bulbs we shall find inside what at first appears to be farina, but if we examine the contents carefully we shall discover myriads of eggs which represent the product of an insect known as the white waxworm.

The latter part of April the Chinese gather these bulbs and put them into little bags—each containing about one-half pound in weight—after which they are carried to the town of Chiating, where there is a regular market for this queer product. At Chiating the bags are emptied and the contents redistributed in little sacks made of leaves, about twenty of these bulbs being placed in each bag, and after the leaves have been pierced with holes they are suspended from the branches of a tree, which botanically named is the *Fraxinus Chinensis.* Of these trees we find large plantations around the town of Chiating, this tree being the feeder of the worms as the *Ligustrum* was the producer.

It generally requires about fifteen days for the larvæ to complete their transformation, after which—having become full grown insects—they abandon their artificial homes and install themselves upon the trees reserved for them. The females at once begin to lay eggs, and in order to protect them these tiny mothers place them under the bark itself. The males complete this work of preservation by secreting a greasy matter, which in time completely covers the trunk and branches of the trees with a brilliant, moisture proof varnish. This varnish, however, is the product sought by the Chinese, and is the purest of white wax.

The wax is now gathered, and in order to do this the inhabitants of the country carefully scrape the trunk of the tree and cut off the branches and throw them into boiling water. The wax is thus melted, and after the water has been cooled, it is refound in a thick deposit on the bottom of the vessel in which it has been boiled. The wax is sold for about sixty cents a pound, and is equal in quality to the best product of our native bees.—*Public Opinion.*

The Highest Mountain Climb.

Mountain-climbing has become to a certain extent a scientific undertaking. Careful preparation, selection in physique and diet, the use of appropriate stimulants and the management of scientific instruments of observation characterize all attempts to ascend the higher peaks of the globe. The record highest ascent to the present time was achieved last summer in the western Himlayas by Dr. Wm. H. Workman, who reached the summit of a peak of the Chogo Lungma, 23,394 feet above sea-level. This is about 300 feet higher than Aconcagua, in South America, the ascent of which has heretofore ranked as the highest on record. Mrs. Workman reached a height of 22,567 feet, the highest point reached by a woman mountain-climber.—*Youths' Companion.*

The Monkey's Reasoning Powers.

The monkey's intelligence has never been able to arrive at a point which enables that animal to achieve the untying of a knot. You may tie a monkey with a cord fastened with the simplest form of common knot, and unless the beast can break the string or gnaw it in two he will never get loose. To untie the knot requires observation and reasoning power, and, though a monkey may possess both, he has neither in a sufficient degree to enable him to overcome the difficulty.

Anthropologists have also re-marked that taking aim is a human characteristic which even the anthropoid apes cannot be said to share. Apes and monkeys frequently throw nuts and sticks, sometimes with un-pleasant consequences to others, but they show little or no ability to take accurate aim. The accuracy of eye and judgment of direction and distance which are involved in real aiming have only been developed by man and are among the tokens of his intellectual superiority.

It is singular, too, that no monkey builds itself a shelter with the express object of keeping off the rain, which they all so much dislike. They are miserable in wet and could easily build shelters if they had the sense to do so. "As the creatures hop disconsolately along in the rain," writes Mr. Kipling in his "Beast and Man in India," "or crouch on branches, with dripping backs set against the tree trunk as shelter from the driving storm, they have the air of being very sorry for themselves." But even the orang outang, which builds a small platform in the trees on which to sleep at night, never seems to think of a roof, though the Dyaks say that when it is very wet it covers itself with the leaves of the pandanus, a large fern.

Another radical point of difference is in regard to fire. Not even the instinct of imitation has caused any of the monkey tribe to build or even add fuel to an existing fire. Travelers have told how that the orang outang and gorilla, as well as other apes, will come and warm themselves by the side of a fire they had left but with plenty of branches about they had never been known to replenish the dying embers.

California Frog Ranches.

Frogs while interesting as specimens of animate nature may be and often are made a source of commercial profit. *Collier's Weekly* tells of a frog ranch located at Stege, near San Francisco, California. In the lower portions of the ranch a great number of springs gush out of the soil in copious volumes. It was the springs that determined the first location of the ranch. The site, over-looking an expansive view of the beautiful bay, was capable of vast improvement. A dozen acres, enclosing the springs, were surrounded with a hedge of cypress. The grounds were laid out with taste, and soon presented the rare beauty incident to the profuse vegetation of a semi-tropical climate. These ponds were formed by confining the waters of the flowing springs, some acres in extent, and stocked with frogs. A fence, high enough to prevent the escape of the inmates, surrounded each, and the ponds were filled with aquatic plants and mosses. Hundreds of frogs were placed in the ponds, and from the original stock the increase has been so great that, though thousands are sent to market yearly, the withdrawals have no sensible effect upon the vast numbers remaining. The successful frog raiser always keeps the young ones separate and apart from the full grown, which are cannibals of the first rank, and eat all which are not able to protect themselves. The four-year-olds are considered ripe for the market, though the gourmand in frogs prefers those that are a year or two younger. A frog's life is twelve years. There are some at that age at Stege. They are of monstrous growth, being fourteen inches in length and weighing as much as four pounds.

In California, as in colder climates, frogs hibernate in winter, and in the spring emerge after their long sleep emaciated to the last degree. Then they are fed with a mixture of oatmeal and blood; and again at the spawning season, but only for a short time. They are, most of the time, self sustaining, feeding upon the insects which they cleverly catch.

. Like most creatures of the animal world, frogs are capable of affection for their keeper, and demonstrate it by coming at call and allowing themselves to be handled, showing much delight in being stroked. Placed upon the ground, they readily follow their mistress for a long distance. At night the noise made by the ten thousand frogs, which, it is esti-mated, are contained in the three ponds, is tremendous.

Animals and Poisons.

Certain substances which are deadly in their effects upon men can be taken by the brute creation with impunity. Horses can take large doses of antimony, dogs of mercury, goats of tobacco, mice of hemlock and rabbits of belladonna, without injury. On the other hand, dogs and cats are much more susceptible to the influence of chloroform than man, and are much sooner killed by it. If this invaluable anæsthetic had been first tried upon animals we should probably have never enjoyed its blessings, as it would have been found to be so fatal that its discoverers would have been afraid to test its effects upon human beings. It is evident, then, that an experiment upon an animal can never be the means of any certain deductions so far as man is concerned.—*Family Doctor.*

Sound in the Clouds.

If, when riding in a balloon, at a height, say 2,000 feet, a charge of gun-cotton be fired electrically 100 feet below the car, the report, though really as loud as a cannon, sounds no more than a mere pistol shot, possibly partly owing to the greater rarity of the air, but chiefly because the sound, having no background to reflect it, simply spends itself in the air. Then, always and under all conditions of atmosphere soever, there ensues absolute silence until the time for the echo back from earth has fully elapsed, when a deafening outburst of thunder rises from below, rolling on often for more than half a minute.

RANDOM NOTES.

Small but perfectly formed diamonds have been found in meteors.

A toad watched for one-half an hour during that time devoured one hundred and twenty-eight flies.

The sun's volume is 1,407,124 times that of the earth, and 600 times greater than that of all the planets combined.

The original carnation was a five-petaled bloom native in the south of Italy. It was imported into England about the time of the Norman conquest.

A pains-taking survey of the fishes of the Nile, extended far up both Blue and White Niles, has recently been completed. It adds 14 new species to about 90 known before.

There are, as is well known, certain fish fond of oysters and clams. A codfish will take a clam or oyster in its mouth, crack it and eat the meat. The crab and lobster will crack them or put a stone between the shells when partly open, scoop out the meat and leave the shells.

That dust should settle in regular figures—crystallizing, so to speak, like the snow-flake—seems rather surprising. Using plates heated 10 degrees or 15 degrees above the atmosphere, it has been found that the settling dust always tends to produce regular geometric forms, which are always star-like, but are made by the shape of the plate to vary from three-rayed to eight-rayed stars. In each instance the rays are of uniform length, and form a perfect pattern, while super-imposed stars often produce very beautiful figures which appear under a microscope.

There is a little flea somewhere in the Arctic region that is worth $5,000. The Arctic fox carries about an especial kind of flea found on no other animal. Hon. Charles Rothschild, of London, who has one of the most famous collections of insects in the world, has offered that sum for a single specimen. There are but two specimens in collections in the world. A year ago an expedition was sent by him to the polar regions especially to get one of these fleas, but failed to secure one, and he is now sending another ship to the north to make another effort.

The Greenland whale, it is said, sometimes attains the age of 400 years.

Fossil remains of a frog as large as an ox are said to have recently been exhumed in Oklahoma.

The boa and python have the largest number of ribs of any animals, the number being 320 pairs.

With an abundance of water the Eucalyptus tree will attain a height of one hundred feet in ten years.

Fish have been resuscitated after freezing at 12 or 14 degrees Fahrenheit below freezing point, but do not survive zero temperature.

Eros, the little planet now being watched with so much interest, is about 17 miles in diameter, and at its nearest approach will be only 10,000,000 miles away.

Our knowledge of the 360,000 living animal species now known is being increased by 10,000 descriptions yearly. As an illustration of Zoological progress, Prof. G. B. Howes notes that few earthworms were suspected to exist in 1874, but more than 700 species, belonging to 140 genera, have been recorded since then.

Fossilized tropical fruits have lately been found in coal mined in Spitzbergen. The discovery opens up a marvellous line of geological speculation. Spitzbergen is 400 miles northwest of the northernmost point of Norway, and is subject to extreme cold and lies for half the year in the gloom of the Arctic night. These conditions add to the mystery of the existence of tropical vegetation in the region.

In spite of the efforts to trap the animals of the deep sea, many forms—perhaps some of great size—must still be unknown. The Prince of Monaco, one of the greatest of marine naturalists, has shown that life of some kind probably reaches the deepest ocean bottom, and in a very ingenious way he has proven the existence of an enormous octopus that appears to frequent the middle depths of the Atlantic. Noticing that the dying sperm-whale rejects some of its latest food, he hastened to secure some of this. It included fragments of such an octopus, and one of the antennæ, though incomplete, measured not less than 39 feet in length.

The Amateur Naturalist.

"To him who in the love of Nature holds communion with her visible forms, she speaks a various language."

VOLUME 1.   BINGHAMTON, NEW YORK, MAY, 1904.   NUMBER 3.

THE CHAMELEON.

BY CHARLES D. PENDELL.

ONE of the most peculiar in form and structure, and most surprising in action and mode of life of all living creatures is the chameleon, a small, slow moving, defenceless reptile with harmless teeth and no venom, and constituting a distinct family in the animal kingdom (*Chameleo*), which naturalists divide into upwards of thirty species. Chameleons, though most abundant in Africa, are also found in southern Europe, Asia Minor, Hindoostan, Ceylon, Madagascar and Australia. A lizard in many respects similar though more slender, classed as a separate family (*Iguanidæ*), is found in the southern part of the United States and in Mexico.

The tail is long and prehensile like that of the spider monkey. The toes are so divided that it has the power of grasping with each foot like a hand. There are five toes on each limb, but, unlike most lizards, these are not free, but bound together in two opposing bundles. In the front legs the thumb and two fingers form the inner bundles, but in the hind legs only two, the great toe and the next one are similarly tied together, so that at first glance he seems to have no toes: it is as if the stumps of the legs had been slit up, the sides of the slit closing around the branch, serving as feet and toes. The lungs are very large, and this strange saurian thus possesses the power of inflating itself with air so as to appear about twice its natural size. This circumstance, together with their ability to endure long fasts, gave rise to the ancient fable, not yet wholly eradicated from the popular mind, that they lived on air. Even the learned Roman naturalist Pliny really believed this, remarking: "It always holds the head upright and the mouth open, and is the only animal which receives nourishment neither by meat nor drink, nor anything else, but by air alone." In fact, however, the chameleon, living among the branches of the trees, feeds upon insects, for which it will watch long and patiently. When an insect passes sufficiently near—within five or six inches—this peculiar lizard will dart its remarkably extensile tongue with lightning like rapidity and unerring aim; and, held fast by a viscous saliva, the doomed insect is engulfed in the mouth of its captor. The tongue is club-shaped at the tip and covered with a sticky substance. Ordinarily, when a chameleon opens its mouth the tongue is not especially conspicuous, but when six or seven inches from a fly this organ will be shot forth so quickly that the eye can scarcely follow it, and yet with unerring aim the tip strikes and snatches the fly down the chameleon's throat. The secret of this little bit of magic is the elastic stem or base of the tongue, which telescopes upon itself when not in use. Remarkable indeed is a creature with a tongue which can be thrust out a distance equal to the length of the entire body of the animal. Mythology itself can offer little that is more extraordinary.

Bodily, the chameleon is slow and rather clumsy; and, owing to its extremely short neck, it is impossible for it to turn its head. It has, moreover, no external organ of hearing. Its eyes, however, are very remarkably developed and adjusted, each eye being able to move in every direction, wholly independent of the other. "Thus, while one of them attentively gazes upon the heavens, the other minutely examines the ground, or while one of them rolls in its orbit the other remains fixed; nay, its mobility is so great that, without even moving its stiff head, like Janus, the double faced god of ancient Rome, it can see at the same time all that goes on before and behind it." It has even been asserted that it "may be asleep on one side and awake on the other." This independent movement of the eyes is more or less characteristic of lizards and other reptiles but in chameleons the fact is made more evident by the eyelids having become fused, growing as one except for a tiny round opening in the center. The eyes are conical and protruding, and the general appearance has been aptly compared to "a boiled pea with an ink spot on it." The "ink spot" is the tiny opening between the lids, and, like the telescope hole in an astronomical observatory, it has to move towards the object looked at. This independent action of the eyes is owing to the imperfect sympathy which exists between the lobes of the brain and the two sets of nerves which ramify throughout the opposite sides of its frame.

The most remarkable thing about the chameleon, however, is its marvelous power of changing color under various influences and surroundings. At the sight of a serpent it at once inflates its body, sways itself as it walks away from what it regards as its natural enemy, opening its mouth, and suddenly snapping its jaws together; the body at the same time undergoing rapid changes of color, from brown, bottle green, violet, blue, yellow and red. The same symptoms are exhibited in the presence of other enemies. In its natural state this peculiar saurian changes its color to correspond to the surrounding foliage or other objects. Thus one seen by the writer while in Georgia some years ago, was when first observed near the foot of a grape vine and was of a brownish hue, similar to the bark of the vine; climbing higher among the leaves the color became green; and later, coming where the rays of the sun shone directly on it, it changed to a bright scarlet color. Under certain circumstances the fore part of the body may be of one color and the hind part another. Or one side, even, may be of a light tint and the other of a dark hue of the same or entirely different color. There are numerous explanations of this phenomenon given by different writers, but they are generally as different from one another as the colors of the chameleon itself. The following seems to the writer the most probable of any explanation that has as yet come under his observation: "The outer layer of the skin is colorless, but beneath this at varying distances from the surface are certain iridescent cells, then some containing drops of oil, others with crystal granules, and still others with brownish and reddish pigment. When the crystal filled cells are brought near the surface, they refract the light and make the creatures very pale—almost white; the oil-drop cells, in turn, cause another color; when all the pigment is forced upward, a dark hue is imparted to the skin, and when the light is diffracted through the yellow oil and iridescent cells a green tint results. These pigment cells are under the control of the chameleon, and thus he can copy his surroundings so perfectly and immediately that when one portion of his body is in shadow and the other in sunshine he is bi-colored, the dividing line corresponding to the edge of light and shade."

The young of the chameleon are produced from eggs, which are white in color, very spherical in form. They are hatched by the heat of the sun combined with that generated by the decomposition of leaves under which they are placed. The period of incubation is said to be 130 days. The baby chameleons are white in color and it is said are not able to produce the chromatic changes after the manner of their parents until several weeks old.

HOW A TOAD SHEDS HIS SKIN.

BY FRANCES BROWE MORSE.

NE of the most curious and at the same time most interesting of Mother Nature's provisions for the care of her children is evinced in a toad's disposal of his cast-off skin. Naturalists tell me that the reason we never find the skin of a toad as we sometimes do that of a snake is because a toad swallows his skin, while a snake crawls out of his turning it inside out as he goes. Most persons living in the country have found these rejected snake-skins, but comparatively few have seen a toad dispose of his last season's coat. I never saw it but once, myself, and the odd sight amused me so much, I want to tell those who have never seen it how the dingy little fellow swallows his huge mouthful. He does not, as one might suppose, crawl out of his skin, snake fashion, and then turn around and proceed to swallow it. I did not see him commence his odd meal, so just how he began still remains a mystery. When I first saw him one hind leg was already a brilliant green, contrasting ludicrously with the rest of the body while one end of the skin pulled from it was in his mouth. For a moment or two after I sat down near him, he made no movement except to blink his eyes stupidly, and then, quicker than the proverbial wink of a cat's eye he dexterously threw one fore leg over his head, pulling the skin from his head, or from half of it, I should say, for the skin was neatly slit lengthwise through the middle, and but half came off at once; a second later he gave two or three powerful gulps, allowing the skin already in his mouth to slip down to make room for the fresh mouthful. His next move was to get rid of the skin on his fore leg and to do this he held it well back and shook and pulled vigorously until it slipped from the last toe, when it shared the fate of the rest of that side and went into the capacious mouth. Then he commenced on the hind part of the other side, while all this time he had not completely swallowed any portion for there was always some hanging from his mouth. He proceeded in the same manner on this side until he came to the last bit clinging to the toes of the front foot, and he seemed to find the greatest difficulty in freeing the skin from them. He shook, pulled and tugged, yet still it clung fast until by one great last effort, he tore it loose and swallowed it, when his curious meal ended. As far as I could see, he had not breathed once during the whole operation. A toad breathes by swallowing air in mouthfuls, as we do food, and the movement of the throat in so doing is plainly visible. It seemed difficult to understand how he could breathe with his throat full of the old skin, and yet how could he exist without doing so during this time, for it must have taken some minutes? As soon as he was through, the pulsations of his throat began again and he was ready to take up life anew.

Athens, Pa.

PORTO RICAN MINERALS.

BY O. W. BARRETT.

UP to about two thousand feet above sea-level, the bulk of the rock is limestone overlaid with a rotten "tosca" which at once forms red clay upon exposure to the air; this, of course, contains little of interest and even good calcite speciments are rare. But above the calcareous series we find a fair variety of the granitic and metamorphosed rocks.

There are still many problems for the geologist to solve; for instance, the reported occurrence of bituminous lignite at Utuado and two other places, of graphite at Adjuntas, of jet at Maricao, and of amber at Moca. But much good work has been done in the last few years along these lines and we now have a fair knowledge of the mineralogical topography of the island. Moreover, a strip ten miles wide across the island from Arecibo to Ponce has been surveyed by the Bureau of Soils of the United States Department of Agriculture; this gives us a definite knowledge of the many kinds of soils, their origins and composition.

In the northeast part, in the "Luquillo" district, the granites and syennites contain quartz veins which bear considerable gold; in fact, it is said that every stream which flows out of the region "runs over sands of gold." While the placer areas are small, they are often exceedingly rich in the shining flakes, and the lazy native sets out with his pan whenever he feels the need of a purchasing medium, confident that his time will not be wasted. But when the "Americano" tries his hand at it the weather—constant rains, bad transportation facilities,—no roads, or some other serious difficulty turns him back in short order.

Millions of dollars in gold were produced in the sixteenth century; since then until recently, little interest has been shown in this ever precarious occupation. But now this Corozal district is "staked out" and we hope it will regain its old fame with modern apparatus and live engineers.

Platinum was discovered about three years ago at Corozal in considerable quantities associated with gold and, stranger still, with mercury.

Copper occurs at several points and has been mined at Jayuya and Rio Blanco. Nickel occurs at Naguabo. Lead, as a sulphuret, is found in various localities. Bismuth has been reported from Ponce. Tin turns up in the gold washings at Guayama. Manganese, as pyrolusite, mingles with the more aristocratic elements at Corozal.

Mayaguez, P. R.

ભ પ

A RAMBLE AROUND KANDY.

TO my mind the Kandyan district of Ceylon is one of the prettiest spots in the whole of the tropical world. The town itself lies in a valley of the most luxuriant vegetation, and is surrounded by a regular ampitheatre of palm-clad hills, overlooking a magnificent lake below. Around this lake and over the hills are some of the most beautiful walks and drives it is possible for the mind of man to conceive, while the rich tropical scenery that greets the eye at every turn is magnificent beyond description. Here almost every variety of palm tree flourishes, while fruit and spice laden trees fill the air with a fragrance both sweet and refreshing. Gigantic tree ferns and flowers of many varieties grow in rank profusion on the road sides and jungly parts, while bright-colored birds and butterflies flit around the evergreen trees and undergrowth in endless variety. Here it is that Nature seems to put forth all her energies, and encouraged by a salubrious climate as well as a rich and a fertile soil, clothes both hill, wood and valley in robes of varied green the whole year round. The seasons come and go almost unnoticed to the casual observer, yet the leaves still cling to the trees, the young bud forcing off the old leaf before it has time to decay, or even become tinted with those autumnal lights and shades which lend such color to the landscape at home as harvest time approaches, so that throughout the year there is one long delicious round of spring and summer. At night too the air is filled with the monotonous music of a thousand humming and chirping insects, the hoarse croaking of the frog is heard from the marshy rice fields, and the noisy jackal from the adjacent hill sides. Gigantic bats flit hither and thither in silence through open glades, numerous moths dance round the succulent herbage and undergrowth, while the lights of innumerable fire-flies twinkle dreamily amongst the trees like so many tiny fairy lamps.

The botanist who visits this garden of the world for the purpose of studying its flora will find boundless specimens to interest and instruct him, for here are represented almost every plant and tree known to the scientific and commercial world, while a large variety are found here which inhabit no other part of the known world. The extensive botanical gardens at Peradeniyia, near Kandy, are said to be the finest in the world, and present a wealth of varied interest to the traveller.

Amongst the innumerable variety of trees and plants pointed out to the visitor, the following few may be mentioned: the talipot palm, a magnificent tree which blossoms on reaching the age of fifty years, then slowly decays; the areca nut and cocoa nut palms; the toddy palm, which yields an intoxicating spirituous liquor; the traveller's palm, which by tapping the base of its branches yields a copious draught of water; the palriyra palm, much used in the manufacture of native basket work; the bread fruit tree, and jak tree, the latter producing a species of bread fruit much larger and coarser than the former, and much used as food by the natives; the plantain or banana, of which there are several varieties; cinchona tree, the bark of which yields quinine; the strychnine tree; the deadly upas tree, of which it is said by the natives that those who sleep under its poisonous branches never wake in life again; the sacred boe tree, under which the Buddhists believe that several of their ancient high priests, devoted followers of Buddha, were endowed with supernatural wisdom and learning; satin wood and ebony trees; the cotton tree, yielding a woolly substance resembling cotton wool, and used for making pillows, cushions, &c.; the sack tree, the inner bark of which is flexible and resembles a thickly woven sack when sewn at one end; the mango and mangostine trees; besides tea, coffee, cocoa, vanilla, pepper, cloves, nutmeg, cinnamon and others in endless variety.

In a country so congenial to the growth of tropical vegetation one naturally expects to find a variety of bright plumaged birds, and some of these are familiar to us as cage pets, notably the parrot species. Amongst the many which I have observed around Kandy are several species of green parroquet and woodpecker, the weaver and tailor birds, barbet, Indian pitta, oriole, orange minivet, white breasted and common kingfisher, all beautifully colored species, the tailor and weaver birds excepted. There is a great variety of duller plumaged birds not familiar to Europe, which entrance the tropical woodlands with sweet and melodious song.

Protective coloring is seen here to great advantage, the color of many species of birds being in complete uniformity with their evergreen surroundings. The same law applies to several species of leaf insects, one variety in particular so closely resembles the shape and color of a leaf that it is difficult for the most practised and experienced eye to detect its presence on the foliage of the trees and shrubs it rests upon. There is a species of green lizard which takes full advantage of its natural protection, allowing one to approach it so closely that it could easily be touched by one's hand. It sits motionless, except for an occasional twinkling of its beady eye, amongst the leaves of some jungle shrub or plants, apparently feeling quite secure and safe from observation in its protective surroundings. Here also we have the chameleon, which, as every schoolboy knows, possesses that wonderful power of changing its color to suit its surroundings. I have watched the chameleon on the tiled roof of a bungalow changing color to suit the various tints of red the tiles assume through long exposure to the weather. On this roof some of the tiles were red, some almost black, others covered with grey and yellow lichen, and some almost new and brick red, yet the chameleon as it passed over the various shades of color, assumed each color likewise. Again I have watched the chameleon on the green slopes and yellow sandy patches around Kandy assume the color of the various objects it passed—the green plant, the decaying leaves, flowers of varied color, the yellow sand and the dull grey rock or stone. On one occasion I saw a chameleon resting on a sandy ledge; the red blossom of a drooping flower hung down behind, and was almost hidden by the upper part of the chameleon's body; that part of its body which concealed the bloom assumed the red color of the hidden flower, the lower part of its body still retaining the yellow color of the sand.

There are, however, other creatures in this fair island, which are perhaps not quite so attractive, and are looked upon with a considerable amount of disgust and dread, yet withal equally as interesting as the foregoing. Several large varieties of centipedes are plentiful in the Kandy district, and some of them nauseous. I have here before me as I write, a large specimen nine inches long, which is regarded by the natives with considerable dread. Its body is composed of thirteen alternate black and brick red segments, thirty-six sharp pointed feet, eighteen on each side, all of which are said to inflict a poisonous sting. There are also several species of scorpions the larger averaging between four and five inches in length, and of a metallic greenish black color. Tarantulas are also common and much dreaded by the natives. A large variety of snakes inhabit the vicinity of Kandy, many of them harmless and of attractive color, while others are fatally poisonous. The most to be feared is the cobra, several of which I have personally observed in the woods and jungle around Kandy, while one was brought to me which had been killed in an engineer's yard on the outskirts of the town The voracious little land leech abounds in the jungle grass and fields around Kandy. It is about an inch long, yet it is almost impossible for one to ramble through the jungle or cultivated fields without a number of these little gluttons attaching themselves to some portion of the body, but princi-pally the legs. They inflict no pain and very often their presence is not detected until perhaps on going to bed you find your legs and feet covered with blood, and the little leaches gorged to three times the normal size. To the inexperienced such discovery is somewhat alarming, but these tiny creatures are quite harmless, and are easily washed off by means of salt water.—*Sergeant Hugh Mackay in Nature-Study, pub. Huddersfield, Eng.*

ﻙ ﻙ

SOLILOQUIES OF A MINERALOGIST.

"Full many a gem of purest ray serene.
The dark, unfathom'd caves of ocean bear;
Full many a flower is born to blush unseen
And waste its sweetness on the desert air."

"Gray's Elegy," from which the above lines have been extracted, is a gem of the highest literary order, and, in point of beauty and rhythm, is perhaps unsurpassed by any other poem in the English language. In the first three lines of the quotation is expressed a truth of which we all are sensible, but does the flower exhaling its perfume in the solitude of the wilderness *waste* its sweetness?

It is true that its richness of *color*, its delicacy of structure, and its fra-grance are lost to man, and can never be interpreted by him unless the flow-er shall become an object of his vision; but, like all other created things, man excepted, it unquestionably fulfills the purpose of its creation.

In may be remarked, in passing, that it has been shown by Darwin that the color and fragrance of flowers have a use in attracting the insects that fertilize the flowers. The sweetness that the poet supposes to be wasted, is thus the very means by which the species is preserved. That they serve a much higher purpose will be shown further on.

Buried deeply below the surface of the earth, and hidden for untold ages in rock bound seams, and lining cavities in the rocks, exist magnificent min-eral crystallizations, rivalling the beauty of the solitary flower. By far the greater number of these will never be revealed to the eye of man; they will continue undisturbed, probably so long as the earth, itself, shall endure; subject, of course, to the changes from which nothing is entirely exempt. Very probably many of them in loveliness of color and symmetry of form, surpass any which have been brought to the light of day.

Man, in excavating tunnels and railroad cuts, in quarrying for building and road materials, in mining for the precious metals and the various industrial minerals, merely scratches the earth's surface, and, in doing so, reveals the many exquisitely beautiful minerals which adorn our museums and the cabinets of the mineral fraternity.

We often wish the minerals were less rock-bound and therefore more accessible; but like many other desirable things, to obtain them, good, hard work must be put in. We value things in proportion to what we have to pay for them.

The older mineralogists will remember the Rev. E. Seymour, of Bloomfield, N. J., than whom no lover of minerals was ever more enthusiastic. He used to say that he would it were possible to begin at the head of Bergen Hill, and, with a gigantic plough, buried deep in the refractory rock, proceed down the center of the ridge to its opposite extremity, turning a furrow which should reveal the vast wealth of the showy zeolites and kindred minerals, which are known to lie in great profusion along the seams of this famous trap-dyke.

The origin of mineral crystallizations is commonly referred to the operation of natural law; it is the property of matter to crystallize from a state of fusion, or of vapor, or from a solution; and in obedience to the same law, definite mathematical forms result, and these laws are such that, in any given species, constancy of angle is preserved; but back of all is Nature's Creator, the framer of what we term "natural law." These laws we can hardly believe are automatic in their action. Rather let us adopt the view that the God of Nature directs, in person, every movement of the energetic molecule as it hastens to its position in the construction of the crystal, and superintends the arrangement of the cells in the plant and its flower.

"All things were made by Him; and without Him was not anything made that was made."—John I, 3.—*Geo. O. Simmons in The Mineral Collector.*

ॐ ॐ

The danger from electricity, particularly for the firemen in directing a stream of water upon an object carrying electric current, was the subject of a number of experiments the results of which are described in the *Scientific American:* A man wearing wet shoes and standing on a wet plank flooring, threw a jet of water on an electrified plate. At 500 volts and an aperture of 0.74 inch in the nozzle, he felt the current at a distance of 2¾ feet, and with an aperture of about 2 inches could not get nearer than about 3¼ feet. Under the same conditions, but with alternating current, he could not stay within 8.2 feet, and at 3,600 volts he had to remain at a distance of 26¼ feet.

The Amateur Naturalist.

A Journal for those who Study Nature from a love of it.

ISSUED BI-MONTHLY.

SUBSCRIPTION, 50 CENTS PER YEAR.   SINGLE COPIES, 10 CENTS.

ADVERTISING RATES ON APPLICATION.

————————EDITED AND PUBLISHED BY —— —— —— —— ——

CHARLES D. PENDELL,

85-87 STATE STREET,   -   -   -   BINGHAMTON, N. Y.

No other one man has done more to throw the light of civilization and open the way for Christianity into Africa than Henry M. Stanley. He died May 10th. His was a master mind in the galaxy of great naturalists.

That the English sparrow is an injurious pest with scarcely a redeeming trait seems to be proven, if proof were needed. *American Ornithology* invited opinions from its readers on the subject and received one hundred and fifteen postals, besides many letters, some of which are published in the May number, of which number only three took a decided stand in favor of the sparrow. As an insect feeder its value is minus, as it drives away many other birds that are insect feeders, while of the food consumed by it about eighty-five per cent. is of vegetable character. They are filthy, noisy, de structive to grain, enemies of the song birds, destroying the eggs, killing the young and quarrelling with and driving away the adults. The indictment against them is serious, but the proof seems to be abundant.

Newspaper science is a peculiar thing and some of the mystic creations of the newspaper sanctum are to be wondered at. Among other fantistic discoveries the editor has noted the following: "A spider that preys upon snakes," "a new kind of bug that has eaten out the foundations of a large church," "the skeleton of a mastodon with the skeleton of an Indian found within the ribs of the mastodon," "a living frog found imbeded in a granite boulder," and several times the undiscovered "connecting link" has been found (?) in some unknown portion of the world. (It is remarkable, anyway, the effort some scientists make to prove their ancestors to have belonged to the *Simiadæ!*). Science possesses facts in abundance that are even more wonderful than the creations of a newspaper man's mind, and to the student of nature who will devote but a small part of his spare time to systematic research, the discoveries of actually existing marvels will be astonishing. This brief editorial could easily be lengthened into an extended article were we disposed. Our object, however, was but to call attention to the utter unreliability of much that passes for science, and to open to the mind a vista of the themes of absorbing interest which might accrue to the mind were a faction of the time often spent in useless smatterings of generalities devoted to systematic study of any one of the sub-divisions into which the realm of nature study is divided.

In our March number we quoted a newspaper dispatch relative to the disappearance of Bald Mountain, Me., and the appearance of a lake in its place, following the earthquake shock of March 21st. The newspaper from which the dispatch was taken has in the past claimed Associated Press franchise or we should not have credited the item to that association, nor have given so much credence to the item. A subscriber in Caribou, Me., who is Associated Press correspondent for that section, disclaims the responsibility and assures us that the item was pure and simple "fake."

Contributions for THE AMATEUR NATURALIST are solicited from all our readers. As stated in our first number, "articles that state facts interestingly," relative to some branch of natural science, are those most desired. The large amount of fiction published is evidence that facts are not alone interesting, while many a dust-covered volume shows that facts are not always interesting—at least not described in an interesting manner. Several manuscripts have been received which we regret we were not able to use; good in themselves but not adapted to the plan or purpose of this magazine. Others we have which will appear in future numbers.

Notwithstanding the tendency of the age to "commercialism," there is also a strong current toward nature study that is growing every year. As a result of this, summer schools are being established where text-books are mere adjuncts and Nature herself furnishes the material for study, under the direction of those proficient in special lines of work. The Bigelow School of Nature Study, held near Forestville, Conn., the last two weeks of July, is one of these and its prospectus portrays what must be two weeks of most profitable study and recreation, and a drawing near to Nature's heart in a manner ideal. Mr. Willard N. Clute, publisher of *The American Botanist* and *The Fern Bulletin*, has charge of the botanical work, and as one who has for years been on intimate terms with Dame Nature he knows how to make the work most pleasurable.

We have received several letters from subscribers from widely separated localities—Connecticut, Texas and British Columbia—giving valuable suggestions as well as words of appreciation. "It is all right, enlarge it, illustrate it, make it a monthly," are among the suggestions which with several others will all be followed out in due course of time. But to those who would like to see these improvements we suggest that they assist by aiding us in building up our subscription list to that point where the financial outlay can be reasonably incurred. THE AMATEUR NATURALIST has good reason to congratulate itself on its success thus far, and as an incentive to our friends to do a little missionary work, we propose this plan: Secure for us three subscriptions at 50 cents per year, send us $1. and keep the other 50 cents for your trouble. Or if you are not a subscriber, send us two subscriptions at 50 cents each and we will send you the magazine a year free.

A BLOODLESS SPORTSMAN.

BY HATTIE WASHBURN.

As I in guarded silence stray,
A vision or a song to gain,
Lest breaking twig my step betray
I bring to none no death or pain.

No deadly gun or rod I bare
For a bloodless sportsman am I;
At my approach no plumage rare
Is stained by life blood's crimson dye.

The wild bird sings his merry lay,
The rabbit 'neath the bushes hides
And where the brooklet's eddies play
The shinning trout securely glides.

Yet the best Nature e'er bestowes,
The visions fair, the songs I gain,
To me her sweetest mood she shows
Nor knows a loss or throb of pain.

Would you know sport simple and pure?
Hunt with naught besides ears and eyes,
Wander where Nature's charms allure
And gain her love, her fairest prize.

Goodwin, S. D.

The Colorado River.

BY LUMAN C. PENDELL.

IN speaking of a river, one naturally expects to find the surrounding country either a well timbered or an agriculture country, but a trip down the Colorado or Spanish "Red River" as its name implies, from the Needles to Yuma would convince him that such was not always the case. With the exceptions of the "overflow lands" the country is practically barren. The valley is about ten miles on either side of the river excepting where the river has cut its way through the mountains, as below the Needles and several other places the mountains come very near. The river in places, even in low water, is quite wide and also very shallow, the writer having waded across it. It is called a treachous river in this portion, in that it changes its channel at will from one bank to the other, throwing up a sand bar here and a mud bar there, and also has large whirls more especially dangerous in high water. Its banks also in places are pure slimy muds or "Soquite" in which many a horse and cow has lost its life. Acres of well timbered banks with cottonwood trees six or twelve inches in diameter have been wiped out and sunk in the sand and mud of the river,—the river making its channel where they once stood. The banks of the river are for the most part lined with a weed called "Cochinia" commonly called arrow weed which attains a height of from six to twelve feet, and so thickly does it grow that one can hardly penetrate it; and back of this is a low brush called "greese wood." In other parts it is well lined with cottonwood and willow, and the mesquite trees, the later bears a bean similar in looks to our vegetable, the string bean which when ripe has a very sweet taste and quantities of them are gathered and fed to stock in lieu of grain. They are also used by the native Mexicans and Indians as an article of food, prepared as a gruel called a'tol.

A trip down the river is very interesting, being full of ever changing scenery and plenty of hunting and fishing. There are several varieties of fish such as catfish, salmon, carp, hump-back sucker, and boney tail. The larger game animals are mostly mountain lions, wild cats, beaver, badger, coon, cyote, deer, mountain sheep, rabbits; also quail.

Douglas, Ariz.

TWO SLAYERS.

The jewel-winged bird on your bonnet
    Last summer was happy and free;
Was flashing across the blue heavens,
    Or filling the treetops with glee,
He died in the midst of a love song—
    Oh, woman's soft heart, think of that!
He died never dreaming you wanted
    His beautiful corpse for your hat.

Each bird that is worn for adornment,
    Each heaven-taught singer that dies
For vanity's sake, has two slayers—
    The hunter, the woman who buys.
One kills and one pays for murder;
    Both equally guilty I hold;
Because the sad slaughter would slacken
    If woman paid not with her gold.
                —Our Dumb Animals.

A Vulture and Rattlesnake.

When the international boundary commission resurveyed the lines between the United States and Mexico, there were naturalists in the party. Dr. Mearns, who, with his assistants, collected many specimens of birds and mammals, tells of a fight in the air between a California vulture and a rattlesnake which he saw while exploring the Cocopah mountains of Lower California.

It was in the early morning. The big bird had seized the snake behind the head and was struggling upward with its writhing, deadly burden. The snake's captor appeared aware that its victim was dangerous. The burden was heavy, as the reptile was nearly five feet long.

The grip of the bird on the snake's body was not of the best. The snake seemed to be squirming from its captor's talons, at least sufficiently to enable it to strike. Its triangular head was seen to recoil and dart at the mass of feathers.

It did this once or twice, and then, with a shriek, the vulture dropped its prey. The bird was probably 500 feet or so above the observers. The astonished men were then treated to a spectacle seldom seen. Few birds but a vulture could accomplish such a feat.

The instant the snake escaped from the bird's clutches, it dropped earthward like a shot, and, like a shot, the bird dropped after it, catching it in midair with a grip that caused death. At any rate, the snake ceased to wriggle, and the vulture soared away to a mountain peak to devour its hard earned meal.
—Youth's Companion.

The Tragedy of an Insect.

According to Prof. C. B. Davenport, of the University of Chicago, the brief existence of the sand fly is full of interest.

The sand fly is known to scientists familiarly as the May fly. In scientific terms, it is called *Ephemerida*. This name is taken from the Greek word ephemeros, which means lasting only for a day. To the scientists the sand fly is one of the most interesting and beautiful of insects. The fly lives but a day at most, but before it sees the light it has lived for from one to three years under the water in the form of what scientists call a nymph. This nymph can both walk and swim. As it grows it molts, and after about the ninth molt tiny wings appear on its thorax. These grow larger until the insect comes forth from the water a sand fly. It then has but one duty—

to lay its eggs. This done, the sand fly zigzags through the air until its brief life is ended.

The Wild Flower Garden.

The writer of this article has always been a lover of native plants. Not simply because they are native, but because they are quite as beautiful as many of the plants brought here from foreign countries. This being the case, why should we not take pride in our home gardens?

Many otherwise intelligent persons are under the impression that we have few, if any, flowering plants and shrubs that are worthy of cultivation. They have come to look upon them as "weeds" or "wild things," as if all plants were not weeds and wild things somewhere, and so unfamiliar are they with them that they cannot recognize them when they meet with them outside their native haunts. I remember that some years ago I transplanted a goldenrod from the fence corner of the pasture to a place in my garden. There it grew luxuriantly, and soon became a great plant that sent up scores of stalks as high as a man's head, each season, each one crowned with a great plume of brilliant flowers. It was a sight worth seeing when in full bloom—a mass of floral sunshine, that brightened the whole garden. One day, in the fall, an old neighbor came along and leaned over the fence where I was at work among my plants.

"That's a beauty," he said, looking at the goldenrod. "I never saw anything like it before. I s'pose,

now, you paid a good deal o' money for that plant."

"How much do you think it cost me?" I asked.

"Oh, I don't know," he replied, looking at the plant admiringly, and then at some of foreign origin, growing near by. The price of these he knew something about, for he had bought some for his own garden. He seemed to be making a mental calculation, based on the relative beauty of the plants. Presently he said:

"I wouldn't wonder any if you paid out as much as two or three dollars for that plant. How near right am I?"

"That plant cost me nothing but the labor of bringing it from the pasture, where I found it growing," I answered. "Don't you know what it is? There's any quantity of it in your pasture, back of the barn."

"You don't mean to say that's yellow-weed?" exclaimed the old gentleman, with a disgusted look on his face. "I wouldn't have it about my house! There's weeds enough, as it is, 'thout settin' 'em out." And away he went, with a look in his face that made me think he felt as if he had been imposed upon.—*Home and Flowers.*

The Pygmies of Africa.

Reports of a race of dwarfs or pygmies have from time to time been given by travellers on their return from the interior of the "Dark Continent." Such reports, however, have been regarded with more or less suspicion; but coming from so many different sources are beginning to be believed, incredible as they may seem, and furnish another object lesson of the trite proverb, "Truth is stranger than fiction." The following extract from "Dwarf Land" by A. B. Lloyd is quite apropos:

We had now been in the forest for six long days and I began to believe that, after all, the pygmy stories were not true. But one day my boy, who was just behind me, suddenly stopped and pointed to what he described as a "man-monkey." I thought it must be a gorilla.

I could only see that it must be a creature of large dimensions to be so near the top of a high tree. I therefore raised my rifle to my shoulder, took careful aim and prepared to fire. I had very nearly pulled the trigger, when my boy called out: "Don't fire! It's a man!"

I almost dropped my gun, so great was my astonishment. Could it be a man? Yes, there he was; I could clearly distinguish him. He had discovered us, and as we stood there gazing, the little man ran along the branch on which he had been standing and, jumping from tree to tree, soon disappeared. It was a pygmy, and how nearly had he paid the penalty of climbing trees!

Late in the afternoon, while casually looking up from my book, I became aware of a number of little faces peering through the thicket. Just in front of me was the huge trunk of a tree and from one side of it peeped a tiny figure. For a moment I was taken aback; it seemed like being in fairyland and receiving visits from fairies. My boys caught sight of these strange little beings and came at once to my side.

I told one of them to go and fetch the little people, that I might talk to them; but he was afraid and refused to leave my side. At last I called out in the language of the people of Toro, and to my pleasure one little man returned my greeting. I asked him to come to me, and very slowly and shyly he crept along, hiding his face behind his hands.

I now had a complete view of my visitors. Although they are very short—about four feet high—they are broad-chested, with muscles finely developed, short, thick neck and small bullet-head, with legs massive and strong. The chest is covered with black curly hair and most of the men wore thick black beards. Each carried a bow and arrows or short throwing-spears.

They never cultivate the ground but wander from place to place gathering fruits and nuts from the trees. Often they follow a wounded elephant for days, shooting into it hundreds of little iron-tipped arrows, until the poor creature dies from sheer exhaustion. They make their little camp and live upon the fleeh as long as it lasts; then away they go again to seek other food.

How a Mockingbird Learns a Tune.

A nest full of very young mockingbirds was bought of an Indian boy on the wharf at San Diego, California, and brought home on the steamer in a cigar box. . . . . . One of them proved to be a fine male and for eleven years was the delight of our household. . . . . . .

I wished to see if he could learn to sing a strain of human music in addition to his own wild melodies, which held us fascinated in the moonlight nights of spring. So I kept his cage beside me while at work and whistled over and over two lines of Bonny Doon, "Thou'll break my heart, thou bonny bird, A warbling on the greenwood tree." I thought the intervals in that strain had something of the "woodnote wild" and ought not to be hard for him. All day, and day after day I kept it up, and still Mockie showed no signs of interest. He kept unusually still, however, with his head often on one side and his eyes half closed, and never interrupted me once with his hilarious outbursts, so I was encouraged to persevere.

After several weeks of this, I was one day called by the maid "Come quick," she said "the bird is singing your tune." I went with her to the door and peeped in. There sat Mockie on the back of a chair singing over to himself, but perfectly correct, the whole strain. He sang it very softly, and seemed shy about his accomplishment, for as soon as he saw he was observed he interrupted the sweet notes with an impatient "chack, chack." After a few days he gained confidence and sang out boldly and loud, even before an audience of strangers. But he was always prone to interrupt himself mischievously, at the very climax of the song, with some droll squawk, the imitation of a wheelbarrow, or other uncouth sound. This song he never forgot till his death, and taught it to his young birds, who,

however, never equally him in their performance of it. Another indication of his ear for music was that he usually kept silent while the piano was being played, and seemed to listen with interest, as he had done while he was learning the song. Sometimes he would sing a sort of accompaniment of soft, single notes, quite different from his usual song. These were in harmony with the piece played, and I was so much struck with this fact that I wrote them down on the score of a Beethoven Sonata. The notes were not continuous, but came in tentatively now and then, as a novice with the violin might try to strike a note in harmony from time to time. I believe if a simple composition had been played to him often enough, these notes would have assumed definite form, and the bird would have appeared with assurance in the role of a composer.

The fact that he still sang the song characteristic of the race, though taken so early from the nest, might be thought to have some bearing on the vexed question discussed by Lloyd Morgan in "Habit and Instinct" on whether song is an inherited instinct or learned by tradition, from the parents. But it should be remembered that night and day from the time he chipped the egg till the Indian kidnapped him, he had heard his father's song, which may have well made an indelible impression on so retentive a memory.—*Anna Head in American Ornithology.*

Coral reefs are formed by the petrified bodies of tiny polyps.

From Orchids to Snow.

There are two places in the world where a person can pass through the tropical, subtropical and temperate zones inside of an hour. Hawaii is one and Darjeeling, in northeastern India, is another. In both these places this is done by climbing up the high mountains.

In Hawaii the traveller starts with the warm breath of the Pacific fanning him amid the smell of palm-trees. He passes by great clusters of tropical fruit, and, as he mounts, the trees change until he is in the kind of scenery that may be found in the southern United States.

Still he climbs, and soon he notices that it is much cooler and that the character of the scene has changed to one that reminds him of the temperate zone, with fields in which potatoes and other northern vegetables are growing.

In Darjeeling the change is still more wonderful. The entrance to the tableland on which the little mountain city stands is through a dark, sombre, tropical pass, full of mighty palms and hung with orchids and other jungle growth.

After a while the trees change from palms to the wonderful tree-ferns. These alternate with banana trees, until, after some more climbing, forests are reached of magnolias and similar trees.

Through these magnolias the way leads ever up, and all at once, over an open pass, there come into view immense thickets of Himalayan rhododendrons and the evergreen of firs and cedars; and beyond stand the white, grim, snowclad, frozen moun-tain-peaks like arctic icebergs on land.

In less than two hours a traveller can ascend from orchids through jungles to tea plantations, and thence to a climate of northern roses and violets.

Have Crows a Language?

There is some reason for calling an owl the bird of wisdom; and yet there is cause for wondering if the crow is not mentally his superior. Crows are not disheartened by the gloom of late autumn. If the fog is too dense to fly through it, they rise above it or trot about the ground, discussing the situation with their fellows. Is this speaking too positively? I have long been familiar with an observing man who has lived all his days within sight and hearing of crows. He claims to understand their language, and can repeat the "words" that make up their vocabularly. Certainly crows seem to talk; but do they? Does a certain sound made by them have always the one significance? Year after year I have listened and watched, watched and listened, and wondered if my friend was right. He believes it. I believe it—almost. Are there limitations to ornithological interpretation? And is this an instance where truth is unattainable?

We know that crows are cunning and by their mother wit have withstood the persecutions of mankind; we know that they have a wide range of utterances, and not one is put forth merely to gratify the ear, as in the case of a thrush's song;

yet we hesitate to say plainly that crow talketh unto crow and that they take counsel together. There is no physical or metaphysical reason why this should not be the case; there is abundance evidence pointing in that direction, but no actual demonstration, satisfying everyone, has taken place.

Were we less theory-ridden and more observant, the question would have been settled before this. In such a case the opinion of the farmer is worth more than that of a professional ornithologist. — *Lippincott's Magazine.*

The Sanitation of Ant Cities.

Insects are scrupulously clean in their personal toilet and often brush, comb and wash themselves, a service for which they are admirably provided with natural implements. This habit is transferred to communal affairs. The streets within the city bounds and the gates and external plaza and "country roads" leading into the foraging fields, as with agricultural ants, are kept free from filth and obstructions that might gather filth. The constant washings and combings of baby ants by the nurses would satisfy the most fastidious maternal taste. One may not say that sanitation is an exact emmetonian science, but it certainly is an art thoroughly practiced in every department of the formicary and brought to perfection as far as natural conditions will permit. Every insect citizen takes part in this service. All ants unite to keep their civic precincts clean.—*H. C. McCook in Harper's Magazine.*

Migrating Birds.

The distances over which birds migrate vary between wide limits and are often surprisingly great. The bobolinks, which rear their young on the shores of Lake Winnipeg and go to Cuba and Porto Rico to spend the winter, twice traverse a distance exceeding 2,800 miles, or a distance equal to more than a fifth of the circumference of our earth, each year. The kingbird lays its eggs as far north as the fifty-seventh degree of latitude and is found in the winter in South America. The biennial pilgrimages of the little redstart exceed 3,000 miles and the tiny humming bird 2,000.

Long Distance Swimming Fishes.

For long distance swimming the shark may be said to hold the record, as he can outstrip the swiftest ships apparently without effort, swimming and playing around them and ever on the lookout for prey. Any human being falling over-board in shark frequented waters has very little chance of escape, so rapid is the action of the shark, the monster of the deep. The dolphin, another fast swimming fish, a near relative of the whale, is credited with a speed of considerably over 20 miles an hour. For short distances the salmon can outstrip every other fish, accomplishing its 25 miles an hour with ease. The Spanish mackerel is one of the fastest food fishes and cuts the water like a yacht. Predatory fish are generally the fastest swimmers.

Large deposits of nickel have been discovered in southern Oregon.

The California Big Trees.

In 1900 Professor Dudley made an extensive study of the California big trees. He obtained data by counting the concentric rings of growth on the cross sections of the felled trunks. The oldest tree that he examined began its existence in 525 B. C. His most interesting discovery, however, relates to the remarkable recuperative properties of these gigantic trees. The trunk of one tree that he studied was 2,171 years old. Here is its history as detailed by Prof. Dudley:

"271 B. C., it began its existence.

"The first year of the Christian era it was about four feet in diameter above the base.

"245 A. D., at 516 years of age, occured a burning on the trunk three feet wide. One hundred and five years were occupied in covering this wound with new tissue. For 1,196 years no further injuries were registered.

"1441 A. D., at 1,712 years of age, the tree was burned a second time in two long grooves one and two feet wide, respectively. Each had its own system of repair.

"One hundred and thirty-nine years of growth followed, including the time occupied in covering the wounds.

"1580 A. D., at 1,851 years of age, occured another fire, causing a burn on the trunk two feet wide, which it took fifty-six years to cover with new tissue.

"Two hundred and seventeen years of growth followed this burn.

"1797 A. D., when the tree was 2,068 years old, a tremendous fire attached it, burning a great scar eighteen feet wide.

"It is to be noted that in each of the three older burns there was a tiny cavity occupied by the charcoal of the burned surface, but the wounds were finally covered and the new tissue above was full, even, continuous and showed no sign of distortion or of the old wound."

Prof. Dudley says that if these trees were protected from fire and from the lumbermen they would live many hundred of years longer, but so long as they are not in charge of the government they are not safe. "We ask for their protection," concludes Prof. Dudley, "becauce the Calaveras trees are historically by far the most interesting of the big trees, because their preservation will afford the highest and most innocent gratification to the thousands of people who will visit them, and, lastly, we believe their preservation will be most useful to the scientific observer of the future in his work on problems in the origin and history of species, in climatology, in the laws of growth. All this work has a bearing on the problem how to treat our forests so as to equalize the varying amounts of precipitation of moisture in the semi-arid region to the best advantage of our water supply."—*Vick's Magazine.*

The Lightest Metal.

Lithium is the lightest of all known metals, its specific gravity being little more than half that of water. The metal is of a silvery white appearance but is softer than lead, and inferior to it in tenacity.

RANDOM NOTES.

Fossils of cuttlefish twelve feet long have been found in chalk formations.

Not a drop of water ever falls on the Red Sea, and only dew on the surrounding shores.

There are about 16,000 islands between Madagascar and India, of which only about 800 are inhabited.

The surface of Lake Superior is 600 feet above sea-level; the bottom is on an average of 400 feet below sea-level.

A single mass of copper was found in the Lake Superior region in 1853 that weighed 400 tons. It was 40 feet in length.

The city of Santa Fe, N. M., it is said, has never had a rat or mouse or a cat within its corporate limits, the altitude being too great and the air too rarefied and dry for rodents and felines.

Australia now has 160 species of marsupials, while the rest of the continents, tenanted by about 1700 species of mamalia, contain only 46 species of marsupials,—namely the oppossums of North and South America.

Nearly four thousand species of ferns are known, and there is scarcely a locality on the globe, unless it is an absolute desert, without one or more species. Many species are evergreen, even in the more northern latitudes.

One feature of the river Nile is without parallel in the physical geography of the world: From 17° south latitude it flows 1350 miles to the sea without an affluent. Not so much as a trickling brook contributes to its waters for that distance.

So perfect were the ancient Egyptians in the manufacture of perfumes that some of their ointment preserved in an alabaster vase in the museum at Munich still retains a very powerful odor, though thousands of years have elapsed since it was originally compounded.

Over fifty species of fish never before known to scientists were discovered by the United States Fish Commission steamer in the Hawaiian waters. Most of the specimens were hauled from depths to which it is thought the light of the sun can never penetrate. Still the fish were equipped with eyes.

Many plants have blossoms in the spring before their leaves appear. Had you noticed it?

The velocity attained by a water-spout at sea-level has been carefully estimated to be six miles a minute.

There are in the Thousand Islands in the St. Lawrence River 1692 islands, according to the count of the International Boundary Commission.

Lake Titicaca, Peru, has the highest altitude of any known lake, being 12,846 feet above sea-level. It is 115 miles long and 30 to 60 miles broad and an average depth of 125 feet.

The world's chief supply of alabaster comes from the quarries of Volterra, some thirty miles southeast of Pisa, in Italy, where this industry has been handed down for generations.

The true fishes are estimated by Drs. Jordan and Evermann to number 12,000 species, belonging to 200 families. Of these, 3,300 species have been distinguished in the waters of North and South America.

A most surprising property of aluminum is its newly discovered power of giving a fine razor-like edge to steel cutlery. Magnified a thousand times, the knife-edge produced on the ordinary whetstone appears rough and jagged, while that yielded by the aluminum sharpener is straight and smooth.

It has been known for some years that ants see in the ultra-violet rays, a color unknown to human eyes, and it is suggested that the presence of this color, alone and in mixtures, doubtless transforms the whole aspect of nature. Other animals preceive vibrations that do not affect our ears, thus hearing sounds and melodies to which we are deaf. It is in the sense of smell, however, that many creatures surpass us, and this sense, so strikingly seen in dogs and some other mammals, is a most extraordinary endowment of insects. A female gypsy moth is known to attract males from a mile away. Males of other moths have found females at a distance of several miles, and when some females were enclosed in boxes in a glass building, the subtle odor confined and masked by thousands of other odors soon drew male moths from afar.

The Amateur Naturalist.

"To him who in the love of Nature holds communion with her visible forms, she speaks a various language."

VOLUME 1.   BINGHAMTON, NEW YORK, JULY, 1904.   NUMBER 4.

FRUITS AND VEGETABLES.

BY WILLARD N. CLUTE.

EVEN in these days of Nature study clubs one may occasionally over-hear a debate as to whether a certain edible part of a plant is a fruit or a vegetable. Our ideas of what constitute a fruit are expressed pretty clearly when we speak of a certain class of trees as "fruit trees" and yet, from the botanist's point of view a walnut, an ash or a maple is as much of a fruit tree as any other. The botanist defines a fruit as "the ovary brought to perfection" and we are thus warranted in consid-ering the dry seed capsules of the arbutus as much of a fruit as are the juicy berries of its relatives the huckleberry and cranberry.

Seed and fruit should not be confused. Sometimes the seed is almost the entire fruit as in the dry achenes of the dandelion and thistle; at others it is but a small part as in the orange, melon and gooseberry. This matter can better be understood if we remember that the ovary is the part of the flow-er containing the embryo seeds and that it often becomes thick and juicy after the flower has fallen. But whether juicy or dry it, together with the enclosed seeds, is the fruit of the plant.

To make a literal interpretation of the botanist's definition would rob us of many of what we now consider fruits. For instance, the strawberry is not a ripened ovary, but the red juicy part, at least, is an enlarged recep-tacle with the seeds embedded in it. The fleshy part of the apple and pear, also, are enlarged receptacles that have grown up and surrounded the seeds. Stranger than either of these, is that remarkable relative of the sumac, the cashew-nut, which has a thickened pear-shaped edible receptacle the size of an egg but which does not surround the seed. The latter is found at the apex just outside of the receptacle as if the stem with the seed upon it had grown so rapidly that the receptacle could not overtake it. It is likely, therefore, that we shall have to modify the botanist's definition somewhat, for it is certain that the receptacle would not increase in size if the ovary and seeds were not developing. We shall find it more in harmony with the facts to consider the receptacle part of the fruit, else the apple would come dangerously near being a vegetable !

The housewife is likely to call cucumbers, squashes, beans and peas vege-tables, but the botanist ranks them as fruits. Corn and tomatoes, also, are fruits; but carrots, turnips, artichokes and onions are barred. A captious critic may insist that the definition only holds good one way, for while beets, potatoes and lettuce are not and never can be fruits, all fruits are vegetables in the sense that they belong to the plant kingdom. But regardless of the critic we shall be warranted in considering as a fruit, the structures resulting from any pollinated flower.

According to the botanist, the blackberry and raspberry are not single fruits but clusters of fruits. The pine-apple, too, is a fruit cluster. The fig, however, must be classed as a vegetable, for it is not an enlarged receptacle nor yet a fleshy ovary but the thickened and hollow tip of a branch bearing the flowers on its inner surface.

Binghamton, N. Y.

THE BAD LANDS.

BY CHARLES D. PENDELL.

THOUGH nearly every one has heard of the Bad Lands, not so many could give an explanation as to their character or origin. The name is applied to several wild, desolate, treeless and barren tracts of land in Colorado, Nebraska and Montana; but is especially applicable to the southwestern portion of Dakota, along the White River.

This region consists of immense beds of clay, cut out by the combined action of frost and water and of rivers which were extinct ages ago, into thousands of columnar masses often one or two hundred feet high. These columns are sometimes round, smooth and tapering, like the small end of an egg. Others, as Winchell happily remarks, "in their endless succession, assume the appearance of massive artificial structures decked out with all the accessories of buttress and turrett, arched doorway and clustered shaft, pinacle and finial and tapering spire. On nearer approach the illusion vanishes and all the forms which fancy had conjured are resolved into barren desolation." The traveller lost in the confined labyrinthian passages might wander for days and in the voiceless and motionless solitude, under the scorching rays poured down from above and reflected from the white soil and walls, distitute of tree or shrub to shelter him, and naught to quench the thirst which overpowers him, finally mingle his bones with the titanic remains of primeval monsters.

Those clayey walls are built up mostly with the fragmentary remains of the animal life of the Tertiary period. The Bad Lands are, in fact, a literal Golgotha. At every step we tread upon the remains of former ages; at every blow of the pickaxe the bones of unknown species are revealed. Hundreds of fossil turtles lay about on every side, single specimens often weighing over a ton.

Entering this valley of dry bones and calling comparative anatomy to our aid, we again unite the broken skeletons and erect once more the frame work of an animal organism. Now imagine the skin once more to cover this frame and life to invigorate this system, and lo! we are in an ante-diluvian museum. There stands the gigantic mastodon; here is an animal resembling the modern tapir, but its head is surmounted with a pair of horns and it is eight feet high. This strange animal is called the *titanothere*. Next we come to the *dinoceras*, an animal rivaling in size the elephant. It has a longer neck, however, and consequently no trunk, and the tusks are replaced by three pairs of horns. Scores of other animals equally strange meet our gaze, together with the rhinoceras, elephant, camel, horse, wolf and other modern animals.

Fossil fish* and mollusk are everywhere scattered around; and the abundant fossil flora prove that an exuberant vegetation once existed on these now barren wastes. The leaves of many trees common to our latitude and those of the torrid zone—fig, cinnamon and palm—have been found. It is probable that this now desolate region was once a vast tropical swamp, and that the numerous fauna made this their favorite feeding ground. Many of these animals, venturing too far in order to reach some tempting morsel became mired and, unable to extricate themselves, perished—their fossil remains alone testifying to their primeval greatness.

൪ ൧

AMBER.

BY DR. B. F. MASON.

AMBER is found in irregular masses with a resinous lustre, without cleavage, and of a yellow, brown, red or even white color. Its hardness is between 2 and 2.5, and its specific gravity from 1.066 to 1.081. It is transparent to translucent, and when scratched with a knife leaves a white streak. It becomes electric on friction and fuses at 287 centigrade. It is a fossil, indurated resin or gum, of vegetable origin, which has undergone some change while inhumed, due partly to acids of sulphur, probably proceeding from the decomposition of iron pyrites. It is usually found in beds of lignite, in alluvial soil on or near the sea coast.

Its composition is found to be by analysis: Carbon, 78.94; Hydrogen, 10.53; Oxygen, 10.53.

True amber is distinguished from the imitations by its becoming electrical when rubbed, by its usual yellowish-green color and toughness—it can be cut into many forms—also by its burning with a yellow flame, and emitting a peculiar odor. This peculiar odor and the white streak which is left when scratched, are very characteristic of amber.

Amber was called *elektron* by the Greeks, from its so readily becoming

---

*One in possession of the editor, broken transversely, shows very clearly the osseous structure. He has seen fossil teeth from this region as large as a man's fist on which the enamel was in perfect condition.

electric when rubbed, and thus it gave the name electricity to science. It was named by some of the ancients *lycurium*, though this name was applied by Theophrustus also to zircon and tourmaline, minerals of remarkable electrical properties. The ancient Greek philosophers, who noticed amber's peculiar electrical powers when subject to friction, held the strange belief that it was endowed with a soul. In Arabia for ages it has been considered a talisman against the evil eye, and in other countries a string of amber beads worn about the neck, has long been considered as a protection against inflammation of the throat on account of their warmth to the skin, and their maintenance of a constant circle of electricity. All the ancient writers speak of amber as a precious gem. The earliest Etruscan jewelry consisted of carved amber, which was called lynx stone. It was supposed to have some relation to the lynx. Tradition, not always to be relied on, says that on one occasion Nero had the amphitheater adorned with amber. It is seldom that a piece of amber weighs a pound, but some notable exceptions are on record. One of the largest masses of amber in the world is in the Royal Museum at Berlin, and weighs eighteen pounds. Another in India is a little larger than an orange and weighs two and a half pounds. Still another mass, weighing twelve pounds, is owed by a Dantzic museum which values it at three thousand dollars.

The greatest quantity and finest quality of amber is found in the Baltic Sea, also in the sand on its shores, particularly after a storm whose violence has washed it up from the deep. This amber often contains insects, and is highly prized as a curiosity. Often the insects appear to have struggled to escape after having been entangled in the soft gum, for occasionally a leg or wing is found some distance from the body.

Amber is mined from the mountains of Prussia; it is found on the coast of Denmark and Sweden; in Galicia, near Lemberg and at Miszan; in Poland; in Moravia, at Boskowitz; in Russia; in Norway; in Switzerland, and in France, near Paris, in clay. In England it has been discovered near London, and on the coasts of Norfolk, Essex and Suffolk. On the American continent it has been found in Mexico, and in the United States at Gay Head, and at Camden in New Jersey. To the geologist there is a peculiar charm about the "golden gum," for it carries him back to the ages when there were primeval forests where man's foot never trod. It tells him that under the stormy Baltic and beyond the marshy coast lines of Northern Europe were once titanic woods, abounding with resinous pines and firs, somewhat resembling those of our own age; and that ages ago these pines exuded from their limbs and trunds masses of half-liquid gums, clinging in balls to their rough barks, and that the odorous gums attracted numerous insects and even small reptiles, and that many of them gradually became embedded in the viscid gum. Ages upon ages swept down the vale of time, the amber-bearing pines and firs grew old, perished and decayed where they fell, leaving the exuded gum to harden, and to finally become altered by fossilization under the deposits of succeeding ages until it lay many feet beneath the accumulated debris. Then the coast gradually sank and the sea swept over the dead forest, and thus it is that amber is found both under the land and beneath the sea.

And from the insects and small reptiles perfectly preserved and buried in their "crystal coffins," the geologist is enabled to tell that some of the flies, bugs and small lizards of that primeval forest resemble those of our own age.

Amber is employed for a great variety of purposes. It is the basis of an excellent transparent varnish; it affords by distillation oil of amber and also succinic acid; and as the preparation of the amber varnish required that the amber be fused, all these products are obtained at the same time. Small pieces and scraps of amber are pulverized and burned as an incense in certain churches.

ᖇ ᖆ

HUMMINGBIRDS.
BY G. D. STORY.

NEXT to the paradise bird in splendor, if not equal to it, comes the fairy little hummingbird, which Audubon described as the "glittering fragment of a rainbow." This feathered firefly, the jewel of the woods, is very common both in North and South America. Its tongue is a long tube, through which the little fellow can draw the contents of each flower chalice as well as the bee, with which, indeed, the little hummer must sometimes fight for the mastery.

There are about seventy species of these birds in our western world, and the early navigators and adventurers, who penetrated to the tropics, wrote home the most extravagant and delightful descriptions of these wonderful little creatures, as they saw them hovering above the flowering masses or nestling amid the petals of the splendid orchids, not a whit more beautiful then themselves. The tribes of the West Indies and American mainland called them by various names, such as "shooting-stars," "will-o'-the-wisps," etc., and wove head-ornaments, bracelets, girdles, mantles, and beautiful pictures, superior in softness of sheene and variety of tint to the richest mosaic, out of the tiny feathers.

In some parts of South America they swarm so thickly in the trees that they might be almost mistaken for brilliant swarming wasps. But the curious traveler only needs to look a little farther to find the Liliputian nests, no larger than a cloven walnut; suspended to the dancing twig of some wild orange, tamarind, or other small tree. The tiny egg looks like blanched peas in a mossy pod. The nest might be mistaken for a bud on the bough, but, by and by, glittering little green heads and crimson gorgets that peep over the side tell a different story.

The flight of these birds is inconceivably rapid—so rapid, indeed, that the eye cannot follow it when the full speed is put forth; and with such wonderful rapidity do the little sharp-cut wings beat the air that their form is quite lost, and while the bird is hovering near a single spot the wings look like two filmy green fans attached to the sides. While darting from one flower to another, the bird can hardly be seen at all, as it seems to come suddenly into existence at some spot, and as suddenly to vanish from sight. Some hummingbirds are fond of towering to a great height in the air, and descending from thence to their nests or to feed, while others keep near the ground, and are seldom seen at an elevation of many yards.

The food of the hummingbird is much the same as that of the honey-sucker, except, perhaps, that they consume more honey and less flies. Still they are extremely fond of small insects, and if kept away from this kind of diet, soon pine away in spite of unlimited supplies of syrup and other sweet food.

The Ruby-throat is a variety most familiar to us, and never attain a length of more than three and a quarter inches. The throat of the male bird has a ruby-colored gorget, shading off into deep black and then to firy crimson and burnished orange. The female bird, it is hardly necessary to say, is always dressed in more sober colors.

This little fairy bird, in spite of his courage, is sometimes driven from its pleasant pastures by the humble-bee, whose sting is too much for the other's long bill; and yet the little fellow is daring even to rashness. His shape indicates a small stomach, a large brain, and a bigger heart.

An eminent naturalist relates that he had seen two hummingbirds fighting with a crow, and by their inconceivably swift motion and long needle-like bill actually succeeded in killing their antagonist. Hummingbirds in many cases have been tamed and become much attached to their mistresses, learning to alight on the finger and sip sugar-water presented in the calyx of a flower. But they crave something more than sweet juices, and range through the air in search of insects. There is one insect—the great black spider of South America—which retaliates and hunts the hummingbird as a dainty tidbit. But the little bird has an ally and avenger in the big-headed South American ant, which hunts the black spider and mercilessly destroys him.—[Humming birds are found only on the American continent and the adjacent islands. Some authorities give the number of species as over three hundred, instead of seventy as stated by Mr. Story. These birds are very capricious in their habitat, some species being found from the equator to the confines of the Arctic Circle; others confine themselves to a very limited area, one species, for instance, being found in a zone five or six hundred yards in width; some species are very sensitive to any cold while others are only found at high elevations on the very edge of the limits of perpetual snow. No genus of the feathered races possess a greater variety of gorgeous coloring.—ED.]

FLINT IMPLEMENTS AND WEAPONS.

MANY persons are apt to associate the flint implements, which are found in such large numbers in the United States, with our North American Indian and overlook the fact that they are found in even greater numbers in Europe, Asia, and, in fact, all parts of the known world, and that they are even used at the present day at some of the out-of-the-way corners of the world.

In the Scandinavian peninsula they are found in great abundance and of exquisite workmanship. Denmark, also, abounds in fine specimens of these relics. France has furnished some of the finest specimens ever seen, and Switzerland, also, gives many fine examples from her caves, and from the lakes, where lived, in unknown ages, the Lake Dwellers. These weapons are found in caves, associated with the remains of extinct animals, as well as those which live at the present time.

Of the many kinds of stone implements found, arrow-heads are by far the most numerous. They are of all sizes and shapes and made of many different kinds of material, but flint is the favorite with all and in every country. Fine specimens are made of jasper, quartz and, in some instances, slate is used.

In England these arrows are commonly called elf arrows, from an old tradition, and in Germany they are referred to as thunder stone and are often looked for after a heavy rain by people who are uneducated. This is accounted for in the fact that you would naturally find the points after a heavy, dashing rain had washed them free from the soil in which they were enclosed.

In the United States, and particularly on the Atlantic side of the continent, they are found in great numbers and of many different kinds and sizes, and, while they occur more abundantly along the rivers, they are occasionally met with far from any stream of importance. Large numbers are found along the Connecticut, the Delaware—both in New Jersey and Pennsylvania —the Susquehanna and the Ohio. The points from Ohio, Indiana, Tennessee, and, in fact, from all the interior states, are generally flint and of superior workmanship. Besides arrow-heads, large numbers of spear-heads, axes, celts, and other objects are found in nearly all the localities mentioned. Spear-heads from two to six inches long, are often found and at the Museum of Natural History at Central Park can be seen some fine specimens, eight, ten, and, in one case, eleven inches long, a splendid specimen, found at Lake Luzerne. And one was found in a grave in Georgia which is fourteen inches long.

Axes are found in great variety, both in shape and size, but nearly all have the one distinguishing feature which consists of a groove for fashioning the handle.

In some cases the axe consists merely of a water-worn pebble with a roughly chipped edge, while in other cases they are finely finished and even polished, showing a great amount of patient labor in their manufacture.

In digging a cellar in Trenton, N. J., a few years ago, 125 stone axes were found huddled together about three feet below the surface, and other lots have been found under about the same conditions in other parts of this state. At the museum of Rutgers College may be seen an axe which weighs over nine pounds and is about ten inches in length. This axe was found in the city of New Brunswick, and is a very finely finished specimen. Celts are also abundant in nearly all localities where other stone relics are met with.

The size and style of all these objects vary in different localities, also in the material of which they are made. On Long Island nearly all the specimens are made of milky quartz which is abundant on that island. In New Jersey many are made of the trap rock, which abounds in that locality, but by far the larger number of those from the interior are made of flint. New Jersey is not noted for the fine quality of the points found in the state, but she can hold her own when it comes to quantity.

Much more could be said of the different kinds of arrow-heads, some having serrated edges; others which are so made that they will rotate when shot from the bow, some having a stem to attach the point to the shaft, and others having none; others triangular in shape, beautifully wrought and exceedingly regular in outline.

When we consider that all the various forms were wrought without the aid of any tool other than stone, we marvel at the amount of skill and patience displayed by the men who fashioned these objects.

∝ ∾

THE COMMON HOUSE-FLY.

FLIES force themselves on our notice in various ways. It is not generally known, however, that there are several different species of flies, and it may be well to consider the characteristics of a few of the more conspicuous kinds, noticing how one kind differs from another, not only in appearance and structure, but in habits of life. It is desirable to take as the first example the species which is properly entitled to the popular name of "common house-fly"—*Musca domestica*.

That flies grow in the ordinary sense of the term, and that the size of any fly merely depends upon its age is a prevalent error. Nothing could be further from the truth, for when a fly becomes a fly—in other words, when it escapes from the pupa-case and acquires the use of wings—its development is completed and all its growth is at an end. It follows, then, that where there is a marked difference of size between the flies we may be sure they belong to distinct species.

Without going minutely into the structure, either internal or external, of flies, it may be useful to mention that the great characteristic of all insects belonging to the *diptera* (as the order of flies is called), marking them off from all other insects, is the possession of only one pair of wings. The second pair of wings, found in butterflies, moths, beetles, etc., is represented among the flies by a pair of small balancers, known as *halteres*, which are attached to the body, one on each side, just behind the true wings, and which in shape resemble a pair of miniature drumsticks.

In its general appearance the common house-fly is very somberly dressed and seems to be without adornment of any kind, but on a closer examination it will be seen that it is really quite an elegantly marked insect. When looked at from above, against the light, the front of the head is seen to glisten with two resplendent silvery-yellow patches; the thorax, or middle part of the body between the wings, is stripped, while the abdomen or hinder part is checked with yellow and black. The wings are transparent and tinged with grey, with a very brilliant iridescence in certain lights. All these points give the little creature a beauty of its own, entirely lost to the majority of people, merely because the insect is a common and insignificant one, and seemingly not worth the trouble of examining.

The head of the fly is a very pretty object. The greater part is occupied by two large, reddish-brown hemispheres, one on each side. These are the compound eyes, and each of them consists of several separate hexagonal lenses, arranged so as to cause an appearance under the microscope like the "engine-turning" on the back of some watch-cases. Between these compound eyes, and quite on top of the head, are a trio of small, clear dots arranged in a triangle, like set jewels. These are the simple eyes, and their exact purpose is not understood. In front of the head are the antennæ or feelers, and each consists of three joints, with a feathered bristle arising from the back of the last joint. This bristle is an important aid in the identification of the various species of flies, in some kinds being quite simple, in others feathered, as in the common species which I am describing.

Below the head of the fly may be seen projecting the long thick tongue or proboscis, which is a wonderful structure. The proboscis is a true sucker, but a very complicated one, made up of a number of pieces united so as to form a tube, which not only serves for the conveyance of the food to the mouth, but also for the passage of saliva from the mouth in order to moisten and dissolve particles of the substance upon which the fly is feeding. At the tip of the proboscis are to be found hardened rings which aid in triturating the food.

The eggs of this fly are about one hundred and twenty in number. From the eggs are hatched small, white, footless grubs, which soon become pupæ inclosed in a hard skin. From this pupæ emerges the perfect fly. The periods of development are as follows: Egg from deposition to hatching, eight hours; first to second molt, one day; second molt to pupation three days; pupation to issuing of adult, five days; total life about ten days.—*Abridged from article by L. W. Irwell in Western Field.*

The Amateur Naturalist.

A Journal for those who Study Nature from a love of it.
ISSUED BI-MONTHLY.

SUBSCRIPTION, 50 CENTS PER YEAR.   SINGLE COPIES, 10 CENTS.
ADVERTISING RATES ON APPLICATION.

————————EDITED AND PUBLISHED BY ——————

CHARLES D. PENDELL,
85-87 STATE STREET,   -   -   -   BINGHAMTON, N. Y.

THE MAKING OF AN HERBARIUM is the title of a book just issued from the press of the publisher of this journal. It is, as its title indicates, a complete guide as to the method and requirements of preparing an herbarium. The author, Mr. Willard N. Clute, is exceptionally well prepared for the preparation of a work of this kind. He is the author of "The Flora of the Upper Susquehanna," "Our Ferns in Their Haunts," and several other works of interest to nature students, and his practical experience as for three years assistant curator in the New York Botanical Gardens, besides his private collection of a most extensive sort, has given him a most practical insight into just what is needed. The contents may be briefly indicated by reference to the various departments treated: the herbarium and its use, collecting, data, drying, mounting, strapping, labels and arranging for use. The book is illustrated and bound for service. It will be mailed by the publisher on receipt of 25 cents.

"When I began to make a study of the common plants about me I was astonished to find how very little I knew about them; and when I made inquiries among my friends in regard to them I was surprised to find that most of them knew even less than I did." So wrote a member of the American Botanical Club and the truth contained therein is particularly pertinent. In no other branch of nature are the specimens for study so abundant and available. For minerals we must delve in the earth and perchance blast our way through massive rocks to obtain the showy crystal; the birds we must follow through wood, field and marsh; insects are everywhere about us but always elusive; the smaller of the wild animals are mostly beyond the reach of careful study and the larger ones most of us do not care to follow to their wilderness homes; the stars are to be reached only through the telescope and mathematical calculations not usually pursued by the amateur. Of all of these we enjoy reading the results of the studies made by specialists and so far as practicable each of us may have some one of them for a hobby and in a superficial way make a study of it. But in the study of plant life, specimens are strewn about us in such abundance that the existing indifference is astonishing. Inquiry reveals the fact that many are deterred from study by the fear of "long Latin names." But long Latin names and the study of the plants themselves are two entirely different things, and when one does become interested in plants for their own sake, the wondrous beauties of form and flower and adaptability to environment will cause many a pleasant revelation; and hundreds of plants, seen from earliest childhood, but as yet unrecognized, will present beauties undreamed of; and still others, more beautiful still, of whose very existence we may as yet be unaware, we will find only awaiting our acquaintance to add much to the fullness of our lives.

In the study of plant life as in any other branch of nature study no other one thing makes it so interesting as a good collection of specimens—specimens collected by our own selves. This may seem difficult at first, especially to those who have never tried it, but once a good herbarium is started the additional pleasure derived will more than compensate us for the time and trouble. Gathered in the ordinary way the plants are brought home wilted and faded, and by the next day they are dry and useless and are thrown out as rubbish and the desire for their further study is thrown out with them. Collected in the proper way their study becomes a lasting pleasure, and the identification can be pursued at leisure or postponed until winter, if need be, while the preserved specimens are even more interesting to while away an hour with a friend or visitor. Those "long Latin names" can be added later—or omitted—and our collection will have a permanent value and place in our home. "THE MAKING OF AN HERBARIUM" is just the book for the beginner, as well as advanced student, and until our next issue of THE AMATEUR NATURALIST we will send a copy free to any person sending us ONLY ONE new subscriber—or will mail it to any address for 25 cents.

In closing this line of thought we can not do better than to quote the following editorial in a recent number of *The American Botanist:*

If you are accustomed to think that you know the flowers you may test the extent of your knowledge in this way: Select the spring flower that you know best and without again examining it, answer the following questions: Is it an annual, biennial or perennial? Does it store up food against the blooming season? How? How is it protected against the cold? Since the seed fall on the surface of the earth, how do the underground parts get so deep in the soil? When are the flower buds formed? How protected? Is the flower pollinated by wind or insects? Does it secrete nectar? Where? What insects visit it? For what purpose do they visit it? What part do the petals and sepals play in pollination? How have they been modified for this purpose? When are the seeds ripe? Of what shape and color are they? How are they disseminated? In what kind of seed vessels are they borne? How does the color of the flower aid in the struggle for existence? The fruit? How does the plant secure a proper amount of light for its leaves? How does it avoid too much light or heat? How is the pollen protected from cold, wet and from pilfering insects? How—but what's the use. Do you really know any of the wild flowers?

THE CLIFF FERN.

Far upwards 'neath a shelving cliff
    Where cool and deep the shadows fall,
The trembling fern its graceful fronds
    Displays along the mossy wall.

The wildflowers shun these craggy heights—
    Their haunts are in the vale below;
But beauty ever clothes the rocks
    Where Nature bids the ferns to grow.

Let others cull the flowers that bloom
    By wood and field, by stream and hedge;
For me there grows the dainty fern
    That droops upon the stony ledge.

The Baltimore Oriole.

BY LYMAN J. PENDELL.

OF all the feathered songsters which are inhabitants of this country, but few surpass the Baltimore oriole (*Icterus galbula*) for richness of plumage and melodiousness of song, the latter consisting of from four to ten full, loud and mellow notes. The Baltimore bird, or Baltimore oriole as it is called from its resemblance to the European oriole, is peculiar to this continent, being found from Canada to Brazil. It is the most beautiful of our summer visitors, the plumage being very brilliant, particularly so in the male, which has its head, neck, fore part of back and the tail glossy black; its quills, excepting the first, are margined with white; the whole under part of wing coverts and posterior part of back is a happy combination of bright orange and vermillion; the breast, under part of neck and the end of the tail feathers are tipped with dull orange. Its bill and feet are of a bright blue color. The above plumage is when the bird is three years old, before which time it is mixed with olive brown. The female oriole is, as in the case of most birds, less beautiful than the male, though it still presents a very charming appearance, being brownish-black mixed with dull yellow on the neck and fore part of back, while on the hind part of back, it is covered with brownish-yellow, brightest on the rump. The Baltimore oriole builds a very curious, ingenious and wonderfully interesting nest, it being a pendulous cylindrical purse-shaped pouch of six or seven inches in depth, and suspended from the end of a lofty branch. This remarkable structure is generally made of long grass, although other material, such as horse hair and thread, is sometimes used, and is woven with great nicety. The bottom of the nest is lined with some soft material, such as thistle blows and the like. The eggs of this marvelously beautiful songster are from five to six in number, about an inch long, pale brown in color and spotted and lined with dark brown, making a very handsome egg. The orchard oriole, which arrives in May, is nearly the same in plumage and general appearance. It lays five eggs, of a whitish-pink, dotted at the end with purple spots.

Caribou, Me.

American Lumber.

BY O. W. BARRETT.

OF course we have stripped our mountains of a great part of their forest wealth and we are beginning to lament the high prices of building timber; we are also establishing forest reserves and trying to prevent forest fires. But we still have something left.

If our trees—not reckoning the vast forests of Alaska and the Philippines—were sawn into boards one foot wide and one inch thick, there would be enough lumber to lay a board walk two miles wide around the earth at the equator, over land and sea; or we might take the same boards and cover every square inch of the State of Pennsylvania and still have sufficient left to build a tight board fence one mile high around the border; or we could lay a two-foot bridge to the sun and build a driveway fifteen rods wide from here to the moon besides.

1,300,000,000,000 feet of lumber don't grow in every country.

Mayaguez, Porto Rico.

Anent Mosquitoes.

THOSE who are immune from mosquito) bites and there are some) can look with interest and some amusement upon the efforts being brought to effect the extermination of this insect. One discovers a germ that will carry disease and ruin into the ranks of the mosquito; a promising and vigorous specimen is captured and innoculated and let loose to carry the germ to its fellows —but they sing the merrier. Another discovers "a parasite that is a natural enemy of the mosquito" and the breeding of parasites is seriously considered. Still another suggests covering the surface of each swamp, pool and mud-hole with petroleum and thus effect the pre-natal effacement of the germs; but this plan gets no further than the newspapers —and the mosquitoes do not read and so are not anxious on this score.

There is no denying, however, that the mosquito is a great pest, and one almost as annoying in the most northern lands as within the tropics. Thirty different species of the genus *Culex* are known to North America. The female mosquito usually deposits her eggs in stagnant water, laying from two hundred to four hundred. These hatch into "wrigglers" on the same day as laid. In from seven to fourteen days (according to the weather being warm or cold) these emerge as adult mosquitoes, ready to do as they have been done by—or otherwise.

Sound passes through air at a velocity of 1,142 feet per second; through water, 4,000 feet; through iron, 17,500 feet.

A Lesson for the Farmer.

A local paper published in Oklahoma relates the following in which the moral is self-evident:

One of our best practical farmers related to us the other day how he came to change his mind about killing birds. He said he formerly took a great deal of pleasure with his gun and dogs. About six months after coming to the territory he told his wife he would go out and kill a few quail. It was about four o'clock; so calling his dogs he started out on his own farm. He soon shot three quail, and his wife, knowing that if he got thoroughly interested in the pursuit of game he would be out till long after supper time, persuaded him to come back to the house and they would have supper, when he could go again. "All right," said the farmer; "I will dress these and we'll have them for supper." His wife remarked on the fullness of the craws of the birds, and on opening one it was found packed full of chinch bugs! Out of curiosity they counted and found over four hundred dead chinch bugs in the craw of one quail! Said the farmer in relating the circumstances to us: "I just cleaned up the gun and have not shot a bird since, and if you'll come down to my place of a morning or evening and see the birds coming to my farm you'll think they know their friends."

Sponges of the Deep Sea.

Some of the most beautiful things that live in the ocean are the sponges of the great depth, which have often very curious and interesting forms. Not least remarkable are the so-called "sea nests," which are in the form of spheres or sometimes egg-shaped. The outer coat of one of these specimens is a complicated network, over which a delicate membrane is spread. An ornamental frill adorns the upper part, while the lower portion throws out a maze of glossy filaments like fine, white hairs. These hairs penetrate the semi-fluid mud in every direction, thus holding the sponge in its place, while a continuous current of water is drawn by waving "cilia" through all parts of the mass, passing out by a hole at the top. In this manner the animal absorbs whatever food may be afloat. Another singular sponge is the "glass rope," which sends down into the mud a coiled wisp of filaments as thick as a knitting needle. The latter opens into a brush, fixing

the creature in place after the manner of a screw pile. Still another remarkable sponge is found in the deep water off the Loffoden Islands. It spreads out into a thin circular cake, surrounded by what looks like a fringe of white floss silk. Yet another curiosity is the "eupectella" sponge of the Philippines, which lives embedded to its lid in the mud, and supported by a lovely frill.

Life on Other Planets.

Upon the question whether life-bearing planets can exist in other solar systems than our own the answer of science is clear and distinct. It is precisely the same which Prof. Newcomb recently gave concerning the possible inhabitants of Mars: "The reader knows just as much of the subject as I do, and that is nothing at all." Within our solar system we can indeed form some crude estimate of probabilities; beyond it, nothing.

All the amazing progress of modern science, all the revelations made by the spectroscope or by photography, all the advance in biology have not brought us one step nearer an answer to the question, "Is this the only inhabited world?" We stand essentially where Whewell and Brewster did half a century ago, or we might indeed say where Galileo and Capoano were three hundred years ago. We can indeed spin out the discussion at greater length than our predecessors, and can introduce a far larger number of more or less irrelevant facts, but of serious argument, either for or against, we are entirely destitute.—*Knowledge.*

Rubies and Sapphires.

The ruby, sapphire and oriential topaz are properly called corundrums being identical in every particular but that of color, which difference may be said to be the only cause of a change in the name. The red sapphire is a ruby, the blue ruby is a sapphire, the yellow a topaz. The name corundrum, itself, is of Indian origin, derived from the Sanskrit, *korund*, and is applied only to the opaque massive varieties, which, however, present the characteristics, hexagonal crystal, and are generally of a dull color.

The first and most important variety is the ruby, or red sapphire, which is the most valuable of all gems when of large size, good color and free from flaws, exceeding even the diamond itself in value; its hardness is superior to any known substance except the diamond; it is susceptible of electricity by friction, and retains it for a considerable time; it is possessed of double refraction, although not to a very high degree. The lustre is vitreous. Rubies are found associated with sapphires, zircons, spinels, oxide of tin, etc., sometimes in perfect crystals, but slightly abraded. Often the crystal exhibits various colors in section across the prism, perhaps blue at both ends and white and red in the center, sometimes reversed, sometimes with yellow instead of red.

Where rubies and sapphires are met with, gold is almost sure to be present. The finest rubies occur in the kidgdoms of Ava and Siam, in the Capelan Mountains; they are also found in Ceylon, at Hohenstein on the Elbe, in the Rhine and Danube, in Brazil, Hindostan, Borneo, Sumatra, in Australia, in France, in the rivers Espailly, in Auvergne, in Iser, the Bohemia, etc.

The ruby mines of Burmah, whence come the finest stones, have long been known. The mines are rigorously guarded, no European being allowed to approach them on any pretence. Fine stones can only be smuggled away. When a particularly large and fine stone is found it is usual to send out a procession of grandees with soldiers and elephants to meet them.

The color of the ruby varies from the lightest rose-tint to the deepest carmine. Those too dark or too light are not esteemed. The most valuable tint is that particular shade called by jewelers the "pigeon-blood" which is a pure, deep, rich red, without admixture of blue or yellow.

Brahmin traditions speak of the abode of the gods lighted by enormous rubies and emeralds. In China rubies have been used from the earliest times for the ornamenting th slippers of women, and there, as in India, they are to be met with in incrusted jade vases, sword handles, or pipe-mounts. In the Bible they are spoken of, and there can be no doubt that the ruby was well known to the ancient Greeks and Romans. Pliny and Theophrastus ascribe to the ruby the power of giving light in the dark. In later ages, the magical properties assigned to the ruby were that it was an amulet against poison, plague, sadness, evil thoughts, wicked spirits, etc. It also kept the the wearer in health, and cheered his mind, and it is thought that if he or the donor were in danger, it would become black or obscure, and would not resume its pristine color until the peril had passed away.

The number of large rubies in existence of fine quality is very small. One of the largest in the old French crown jewels adorns the Order of the Golden Fleece, and is cut in the form of a dragon, with extended wings.

The two large jewels which were shown amongst the jewels of Queen Victoria, at the Exhibition of 1862 as rubies, are simply spinels.

In Travernier's travels, he speaks of a ruby in the possession of the King of Vishapoor, weighing fifty carats and of fine quality. The King of Burmah is said to possess a ruby as large as a pigeon's egg, of extraordinary quality. In the Russian Treasury is said to be one of very large size, which was presented by Gustavus III, King of Sweden, and among the crown jewels of Austria are several of fine quality and considerable size. The value of the ruby, as before mentioned, exceeds, when perfect, that of any other gem. The rare occurence of specimens of the desired pigeon's-blood color of any size, causes the value to increase in an even greater proportion than the diamond, as for example: a ruby of one carat weight, of the finest and purest, is worth $100, while a four carat would be worth $2,500.

Of course, rubies which are flawed, specky, or which have any so-called silky or milky appearance, either on the table or beneath it, or which are of too deep or too pale a color, are worth far less.

The oriental topaz or yellow sapphire is of a yellow tint, seldom deep, but generally of a light straw-color shade, and is extremely brilliant; it is frequently mistaken for a yellow diamond, and is of very little value in commerce; even jewelers often confound it with the ordinary topaz.

The sapphire, as already mentioned, is identically the same stone as the ruby; it has the same composition, hardness, electrical and other properties, it differs in name from the ruby on account of the color, which varies from white to the deepest blue or black. The blue of the sapphire is very seldom pure or spread over the whole substance of the stone; sometimes it is mixed with black which gives it an inky appearance, sometimes with red, which although imperceptable by daylight, yet by candlelight gives an amethystine appearance. Two sapphires, which by daylight may appear of the same hue, often differ extremely in color by night. The asteriated varieties, called star sapphires, are usually of a grayish-blue, and the star is exhibited in its greatest perfection when looked at by the light of the sun, or of a candle; the sapphire is found in all shades of blue, but the color which approximates to blue velvet, of the shade formerly called "*bleu du roi*," is the most valuable. A really fine sapphire should appear blue by candlelight as well as by day. The name sapphire is, perhaps, one of but a few which runs through all languages with very slight alterations.

To the sapphire has been ascribed the following magical properties: that it prevents evil and impure thoughts, that it is such an enemy of poison, that if put into a glass with a spider or venomous reptile, it will kill it. St. Jerome, in his exposition of the 19th chapter of Isaiah, says that the sapphire procures favor with princes, pacifies enemies, frees from enchantment, and obtains freedom from captivity. This gem was sacred to Apollo, and was worn when inquiring of the Oracle at his shrine. It was esteemed as a remedy against fevers.

Bœtius says that on account of its attachment to chastity it was worn by priests. The ancients called sapphires, male and female, according to their colors; the deep color, or Indigo sapphire, was the male; the pale blue, the female. The value of the sapphire does not, like the ruby, increase so enormously in proportion with its size. A fine, perfect, evenly colored, spread sapphire, weighing one carat, of a deep rich blue color, by night as well as by day, is worth $100, whilst a sapphire, equally fine, of one hundred carats, would not be worth more than $25,000. A ruby of the same size and perfection, would be the most valuable gem in existence, surpassing even that of the finest diamond.

The treasuries and regalias of Europe possess sapphires of a very large size. In the green vaults at Dresden are or were several of remarkable size and beauty. In the Russian treasury are some of an enormous size, amongst them, one of a light brown tint. In the Vienna Kronenschatze there is one of marvellous beauty and great size. At the last Paris Exhibition there might have been seen an oval sapphire, and drops of enormous size and great purity belonging to a Russian Countess.

The white sapphire resembles the diamond to such a degree that when well cut and polished, it has been sold to persons conversant with the trade as a diamond.

Malachite.

Malachite is a proto carbonate of copper, and is found by analysis to yield 71° of protoxide of copper. It is distinguished for its beautiful blue and green color, and is variegated in many ways.

This valuable substance is found in copper mines. Specimens of it are found in the Lake Superior district, in Australia, and sometimes in England. But the only quantities of any importance are in the Ural Mountains, in Russia. In the town of Tagilsk, in that region, there is a valuable copper mine which produces immense quantities of malachite. In the mine of Tagilsk, about forty years ago, an enormous mass was discovered, which it took several years to remove. If it could have been taken out in its natural state, it would have been one of the greatest curiosities in the known world. It is estimated to have weighed seven hundred and twenty thousand pounds. The origin of this mass is supposed to have resulted from copper solutions emanating from all the porous, loose, surrounding mass, and which, trickling through it to the lowest cavity in the subjacent rock, have in a series of years, produced this wonderful subterranean incrustation.

Malachite will receive a high polish, and is used for jewelry, tables, vases, and many ornamental articles of great beauty. Large doors have been made of it, highly polished and very beautiful, and it is used in interior furnishing of public buildings, mantels, etc. In some of the Russian churches there are pillars twenty, thirty and fifty feet high, apparently of solid malachite, though in reality they are of granite veneered.

The annual production is about eighty thousand tons.

Obsidian.

Obsidian or volcanic glass, as it is sometimes called, is a stone of glass-like appearance and of volcanic origin. It is most abundant in Mexico, where it was extensively used by the Aztecs in making mirrors, knives, razors, arrowheads, spearheads, etc.

It is also found in limited quantities west of the Rocky Mountains, but as yet has never been discovered on the eastern side, although arrow-heads made from it have been found in Ohio, which must have been transported by the aborigine at least 1,500 miles. Obsidian has both black and smoky tints. It contains 78 per cent. of silica, and is thus very hard and flint-like.

Sapphires in Montana.

Sapphires have been occasionally found in several localities in Montana but in no place very abundantly except in a locality some sixteen miles east of Helena. Here they have been found in the auriferous gravel while sluicing for gold, but have never been systematically mined. This may be because the colors of the gems obtained, although beautiful and interesting are not the standard blue and red shades generally demanded by the public. The stones embrace a greater variety of the lighter shades of red, yellow, blue and green. The latter color is found quite pronounced, being rather a blue green than an emerald green. Nearly all the stones when finely cut, have an apparent metallic luster.

Back to Nature.

The current jest that the next outdoor manual is to be entitled "How to Tell the Animals from the Wild Flowers," emphasizes the extent to which the systematic study of nature is being carried on in America. Hardly a phase of wood or field or marsh or coast life, whether flowers, trees, mushrooms, insectivora, sea shells, big and little game, or pets, but has had its turn of late years in the scrutiny and classification of some devoted student. The often arid regions of botany and zoology have increasingly been under literary irrigation, and have taken on a new fertility and charm. From the middle of the last century to the present time we have always had some voice of power calling us back to nature: Audubon, Emerson, Bryant, Thoreau, Muir, Burroughs, Torrey, Gibson, Seton, Shary, but in the last decade the general impulse has taken on the aspect of a cult which we fancy, has no counterpart elsewhere.—*Century.*

WHERE GOD STILL REIGNS.

S. E. KISER.

Come to the woods, O weary one,
　For faith and hope are there;
Under the leaves God's will is done,
　His glory fills the air;
There is joy in the piping from the pond,
There is triumph in the velvet frond.

Come to the woods, O doubting heart
　And learn that earth is fair;
The city and Heaven are far apart,
　But God is near, out there.
Where all is obedient to His will—
The woods are His, as He made them, still.
　　　　　　—*Chicago Record Herald.*

Some Ancient Trees.

On a hillside in Waltham, Mass., not far from the depot, though the immediate spot is a sylvan solitude, are three huge white oak trees, monarchs of the woodland. There those sentinels have stood for ages; the Indian children played beneath their branches long before Columbus planted the standard of Castile and Aragon upon San Salvador; long before the Pilgrims set foot on Plymouth Rock. They attained their full gigantic stature many and many a year ago, but in summer their raiment is still of the brightest green, and their limbs as strong and un- yielding as the solid rock.

An incident of the Revolutionary War which is authentic, though not included in our histories, nor widely known, is the story of the Liberty Tree which stood in Charleston, South Carolina. It was a huge live- oak which grew in the center of the square between Charlotte and Boundary Streets.

When the popular excitement over the Stamp Act was at its height in Charleston in 1776, about twenty men, belonging to the most influen- tial Carolinian families, assembled under this tree, and were addressed by General Gadsden. He denounced the measure with indignation, and prophesied that the colonies would never receive justice from the mother country. He then, after a moment's solemn pause, declared that the only hope for the future lay in the sever- ance of all bonds with England, and in the independence of the colonies. This, it is asserted, was the first time that the independence of this coun- try was spoken of in public.

The men assembled then joined hands around the old oak, and pledged themselves to resist oppres- sion to the death. Their names are still on record. Most of them were distinguished for their courage and patriotism during the struggle which followed.

The Liberty Tree was regarded with such reverence by the enthusi- astic Carolinians that Sir Henry Clinton, after the surrender of Charleston to the British, ordered it to be destroyed. It was cut down and afterwards its branches were formally heaped about its trunk and burned.

The great oak tree at Woodbridge, which was cut down not long ago, after an existence of nearly 2,000 years, has been made into chairs for the members of the Quinnipiac Club of New Haven, the tree being a pro- duct of the state of Connecticut. This tree was doubtless the oldest along the Atlantic Coast, and the largest oak in the world.—*George B. Griffith, in Vick's Family Magazine.*

RANDOM NOTES.

The unexplored Antarctic region, which equals Europe in size, is the largest unexplored area in the world.

The eggs of the fireflies of the tropics when dried will retain their luminosity for a week. The light will reappear when they are placed in water.

The whale moves through the water with a velocity which if continued at the same rate, would enable him to encircle the whole earth in less than fourteen days.

The only deposit of white onyx known to exist is in Yavapai County, Arizona. It is found under-lying a bed of limestone, and is pure white. The vein is five feet thick.

Tradition has it that the Milesians first brought from Egypt a knowledge of the cultivation of flax, also of spinning and weaving, introducing these arts into Ireland about 1200 B. C.

One of the rarest metals of the world is platinum. About 95 per cent. of the world's supply comes from the mines on the west side of the Ural Mountains. It has recently been discovered in the State of Washington, and it is thought in paying quantities.

Tests to deter minethe durability of various kinds of wood when buried underground show that the birch and aspen decay in three years, the horse chestnut and willow in four years, maple and red beech in five years, elm and ash in seven years; the larch, juniper and arbor vitæ were uninjured at the expiration of eight years.

Many bird form their sounds without opening their bills. The pigeon is a well-known instance of this. Its cooing can be distinctly heard, although it does not open its bill. The call is formed internally in the throat and chest, and is only rendered audible by resonance. Similar ways may be observed in many birds and other animals. The clear, loud call of the cuckoo, according to one naturalist, is the resonance of a note formed in the bird. The whirring of the snipe, which betrays the approach of the bird to the hunter, is an act of ventriloquism. Even the nightingale has certain notes which are produced internally, and which are audible while the bill is closed.

Nearly 85 species of palms have been found growing in the valley of the Amazon.

A canary bird has been known to continue a single trill for 85 seconds, with 20 changes of note in it.

A beautiful jet-black lioness has been added to the collection of animals in the Jardin des Plantes in Paris. Black lions are found only in the interior of the Sahara, and are scarce even there.

There is a deposit of clam shells near Astoria, Oregon, which is said to cover an area of over four acres, and is piled in places to a depth of ten feet. The amount of shells is incalculable. Over a thousand loads have been hauled away to make roads, but that amount is hardly noticed in the diminution of the immense heap. From time to time relics of the old clam-eating tribes that made the place their headquarters are found. There are some sixteen inches of soil on top of these immense clam-beds, on which grow fir trees, some of them four hundred years old.

Census Bureau figures indicates that in 1902 this country produced more than a quarter of a billion tons of bituminous coal, valued at nearly $300,000,000; anthracite coal worth more than $76,000,000, copper with a valuation above $71,000,000, gold of a coining value exceeding $67,000,000, iron ore reached a total value of nearly $67,500,-000, silver at coining figures surpassed $70,-000,000, and the petroleum total was more than $71,000,000. Mines and quarries and oil wells, together with smelters, reducing and refining works, turned out the almost fabulous total of $884,040,869.

There are sixteen species of trees in America whose perfectly dry wood will sink in water. The heaviest of these is the black ironwood (*Condalia ferrea*), of southern Florida, which is more than thirty per cent. heavier than water. Of the others, the best known are the lignum vitæ (*Gulacum sanctum*) and mangrove (*Rhizphora mangle*). Another is a small *Quercus grisea*, found in the mountains of Texas, southern New Mexico and Arizona, and westward to the Colorado Desert, at an elevation of 5,000 to 10,000 feet. All the species in which the wood is heavier than water belong to semi-tropical Florida or the arid interior Pacific region.

The Amateur Naturalist.

"To him who in the love of Nature holds communion with her visible forms, she speaks a various language."

VOLUME 1.　　　BINGHAMTON, NEW YORK, SEPTEMBER, 1904.　　　NUMBER 5.

ENTOMOLOGICAL NOTES.

BY ADDISON ELLSWORTH.

"ALMOST one-half of the species of insects are beetles. Lepidoptera comprises about twenty-five thousand species." The above statement which has made the rounds of newspaperdom and found its way into many of the scientific journals of the country, might have marked the extent of our knowledge of the subject a quarter of a century ago, but is far from being a correct estimate of the number of insects. For the past two decades entomologists all over the world have been actively engaged in bringing to light new or unknown forms, until now more than half a million species are known to exist. Of these, about one hundred thousand are beetles or Coleoptera, as many, or more, are Lepidoptera, while the great order Hymenoptera, including bees, wasps, ants, sawflies and ichneumons, contains at least one hundred and twenty-five thousand species. The rest are made up of the other orders Orthoptera, Neuroptera, Diptera and Hemiptera. Of the Lepidoptera, more forms are known among the diurnals or butterflies alone than are mentioned above, while there are at least five times as many moths. The great collections of the Grand Duke Nicholas of Russia, a private museum of Berlin, Germany, and the collection of the Rothschilds, in England, contain respectively trom twenty-five thousand to forty thousand species of butterflies, while the magnificent collection of the late Herman Strecker, of Reading, Pa., comprises more than two hundred and fifty thousand specimens or something over one hundred and thirty-five thousand species and varieties.

We are wont to consider insects as small and insignificant creatures; and perhaps when taken singly in comparison with our domestic and other animals, they are. Yet it has been computed that the average size in the animal kingdom—with the smallest protozoan at one end of the line and the flat-back whale of the Pacific, with its ninety-five teet in length and two hundred and ninety-four thousand pounds, at the other—is to be found in the common house-fly (*Musca domestica*). Taking this estimate as a basis, if all the insects of the upper Susquehanna Valley to the Pennsylvania line, in any one season, could be compressed into mammals as large as the mastodon, they would form a herd ten deep and more than a mile in length, and possessing five times the strength and ferocity of any mammal living or extinct.

Indulging in figures—one dark, lowery night in August, 1900, while collecting moths under one of the arc lamps near Floral Park Cemetery there seemed suddenly to arise a vast cloud of Neuropterous insects which poured in towards the light from three directions. These extended back as far as the eye could reach, but soon became so dense as to make retreat necessary. The large, old-fashioned, open top globes were at the time in use, and it was but a few minutes before the globe was filled with the ashes of their dead bodies, and the ground underneath completely covered with them. Other lights in different parts of the city were choked out in the same way while every lamp in this city and Lestershire were visited by immense swarms of them. If all the insects that were burned to death on that occasion could have been strung out, twelve to the inch, they not only would have measured the earth's orbit about the sun, but also that of all the other planets including the asteroids and the problematical Vulcan and Neith.

The rapidity with which propogation is carried on in some insects, especially among the aphides or plant lice, is truly marvelous. In these insects, successive generations, all of which are females, continue to be produced throughout the summer months without the presence of the male, by a process called budding. Professor Riley observed thirteen successive generations of the hop-vine aphis, (*Phorodon humuli*) in a single season. In his report for 1891, A. J. Lintner, Ph. D., then State Entomologist, figures that "if each female produced one hundred young (a small average), at the end of the thirteenth generation there would be ten sextillions of individuals." A number so vast that if all the people on earth to-day spent their whole time in counting—from the crade to the grave—they would fail in enumerating them. Now take as a starting point the countless millions of such insects that weather the frosts of winter—figures here fall flat, there is no use speculating in them !

Binghamton, N. Y.

ᖇ ᖯ

BIRD-SONG STUDIES.

BY NORMAN O. FOERSTER.

ALL in all, June is the best month of the year to study bird-songs. Then most of the birds are nesting and sing most typically and frequently. In May conditions are still unsettled; besides, our time would best be spent with the migrants. When July brings its hot days nesting is almost over, and one by one the birds drop out of the chorus; the bobolink's rollicking song is one of the first to be missed, and the thrashers and chat soon follow. August announces the advent of the molting season, and, consequently, an almost total muteness among the birds; and the disappointed ornithologist must seek refuge in botany and entomology. Late September marks a brightening, a short period of song preceding migration; but the young of the year join in with their unpracticed voices and hopelessly confuse the student. This period is so soon over, and with it the migrations, that before we are aware of the fact that all the robins have left, goldenrod and boneset are fast fading and another cold season is at hand.

Among the great variety of songs, the student will first begin to pick out those that seem to exhibit sentiment and feeling. It is not likely that because the pewee's note is pathetic and doleful that he partakes of these feelings. If this were so, the screech owl, Nature's chief mourner, would be the most unhappy being in existence. Yet we are prone to contemplate on the various songs in this way, and refer to the mournful cooing of the turtle dove, the merry laugh of the flicker, the petulant dissuasion of the phœbe, the plaintive chant of the field sparrow, the drowsy notes of the warblers, the uncouth monosyllables of the chat, the sad-voiced meadowlark and the like. But such adjectives are very good from a literary standpoint, and unless they are taken too literally (I have known persons who did take them so) are more colored in a descriptive sense than such trite expressions as clear, or loud, or sweet.

Mentioning the variation in songs, it might be noted that the value of a song as a thing of beauty is determined only from our cultivated human standpoint, and that therefore to the ears of the grackle his coarse, rusty notes are inestimably better music than the spiritual chants of the thrushes. Were it not so that each species possesses its peculiar musical-sense, and acknowledging the hermit thrush as the finest singer, evolution would produce a tendency to sameness among the birds, the thrush song being the object to be attained. For in courtship the iconoclastic finch or vireo would assume a higher form of music, nearer related to the thrush. This would be more pleasing to the female finches or vireos (for by hypothesis, they have a common musical sense, with the thrush as the highest form) and the radical-voiced male would meet with success. Others of his tribe would do likewise, until the very existence of the said finch or vireo would force him to adopt the betterment. Thus a gradual evolution resulting in the thrush form of song becoming almost universal. Now, of course, this is not and will not be the case. The chipping sparrow's unbeautiful trill (unbeautiful, of course, from our human standpoint) wins the heart of the female as well as do the male hermit thrush's sublime notes call forth the admiration of the opposite sex.

Another feature of bird-song that elicites speculation is the morning chorus. . . . . . It is a quarter before four o'clock on a May morning. Not a vestige of light is tinging the eastern horizon. Not a sound disturbs the still air. Fifteen minutes pass thus. Suddenly a few subdued notes issue from a tree. They sound ghostly, as if the bird were frightened by the sound of his own voice. But another robin hears the song and joins in with greater vigor, a full carol. Then the first robin starts with fresh spirit. Another bird sings afar off, and another, and another, till a half hundred, a mighty throng, swell the chorus. Gray light is appearing in the east, but the chorus continues for a half hour. No thought of seeking food, hungry as the birds may be after the night's fast. Each robin must partake in the matins. . . . . . What causes this morning chorus, as regular as the rising of the sun? Why do not the birds feed first and then sing? My theory may be fanciful, but I trust there is a spark of reason in it. At one time the birds did not sing in a great chorus like this in the morning. They fed first. But one day in wooing season an experimental individual started to sing as soon as he awoke. The subdued, religious light of dawn and the absolute stillness formed an effective background for his carol. His beloved at roost awaking and hearing the stirring notes, admired them so truly that he won her. Meanwhile the rival males, spectators of this, one after another commenced to sing to exhibit their ability. Thus in time it became a regular custom, when courting, to sing in the morning. In time also this became a habit, and every morning the matins were sung. All this sounds very fanciful; but who will suggest something better?

Which is the earliest songster of the day? I think the robin, undoubtedly. The chipping sparrow has often been suggested as the first bird, but I have never heard it before the robin. The following table of a morning chorus indicates at what time the given birds enter the chorus on a June morning in the Alleghany Mountains. The point from which I listened was constant.

3:45-4:00 A. M.—robin, vesper sparrow, field sparrow; 4:00-4:10 A. M. —song sparrow, wood pewee; 4:10-4:20—chipping sparrow, towhee, catbird and crow.

The turning point of the chorus is earlier with the field birds, I believe, than those of the woods. Perhaps the degree of light has something to do with it, for it is as dark in the woods at 4:30 as outside at 4:00 A. M. At any rate the highest point of the chorus is reached by the field birds at about 4:15, but by the wood birds not until 4:45 A. M. When heat begins to be felt, about ten or eleven o'clock, there is a very marked decline. From twelve to four few birds sing frequently. Then there is another marked change, an increase in the number of voices which attains its climax just before the sun sinks, and dies out rapidly at twilight.

During the middle of the day, when few birds are singing and each can be heard distinctly, go forth to some field or pasture where the meadowlark is found. Listen to two birds in different parts of the field. One sings a few notes which seem incomplete, leaving the musical sense suspended, when from the opposite part of the pasture come the answering notes that completely satisfy the ear. It is as fitting and expected as the apodosis after the protasis. Such singing is termed antiphonal, and is common among the birds. The towhee and wood thrush are also notable in this respect. From this it would seem that the birds possessed some inherent harmonical sense. Another evidence in favor of this belief is illustrated by Mr. Henry Oldys, who tells of a meadowlark that habitually sang the first four notes of the toreador song in Carmen. Other similar instances might be cited but, in my opinion, these do not go to show that the birds possess our laws of harmony but have distinct laws, and that these resemblances are merely coincidental.

It is often interesting to note the places birds frequent in delivering their songs. Harmony with its surroundings most often decides this. For instance, the meadowlark, when it arrives here in the spring, finds the grass short and light green, where its brown back and light yellow breast would be ill-protected. So in spring the meadowlark sings in tree-tops like most other brilliant birds. But when the hay is almost high enough to be mown, perfectly concealed in the tall, brown grass, the lark sings in the fields, or on a jutting fence-rail from which he may readily descend into the covert of the dense grass. As a general rule we will find that soberly-plumaged birds like the sparrows, sing near the ground, and brightly-colored tanagers, indigo-birds, cardinals, orioles and the like are more partial to higher situations. The Baltimore oriole, chat, bobolink, meadowlark and song sparrow and occasionally the indigobird, prairie horned lark, ovenbird, Louisiana water-thrush and Maryland yellow-throat sing on the wing. Courtship is the primal motive here. The prairie horned lark and bob-white sing on the ground. Robins are familiar singers on house-roofs. As to telegraph wires, —robins, song sparrows, indigobirds, catbirds, chipping sparrows, blue-birds and phœbes are often seen singing there; and occasionally the wood thrush so far forgets his dignity as to sing on a wire. Many birds are partial to the high dead branches of living trees; such are the indigobirds, Carolina wren, cardinal, crested flycatcher, cowbird, meadowlark (in spring), red-winged blackbird, pewee, kingbird, thrashers, etc. The fly-catchers have especially good motives as they use these situations as points from which to sally.

The frequency of the song is also an interesting point. As a rule, if the song is long there are fewer repetitions per minute than if it is short. Five times per minute seems to be the song sparrow's average. On a quiet June evening I listened to a vesper sparrow's inspiring notes; his song averaged seven times to the minute. Imagine a meadow that contains about six song sparrows and six vesper sparrows. Together, one of each species sing twelve times per minute and six of each seventy-two times per minute. In five minutes then we will have heard three hundred and sixty songs from these two species alone, not to mention others that sing at the same time!
. . . . . The maximum number of repetitions is given, I believe, by the short-songed whip-poor-will, fifty-nine times per minute being his aver-

age. Generally he commences to sing about 8:00 P. M. and for a half hour at least continues almost uninterruptedly. This means three thousand five hundred and forty repetitions in that brief time. Including the almost inaudible "cluck" that precedes the song, he sings in a single hour seventeen thousand seven hundred notes. We are apt to wonder where he gets the breath for that effort!

We often speak about certain songs having a "woodsy" flavor, and of others that are "songs of the pasture." This is because in most cases there is a subtle harmony between the song and its surroundings. Imagine, who can, a veery instead of rolling out his ethereal strains while in a pensive, meditative mood, sing while gyrating in aerial evolutions! Take the demuse wood pewee into the city and he loses half of his charm; and the wood thrush beside a city "artery" (where I have heard him) is very different from the wood thrush of the woods.

Pittsburg, Pa.

A DATE-LEAF BOAT OF ARABIA.

BY D. F. FAIRCHILD.

WHILE traveling up the coast of Arabia, last February, the writer's attention was attracted to some curious craft made entirely of date leaves that came along side as the "Pemba" steamed into the desert harbor of Jask on the Arabian coast. The coast of the Persian Gulf is so barren that one can travel for many days along it

without finding so much as a stunted tree or shrub, and at this place the only plants of any size were some groves of date palms and a few acacias which had been planted by the English employees of the Persian Gulf Cable Company which has a station at Jask.

Wood is so scarce in the region that even the roots of such small desert shrubs as are to be found are dug up for fuel, and timber large enough for boat-building would have to be brought by water from Bombay. It is necessity, therefore, which has invented these curious date-leaf boats of Jask. They are made of the mid-ribs of the date palm leaf, which are about an inch and a half in diameter and ten feet long. These tough mid-ribs, from which the leaflets have been removed, are fastened together by means of wooden pegs and strong twine in the form of a boat. No attempt is made to match joints, but a false bottom is built to the craft, and the mass of light mid-ribs that lie beneath this bottom buoy the boat up out of the water, so that the inside remains quite dry. Though in the form of a boat, this curious date-leaf affair is really a boat-shaped raft, for nothing but the fact that the bottom stands high out of the water prevents the waves from entering and flooding it.

They are not pitched or painted in any way, and would doubtless be short lived were they not dried out carefully on the beach whenever the owners are not using them. The paddles are the only parts of the boat which are not made of the date palm, being crooked, irregular poles with the sides of some dry goods box for blades. They indicate the remarkable dearth of wood in the region. They are wierd little crafts, and add one more use to the list of things which can be made from this remarkable desert palm.—*Botanical Gazette.*

ELECTRIC FISH.

BY CHARLES D. PENDELL.

THE study of the electrical properties of the muscles and nerves of animals dates from 1786, when Galvani made his wonderful discoveries. The phenomenon which first called the attention of the Italian philosopher to this subject, may be illustrated in the following manner: Expose the crural nerve of a recently killed frog, and touch it with a piece of zinc, at the same time touching the surface of the leg with a piece of copper wire. Now bring the two metals in contact with each other, and the leg will be thrown into violent spasmodic contortions, which will cease when the metals are separated; and be renewed again on bringing the metals together.

From this and similar experiments, it is evident that animal magnetism pervades animated nature. Further investigation shows that in the living animal an electric current is perpetually circulating between the internal portion and the external surface of the muscle. Though common to all animals this phenomenon is remarkably developed in certain fishes. The species first noticed as possessing this peculiar power, and which has been longest known, is the electric ray (*Raia torpedo*). This fish is common in the Bay of Biscay and the Mediterranean Sea, where it grows to a considerable size, specimens having been found weighing eighty pounds or more. The electric organs of batteries are situated on each side between the pectoral fins and the gills. Each battery consists of several six-sided prisms, which in form and arrangement resemble the cells of a honey-comb. By means of this battery, the fish when disturbed or in search of prey, gives a succession of strong electric shocks which have a paralyzing effect upon the intruder or intended victim.

A very similar species of the ray, or torpedo as it is often called, may be found on the southern coast of England where it is locally known as the "numb fish," and "cramp fish." On being touched it discharges its battery, so to speak, and the person handling it receives a shock which usually banishes all desire for further personal investigation in that particular line of ichthyology.

Another electrical fish, and one comparatively small,—the largest not measuring more than fourteen inches in length—is the raash or thunder-fish as it is called by the Arabs. It is extremely plentiful in the River Nile, and, possessed as it is of two distinct batteries capable of giving a very considerable shock, undoubtedly was an object of worship by the early Egyptians.

The gymnotus or electric eel (*Gymnotus electricus*) is a greenish colored fish with an eel-like body, probably more widely known than either of the foregoing. It is common to all the streams flowing into the Orinoco, and frequents other rivers of South America. This is the most powerful of all this class of fishes, the electrical apparatus occupying seven-eights of its entire length which is usually about four feet, though the length of six feet is occasionally attained. An idea of the intense power of these batteries may be conveyed by the fact that they are supplied with eight hundred and ninety-six distinct nerves. The shocks produced are so powerful that wild horses driven into the streams inhabited by the gymnotus are so affected by them as to be easily captured. The shocks have sufficient power to stun and even kill fish in the immediate vicinity. The shock which would only stun a small fish will kill a larger one; evidently because the larger exposes a greater conducting surface to the water through which the electricity passes and a much more severe shock is received.

Faraday on one occasion put a fish in a tub with an electric eel. The eel coiled into a semi-circle around the fish and gave forth a shock. A moment after, the fish floated dead upon the surface. The gymnotus is capable of being tamed and may then be handled with impunity. Some others might be mentioned, but comparatively nothing is known of them more than that they exist; one in India, another in Africa.

COLLECTING SEEDS.

BY DR. WILLIAM WHITMAN BAILEY.

 EEDS are not only fascinating to collect, but are most instructive to study. Amassed perhaps in the first place simply in response to the individual's desire to collect—a tendency apparently inherent in the race—closer inspection endows them with varied attributes of interest.

At Brown University we have quite a large collection of seeds gathered either personally or by exchange, by a former curator Mr. J. L. Bennett. They illustrate a wide range of families, genera and species. They are preserved in bottles with a loose label, easily read in any position the bottle may assume and containing full data. The preparation of the seeds often entailed much labor, as in the separating the seed from surrounding parts. Indeed, in case of achenes, or where the calyx permanently persists, or when the ovary wall adheres to the seed, this was not done. It would be next to impossible and not specially desirable.

The bottles, arranged in drawers, are kept in a convenient cabinet. This allows the arrangement by families. In the case of very large seeds, special drawers must, of course, be provided, nor would these be bottled.

In such a collection color is perhaps the first thing that attracts attention. Nearly every hue is seen here, pure white, jet black, azure blue, yellow, orange and intense scarlet or vermilion. Some beans and peas, as every one knows, are a brilliant red with a black eye and are strung together in necklaces. Indeed, among savage tribes always enticed by beads, they are constantly employed as ornaments. No coral can surpass them in brilliancy. The outer surface or testa of the seed may be smooth and highly polished or roughened, embossed or sculptured in many marvelous ways. Then there is a long range of seeds provided with wings, hooks, grapnels or other mechanical contrivances to aid in distribution by wind. Of parachute arrangements there is no end, as in the achenes of Compositæ and the seeds of milkweed and Epilobium. These contrivances, alone, will afford months of study. Again, while but four technical forms of seeds are recognized, such as the orthotropous, anatropous, *etc., these are constant to their belongings; they help to distinguish or classify large groups of plants. But apart from the shapes to which these long names are applied, each seed has a geometric form of its own. Hence, the fine globular, ovoid, cylindric or polyhedral seeds. The size, too, varies from the cocoanut on the one side to the dust-like seeds of orchis or poppy on the other. Any group of seeds will afford profitable study. Much remains to be accomplished, not only as regards the externals, but the anatomy of seeds.—*The American Botanist.*

---

*The four forms are anatropous, orthotropous, campylotropous, and amphitropous.—ED.

The Amateur Naturalist.

A Journal for those who Study Nature from a love of it.

ISSUED BI-MONTHLY.

SUBSCRIPTION, 50 CENTS PER YEAR.   SINGLE COPIES, 10 CENTS.
ADVERTISING RATES ON APPLICATION.

————————EDITED AND PUBLISHED BY ——·————

CHARLES D. PENDELL,

85-87 STATE STREET,   -   -   -   BINGHAMTON, N. Y.

A subscriber to THE AMATEUR NATURALIST in a recent communication expresses the opinion that "specialists are all right and those who accomplish the most in any one thing are specialists." The asservation is granted. This magazine has no complaint to make against specialists. The fact remains, however, that the large majority of people are not specialists; and furthermore, most people are interested in one or more branches of nature study, but many have been deterred from anything like systematic or persistent study of nature through fear of the bug bear of "long Latin names" which specialists have given us; But happily that fear is being removed and nature study is becoming more and more popular, and in the awakening of the popular mind to the many features of interest in nature's wonderful book, we believe THE AMATEUR NATURALIST holds a position that should not be left vacant. Every person should have his vocation and avocation. The greatest results, as our correspondent rightly affirms, are achieved by those who devote their time and attention to the one thing in hand. But how intimately associated are the artificial divisions and subdivisions of nature study. Who can study one division without constantly coming in contact with the others? The thorough study of either birds, plants or insects requires a knowledge each of the others, and astronomy embodies geology and so on. Primarily this journal was not especially designed for the restricted specialist; but, as if illustrating the truth of our position, is taken and read by many; in fact, most of the leading articles are by those who have made a special study along their respective lines, but, with minds broad enough to reach out beyond the immediate horizon of their particular line of study, they recognize the intimate association of the varied subjects treated in this journal, and hence their appreciation of it. Our correspondent incloses a clipping which he requests us to publish. The "internal evidence" of the article would indicate that his own reading was somewhat diffusive notwithstanding his assertion that "diffusive effort intermittently exerted compasses comparatively insignificant results," and withal he says he likes THE AMATEUR NATURALIST and reads it with interest. The clipping we think confirms our own opinion, and, though it lacks names and other data, has a point worth remembering; we therefore give it place:

Many years ago a boy who lived in the far West of America was suddenly thrown on his own resources by the death of his parents. His eye chanced upon the statement that every man should know something about everything and also be a specialist in addition to his occupation. The boy decided to make the idea his own, and because the willow was the tree that was nearest him, he decided to become an expert upon willows. He found willows that were red and willows white, and willows gray, and willows yellow, and willows blue; willows that stood up straight, and willows that bowed themselves down weeping. He collected choice specimens of willow seeds and leaves and exchanged with agriculturists in all parts of America. Then he gathered specimens of willows from China and Japan, from England and Russia. The time came when teachers of forestry in lands beyond the sea sent to this farmer strange specimens of the willow for examination and classification. He lived and died a farmer, but if his occupation confined him to his fields and meadows, his hobby made narrowness impossible, broadened the scope of his study and observation, lent him sympathy and made him friends in all the countries of the earth.

Amateur naturalists need not fear that all the work of discovery or investigation will be accomplished before they arrive at the state of proficiency necessary to accomplish something in the way of original research. It might be mentioned in this connection, in insect life, as might be expected, there are no doubt thousands of forms unknown; but even among those comparatively well known, much remains to be discovered. For centuries the transformation of a genus of flies very common in Europe was a mystery, but about thirty years ago it was learned that they live upon the eggs and young of spiders. Until 1890 the life history of the common bot-fly was entirely misunderstood. But more singular yet, old and populous England possessed a serpent (*Coronella lævis*) undiscovered until 1862. The discovery of radium is still fresh in the public mind. There remains plenty to be discovered and we need not go far from our own homes to make the discovery.

In the article "Three Common Flies" (page 96) occurs a statement which should have a word of explanation. The flesh-fly referred to is undoubtedly the *Sarcophaga sarraceniæ* rather than *S. carnaria*, the latter being an European species so closely allied that one might easily be mistaken for the other. The statement that these flies are viviparous is also misleading. That they produce their young alive (in the larval state) is true, but this is because they are ovoviviparous, the young being formed and developed in the egg, but hatched before the egg is deposited and being thus produced as living larvæ.

The season usually taken for naturalist's field work is nearly over for 1904, and the question naturally suggests itself, what has been accomplished? Have you added to your practical store of knowledge? Have you learned to know one more plant, bird or mineral than in the earlier days of the year? Or to know any of the characteristics, habits or distinguishing features of any one already known? If you have, well and good. If not— the season has not wholly passed, let what remains be improved.

NATURE'S ORCHESTRA.
BY HATTIE WASHBURN.

I wandered through the woodland wide,
　　I lingered 'neath the trees,
And heard the wild birds sing their songs
　　With sweetest melodies.
From o'er the grassland decked with flowers
　　The meadow lark's clear call
I heard, like some old anthem grand,
　　In sweetest cadence fall.

Entranced, I heard the robin sing
　•　To me his song of cheer;
The warbler's soft and lisping notes
　　Fell on my list'ning ear,
And from a lowly bush nearby
　　I hear the sparrow sing;
The goldfinch swiftly flitted by
　　And caroled on the wing.

The veery sang an anthem sweet
　　Within the woody dell,
I heard the dove in softest tone
　　The world's old story tell.
The catbird heard each song they sang
　　And caught each wild refrain,
The robin's song, the veery's lay,
　　And echoed back the strain.

Then throughout all the woodland wide
　　As when the night is gone
The stars fade softly one by one
　　Before the coming dawn,
Each woodland song was lost to me
　　Before the thrasher's lay:
I heard naught but the king of song
　　Sing on the verge of day.

He seemed to sing at Heaven's gate,
　　While through those portals with
The angels sang again to strain
　　Upon the other side.
If sorrow lurks within your breast,
　　If some sweet joy is gone,
Put thoughts of earthly care away
　　And wander forth at dawn.
　　　　Goodwin, S. D.

Animal Intelligence.
BY ASA A. EBERHART, M. D., LL. D.

WHILST we all acknowledge a certain kind of intelligence in animals, the suggestion that it approaches very near to human intelligence is apt to awaken a kind of skeptical frown. A friend of mine to whom the suggestion was made almost sneered and said, "There is no comparison at all." But the way to tell whether you are more intelligent than another is to put yourself in his place and see how much more of wisdom you would show. So I said to my friend, "Well, suppose your body could be suddenly changed to the body of a fly—with all the intelligence you have now—what could you do more than the fly does?" He looked a little confused, and hesitated. To relieve him, I said, "Well, if I were suddenly changed to a clam, with no hands or feet, and no wings to fly, but with a power to exude from my flesh a fluid that would form a shell, I would look the situation over, and would say, 'I can't run away like a mouse, I can't fly like a bird or swim like a fish, but I must do something to protect myself.' So I would form a shell around my body, and by my fleshy muscles would move myself along through the water and get food to sustain life, and do very much as the clam does, and would probably show no more intelligence."

It is true that no animal can do what man can do. They can not even approximate man's achievements in general. But this is in part due to the difference in physical structure, for neither can man do what the animals can. He can not swim like a fish nor fly like a bird nor eat through iron like a certain worm does, because he is not physically adapted to do so. But it is also true that some things he cannot do so well for want of the same mental ability. Take the little tailor bee, for instance. When its leaf-cell is complete and filled with honey it needs a lid to fit into it exactly. It flies out (often to a rose-bush) and, selecting a nice, perfect leaf, it cuts out a circular lid that will exactly fit into the top of the cell—that will fit it so nicely that the honey will not leak out. Now, what man is there who could look at the top of a can, for instance, and then go down town and cut out a lid that would exactly fit into it—that would fit so nicely that the honey would not leak out?

The man may have as good a pair of scissors as the bee, but he has not the material skill. The little bee is in advance. It might be thought, perhaps, that the little bee does it by mere mechanical instinct; but it has been found that the cells are not all of one size, so that could not be, and it must be that it does it by some mental skill that exceeds the ordinary power of man.

The wood bee gives us another illustration. It cuts a small circular hole into a tree, going in perhaps four to five inches; then downward twelve to eighteen inches. It then begins at the bottom of the hole, fixes a nice place, lays an egg, then fills in a bee's lenght of honey, puts a nice lid over it, lays another egg, and so keeps on till the hole is filled up. But the egg first deposited will hatch first. Then how can the young bee get out? And here comes the skill to which I wish to call attention. When the eggs are all laid it begins again on the outside of the tree opposite the bottom of the first hole, and cuts a hole in to meet the bottom

of it. And it does its work so well that it strikes it exactly, giving the young bees a chance to come out one at a time as they become mature enough to do so. In the examinations I have made, I have never found a hair's breadth of meeting the bottom of the first hole. Here is a piece of engineering that is not easily accomplished; even with the instruments of the engineer, and by mere mental power, who could accomplish it? We are not quite equal to the little bee in mental engineering, and these are only a few of the many instances that might be given. —*The Pacific.*

Habits of the Scorpion.

A few years ago, writes a traveler in the island of Jamaica, it was my fortunate chance to have an opportunity for observing some very curious facts in connection with that genus of the Arachnida class commonly known as the scorpion, and the curious traits of character in these insects. Turning over some old papers in my office one day, I suddenly came upon a large black scorpion, who promptly tried to beat a precipitate retreat. Having read or heard somewhere that if you blow on a scorpion he will not move, I tried the experiment, and was greatly astonished to find that it had the desired effect. The scorpion stopped instantly, flattened himself close to the paper on which he had been running, and had all the appearance of "holding on for dear life." While I continued to blow even quite lightly he refused to move, though I pushed him with a pencil and shook the paper to which he clung so tenaciously. Directly I ceased blowing, he advanced cautiously, only to stop again at the slightest breath. I was thus able to secure him in a glass tumbler which happened to be within reach, and then I determined to try another experiment as to the suicidal tendencies which I had heard ran in the veins of the Pedipalpi family.

On the stone floor of the kitchen attached to my office, I arranged a circle of burning sticks about three yards in circumference, the sticks being so placed that there were no means of exist through the fire. It was not intense, but small and quite bearable as regards heat within a few inches, so that the central part of the circle was perfectly cool. Into this center I accordingly dropped my scorpion, who, on touching terra firma, darted off in a great hurry, only to be quickly brought to a halt on reaching within a few inches of the periphery of the circle. After a short pause of reflection he deviated to the right, and ran once completely round the circle as near to the firesticks as it was prudent to venture. This he did three times, often approaching the burning sticks quite closely in his anxious endeavors to escape. In about a quarter of an hour, finding that his efforts were useless, he retired almost into the exact center of the circle, and there in a tragic manner raised his tail till the sting or spur was close to his head, gave himself two deliberate prods in the back of the neck, and thus miserably perished by his own hand. As I placed the body of the

suicide in a bottle of spirits, I almost regretted that I had not let him escape before he had resorted to such an extreme measure.

My last experience is even more curious than the preceding, and it shows a remarkable provision of nature that is almost incredibable. All I have ever read on this point is contained in the following words: "The young scorpions are produced at various intervals, and are carried by the parent for several days upon her back, during which time she never leaves her retreat." I was playing a game of billiards in a small village in the Blue Mountains; there was no ceiling to the room, the roof being covered, as is the custom in Jamaica, with cedar wood shingles. My opponent was smoking a large pipe, and suddenly, just as I was about to play a stroke, what I thought was the contents of my friend's pipe fell on the table close to the ball at which I was aiming. Instinctively I was on the point of brushing it off with my hand, when, to my amazement, I saw it was a moving mass, which, on closer inspection, turned out to be a very large female scorpion, from which ran away in every direction a number of perfectly formed little scorpions about a quarter of an inch in length. The mother scorpion lay dying upon the billiard cloth, and soon ended her feeble struggles, the whole of her back eaten out by her own offspring, of which, as they could not escape over the raised edge of the billiard table, we killed the astonishing number of thirty-eight. They had not only been carried by their parent, but they had lived on her, cleaning out her body from the shell of her back, so that she looked like an inverted cooked crab, from which the edible portions have been removed. She had clung to her retreat in the shingled roof until near the approach of death, when she had fallen and given us this curious spectacle. I was told by the attendant that the young scorpions always live thus at the expense of their mother's life, and that by the time her strength is exhausted, the horrid offspring are ready to shift for themselves.

The Magnetic Poles.

The location of the magnetic poles of the earth has never been determined with precision. An expedition prepared to be absent three years is now engaged in the effort to locate the north magnetic pole. We may on its return have definite knowledge concerning the matter. At present we can only say that the north magnetic pole is in British America, to the north of Hudson's Bay. The north and south magnetic poles are of equal strength. The earth behaves magnetically as if it had a bar magnet within it some 4,000 miles long, making an angle with its axis, and this magnet slowly oscillating, causing the declination of the needle. Both poles of this magnet attract and repel magnetic needles on the surface of the earth. This attraction and repulsion are not affected by the position of the compass. If it is in the northern hemisphere, the north pole attracts its north and repels its south end, and the south pole of the earth does the same. So also a compass in the southern hemisphere is affected by both the north and the south pole of the earth. The dip of a compass needle is affected by the pole to which it is nearer. In the northern hemisphere the north end of the needle dips, and in the southern hemisphere the south end of the needle dips, but the swinging of the needle in a horizontal plane is not caused by the pole of the hemisphere in which the needle is, to any greater extent than by the other pole of the earth.

The Ocean's Floor.

While carrying on her work for the Bureau of Fisheries, says the *National Geographic Magazine*, the Albatross has made more than 10,-000 soundings and more than 400 dredgings, and has brought up from the bottom of the sea hundreds of tons of fishes and other animals and mud.

The greatest depth from which the Albatross has secured any life was 4173 fathoms. This was in the South Pacific between Tonga and Ellice Islands. The dredge brought up siliceous sponges, radiolarians and brown volcanic mud. The greatest depth from which she has brought up fishes is 2949 fathoms, or about one and a third miles. This was in the edge of the Gulf Stream off the coast of Virginia. The deepest sounding ever made by the Albatross was at Station 4010, near Guam, where the enormous depth of 4813 fathoms, or nearly five and a half miles, was found.

The deepest sounding ever made

by any vessel was by the U. S. Nero while on the Honolulu Manila cable survey, with apparatus borrowed from the Albatross. When near Guam the Nero got 5269 fathoms, or 31,614 feet, only sixty-six feet less than six miles. If Mount Everest, one of the highest mountains on earth, were set down in this hole, it would have above its summit a depth of 2612 feet, or nearly half a mile of water.

Three Common Flies.

The only kind of house-fly that "bites" or "stings" is distinguished by having its weapon of offense, the proboscis, standing straight out horizontally in front of its head. Moreover, the fourth vein of the wings is gently curved toward the third, and neither straight, as in the "smaller," nor bent at an angle, as in the "common" house-fly. On the whole it is a more prettily marked insect than either of the others, though its beauty cannot be said to compensate for its viscious habits. It is a veritable blood-sucker, attacking our hands and faces, and well merits both its popular and scientific name—"the sharp-mouthed stinger," or *Stomoxys calcitrans*. Its thorax is similarly striped to that of the common fly, but the abdomen is very differently adorned, being yellowish-gray with six black dots, three on the second ring and three on the third. Its life history is similar to that of the common house-fly.

Quite different both in habits and appearance from others, is the common blue-bottle fly, called scientific-ally *Calliphora erythrocephala*. It is almost too well known to need description. It is a large fly—large as compared with the common house-fly—of a metallic blue color, with a lustre that changes position as we turn the fly around in various lights. The front of the head on its lower part is of a reddish color, and the fourth vein of the wings, so often alluded to, is bent at a very sharp angle toward the third. The eggs of the blue-bottle are laid in flesh of various kinds. Even living wounds have been selected by these flies for the purpose of depositing their eggs, and the pain caused by the maggots which hatch from them must be great. These maggots are ready to escape from the eggs in a very few hours after the latter have been laid, and themselves soon enter the next or pupa stage. As to the duration of life of the perfect fly, it is probably much longer than that of either the larva or pupa, and some blue-bottles may even hibernate during the winter, and so live on from one year to the next.

Another fly, worthy of passing notice, although not found in houses, like those already described, possesses some interest from its habits. This is the common flesh-fly, *Sarcophaga carnaria*. It is about the size of the blue-bottle, but of a more slender build, of a gray color, and perhaps the most handsome of the flies which have been mentioned. The face is silvery, the veins in the wings are similar in arrangement to the wings of the blue-bottle, the thorax is beautifully striped, alternately black and gray, while the abdomen is brilliantly checkered with black and silvery gray. The females of this fly are viviparous, that is to say, they do not lay eggs, but produce their young alive. These are deposited upon all sorts of vegetable matter, and in great numbers. It has been calculated that if a single female produced fifty young ones, by the end of October, by the same reckoning, would be produced from this single fly a progeny of no less than five hundred and eight millions of separate individuals. It is easy to see that if Nature had not provided ample means for the extermination of these insects, more especially in the form of insectivorous birds, little meat would be left for man after the flesh-flies had consumed what they regard as their proper food. Indeed, if even one-fourth of the flies which are hatched lived for three days they would constitute a serious menace to health; but, fortunately for us this is not the case, and their natural enemies devour them in great quantities before they have had time to do much harm.—*L. W. Irwell in Western Field.*

Screech Owls.

While the screech owl does occasionally destroy a small bird, the fact remains that its principal food is mice. Of ninety-four stomachs of the screech owl, from several states examined by the United States Department of Agriculture, forty-one contained mice, thirty-five contained insects, seven contained English sparrows while only twelve contained other birds, and some stomachs were empty. A few contained both mice and insects. This teaches

that the proportion of birds taken is so small as to have little weight as against the noxious creatures destroyed. As a rule when we kill our native birds, even owls or hawks, we have to pay the penalty by being compelled to provide artificial means to do the work that the Creator designed them to do.

Whistling Trees.

A species of acacia, which grows very abundantly in Nubia and the Soudan, is called the "whistling tree" by the natives. Its shoots are frequently distorted in shape by the agency of larvæ of insects and swollen into a globular bladder from one to two inches in diameter. After the insect has emerged from a circular hole in the side of this swelling, the opening, played upon by the wind, becomes a musical instrument suggestive of a sweet-toned flute. The whistling tree is also found in the West Indies.

A Great Salt Field.

The great field of crystalized salt at Salton, Cal., is in the middle of a great desert, and is two hundred and sixty-four feet below the level of the sea. Its surface, covering hundreds upon hundreds of acres, is as white as snow and, when the sun shines upon it, its brilliancy is too dazzling for the eye. The field is constantly supplied by the many salt springs in the adjacent foot-hills. That the whole region was at one time under the ocean is evident.

A man turns 112,000 spadefuls of earth in digging an acre of ground, the soil moved weighing 850 tons.

NATURE'S LESSON.

The pine that stands upon the wooded
    mountain
Gains not in stature in a single day;
The noble river springs not from one fountain,
    But gathers up its strength along its way.

The aloe hears for years the autumn's dirges,
    Before it shows its blossoms to the skies;
The coral reef that breaks the ocean's surges
    Through centuries of growth alone can rise.

Thus, through her works, Dame Nature offers
    ever
For our acceptance one persistent thought,
'Tis but by patient, sturdy, brave endeavor
    The greatest, best and grandest things are
        wrought.
                    —*Housekeeper's Weekly.*

A Veritable "Floating Island."

Away up in the wild Sierra
Nevada Mountains of California
may be found a veritable floating
island. This islet is small, but it is
nevertheless a floating one. Surrounded by lofty mountains is a
small lake known as Mirror Lake.
The waters of this body are wonderfully clear and reflective, and the lake
is very deep. Floating about on the
surface is a mass composed of plants,
roots and earth. This mass is about
twenty-five feet across at the top,
and is nearly circular in shape. How
far it extends downward is unknown. The roots of the plants are
so interlocked and filled in with earth
that the whole mass is firmly attached. Where the earth came from
is largely conjectural, but it is supposed to be the accumulations of
dust blown from the surrounding
mountains. So far as is known, this
floating island has existed for an indefinite period.

A great many persons have been
on the islet. The lake abounds in
fine trout, and its waters are much
fished. By means of long poles and
oars, the island may be slowly "navigated" about the lake. Many fish-
erman get on the floating mass, drift
about, and use their lines. Mirror
Lake is much visited, and the floating island is one of the chief attractions of the scene.

Uses of Cornstalk Pith.

To read of the variety of useful
things that are today being manufactured from Indian corn pith,
neglected for centuries as worthless,
is like delving into the mysteries of
an Indian fairy tale. There are three
cellulose "plants" in the United
States. The largest has just been
completed in Indiana, and has a
mechanical equipment costing over
one hundred thousand dollars. Here
is an interesting list of some of the
numberless articles that corn pith
will become on its devious progress
through the machinery: A product
for protecting battleships, smokeless
powder, dynamite, face-powder, pat-
ent-leather finish, kodak films, varnish and car-box packing-filler. It
sounds like a modern Aladdin's
lamp, as though one had only to put
in the corn pith, start the machinery,
murmur an incantation, and presto,
the desired article is at hand, from
dynamite to face-powder. The outer
lining of the cornstalk, that incloses
the pith, furnishes a separate reve-
nue of its own, as it is converted into a flour that is used to feed and
fatten cattle and chickens. Over one
hundred and sixty million tons of
cornstalks have been annually going
to waste; today this farm product
is worth three dollars a ton.

Fish Caught in Our Waters.

The vast amount of nutritious, wholesome and delicious foodstuff resulting from the fisheries of the United States is not generally realized.

The total catch of food-fishes in the United States and Alaska, as shown by the last census, was 1,733,-314,324 pounds, valued at $45,531,-165. The number of men employed was 214,056 and the capital invested was $72,261,646. The salmon pack of Puget Sound alone in 1901 exceeded $4,500,000, an amount more than four times as great as the entire silver output of the whole region drained by the Columbia River. The salmon output of Alaska for 1903 is valued at $10,000,000, which exceeds by more than $2,500,000 the amount which Alaska cost us, and if we add to the salmon the value of the cod, halibut and other fisheries of Alaska, the total greatly exceeds all the other resources of Alaska combined.

Pruning Shade Trees.

The object of pruning it two-fold. First, to remove low hanging boughs which annoy the passer by. Second, to preserve the natural form of the tree. Our shade trees are largely elms and maples. The former naturally grow tall with branches at a sharp angle to the main stem, which latter is adorned with twigs and branchlets, giving the appearance of a vine. *Do not disturb this growth.* It will always remain close to the tree and adds much to its beauty. It is not difficult to distinguish between this growth and the genuine branches. Maples on the other hand should have one erect stem branching symmetrically twelve feet or more from the ground. Limbs below that should at the proper time be sawed off. *Do not use an axe* to trim trees. Branches above that which show a tendency to outgrow their fellows should be shortened.

Erect branches should be pruned by cutting at an angle to prevent rotting from the rain. Side branches should be cut perpendicularly for the same reason. Large branches should not be removed at one cutting. It is better to cut back one-half or two-thirds the first year; repeat the second year; remove entirely the third year. Branches thus entirely removed should be cut even with the tree, smoothed with a knife and a dressing applied to the wound. Lead paint, or coal tar are recommended as suitable dressing, and Mr. Von Hoffman, a prominent forest engineer of New York City, in his book soon to be published recommends a dressing made of equal parts of coal tar, raw linseed oil and white lead.

Tree pruning should be done when the tree is dormant. Small twigs and branchlets may be removed with care at any time, and the dead limbs should be removed when observed, but no branch larger than three inches should be cut off while the tree is in sap. The best time for general prunning in this locality is in the spring before growth begins — or autumn just after the leaves fall. Maples, however, are best trimmed between the middle of May and the middle of June.

RANDOM NOTES.

Almost every county in the eastern part of Tennessee has deposits of galena.

Sand pits with a depth of 200 feet and extending 600 to 700 feet across are sometimes excavated by the whirling winds in Arabia. It may be entirely obliterated in a few hours and another excavated within a short distance of it.

A writer in the *Scientific American* says: "In collecting bird skins I have found innumerable air cells, forming a most delicate and wonderful network, between the body and the skin. In the pelican, one of our largest birds, this network of cells practically covered the whole body and was very noticeable. Now if these cells work automatically, like the lungs or like the circulation of the blood, being filled with or emptied of hot air, according to the purpose of the bird to rise, float or descend, then surely we can better understand the ease with which birds seem to sustain themselves in the air during their long flights."

Alaska is likely to prove a prolific source of that much used metal, tin. A late report from an assay of samples of this ore pronounces it a very high grade, and needs no concentration whatever. Several owners of claims have sent to the office specimens which average nearly fifty per cent. tin. In view of the fact that hitherto no tin has been profitably mined in the United States, and that for the years 1890 and 1902 tin imported was worth about twenty-seven cents a pound in New York City on a consumption of over 85,-000,000 pounds, the importance of this discovery is apparent.

In his balloon experiments, Mr. J. M. Bacon has been able to see the sea-bottom under clear water from a height of five hundred feet, all waves seeming to be blotted out, with no apparent scattering of light from the surface. At one thousand feet or higher, all water—whether deep or not—seemed opaque. Photographs taken during the ascent on a clear day became gradually blurred until at four thousand feet good pictures were made impossible by the dust particles that reflected the sunshine, the definition over water being better than over land.

Mosquitoes were unknown in Switzerland until the completion of the St. Gothard tunnel under the Alps. The tunnel gave them a short cut to the land of William Tell.

There are in the southern states east of the Mississippi River six coal areas entirely separate and distinct; some of them formed at the same period but not now showing any trace of ever having been connected.

A new use has been found for radium. If radium be placed near the receiving end of an ocean cable the message will be received much more clearly and distinctly than without it. This would be a great advantage in ocean telegraphy. The price of radium has gone up forty per cent. within a few months on account of the large demand and comparatively small supply.

A number of the huge war galleys of the Roman emperor Tiberius are known to have been sunken in Lake Nemi, in the Alban Hills, where they have lain for about 2,000 years. Unsuccessful attempts were made in 1400, 1535, 1827 and 1895 to raise these huge boats. It has been proposed to temporarily drain the lake, but the expense of this project has caused it to be declined by the Italian government.

How does it come about that so many take alcohol to keep out the cold? Simply because the nerves of our sense of temperature end in the skin. Be our skin well supplied with warm blood we say we are warm, and visa versa. Furthermore, we normally lose heat and keep our temperature at the proper level by radiation from the skin. Any drug that dilates the blood vessels of the skin will therefore tend to make us feel warmer and be colder.—*The American Inventor.*

A French scientist has recently been compiling a record of curious facts regarding the human body. He finds that among other things it is not only, as every one knows, a sort of ambulatory chemical laboratory, but that it contains enough material to supply a small factory. In its normal state the human body contains enough iron to make seven tenpenny nails; enough fat to make thirteen pounds of candles; enough carbon to make sixty-five gross of pencils, and enough phosphorus to tip 7,200 matches.

The Amateur Naturalist.

"To him who in the love of Nature holds communion with her visible forms, she speaks a various language."

| VOLUME 1. | BINGHAMTON, NEW YORK, NOVEMBER, 1904. | NUMBER 6. |

THE MILKWEED BUTTERFLY.

(*Danais plexippus.*)

BY ADDISON ELLSWORTH.

OF the one hundred or more species and varieties of butterflies which are found in this vicinity, there is none more conspicuous or better known than the large, brick-red insect known as the Monarch or *Danais plexippus*. It has an expanse of wings of about four inches, of a deep orange-red, with a wide margin of black on both the fore and hind wings, more or less dotted with white. The veins, forming the framework of the wings are also traced in black, while across the somewhat falcate tips of the forewings is a broad oblique band of the same hue which merges into the outer border. Within this area are two rows of white spots nearly square in form. The body is also black, but dotted on the thorax and ringed on the abdomen with white.

This species, while belonging to a group essentially tropical by nature, is, nevertheless, found over almost the entire continent, from northern Patagonia on the south to the Hudson Bay Territory and Athabascan region on the north. It is very abundant in the West Indies as well as throughout the whole tropical region on the mainland. A truly American form, it has, however, within the past forty years, become quite cosmopolitan, spreading over nearly the whole habitable earth, including not only the mainlands of Europe, Asia and Africa, but also Australia and the many islands of the Pacific Ocean. This has been accomplished, no doubt, mainly by mercantile and other ships, aided by its own extraordinary powers of flight, for on numerous occasions it has been seen at sea as much as five hundred miles from land. Only one other butterfly, *Pyrameis cardui*, or the Painted Lady, covers so wide an extent of territory.

The eggs of *Danais plexippus* are very pretty objects, a rich amber green in color, and shaped somewhat like an old-fashioned sugar-loaf with the top slightly blunted. It is ornamented with twenty-two longitudinal raised lines and transversed by numerous slightly raised ridges, while it is crowned with a little rosette of cells that are of extreme delicacy. They hatch out in about four days but are sometimes delayed a day or two longer. Upon eclosion from the egg the caterpillar at once devours the shell and then attacks the leaf upon which it was born. After its hunger is satisfied the larvæ retires to the concealed side of the leaf for rest, after which it resumes eating. This it does until its full growth is attained. In a day or two the caterpillar makes its first moult, i. e., sheds its skin, but its habits remain much the same throughout. Three other moultings take place before it is ready to enter the next or chrysalis state. This may be accomplished in eleven days if the weather is suitable, though it usually takes a little longer. The caterpillars attain a length of about two inches, and are green in color with transverse bands of yellow and black. Before entering the pupa state it leaves the food-plant and seeks some secluded place where it undergoes the change. This is accomplished much after the manner of moulting, but instead of the larvæ in a new dress, there appears a compact, rounded object of a deep emerald green color, surrounded at the top by a number of bright golden tubercles. It changes to a deep orange-red just before the

THE MILKWEED BUTTERFLY—Danais plexippus.

emergence of the butterfly, which in this latitude takes place in from nine to fifteen days. In the South there are undoubtedly two broods during the season, but in New York and New England there is but one brood though a number of writers have stated there are two. This error has, without question, arisen from the fact that the mother fly lays but two or three eggs at a time, and this she continues for several days, or even weeks, and the eggs hatching out at different dates makes it appear that there are successive broods. The fact that the Monarch does not put in its appearance until late in the season precludes the idea of a double brood; moreover, no butter-fly of this species has ever been known to lay her eggs here at the North the same season as hatching. They are all deposited by insects that have come to us from further south, and that probably in the second year.

It is now generally understood that our butterfly not only hibernates, but that it is also migratory, going south with the approach of cold weather. From abundant observations we know of massive movements of the species southward in the autumn. One of these was recorded in Massachusetts, October 1, 1876. Another nearly as great, and to us more interesting because of its recent occurrence, was noticed in Kansas, October 3, 1898. The people of Wichita in the afternoon of that day were greeted with the sight of many butterflies moving southward. Swiftly the numbers increased until there became vast swarms. The schools closed and business practically ceased, everybody turning out to view the brilliant spectacle. This vast stream of insects continued until within a quarter of an hour of sunset, and after that were followed by millions of stragglers.

Later still, on the 7th and 8th of October, 1899, one of the largest and most magnificent migrations ever witnessed took place, and was observed throughout New England and the Middle States. Here at Binghamton during the whole of the first day millions of these flies could be seen collecting in and about the woods to the west of the city till every bush and tree was fairly ablaze with their bright colors. Early the next morning they began to rise and fly southward, so that when night came not a one was to be found. These migrations have been observed nearly every year for the past two decades or more, but seldom in such vast swarms as those mentioned.

The evolution and migrations of the Monarch, however, are not the only features that commend it to our consideration, as it takes part in one of the most remarkable and interesting cases of mimicry known to our fauna. Belonging to a favored race which is protected from its natural enemies among the birds by an offensive odor, it enjoys perfect immunity from their attack. This odor, though scarcely perceptable and certainly not disagreeable to our own sense of smell, is, nevertheless, nauseating to the feathered tribes, and therefore avoided by them. It is also a fact, whether from this or some other cause, that they are more rarely attacked by insect parasites than any other of our butterflies. We have another large orange-red species popularly known as the Viceroy (*Limenitis disippus*), which, from its coloration differs from all the other members of the genus, is found here. Instead of being a deep blue-black, with a broad white band as in *L. arthemis*, it so closely imitates *Danais plexippus* as to be scarcely distinguishable from that insect except by careful comparison. The protection thus afforded the Viceroy not only secures it from attack by birds, enabling it holds its own in the struggle for life, but it has thereby become the most numerous and widely spread species in the family it represents. More curious still, there is found in the Gulf States another large Danidæ known as *Berenice*, or the Queen, which is much darker in color than the Monarch. *Limenitis disippus* is also found in the same locality, but is here dimorphic, some members of the species, and even of the same brood, mimicing plexippus and others resembling Berenice. As the Limenitis are among the butterflies most eagerly sought by birds, the importance to the Viceroy of such mimicry can readily be seen.

There is not a little confusion regarding the scientific name of our butterfly as there are some half dozen synonyms, each claiming more or less attention. The writer, however, believes that the *plexippus* of Linnæus will in the end prevail, although that of *archippus* by Fabricus is found in many collections and even in catalogues and price lists. But with this we need not concern ourselves at this time. It is, however, to be regretted that some systematists, eager for self glory, should attack the generic name and try, on the most flimsy pretexts, to break up the Danidæ into several genera. Thus, the name *Anosia* for both *plexippus* and *berenice*, coming as it does from one of our most popular and capious writers, has been quite extensively adopted, yet for no good reason. It is a pity that we have writers who, while doing a good work in entomology, can, nevertheless, see no beauty in an insect unless encumbered with their own cognomen. They fane would seek fame and distinction by pinning their names to the wings of some poor butterfly, thinking they will carry it down to posterity. Alas, for human folly !

Binghamton, N. Y.

∝ ∾

TYBEE ISLAND.
BY GEORGE MIDDLETON.

SAND is perhaps the most important production of Tybee Island*. The almost constant winds blow it up into dunes or hills, which at some points are quite large. The ancient dunes are still visible inland, and they support a scraggly variety of brush, while in the little valleys where organic matter has decayed and formed a better soil, the vegetation is much more luxuriant. This sand is composed almost wholly of quartz fragments, though there are quite a number of other substances represented, including shells, and small scales of mica.

On the beach itself ripple marks are scarce, but at the inlet where the winds have better play, and where the tide does not always reach, they are quite plentiful but they are formed more by winds than by waves. A shell or any object that rises above the level of the beach is quickly covered, only to be uncovered by the drifting sand when dry, until it disappears to form, perhaps, a wonder for scientists in ages yet to come. I sat on a piece of drift-wood, come from nobody knows where, away down the beach, and studied the process I have described—a steady stream of minute particles

---

* Tybee Island, Georgia, is a small low-lying sandy island nine miles long by three broad, situated at the mouth of the Savanah River.—ED.

followed the wind—went before the wind—and in the middle, too,—jumping, skipping, flashing like gems as the proper angle was turned; and ever and anon the fragments of mica showed their bright faces for a moment and then jumping on their edges, sped away, ever moving like restless spirits.

For those who admire marine views that from Tybee Island will be peculiarly charming. The rising of the sun in a blaze of glory is grand; that of the moon trailing its attenuated image away off and flashing its opalescent sheen upon the waters, is a sight not to be forgotten. Then the ships sailing in and out the harbor; the bathers; the strollers on the beach; and the wild roaring of the breakers that rearing their heads higher and higher, finally with a sullen boom, splash over everything within reach. All of these and many more attractions are there. The Tybee railroad makes an almost straight line across the marshes, paralleling the river nearly its entire distance, and crossing two wide creeks. The view from the cars is very attractive at certain points; it is picturesque all the way. The United States Government has a large and powerful fort on the island, and the reservation is quite a community in itself. And it may be worth mentioning that just off Tybee was made the first capture of the Revolutionary War— a British schooner loaded with kegs of powder, which went a long way in the cause of right and justice.

There are many palmetto trees on the island which makes the place, especially in the summer, have a distinctly sub-tropical appearance. Vines, creepers and shrubbery are also abundant.

Bird life is scarce and hardly noticeable except to the close observer. I wonder why.

A few harmless snakes exist on the island. At the inlet fine fishing can be had; also, crabbing and shrimping. Sharks are plentiful off the coast, but cause no alarm to the surf-bathers for the reason sharks do not like the surf and let it severely alone.

Of course, the flotsam and jetsam of the sea is of an inexhaustible variety but is hardly of permanent interest.

Tybee Island does not rise much above sea level and a slight subsidence by a land movement would eliminate it from the map. Some might think that the ending process had commenced and that the waves and high tides would carry the island back to the sea, but I am of the opinion that having endured this combined action of wind and wave for centuries, it will exist for years more unless there is some sinking of the land.

Savannah, Ga.

One of the greatest natural marvels of earth made its first appearance so recently as about two years ago. This is the now largest geyser in the world, the "Waimangu" in New Zealand. The crater is fully a half an acre in extent, and it shoots a huge column of black boiling mud and stones to the height of nearly 1,000 feet, and the steam several thousand feet further.

LUMINOSITY OF INSECTS.

BY CHARLES D. PENDELL.

LUMINOSITY or phosphorescence is common to many substances, especially to decaying animal and vegetable matter. In the tropical seas, is a minute animal resembling a very small cylinder of glowing phosphorous, which sometimes occurs in such numbers that the ocean appears like an immense molten sea of fire. Dr. Phipson, an English naturalist, relates that he has found a species of the rhizopoda, *Noctiluca miliaris*, a minute animal very common in the English Channel, "in such prodigious numbers in the damp sand at Ostend, that on rising a handful of it, it appeared like so much molten lava." These examples illustrate a remarkable phenomenon by no means confined to marine life. It is slightly manifest in a large number of beetles and some moths; but in a certain species of insects this is exhibited to a surprising degree.

The European glow worm is the wingless female of a certain coleopterous insect, *Lampyris splendidnia*. The male emits this phosphoresence slightly, but in the female it is quite strong; and it is probable that it can display or extinguish its light at pleasure. The habits of the insect are nocturnal and it is generally to be found during the summer months among grass or on mossy banks. If the luminous portion be placed in hydrogen gas it causes quite a detonation.

Every one has seen the common fire-fly, which causes our lawns on summer evenings to assume the appearance of a starry firmament. This interesting insect is widely scattered on this continent and a similar variety is found in Europe.

But in the tropical America, where insect life reaches the acme of development, there are phosphorescent insects of far superior splendor. There we find the great lantern-fly which has two prolongations from its forehead that gleam with a brilliancy sufficient to enable one to read the smallest print. By placing several of these luminous beetles together in a glass bottle their monstrous heads will furnish sufficient light for the lumination of a room.

The West India Islands are also inhabited by several species of this remarkable phosgene insect, which the people daily utilize. Travelers there, on a difficult road, illuminate their path by attaching one of these beetles to each of their feet, or by tying several to a stick and carrying it as a lantern. The creoles set them in the curls of their hair, and there, like resplendent jewels, they give a fairy-like aspect to the head of the wearer. The negresses, in their nocturnal dances, fasten these brilliant insects over their robes of lace, woven from soft bark, and in their rapid and graceful movements they seem enveloped in a robe of fire.

Science has not yet succeeded in explaining the cause of this luminosity. Certain centepedes possess this peculiarity but with the singular modification that it must first be exposed to sunlight. Carus, the German anatomist, has discovered that even the eggs of some of the foregoing insects are luminous; which certainly is a very curious fact and one which may throw some light on the cause of their phantom brightness.

ARCTIC TRAVEL IN WINTER.

RECENT news items have mentioned the project of running an overland telegraph line to extend up through Alaska, and by a short cable to Siberia and thence across northern Asia to Europe. The plan is not a new one. Soon after the purchase of Alaska by America in 1867, the plan was contemplated, a company organized and a survey partly made, but the lack of timber for poles proved too serious a draw back, and for that among other reasons the undertaking was abandoned. An account of a portion of this journey, by one who participated in it, is appended herewith:

"It was a land of desolation. A great level steppe, as boundless to the weary eye as the ocean itself, stretched away in every direction to the far horizon, without a single tree or bush to relieve its white, snowy monotony. Nowhere did we see any sign of animal or vegetable life, any suggestion of summer or flowers or warm sunshine, to brighten the dreary waste of storm-drifted snow.

"White, cold, and silent, it lay before us like a vast frozen ocean, lighted up faintly by the slender crescent of the waning moon in the east, and the weird blue streamers of the aurora, which went racing swiftly back and forth along the northern horizon. Even when the sun rose, huge and fiery, in a haze of frozen moisture at the south, it did not seem to infuse any warmth or life into the bleak wintry landscape.

"The thermometer at noon marked—35°, and at sunset it was—38°, and sinking. We had seen no wood since leaving the yourt on the Malmotka River, and, not daring to camp without a fire, we travelled for five hours after dark, guided only by the stars and a bluish aurora which was playing away in the north. Under the influence of the intense cold, frost formed in great quantities upon everything which was touched by our breaths. Beards became stiff tangled masses of frozen iron wire, eyelids grew heavy with long white rims of frost, and froze together when we winked, and our dogs, enveloped in dense clouds of steam, looked like snowy polar wolves. Only by running constantly beside our sledges could we keep any sensation of life in our feet. About eight o'clock a few scattered trees loomed up darkly against the eastern sky, and a joyful shout from our leading drivers announced the discovery of wood. We had reached a small stream called the Oosee'nova, seventy-five versts east of Geezhega, in the very middle of the great steppe. It was like coming to an island after having been long at sea. Our dogs stopped and curled themselves up into little round balls on the snow, as if conscious that the long day's journey was ended, while our drivers proceeded to make rapidly and systematically a Siberian half-faced camp. Three sledges were drawn up together, so as to make a little semi-enclosure about ten feet square; the snow was all shovelled out of the interior, and banked up around the three enclosed sides, like a snow fort, and a huge fire of trailing pine branches was built at the open end. The bottom of this little snow-cellar was then strewn to a depth of three or four inches with twigs of willow and alder, shaggy bear-skins were spread down to make a warm, soft carpet, and our fur sleeping-bags arranged for the night. Upon a small table extemporized out of a candle box, which stood in the center, Yagor soon placed two cups of steaming hot tea and a couple of dried fish. Then stretching ourselves out in luxurious style upon our bear-skin carpet, with our feet to the fire and our backs against pillows, we smoked, drank tea, and told stories in perfect common. After supper the drivers piled dry branches of trailing pine upon the fire until it sent up a column of hot ruddy flame ten feet in height, and then gathering in a picturesque group around the blaze, they sang for hours the wild melancholy songs of the Kamtchadals, and told never-ending stories of hardship and adventure on the great steppes and along the coast of the "icy sea." At last the great constellation of Orion marked bed-time. Amid a tumult of snarling and fighting, the dogs were fed their daily allowance of one dried fish each, fur stockings, moist with perspiration, were taken off and dried by the fire, and putting on our heaviest fur "kookhla'nkas," we crawled feet first into our bear-skin bags, pulled them up over our heads, and slept.

"A camp in the middle of a clear, dark winter's night presents a strange, wild appearance. I was awakened soon after midnight, by cold feet, and, raising myself upon one elbow, I pushed my head out of my frosty fur bag to see by the stars what time it was. The fire had died away to a red heap of smouldering embers. There was just light enough to distinguish the dark outlines of the loaded sledges, the fur-clad forms of our men, lying here and there in groups about the fire, and the frosty dogs, curled up into a hundred little hairy balls upon the snow. Away beyond the limits of the camp stretched the desolate steppe in a series of long snowy undulations, which blended gradually into one great white frozen ocean, and were lost in the distance and darkness of night. High over head, in a sky which was almost black, sparkled the bright constellations of Orion and the Pleiades—the celestial clocks which marked the long, weary hours between sunrise and sunset. The blue mysterious streamers of the Aurora trembled in the north, now shooting up in clear bright lines to the zenith, then waving back and forth in great majestic curves over the silent camp, as if warning back the adventurous traveller from the unknown regions around the pole. The silence was profound, oppressive. Nothing but the pulsating of the blood in my ears, and the heavy breathing of the sleeping men at my feet, broke-the universal lull. Suddenly there rose upon the still night-air a long, faint, wailing cry like that of a human being in the last extremity of suffering. Gradually it swelled and deepened until it seemed to fill the whole atmosphere with its volume of mournful sound, dying away at last into a low, despairing moan. It was the signal-howl of a Siberian dog; but so wild and unearthly did it seem in the stillness of the Arctic midnight, that it sent the startled blood bounding through my veins to my very finger-ends. In a moment the mournful cry was taken up by another dog, upon a higher key —two or three more joined in, then ten, twenty, forty, sixty, eighty, until the whole pack of a hundred dogs howled one infernal chorus together, making the air fairly tremble with sound, as if from the heavy bass of a great organ. For fully a minute heaven and earth seemed to be filled with yelling, shrieking fiends. Then one by one they began gradually to drop off, the unearthly tumult grew momentarily fainter and fainter, until at last it ended as it began, in one long, inexpressibly melancholy wail, and all was still. One or two of our men moved restlessly in their sleep, as if the mournful howls had blended unpleasantly with their dreams; but no one awoke, and a death-like silence again prevaded heaven and earth. Crawling back into my bag as the aurora disappeared, I fell asleep, and did not wake until near morning. With the first streak of dawn the camp began to show signs of animation. The dogs crawled out of the deep holes which their warm bodies had melted in the snow; the Cossacks poked their heads out of their frosty fur coats, and whipped off with little sticks the mass of frost which had accumulated around their breathing-holes. A fire was built, tea boiled, and we crawled out of our sleeping-bags to shiver around the fire and eat a hasty breakfast of rye-bread, dried fish and tea. In twenty minutes the dogs were harnessed, sledges packed, and runners covered with ice, and one after another we drove away at a brisk trot from the smoking fire, and began another day's journey across the barren steppe.

"In this monotonous routine of riding, camping and sleeping on the snow, day after day slowly passed until, on December 20th, we arrived at the settled Korak village of Shestakova, near the head of Penzhinsk Gulf."

ᴈ ᴊ

Naturalists have decided that many insects have senses which human beings lack. That of location, shown by the wasp, for instance, is remarkable. One species builds its nest in a sandbank that is only a part of several acres of such soil, and when it leaves in search of food it covers the nest so carefully that no ordinary eye could discover its location. That is to say, it is just like all the surrounding location, and yet the wasp flies back to it without hesitation and finds it without making a mistake.

The Amateur Naturalist.

A Journal for those who Study Nature from a love of it.

ISSUED BI-MONTHLY.

Entered as Second-Class matter October 6, 1904, at the post office at Binghamton. N Y.

SUBSCRIPTION, 50 CENTS PER YEAR.   SINGLE COPIES, 10 CENTS.
ADVERTISING RATES ON APPLICATION.

————————EDITED AND PUBLISHED BY——— —————

CHARLES D. PENDELL,

85-87 STATE STREET,   -   -   -   BINGHAMTON. N. Y.

The first year of the existence of any publication is in many ways its critical period, and many a journal that has made its salutatory full of hope and filled with bright promises for the future, animated with laudable ambitions, has not lived to see its second birth-day. As a matter of fact several of our contemporaries that were full fledged when the AMATUER NATURALIST made its first bow to the public, have been forced by varying circumstances to make their valedictory, or, perhaps, departed from the journalistic forum without even a good-bye, or an revoir! In the first number of this journal, issued a little less than a year ago, only one promise was made—that of permanence; and of this we can still give our readers the most positive assurance. This publication, as was then stated, is not necessarily dependent upon its subscription list for its maintenance. But it is a pleasure to state that it has from the first been self supporting—a condition of affairs that is a strong testimonial of appreciation. We should like at this time to make the publication a monthly, and have been strongly urged to do so. This would of course double the cost of production, besides which the editors time is so fully occupied that it seems at the present time inexpedient to say the least. In its present form THE AMATEUR NATURALIST is giving its readers fully as much reading as some of the more pretentious monthlies, and it has been suggested that by making our pages smaller, using wider margins, that we could issue a monthly without materially increasing the amount of type composition. This is true. But in adopting the present form for this magazine we did so after long and careful study, and with the idea of making it permanent, so that subsequent volumes as issued would be uniform with the first. As our subscription list grows we hope in time not only to make it a monthly, but to increase the number of pages as well.

In considering the value of any publication, what it contains is a fair criterion of its value. If it is fiction one is looking for, that is cheap and may be bought in car load lots for a nominal sum. It pervades most of the literature of the day—public libraries, Sunday school libraries, and private libraries. It may be found on the street corner, or the palace hotel, in slums and palaces. It is the mainstay of the "great" magazines and pervades the newspapers. But if one wants interesting truths of the great Book of Nature, in a readable, entertaining, understandable form, the search through the sources named would be long and arduous, and withal very unsatisfactory. But fifty cents invested in a year's subscription to THE AMATEUR NATURALIST will bring more information of this character than can be found in any half dozen of the general fiction dollar magazines combined. For instance, this first volume has 120 pages which contain 111 long and short articles, 10 nature poems and 103 short notes, and every one of them interesting as well as accurate. One would have to look far and wide to find an equal amount of similar literature for so small a sum as the subscription price of this magazine.

The organization of "Burroughs Clubs" has reached several states with prospects of its general extension throughout all America and Canada. It is taking a firm hold especially with teachers and the schools. It has for its object the arousing of intimacy with and sympathy for birds, trees, flowers, and the whole out-of-door world, and aims to lead people to the country from the city and town, and to keep country people in the country. It evidently has a great field in which much practical good can be done.

Many and varied are the ways suggested for the preserving of our forests, but so far none of the suggestions have resulted in any perceptable diminution of the continued destruction of our forest area. True, there are still billions of feet of timber standing and thousands of acres of virgin forest yet untouched by the woodman's axe, but these new areas are constantly being invaded, and new and improved methods invented for the cutting of the trees, while the demand is ever on the increase. Recently electricity has been brought into use, and trees are now being cut down by electrically heated wire saws. Forest preserves by the government at the head waters of our principal streams are good in their way, but are only a small item in the aggregate. Most of the suggestions made appeal only to the sentimental view, against which is arrayed the matter of dollars and cents, and in the end finance will prevail over sentiment, and it seems evident that the cutting down of trees will continue, and as yet no practical way seems to to have been devised to restore the destroyed timber land or to replace it with a new growth. Viewed with a financial basis, as is the only feasible way it seems that if the matter could be reached through some method in taxation a long step would be made in the right direction. For instance, let taxes be remitted on newly planted forests containing a specified number of young forest trees. This would encourage the planting and care of trees on many an acre of now barren hillside, now given over to brush-lots and weeds. A portion of the tax could be remitted on timber-land containing a certain number of trees of a specified size and this would prevent the wasteful cutting of small trees in existing forests.

IN THE FROST LAYDEN FOREST.

BY HATTIE WASHBURN.

I stand alone in the forest,
   Beautiful with frost flakes white,
Where Nature in robes of ermine
   Blushes in the morning light.

There is no sound save the moaning
   Of the wind in tree-tops high,
Where the weighted trees wave their arms
   Slow beneath the azure sky.

Or where a tiny crystal form
   Loosened from its lofty height
Falls, and falling carries thousands
   Downward in its giddy flight.

There's music in each crystal's fall;
   The wind breaths a soft refrain;
A song of fondness and longing,
   But all devoid of pain.

'Twas here in the happy summer
   I heard the wood minstrels sing;
It was here the birds were building
   Their homes in the gladsome spring.

Here at my feet the blooming trees
   Shed their petals white as snow,
And here the leaves of red and gold
   Fell to the soft turf below.

Each passing season has its charm,
   But what can surpass the glow
Of the sunlight on the forest
   Decked in robes of frost and snow.

Goodwin, S. D.

Miracles of God's Works.

BY EDMUND EVERETT HOBBS.

TO begin with a majority of the people who read of the ancient miracles, wonderful workings of God, claim that the day of miracles has past. Not so, my friend. God has made many beautiful things which if you study them you will find are miracles which God alone can perfect; and you will enjoy yourself immensely, I can tell you, if you once get on the right sort of study. You need not be a scientific man or woman; all scientists are not lovers of Nature.

If one could put on a diving suit and submerge himself in one of the numerous bogs or swamps, what a wonderful sight he would see. Miracles every thing he saw. To begin with, there is the water: no man, even those who know the chemical composition of water, can go to work and gather the different composites and make or construct water.

Thousands of specimens of algæ are found in every body of water, some so small that it is an impossibility for one unfamiliar to discover them. Every specimen of algæ is a wonder in construction, revealed only when a specimen is closely examined under a good microscope.*

Many varieties of snails are found in the different bodies of water. Please examine a snail shell—see how nicely it is constructed to suit the different purposes of its inhabitant.

The first forms of life of many insects are found in the water. Dragon flies, for instance, spend a long period of their life beneath the surface. One seldom sees a dragon fly without its wings, as it is under water.

What is more interesting than the metamorphosis of a frog from the egg, through the tadpole state up to

---

*Over two thousand species of algæ are known and described, varying in size from the smallest microscopical specimen to great sea weeds which ramify like trees, the *Macrocystis pyrifera* of the Pacific Ocean reaching a height of one thousand five hundred feet. Their color is usually green but not always; brown, yellow, purple and rose colored varieties also exist.—ED.

the complete frog? How wonderful to see the hind legs form, then the front or fore legs form, and then gradually the tail dissappear. Behold, the perfect frog! Is not he and his way of living wonderful?

Go then to the mountains: see how a gigantic tree seventy-five or possibly one hundred and fifty years old grew from a single small seed.

In late summer see how the seeds are arranged so that the wind will carry them to a spot of fertile soil where they will germinate and grow.

When the blossoms are on the trees or flowers, see how the bumble bee carries pollen from one blossom to another to help the flower in the formation of its seeds. Wonderful, is it not?

See how some stones were formed by the waves of an ancient sea out of minute particles of sand. See how a small pebble has rolled (like a snow ball) around in the mud until by the action of the wind and chemical changes of the atmosphere it has become a large pebble or bolder.

All of these are in a sense miracles. We scarcely realize that they are, because they are of such every day occurance; but they are none the less marvelous manifestations of God's handiwork. Enough more could be named to fill a large volume and still mention only a small fraction of God's works.

"God has made all of these beautiful things for you. My friend, if you are not enjoying yourself you have not seen Nature in her grandest form"; which means, if you have not seen the present day miracles it is just because you do not look for them.

"The works of God are fair for naught,
  Unless your eyes, in seeing,
See hidden in the thing the thought
  That animates its being."

Binghamton, N. Y.

A Shocking Experience.

BY O. W. BARRETT.

THE article on "Electric Fish" in the September AMATEUR NATURALIST reminds me of my introduction to His Mightiness *Electrophorus* (*Gymnotus*) *electricus*, the Electric Eel of Venezuela. The place of meeting was near the orchid houses of the Trinidad Botanic Gardens at Port of Spain, Trinidad; the reception was informal.

First, I tried touching him with an iron rod, but although he did his best to shock me, I felt scarcely a thrill. The iron was rusty, but the attendant told me he had received good current through the iron; the eel seemed to know what was expected of him and curved his body partly around the rod, stiffening himself at the time of turning on the current. But this failure to send the lightning along the rod was only one of many mysteries connected with His Mightiness.

The keeper told me a Hindoo "Coolie" woman was in the hahit of coming to the Gardens for the purpose of being shocked by the fish; she believed it would cure her rheumatism. But I do not understand how she could accustom herself to holding such a living battery in her bare hands,—even though the treatment was free. The most I could do was to hold two fingers in contact with his body; and probably I could not have done that if he had been aroused to his best efforts. Now, I used to take pretty big quantities of electricity, and used to know something about resistance, conductivity, etc., but I fail utterly to see just how that fish, entirely under water could fill my arm and chest with static organic electricity to such a painful extent. I stood on dry ground and my other hand did not touch the water or any metal. The water apparently did not carry the current at all. If touched while swimming there was no shock felt; the body was held rigid in a curve when the current was "on."

The color of my lightning conductor friend was an olive brown. There was no tail fin, yet nearly all the body was tail, the vent being situated just behind the throat. He was only a baby—under three feet in length—but I'll never forget the strenuous warmth of his manifestations.

Mayaguez, Porto Rico.

"Balled" Partridges.

The following is certainly a curious freak—either of nature or of some writer. We cannot say that we are fully prepared to give credence to it, but hope some of our English exchanges may enlighten us on the subject. But for the usually reliable character of the paper from which it is taken, we should attach no importance to it. The article is as follows:

In certain districts where the soil is exactly right (or rather exactly wrong) the partridges so carefully preserved in England are likely to be attacked by a peculiar misfortune known as "balling." The word means simply that a partridge hatched out on a clay soil in wet weather may find mud adhering to its feet as it struggles along after the mother bird.

This is a small beginning; but the chances are that the earth accumulates. Sometimes, indeed, the soil attached to the foot of a little partridge will increase from a mere speck to a weight of several ounces. A writer in Badminton says that the heaviest ball he ever knew weighed four ounces, and the bird that carried it was only half its proper size, although the rest of the covey were full grown. The little creature could only move along in a kind of flying scramble, dragging the ball on the ground.

The clay was baked as hard as a brick, so that it was no easy matter to remove it. Finally it was soaked off, and then it became apparent that the bird, without its accustomed ballast, did not know how to fly. With every effort it tumbled head over heels, and learned the natural mode only after long trying.

The fate of a "balled" partridge which is not rescued by some kindly hand is a cruel one. Day by day the burden grows heavier, and the more the chick scrambles after its companions the larger its burden becomes. Finally, it is no longer possible to move at all, and then the little thing can but give up and die.

Naturalists say that this balling of birds is one of nature's provisions for scattering seeds. It is easy to demonstrate this, and the "answer comes true." One experimenter scattered the earth from a three ounce ball over the top of a pan of ordinary dirt, which had been baked to destroy the seeds in it. Ten plants sprang up in due time, and developed into seven varieties.

New York City Minerals.

Every locality can furnish something in the mineral line, though, of course, the mineral resources of some localities are much more abundant than others. But to the experienced mineral collector even the most unpromising fields are worthy of investigation.

One would hardly believe what a lot of *ites* and *ines* and such things there are in New York City alone, but any one can get an idea if he cares to go up to the American Museum of Natural History and examine the cabinet of Manhattan Island minerals there.

The substance of the island seems to be gneiss, but there are more or less interesting things scattered through it, like feldspar of different colors, some varieties of it sparkling like Norwegian sunstone, garnets, brown, pink, and red, mostly found in Harlem now, though one of extraordinary size, weighing 9⅔ pounds, was taken out of a sewer on the east side; brown and black tourmalines, scattered through the white limestone at the place where the ship canal joins the Harlem River and Spuyten Duyvil Creek; mica, in black, yellow, brown, and green colors, the green especially abundant

at Fort George; crystals of quartz near Inwood and Kingsbridge; hyalite, or Muller's glass, a form of opal, that looks as if it had been melted and poured onto the stone while hot, in Mott Haven; epidote, beryl, rose quartz, actinolite and other substances, if you are lucky enough to find them, as you may, in the ballast of the Hudson River railroad track, where you are sure to find large and showy plates of black mica anyway. Then there is gold in Central Park, as there is almost everywhere, but not in quantities that will ever pay for working. Sphene is found near Fort George—a rare mineral that yielded a small gem for the scarf-pin of a local collector. A sphene is one of the most beautiful things in the world—a honey-yellow stone that has the play of color of a diamond, with a steadier light. On the site of the Manhattan Iron Works, at Manhattanville, you may find on the old dumps limonite, hematite, calcite, pyrite, franklinite and, from the limestone used as a flux, a good many fossil shells. Further up the river, at the sites of the lime kilns at Riverdale, may be found long, glistening white blades of tremolite in the dolomite that has been brought down from Sing Sing. Apatite is found on the upper end of the island in small green crystals.

Brooklyn and its neighborhood are interesting to the mineralogist, and likewise to the geologist. A great boulder of labradorite was found on Myrtle Avenue, across the river. There is no other labradorite *in situ* nearer than the Adirondack Mountains, and it is believed that this block of rock was carried by the great glacier, during the last ice age, from its parent ledge and dropped here beside the ocean thousands of years ago. The whole of Long Island is merely the dump of that great glacier—a part of the terminal moraine that extends half way across the continent—and the stuff that has been gathered there has been identified in many instances as coming from various parts of the country to the north and west—New York, New Jersey, Connecticut, and Vermont. The green mica found near One Hundred and Eighty-fifth Street, New York, is frequently found in Brooklyn, and there was no way for it to get over, except on the ice, or in it. There are thousands of boulders of trap rock, or basalt, from the Palisades on the Hudson, in and around Brooklyn, and on top of the Palisades a glacial groove was found a year ago that pointed straight towards Prospect Park. So, with everything north and north-west to borrow from, you are likely to find anything in Brooklyn. Over a hundred varieties of minerals have been found, and the list is growing all the time.

Biggest Grape-vine.

Probably the largest grape-vine in the world is growing in the Car-pinteria Valley, California, and is called La Para Grande. It was started from a cutting sixty-one years ago by a young Spanish woman. It is eight feet four inches in circumference at its base and one of the horizontal branches measures more than three feet in circumference.

The trellis covers about a third of an acre and sixty heavy posts support it. The vine, it is asserted produces as many as five thousand bunches annually, at a conservative estimate, and in good years many clusters measure twelve to fifteen inches in length and weigh six to eight pounds. Its owner estimates that in 1895 the vine yielded ten tons of grapes.—*Green's Fruit Grower.*

In the Grip of an Octopus.

A special cable dispatch to *The New York Journal* from Cape Town, South Africa, says: a series of most interesting photographs, pictures of an octopus that attacked a diver named Palmer, thirty-five feet below the surface outside Cape Town Harbor, have been sent to King Edward. Palmer was fairly covered by the arms of the octopus when pulled to the surface, and the animal was captured in its entirety. This is a rare find, and the King cabled at once to preserve the curious specimen for the Museum of Natural History. At the same time Mr. Palmer, who had such a narrow escape, was ordered to report in full on his experience.

"I was going down the fifth time in the same spot," says Mr. Palmer, "and it seems now that the animal was lying in wait for me, starting from behind a rock, and before I knew it my legs were encircled by his slimy arms. While I felt about me for a hatchet or knife, my left arm was attacked, and I felt the suckers pressing against the flesh.

"As I know that an octopus has one hundred and twenty or more suckers to each arm, my fright was boundless. Of course, I immediately rang the alarm signal and was pulled up."

When Palmer appeared on the surface his whole body was covered by the fearful animal, that exuded a black liquid. The body was pulled into the boat, or rather the two bodies were, and the men went to work with hatchets and knives to cut off the octopus's arms. Its body has now been reconstructed, and measures from the tip of one arm to the tip of the opposite arm eleven and one-half feet. Palmer is slowly recovering. It was first feared that he would die of the fright.

Animal Instinct in Winter.

With many forms of life the readiness for winter, says *St. Nicholas*, is not to secure a place to protect them from cold or even from freezing, but for security against sudden changes of conditions and of temperature. It is a protection in some cases similar to that of the plants on the lawn that were covered with straw by the gardener when he made them ready for winter. In some places of the kind, for instance, in the squirrel's nest, there is undoubtedly real animal warmth and coziness. Fish seek the deepest parts of pools, where the temperature of the water is a little above freezing, and where it remains very near this point until spring.

In the Philippines.

The number of islands which compose the Philippine Archipelago is not less than 3141. They are largely of volcanic origin. New islands are constantly being formed. In a single day, on September 21, 1897, an island 750 feet long, 450 feet in breadth and 45 feet above the sea, was formed, and several others on the same day. These islands were formed by an upheaval from the bottom of the ocean by volcanic action in conjunction with an earthquake. The water surrounding the archipelago is very deep, not far from the east coast the Pacific Ocean being from 4000 to 6000 meters deep. There are twelve volcanoes constantly active, and many more intermittantly so. On one island over 500 very perceptible earthquake shocks have been felt during a period of 18 months.

Mine of Pure Glass.

What is believed to be a mine of pure glass has been found it the neighborhood of Tampico, Mexico, according to mining men who have recently returned from that section.

The information was found in a mound of earth, and tests have demonstrated that with simple melting and running into molds the product comes out as clearly as the best manufactured glass in factories.

Beyond the general statement that the crystal is a remnant of the age of fire, when subterranean volcanoes threw up masses of fused material, no attempt has been made to explain this freak of nature. The component parts of the glass are the same as enter into commercial glass, though in places, it is said to be discolored from a mixture of foreign substances while in a state of semiliquidity.—*The Mineral Collector.*

A WINTER MUSING.

BY C. LEON BRUMBAUGH.

Ghost of bleak winter's night !
No fear to me you bring,
Nor sadness.
Message of summer's light !
I hear the bluebird sing
In gladness.

Wilkinsburg. Pa.

God in Nature.

Yesterday I drove to the nearby park where a band was playing and where thousands of people were innocently congregated for a few hours of recreation and enjoyment. As I sat there in my wagon listening to the excellent music, this thought came to my mind. Here on the platform before me are forty men, all skilled in the use of some one instrument. Each instrument played upon by each of these forty men is different from that used by any other member of the band and is itself a marvelous invention. There is something of the divine in music. Music itself is a marvelous creation. Then I said to myself, how can one witness this simple exhibition and say there is no God ? In saying this he would have to say that the creation of these musicians and their wonderful art was all chance or accident. Then my eyes fell upon the sweet clover blossoms on the green sward before me, upon the forest trees in full foliage, on the birds, horses and other beasts that were nearby. Then I looked at the clouds, upon the blue sky and the sun hanging low in the heavens, and I asked myself again, how can any one look upon these creations and say that there is no God ? Which is as much as to say that the sun, the earth, the creations on earth were not designed by the Creator but came by chance. And yet these things that I have alluded to are some of the more common every day evidences of the fact that there is a God. There are greater evidences. Whatever you do, my friend, never say to yourself or to others, that there is no God, no Creator, no Designer of the great universe.—*E. J. B. in Green's Fruit Grower.*

Antiquity of the Rose.

Flowers have always figured more or less prominently in history, the roses of England, the lilies of France being notable examples. There are some six hundred varieties of roses known. Speaking of the antiquity of this favorite flower, *Success* says:

Rose culture's beginning goes back beyond records. The flower is mentioned in the earliest Coptic manuscript. India's traditions take the rose to the times of the gods on earth, Egypt had roses, wild and tame, before the Roman occupation made it, in a way, Rome's commercial rose garden; yet, curiously enough, there is no reference to the flower in painting, sculpture or hieroglyphics. Japan in our time parallels Egypt. Roses flourish there, but do not serve as a motif for artists. There is this further likeness—neither Egypt nor Japan has a rose song or a love song proper—so it may well be that madam the rose is avenged for the slight.

The Jews, returning from the Babylonish captivity, took with them a recompense of roses. Semiramis, with the world at her feet, found her chief joy in a bower of roses. Mohammed turned back from Damascus after viewing it encircled with rose gardens. "It is too delightful. A man can have but one paradise," said the prophet. Damascus lies in the heart of Syria whose name some geographers derive from seri, meaning a wild rose, and wild roses are abundant there. The damask of our gardens go back to Damascus. They were brought from it at the time of the Crusades—although exactly when, or by whom, nobody can certainly say.

Why a Limpet Sticks.

The limpet has gained notoriety by the strength with which it adheres to the rock on which it decides to rest. The force required to detach the limpet from the rock has lately been tested by a well-known naturalist, who found that more than sixty pounds must be exerted for the purpose. So this little thing, weighing about half-an-ounce, sticks so tightly that a force equal to two thousand times its own weight is necessary to drag it away.

It was at one time supposed that atmospheric pressure had something to do with the adhesive power of the limpet, but it is now generally agreed that the creature exudes a kind of a glue for this purpose. If you place your finger on the rock immediately after a limpet has been detached, you will feel that the surface is sticky, and if you allow your finger to remain there for a short time you will notice that it is beginning to stick quite tightly.

Timber Resources of Canada.

Across the Great Lakes in Canada there lies one of the world's largest reserves of timber. In spite of the tariff imposed, much of this timber is today coming to the United States. The forests of the dominion are beginning to yield abundantly. More than a billion feet of pine sawlogs and square timber, during a recent season, were cut upon territory held under timber license from the crown. Much of Canada's timber land has not yet been explored. In the newly-developed districts of Algoma, which are close to the Great Lakes, it is estimated that there are more than a hundred million cords of spruce and pulp-wood, while in the districts of Thunder Bay and Rainy River there are nearly two hundred million cords more. A belt at least three thousand miles long is believed to exist in Canada between Alaska and the Atlantic.—*Booklovers' Magazine.*

Puff-ball Culture.

Since all the puff-balls are edible, and many of them well flavored and of large size, it is remarkable that nobody has yet attempted to grow them commercially. A single puff-ball is often large enough to furnish a meal for an entire family, and if the family is small or the puff-ball unusually large it is even possible to carefully cut off as much as is needed, returning at another time for the rest which will remain in good condition for some days. The person who first makes puff-ball growing easy may be sure of rich rewards.—*The American Botanist.*

RANDOM NOTES.

Granite liquefies sooner than iron, or at a temperature of about 2400°.

Mercury or quicksilver is usually obtained from the ore called cinnabar, but is found native in Spain and in Mexico.

Bismuth melts at a temperature of 507° lead at 617° and tin at 442°, but a fusible metal made by uniting these three will melt at 201°. Spoons made of it will fuse in hot tea.

Greyhounds are pictured on Egyptian monuments carved 3,000 B. C. The Arab boarhound is thought to be the oldest type of domestic dog at present living.

All spiders are provided with spinnerets, though comparatively few species spin webs for the capture of their prey. One species (*Synageles picata*) lays but three eggs; another species (*Mygale cancerides*)—a spider inhabiting Martinique and so large as to capture small birds—lays from 1800 to 2000 eggs.

The stars are now known to vary greatly in size and brilliancy, as well as in distance from us, many being probably much smaller than our sun. It has been calculated that Aldebaran has a mass of 882 times greater than our sun, and that the red southern star Antares is 215 times brighter than Aldebaran, with a mass about 88,000 times the mass of the sun.

The flexibility of intacolumite—a remarkable sandstone existing in Georgia and North and South Carolina—seems to be surpassed by that of a magnesian limestone found at the entrance of the Tyne in England. This limestone is reported to be so flexible that thin layers, three feet or more in length, may be bent into a circle while damp, retaining that form on drying.

Botanists who grieve at the loss of color in preserved flowers will do well to dip leaves and blossoms in a warm mixture prepared thus, says *Buffalo News*: One part of hydrochloric acid to six hundred of alcohol. If this be done before they are placed between the driers, they will not only retain their natural colors, but will also dry with greater quickness. This is in the proportion of one dram of the acid to 9.025 and three drams of alcohol. It will prove very satisfactory.'

Some species of star-fish will themselves break off ray after ray, if alarmed, hoping, no doubt, that the attention of the intruder will be attracted by these broken members while the star-fish itself escapes.

The metal gallium melts at 81.1 degrees Fahrenheit, becoming liquid when held in the hand. Its specific gravity is a little less than six, or about half that of lead. It tarnishes but slightly in the air. It adheres readily to glass when fused, forming a beautiful mirror, In chemical characteristics the rare element gallium most resembles the abundant element aluminum.

In Ecuador there is a lake at the bottom of which are supposed to repose many great links of pure gold cast into its waters at the time the Inca empire fell. They formed a part of an immense golden chain, and they were so large that when they were carried away to escape the rapacity of the Spanish, each link was a load for a llama, the small South American beast of burden, and a long train of llamas bore them to the shores of the lake.

This world seems large to us who live upon it. It must be large in order to contain the vast oceans, the great lakes and mountain ranges. but the sun is 1,580,000 times larger than our earth. The strongest telescope reveals millions of worlds, or as we know them planets or stars, and there are many more that the telescope does not reveal. Such thoughts as these give us a faint idea of the great Creator.

In the New World, the largest of the boas is the anaconda, or water boa, of tropical South America, a species alleged to attain a length of twenty-five feet or more, but specimens of such dimensions appear to be so exceedingly rare that they never find their way into captivity. Two fine specimens of this aquatic snake are on exhibition in the reptile house. The largest specimen, measuring sixteen feet in length, recently gave birth to thirty-four young. The young snakes are being carefully fed, and it is thought that the majority of them may be reared. At the time of birth they were twenty-seven inches long, and of much the same coloration as the parent. Like the adult, they are vicious and and resent handling.

making it extremely difficult

BUTTERFLIES.—Life-size.—Third Series

Melitæa chalcedon.
Thecla crysalus.
Anthocharis sara.

Papilio thoas.
Papilio philenor.
Argynis idalia.

Limenitis arthemis var. lamina.
Cystineura dorcas.
Thecla halesus.

The Amateur Naturalist.

"To him who in the love of Nature holds communion with her visible forms, she speaks a various language."

VOLUME 2.   BINGHAMTON, NEW YORK, JANUARY, 1905.   NUMBER 1.

A GROUP OF BUTTERFLIES.

BY ADDISON ELLSWORTH.

WE present the readers of THE AMATEUR NATURALIST this month with a group of butterflies, typical of some half-dozen different families, all but two of which are sub-tropical, yet, with a single exception, found within the territory of the United States. A minute description of these insects will not be necessary as our illustration gives an excellent and life-like representation of them, and serves better their identification than any amount of mere words. A little consideration of their habits and generalities of the groups to which they belong, however, may not prove uninteresting, and to which we will confine our attention.

Standing at the head of our list—in point of size and beauty but not structurally—is *Papilio thoas*, Linnæus. This is one of our largest and most conspicuous butterflies, of a deep black ground on the upper surface of the wings, which are traversed by a broad band or subcontinuous series of large yellow spots, and with a similar spot at the end of the great spatulate tails. The under surface inclines to a safron hue. Strictly speaking, this insect is an inhabitant of the tropics, though occuring at rare intervals in the hot lands of southern Texas. It extends southward through the Antillis, Mexico and Central America, and in South America along the Amazon Valley to the Tropic of Capricorn. Throughout all but the extreme southern portion of this range, it is accompanied by a closely allied species, *P. cresphontes*, Cramier. This latter insect enjoys a somewhat wider range within the United States, being quite common along the entire Gulf Coast, and in recent years has worked its way northward even as far as Toronto, Canada. In New York it has been reported from Rochester, Brockport, Poughkeepsie and other points. I have taken it on two occasions here at Binghamton, each time in a badly mutilated condition, as though for a long time on the wing. The larvæ of both species feed on the orange, lemon and other citrus plants, and often become very destructive. They are called by the planters "the orange-puppy," "dog-faced caterpillar" and other equally agreeable names. *Thoas* is distinguished from its cogenitor by the greater and more uniform breadth of the median band of yellow spots and by the almost total absence of the curved submarginal series of spots on the primaries, which are altogether too prominent in our illustration. In this respect the cut approaches much more closely to *cresphontes*. The two forms, however, often blend one into the other making it extremely difficult to separate them. For this reason many writers believe them to be mere varieties of the same insects, *thoas* doubtless being the parent form.

In striking contrast to the above is our beautiful *Papilio philenor*, Linnæus. This large and magnificent butterfly is of an intense black, shading off into brilliant metallic tints of green and steel, as viewed in different lights. With the exception of *P. polydamus*, also belonging to our fauna, this insect stands apart from our other native swallow-tails and approaches more nearly in structure, though not in size, to the gorgeous *Ornithoptera* group of the West Indies. It is a southern fly and its allies are all tropical. Like *thoas* (or rather the form *cresphontes*) it is occasionally found in our northern states, and eastward as far as Massachusetts. In this state it is extremely rare, often not seen for years, and then for a single season found quite plentifully. I have taken but a single specimen near this city during a half-score years collecting, but have captured it in Chenango County and at Heart Lake in Pennsylvania. The eggs are nearly round, covered with a red, waxy secretion and are laid in clusters of about one dozen on Aristoloncha, Ipomea and some kinds of Polygonium, all of which serve as food for the caterpillars.

There are within the limits of boreal America at least twenty-seven species of butterflies belonging to the genus *Papilio*, while throughout all Europe from the Dardanelles to Gibraltar and the North Cape, there are but three known species. The genus, however, is wonderfully prolific within the tropics of both the Old and New Worlds, where there are nearly five hundred distinct forms and many of these are the largest and handsomest of the *Lepidoptera*. They display great diversity in form of wings and coloration, some species mimicing to an astonishing degree other genera widely separate from them, but in all the neuration is nearly the same, while the larvæ and chrysalids reveal very strongly marked affinities.

Our next four figures represent species belonging to the great family Nymphalidæ or brush-footed butterflies. They are readily distinguished from all other forms from the fact that the first pair of legs in both sexes is atrophied; that is, greatly reduced in size, so that they cannot be used in walking and are carried folded up on the breast. This is the largest and most widely distributed family of butterflies and within the tropics includes some of the most gorgeously colored species in the world. In the United States the family is most widely represented by the Fritillaries or Silver spots, represented by the genus *Argynnis*, of which we have no less than sixty distinct forms. These find their greatest development in high latitudes and on mountain slopes to nearly the line of perpetual snow. In Europe there are some thirty-five species, and they are well distributed within the temperate regions of Asia, many magnificent forms being found in Japan, China and the Himalayas. It extends even to Australia, while recently two species have been reported in near vicinity to the great volcanic peak Kilima-

Njaro, in Africa. There are also a few native varieties upon the mountains and table-lands of Chili and Peru, in South America.

Of this group we have figured as typical within our own domain, the lovely *Argynnis idalia*, Drury. This exceedingly beautiful insect belongs to the Alleghanian fauna, though it is somewhat irregularly distributed, ranging from Maine to Nebraska, but particularly at home in northern New Jersey and Pennsylvania and the higher elevations of New York. It is of a rich orange-red and blue-black on the upper surface, marked with black, orange and white or cream color as shown by our illustration. On the under side, the fore wings are fulvous with a marginal row of silver crescents and some silver spots on and near the costa. The hind wings beneath are dark olive brown, with three rows of large, irregular, silvery spots. The female is distinguished by having the marginal rows of spots on the hind wings cream-colored and by the presence of a similar row on the fore wings. It expands from 2¾ to 4 inches and flies from the end of June until into September. As the habits of the *Argynnis* are similar, what applies to this species does so, as far as known, to the entire group. The larvæ feed for the most part on various species of violet during the night and throughout the daytime remain concealed. The eggs are laid late in the season, and hatch out in from ten to twenty days, according to the weather. Upon eclosion from the egg, the young caterpillars, without partaking of food, immediately drop to the ground, when they go into a state of lethergy and there remain till their food plant starts up again the following spring. In other species of butterflies which hibernate in the larval state, the caterpillar usually attains a considerable portion of its growth before entering this trance-like condition, and moreover seeks protection by boring its way into woody substances or by providing for itself a covering, technically called hybernaculum, woven of silk from its own spinnerettes. But here are billions of these tiny specks of life, scarcely a line's length,* scattered broadcast over the cold earth, forced to face the rigors of winter, and with no other covering but such as is provided by the elements themselves. This is the more remarkable from the fact that the great majority of these insects are found in northern latitudes, even to within the Arctic Circle, where summer at best is bleak and of but few week's duration. Why this is so, why the infant larvæ should be deprived of even the small protection afforded by the egg-shell, is more than we can say. It is another of Nature's secrets at which we can only marvel, but serves a demonstration of the wonderful ways she has to accomplish her ends. An attempt has been made by Messrs. Scudder, Holland and others to revive the old Hubnerian genus, *Brenthis*, for some of the smaller Argynids, but with what success we will leave to lepidopterists to determine. There seems, however, no good grounds for the division which only results in confusion.

---

*One-twelfth of an inch.

Closely allied to the preceeding, but differing in some important particulars is the genus *Melitea*. In these insects the markings upon the wings are different and the spots on the under side are not silvered. So far as I am aware the larvæ hibernates after the third moulting, and when it has received nearly its full growth. They are, moreover, gregarious and spin a web into which many retire together to pass the winter months. In the spring they forsake their nest and, although still consociative to a limited degree, wander about restlessly till time for their fourth and last moulting. Our illustration depicts a Californian species, *Melitea chalcedon*, first described by Doubleday and Hewitson. It also extends southward into the sub-tropics. Its nearest eastern ally is found in our beautiful *M. Phœton*, Drury, which is a much handsomer insect, especially in the variety *Streckerii*, recently taken at Binghamton and described by the writer in the *American Entomologist*. As I shall reserve this insect for description in another article, further remarks will not be necessary at this time. The genus is a very large one and well distributed over the whole North Temperate Zone. There are twenty-eight well defined species within the United States, mostly in the mountain slopes and the valleys of the Pacific Coast Range. Only two species occur in the Eastern States, the one mentioned above and *M. Harrisi*, Scudder. There are also many species in Europe, in Siberia, in China and in the northern islands of Japan.

.   Our next species is *Limenitis arthemis*, Drury, which is found throughout northern New England, New York, Quebec, Ontario and the watershed of the Great Lakes. It is rarely taken in northern Pennsylvania. A good idea can be had of its general appearance by a glance at our beautiful colored plate, which shows the form *lamina* of Fabricus. The form *proserpina*, Edwards, differs in the narrower and sometimes almost obsolete white band which crosses both wings. The genus is represented in boreal America by six species, two of which are brick-red and resemble in a marked degree the genus *Danais*, described in the December number of THE AMATEUR NATURALIST. The caterpillar feeds upon the black birch and hibernates as in the preceding insect, about the middle of August while the days are yet hot, but in hybernaculums which it builds by weaving a silken web around the leaf upon which it has feasted, taking the precaution to secure the midrib to the stem by threads passed many times around it. Unlike the *Meliteas*, however, it is solitary by nature and goes into its long sleep alone. I know of no more beautiful sight than a bevy of these butterflies floating with easy abandon about some damp spot by the roadside or in an open bordering of woodland.

Our last insect of the Nymphalidæ, *Cystineura dorcas*, is not found within the domain of Uncle Sam unless, peradventure, it may be met with in our recently acquired territory across the Isthmus of Panama. Seven species are included in this genus all of which are tropical and one only, *Amymone*, is found north of Mexico. They are beautiful, dainty creatures, as light and airy as a sniff of June roses, and as graceful as a fairy's dream.

Three other insects, representative of two families and two genera, comprise our group. One of these, *Anthocharis sara*, Boisduval, belongs to the Perinæ, small or medium-sized, white or yellowish flies; usually bordered with black, brown or orange. They are found everywhere, often collecting in vast numbers around damp places and mud-holes on country roads. There is no country without its Perinæ, while the tropics of both hemispheres fairly swarm with them. There are many genera included in this sub-family, the two most important with us being the *Pieris* or white cabbage flies and the *Colias* or yellow road flies. The genus *Anthocharis* or orange-tips contains eight species within the United States, all of which are exceedingly pretty. With two or three exceptions they belong to the Pacific slope, our example being found in Oregon, California and southward. This is a polymorphic insect, there being no less than four distinct varieties described. Considerable confusion exists in the identification of various members of this group, believed to be the result of hibridization. It winters in the pupæ state as do most of the family.

The two *Theclas* or hair-streaks belong to the Lycænidæ. They are both sub-tropical, the northern limit of *Crysalus*, Edw., being Utah, Colorado, Nevada and southern California, while *Halesus*, Cramer, is common throughout Central America, Mexico and the hotter portions of the Gulf States. The hair-streaks as they are popularly called are small butterflies, the upper side often brilliantly colored with iridescent blue or green, sometimes dark brown or reddish. On the under side they are marked with lines and spots variously arranged and these are frequently of brightest colors. It is another large group, being found in both the Old and New Worlds.

> "These be the pretty genii of the flow'rs,
> Daintily fed with honey and pure dew."

Binghamton, N. Y.

ત ૪

A JANUARY RAMBLE.
BY MARY-LEE VAN HOOK.

WINTER'S walk should be sharp and crisp, bracing as the nipping cold, the stimulating air. Yet often in winter as in other seasons friends whom you meet delay you, stop you to pass the time of day, and your brisk walk is changed into a ramble. So it fell out with me as this afternoon I ventured forth "to take the air" as our grandfathers say. The snow covers the ground in a sheet white and spotless here in the country. The walks which lead to the village are well cleared and the roads with their sand and dirt mixed with snow look like chocolate; but no paths lead into the woodland by the roadside, and the brown weeds, the dried remains of sweet clover, and the grasses, still tremblingly support the flakes of snow received the day before, now looking like the feathery cotton which decks a Christmas tree:

From a distant treetop a jay bird screams his note, carrying well in the clear air; another answers, and from an ash tree just beside me a third calls out until the air rings with the discord of their harsh voices; after a lengthy discussion, seemingly angry, they at last settled the point to their liking and flew away.

There is more color variety in a winter landscape than one sometimes realizes, for the effects are in the browns and dull reds, though there is often much blue as well—and the impressionists love to say a great deal of purple. This last color is often to be seen in the shadows of objects on the snow and there is a great deal of lavender, in the trunks of beech trees particularly. The red cedars proudly pointing to heaven in evergreen grandeur give a sombre touch to any landscape. Some little spruce trees have caught in their outstretched arms heaped up burdens of snow and hug them close to their dark garments. The wind shudders through an oak grove as I pass, and the rustling leaves call attention to themselves. Withered and dry though they are, their soft brown gives a tone to the view and color which could ill be spared. The sumac with dull olive branches covered with soft down and red fruit of velvet lights up the roadsides; and less often the stocky bittersweet trails its bunches of red berries over a fence almost as gayly now as in the autumn.

My eye catches a quick movement at the base of a burr oak and in a moment a red squirrel dashes half way up the trunk, pauses and looking at me expectantly for no reason at all, dashes down again. Frisking about in the snow he begins to brush it aside and finally brings up an acorn which he proceeds to devour. Turning it nervously over and over in his front paws he finally attacks it with his sharp teeth, scattering the shells to right and left. The red squirrel is not a bit afraid of snow and does not think of staying indoors because of it when there is a chance of fresh food. He does store some provisions, I believe, especially nuts with hard shells which he buries, but the acorn that my friend just picked up was one he had only now discovered. Off he is again in his merry runs up first one tree then another, perhaps taking a circuitous route home, a habit which most of us—only the bee likes a short cut, I believe—seem to enjoy.

The sun has gone down and now I, too, hurry home. Through the thousand branches of yonder group of maples, and through the fine lines of the elms beyond, the sky is seen tinged with the dull red and pale yellow of the after glow. To the east I can catch a glimpse of Lake Michigan, cold and white with gleaming heaps of snow and ice, and through a clump of birches, looking like ghosts in the dusk, shines a single star.

Lakeside, Ill.

SOME REMARKABLE NESTS.

BY CHARLES D. PENDELL.

BIRDS' nests wherever found present a subject for an interesting study. There are upwards of five thousand known species of birds. Some, it is true, like the cuckoo and the cowbird deposit their eggs in the nests of other species, and give no further heed to them, leaving the duties of parentage to their foster-parents. Others, like the ostrich, deposit their eggs in a mere excavation in the sand and let the heat of the sun perform the work of incubation, the young being able to shift for themselves when hatched. But most species construct a nest of some sort in which to lay their eggs and rear their young.

Whether we consider the graceful pendant nest of the oriole, the dainty chalice of the humming bird, the lofty eyrie of the eagle, or the innumerable and varied forms of nests constructed by the hosts of the feathered tribes, each and all present a remarkable adaption to the individual requirements of the builder. But there are certain extraordinary forms which have been described by travelers, that are especially deserving of notice on account of their great size or peculiarity of construction.

First in regard to size may be mentioned that of the jungle fowl or mound-building megapodius (meaning "great footed"), a bird of Australia, which in color and size resembles the partridge. A nest of this bird measured by the ornithologist Gould, was fourteen feet high and had a circumference of one hundred and fifty feet. "Compared to the size of the bird the dimensions of such a mountain are almost prodigious, and we ask how, with its beak and claws only for pickaxe and entire means of transport, it contrives to get together such a mass of materials."

The immense structure is constructed by first getting together a thick bed of leaves, branches and plants, the bird being guided in making this collection by a wonderful chemical instinct, selecting only such matter as will in fermenting, by the heat thus generated, hatch the eggs without a tendency to cause their decay. After having gathered sufficient vegetable matter, it heaps up earth and stones above it, and in such a manner as to form "an enormous crater-like tumulus, concave in the middle, the place where alone the materials first collected remain uncovered." The bird having completed its herculean task, deposits its eggs (usually eight in number, and about the size of a swan's,) in the center of the nest among the vegetation left uncovered. They are placed in a circle at equal distances apart with the small end down. This done, the megapodius gives no further attention to its nest or offspring. The young knows how to nourish itself from birth. When it breaks the shell it throws off the leaves that cover it, mounts the crest of its birthplace, dries its wings, (for it is full fledged,) gives a few flaps, and, "having cast a disturbed and inquisitive look upon the surrounding country, the feeble bird takes its flight into the atmosphere and quits its cradle forever."

Another Australian bird, the talegala (*Talegala Lathami*) or bush turkey, whose appearance is similar to the common turkey though somewhat smaller, builds a nest equal in size to a large haycock. The material is collected by grasping the grass with one foot and hopping along on the other until the bird arrives at the prospective domicile, where it deposits the grass, until after many journeys, the nest is completed. Several families often unite in building these remarkable nests and in one that was examined a bushel of eggs is said to have been uncovered.

In respect to ingenuity of construction the social grosbeak, of Africa, excels all of its kind in the complexity of aerial architecture. This little bird, of similar size and appearance to the sparrow, congregates in vast numbers which unite in building one immense nest. There are sometimes more than six hundred birds inhabiting this elevated dormitory, or more than three hundred compartments to the nest. This abode has the appearance of an enormous umbrella of which the trunk of the tree is the handle. "One of these nests," says Patterson, "I had the curiosity to break down, so as to inform myself of its internal structure, and found it equally ingenious with that of the external. There are many entrances each of which forms a separate street with nests on both sides at about two inches distant from each other."

The nest of the tailor bird (*Sylvia sutoria*), of Hindoostan, less remarkable in regard to size, is in one respect more remarkable than that made by any other member of the feathered race. The bird, selecting a plant with two large leaves, gathers cotton or similar material, and spinning it into a thread by means of its slender mandibles and delicate feet, then, with its bill for a needle, sews the leaves together, and within the compartment so formed weaves a delicate nest, which is thus concealed from the observation of its enemies.

Far less ingenious, the nest of the rhinoceros hornbill, an Asiatic species, called korwe by the natives, is too curious not to deserve mention. The female having entered her breeding place, the cavity of some tree, the male plasters up the entrance, leaving only a narrow slit exactly suited to the form of his beak, through which to feed his mate. The female lines the nest with her own feathers, and remains by her young after hatching until they are fully fledged. During this time, from two to three months, the devoted husband provides food for the entire family, reducing himself by starvation to such a degree that a sudden lowering of the temperature is sufficient to cause his untimely death.

The nest of that peculiar swallow, salanganes, belonging to the genus *Collocalia* which inhabits the coast of China and the neighboring islands, are affixed by thousands to the all but inaccessible cliffs and dark caverns, and the gathering of them furnishes profitable employment to large numbers of the inhabitants. They are composed of a glutinous material resembling isinglass which is composed of certain saliva secreted in glands of the mouth. The nests weigh about one-half ounce each, 8,400,000 of these nests have been sold in the market at Canton market at from $10 to $35 per pound.

The nest of the flamingo, too, deserves mention. The adult bird stands five feet high, having very long legs and neck. Of the seven species of flamingo, three inhabit America, being found in Florida and in Cuba and the Bahama Islands. The nests are built of mud, conical in shape and averaging nine to twelve inches in height, though sometimes eighteen inches high. On the top is a slight depression in which the bird deposits its one white egg. The flamingo nests in colonies. Two thousand nests have been found in an area of 27,000 square feet, and eight groups or villages have been found in the radius of one mile, though not all as large as the one mentioned.

Another peculiar nest, which is not a nest at all, is that of the Patagonian penguin, which lives amid the waves, rocks and ice of the frigid Antarctic zone. Like the marsupialia among mammals, which conceal their young in a ventral sack, the female penguin carries her solitary egg in a pouch formed by a fold in the skin of the abdomen, and there holds it so firmly that as he leaps, and sometimes falls, from rock to rock the egg remains unharmed until hatched. To purloin the egg from this singular receptacle it is necessary to engage in a regular battle, not only with the female but also her devoted mate, who, at the first alarm, rushes to the spot and fights so furiously that success for the agressor can only be secured when the noble bird sink dead or totally disabled.

Wonderful indeed is the instinct with which wise Nature has endowed her creatures, and to the observing mind its development is everywhere present in forms as curious and remarkable as those just described. "Wheresoever the naturalist turns his eye, life or the germ of life lies spread before him."

❧ ❧

Flowers secrete honey for the bees, butterflies and moths, and reserve it for them by fencing out creeping insects and other small game. All this, of course, is intended to promote cross-pollination, but the bees often abuse the trust reposed in them by stealing the honey without transferring the pollen. They bite through the tips of long spurs or make perforations at the base of deep corollas and so get at the honey with less effort than if they obtained it in the way intended by the flowers. It is remarkable how accurately they gauge the location of the nectar, never making a puncture in the wrong place, and seeming to indicate a fair amount of reasoning power in apian brains. Sometimes they bite through both calyx and corolla when this is the most direct line to the sweets. Nearly a hundred different species have been thus punctured.—*The American Botanist*.

The Amateur Naturalist.

A Journal for those who Study Nature from a love of it.

ISSUED BI-MONTHLY.

Entered as Second-Class matter October 6, 1904, at the post office at Binghamton, N Y.

SUBSCRIPTION, 50 CENTS PER YEAR.   SINGLE COPIES, 10 CENTS.

ADVERTISING RATES ON APPLICATION.

———— EDITED AND PUBLISHED BY ———— ————

CHARLES D. PENDELL,

85-87 STATE STREET,   -   -   -   BINGHAMTON, N. Y.

The attitude of the subscribers of any publication at the close of Volume I and the beginning of another volume may in a degree be regarded as a test of its merit, or, at least, of its value to those who gave it its initial support. With that for a criterion THE AMATEUR NATURALIST has good reason for self gratulation. Renewals have come to us from all parts of the country accompanied by words of unstinted praise and commendation, and we are more than ever convinced that there is a demand for just such a publication as this journal aims to be. The one great difficulty we have to meet in extending our circulation is to find out just who are the people most interested in popular natural science. Of the 70,000,000 people of America there are undoubtedly 70,000 who would be interested in a periodical of this kind, but could we but have one-tenth of that number as subscribers, much could be added to make this journal better. Our subscribers naturally will feel an interest in seeing improvements made and we believe will be ready to assist in increasing the circulation and usefulness of this magazine. To them, therefore, we make this offer: To each subscriber sending us the names and addresses of ten persons who are interested in one or more branches of natural science and might be interested in THE AMATEUR NATURALIST we will send a copy of *The Making of an Herbarium*, by Willard N. Clute. This book has before been described in these pages and a brief description will be found in advertisement on cover. As spring approaches the natural desire is to form a collection of plants for study or the entertainment of friends, and this book will be especially valuable. Those who already possess a copy can in this way obtain a copy which would make a present to be appreciated by any plant loving friend. On receipt of these names we will mail to each a copy of THE AMATEUR NATURALIST and they will then have opportunity of deciding its value to them. This little effort on the part of our subscribers will be appreciated by the publisher, and as new subscribers are added to our list the improvements which will follow will be still further reward. This offer is also extended to new subscribers; thus any person who remits fifty cents for a year's subscription and also sends the names and addresses of ten persons whom we might interest in this magazine, will be entitled to the premium also.

While THE AMATEUR NATURALIST has not been enlarged or made a monthly, yet we shall strive to show progress in other ways. The frontispiece of this volume, a fine colored plate, is the visible evidence of our intention. While we shall not, at present, have a colored plate in each number, yet we shall use illustrations as required, and probably with greater frequency than in Volume I.

The "Random Notes" published as our last page afford an interesting department, but are merely suggestive texts of what may in many instances be elaborated into a much more exhaustive treatment of the subject matter. In one instance this has been done and two valuable contributions have resulted therefrom. Let others follow. We are ready at all times to give consideration to contributions coming within the scope of this journal, and will publish any which may be in consonance with its plan.

Those interested in the preservation of our magnificent forest domain will be pleased to note that the National Forest Congress, recently held at Washington, D. C., was attended by over eight hundred delegates. These represented all sections of the country and included railroad officials, farmers, lumbermen and mine owners, as well as others. It is a good sign to note that the practical and business interests of the country are being awakened to the need of saving our timber resources from wanton waste.

Among the recent happenings of interest to those geologically inclined is the completion of Dinosaur Hall, in connection with the American Museum of Natural History. This building will be opened to the public February 16th. For the past eight years a special search for fossil reptiles in the Rocky Mountain States has been carried on and with considerable success. The new hall will contain the largest fossil skeleton ever mounted, and from this and others may be obtained some idea of the marvelous animals which populated this earth during the earlier ages.

Dispatches from South Africa state that the largest diamond ever known has been taken from the Premier mine in the Transvaal. The stone is oblong in shape, has a diameter of four inches, and weighs 3,032 carats—equal to about a pound and one-half avoirdupois—and is said to be worth upwards of $4,000,000. This weight is declared to be over three times greater than that of the Excelsior diamond, which was discovered at Jagerstontein in 1893 and weighed 970 carats. Only one diamond of larger size has ever been found so far as is known. This was a large black diamond found a few years ago in Brazil, but being of no ornamental value was cut up and used in making diamond drills. Among the most famous diamonds are the Orloff, owned by the Czar, cut in rose form and weighing 195 carats; the Koh-i-Noor, owned by the British royal family, weighs 102¾ carats, and the Regent or Pitt in the Louvre, weighing 136 carats.

THE FLASHLIGHT.

BY HATTIE WASHBURN.

At night within the forest shade
   There wandered a gentle doe
Where a streamlet sweet music made,
   In its soft and ceaseless flow.

And could there be a thing to dread
   Beside that murmuring stream,
With branches arching over head
   Beautiful as in a dream?

A man stood upon either side
   With a camera and gun;
And each in that dark forest wide
   Thought himself the only one.

The wild doe started in alarm
   As two reports shook the air;
One from the death-dealing firearm,
   And one caused the flashlight's glare.

Unharmed the frightened wild doe fled.
   Next morn on the dewy ground,
The hunter's bullet in his head,
   The photographer was found.

The plate his camera concealed
   Was skillfully brought to light,
And an image was there revealed
   Of his destroyer by night.

Goodwin, S D.

The Porto Rican Pillow Tree.

BY O. W. BARRETT.

THERE seems to be a special kind of pillow tree in use in Porto Rico which is not common elsewhere in all the world. The "stuffing" for these is the fibre of the seeds of the Cork-wood (*Ochroma lagopus*), a medium-sized, large-leaved tree of the Bombax, or Silk Cotton family. This tree grows in the open forests, but not plentifully, and is planted near dwellings for shade, ornament and "goano," as the fibre product is called.

The leaves are roundish, or slightly three-pointed, and are borne only at the tips of the clumsy branches.

The flowers, which stand erect, are six to eight inches long, shaped somewhat like a lily with thick leathery petals, and are creamy white inside, with a yellowish-brown velvety surface outside; their odor is peculiar, but not quite pleasant. The fruit is a five-celled capsule about six or eight inches long by one inch in diameter and clothed with a tawny coat of short hair.

The numerous seeds are about the size of mustard seeds and are densely covered with a brownish cotton-like wool. The "crinkliness" of this fibre prevents its "wadding" and gives it a fluffiness. One of its strongest qualities is that it seldom gets "musty," even where the annual rainfall is one hundred and thirty inches in a high temperature—something which cannot be said of feather pillows. The cost of the "goano" is much less than that of feathers; it wears longer and never "leaks through."

The wood of the tree is exceedingly light and spongy with no heart whatever and may be used for making firm, but slightly porous corks; the pith is very large, lustrous white, and dense enough to also be used for corks.

The Ceiba, or Silk Cotton tree, is the nearest relative of the cork-wood. The seed fibre of this species is exceedingly fine, straight and of a lustrous satiny white; it is sometimes used to adultrate cotton and even silk, and is occasionally used in the East Indies for stuffing pillows and mattresses. It is a majestic tree, but the native Porto Rican always gives it the cold shoulder, so to speak, when his own pillow tree is in sight.

Mayaguez, P. R.

"A Lost Invention."

"Fame and fortune await the lucky individual who can rediscover the combination of metals from which the Egyptians, the Aztecs, and the Incas of Peru made their tools and arms. Though each of these nations reached a high state of civilization, none of them ever discovered iron, in spite of the fact that the soil of all three countries was largely impregnated with it. Their substitute for it was a combination of metals which had the temper of steel. Despite the greatest efforts, the secret of this composition has baffled scientists and has become a lost art. The great explorer Humboldt tried to discover it from an analysis of a chisel found in an ancient Inca silver mine, but all that he could find out was that it appeared to be a combination of a small portion of tin with copper. This combination will not give the hardness of steel, so it is evident that tin and copper could not have been its only component parts. Whatever might have been the nature of the metallic combination, these ancient races were able so to prepare pure copper that it equaled in temper the finest steel produced at the present day by the most scientifically approved process. With their bronze and copper instruments they were able to quarry and shape the hardest known stones, such as granite and porphyry, and even cut emeralds and like substances. A rediscovery of this lost art would revolutionize many trades in which steel at present holds the monopoly. If copper could thus be tempered now its advantage over steel would be very great and it would no doubt be preferred to the latter in numerous industries. It is a curious fact that though this lost secret still baffles modern scientists it must have been discovered independently by the three races which made use of it so long ago."

The above is from a recent newspaper article and is a fair example of much of the newspaper science. It is interesting to read, and contains some truths, and the fact that the "lost art" was independently discovered in three widely separated portions of the earth is especially noteworthy. But may we ask, *why* would the rediscovery cause such a revolution "in the trades in which steel at present holds monopoly?" Is there any evidence to show that such instruments would be better or cheaper than steel? Is anybody mourning over the absence of bronze hand-saws, or longing to be shaved with a copper razor, or is any boy hankering for a brass jack-knife?

And we are not so sure about this process being a "lost art." Prof. R. H. Thurston, of the United States Government Board, appointed twenty-five years ago to test iron, steel and other metals, reported that alloys of copper 72.89, tin 26.85, tin 29.88, copper 68.58, tin 31.26; copper 67.87, tin 32.10; and copper 65.34, tin 34.47 were all so hard that they could not be turned in a lathe with steel tools. These and other hard combinations have been generally known to the trade for years, but of what good are they? Copper and its alloys are more costly than the ordinary grades of tool steel, and the only apparent advantage possessed is that they are incorrodible. This may be an advantage, but is not likely to cause any great revolution in the iron and steel industries.

Egyptian Papyrus, Past and Present.

The papyrus plants of ancient Egypt are not all dead, though papyrus paper making is a long-lost art. As a beautiful ornament plant the papyrus thrives to-day, and is perhaps destined to become a favorite along the banks of our warmer streams and rivers. In Florida or Louisiana in a noiseless electric launch the visitor may then glide up creeks and winding rivers, and drift back some thousand years into the dim and hazy days when the Pharaohs and the Ptolemies and Cleopatra ruled the land of earliest civilization. In the days of paper-making Egypt, the banks of the Nile near the sea must have been covered with great stretches of this wonderful plant. The bass-reliefs on Egyptian monuments show the methods of this culture, while the great Alexandrian library with its half million long papyrus rolls, burned by the ruthless Mohammedans, gives an idea of the extent of its use. Alexandria was the center of its manufacture, and throughout the Nile delta were large plantations of this graceful and lordly plant.

As late as the eighteen century travelers in Egypt found the fella-heen or peasants making mats of papyrus, although the art of paper making has been long dead. To-day you may search lower Egypt in vain for a single plume of papyrus, although on the upper reaches of the Nile you can still lose yourself in its dense forests, which everywhere line the banks of the sluggish river. The few plants now growing in the Ezbee Kieya garden in Cairo are said to have been imported there from Hamburg.

It seems strange that a plant which once played such a role in the world of literature and history should have become so neglected that probably not one in ten thousand of the people of the United States could tell what it is like or would know it if they saw it, except that they would recognize a plant surpassingly beautiful.

The papyrus of old Egypt would add an irresistible charm to our southern waterways. To enthusiasts on beautiful plant forms it were well worth a visit to Sicily just for a look at the miles of papyrus which overhang the Anapo River, as well as its source, a deep clear spring just outside the ancient city of Syracuse. It is difficult to conceive a more brilliant or more fairy-like sight than the thousands of smooth, slender, leafless stems, rising in graceful curves from the water to a height of fifteen feet and bearing at their summits feather-duster tassels of delicate green filaments. As the boat winds in and out among this multitude of smooth stems, or as you separate the tassels which nearly touch overhead, it is easy to believe yourself in a tropical forest, where all the tree trunks are brilliant green and all the leaves are threads of but a lighter vivid hue. This wealth of papyrus on the Anapo is one of the most fascinating sights in the world, and every year thousands of visitors make the excursion from Syracuse to view it.

If the experiments which are being started with the papyrus by the Office of Plant Introduction of the Department of Agriculture are as successful as Mr. Fairchild, the agricultural scientist in charge of the office, hopes that plant may yet become a favorite ornament in Florida, where many streams like the Anapo are to be found, and where thousands of visitors repair annually to look upon and enjoy strange plants and fruits and to thaw the cold and frost from the marrow of their bones.— *Scientific American.*

A Rich Find of Tourmalines.

The value of a knowledge of minerals as well as other products of nature is illustrated by the recent discovery of tourmaline on Kangaroo Island, off the South Australian coast. The discoverer was ridiculed by his companions, but subsequently it was ascertained that the stones were fine specimens of tourmaline and a small syndicate has been formed for the purpose of prospecting in likely places. According to *The Mineral Collector,* these are all situated in country overrun by the yucca, from which large quantities of marketable gum are obtained. In one locality a shaft was sunk 12 feet and a number of valuable stones obtained. Later on, the depth of the shaft was increased to 20 feet and a drive of 35 feet put in. This enabled a fresh lot of stones to be obtained. Then an open cut in the opposite direction was made, followed by the discovery of more stones, which appeared to be very plentiful.

Encouraged by the success of their labors in the vicinity, the prospectors sank a second shaft in the neighborhood of the former one. Here some blue stones were met with. Several were of a light and others of a dark character. Other finds equally valuable have been reported.

The nature of the country is feldspathic granite, and it is easily worked. The best stones are said to occur in pockets in the soft clay, but there is nothing to indicate where these are to be found. When occurring in the decomposed granite, the tourmaline is mostly perished, and in a crumbling state of decomposition.

In the open cut numbers of large quartz crystals, several ten inches in length, were met, mostly pointed downward. In not a few of these blue and green tourmalines were found embedded.

The stones obtained include all shades of green, blue, lilac, pink and red, numerous specimens having pink kernels, with surrounding zones of green, salmon pink, brown and black. The least valuable are the dark green, these being too blackish.

When of a light green color the price rises, according to quality. The pink stones are still more valuable, especially if the color is bright and clear. The blue stones are about the same value as the pink ones.

TRACKS IN THE SNOW.

BY FLORENCE JOSEPHINE BOYCE.

When the moon rides high and the snow is
 white
And the air is frosty and chill,
There's many a traveler out at night
A-journeying over the hill;
Where do they come from? Whither go?
Making tracks on the midnight snow.

There's a path that leads to the squirrel's
 house
At the edge of the hemlock clump,
And here is the track of a bold, brown mouse
On his way to a neighboring stump;
Only the prints of their feet to snow
They passed this way on the midnight snow.

Here are the marks on the snow-covered rocks
Of rabbit feet, light and swift;
And there is the trail of a sly red fox
Where a partridge hid in the drift;
Many a tragedy comes, I trow,
When the red fox prowls on the midnight snow.

Time and again in the morning light,
When the air is frosty and chill,
I see where a traveler's been by night
A-journeying over the hill;
And I wonder why he happened to go
Out climbing the hill on the midnight snow.

—*Forward.*

The Metal Aluminum.

The most plentifully distributed of all the useful metals is aluminum. Iron stands next, a bad second. Iron is common, but aluminum is, almost literally, everywhere. In strict truth, it is almost as common as dirt, because it actually is present in a large percentage of all earthly matter. Nearly eight per cent. of the composition of the earth's crust is aluminum. Iron forms less than six per cent.

Aluminum is the basic metal of all clay, just as sodium is the basic metal of common salt. Whenever you find a clay bank, you have found an alu-minum mine. All that is left for you to do is to find a method of getting the metal out of the clay, and you have won a fortune. It is there; anywhere from 20 to 60 per cent. of all clay is metallic aluminum. The ruby and the sapphire are practically nothing more than aluminum and oxygen. The turquoise, the topaz and garnet confess their constituent aluminum to the analyst. So does the emerald. So would the tiles of your bathroom and the very enamel of your bath tub. The china from which you eat would probably admit being close to 40 per cent. aluminum, if interrogated by a chemist. The metal is plentiful beyond computation, but of all the useful metals it is the hardest to get hold of.

But this beautiful, featherweight, silvery metal, with its glorious possibilities and its tantalizing abundance, which was not discovered as a metal until 1828, has since been a constant incentive to research and invention. What a glittering prospect was that before the man who should devise a process whereby he could extract this precious substance from the mud of his own fields! And so experiment followed experiment, and process followed process, until at last a Frenchman named Deville actually succeeded in putting aluminum on the market—at $90 a pound! This was in 1856, and of course the metal was used only for medals and trinkets and jewel-settings. But the enormous commercial possibilities in sight did not permit the metallurgists to be content with aluminum at a precious-metal price. The Deville process was amplified and improved;

other processes were devised, and the price fell slowly through the next 30 years. In 1886, it was down to $9 a pound, and a half-dozen concerns were producing the metal, more or less pure.

So far, all the processes were chemical, and decidedly expensive. It was about this time that the wonderful development in the dynamo had, for the first time in the history of the world, made electricity actually cheap. Experimenters then turned to electrolysis, rather than to chemical action and reaction, to free the aluminum from its bonds. In 1889 a patent was granted Charles M. Hall, of Oberlin, Ohio, for a process of reducing metallic aluminum from alumina, by electrical means which combine in a remarkable manner the principles of the electric furnace and the electrolytic bath.

The enormous electrical energy derived from Niagara Falls has been applied to the production of aluminum, with great cheapening of prices and increase of output. The Hall process, which has had the market to itself for nearly 10 years, is owned by the Pittsburgh Reduction Company, which has extensive works at St. Louis, at Shawinigan Falls, Canada, at Massena, N. Y., at Pittsburgh and at Niagara Falls, at which latter place the cheap electricity furnished by the Niagara Falls Power Company is utilized.

The points of aluminum most in its favor are its light weight and its cleanliness. It retains its beautiful silvery lustre in the face of conditions that reduce most metals to corrosion. In this respect it is superior to silver, and almost equal to gold. A metal superbly clean and light suggests itself at once as one eminently fit for household utensils. If it costs as much as silver, it would undoubtedly threaten silver itself in its entrenched position on the dining tables of the land. But, being cheap, it goes to the kitchen and squares off at the iron, tin and enamel pots, kettles and pans.

When householders understand the new metal, it is expected that the struggle in the kitchen will be short, sharp and decisive. There can be no question as to the advantage of aluminum utensils.

Water in an aluminum kettle will boil quicker than that in an iron kettle, under the same conditions. Moreover, the scorching of the contents of an aluminum cooking utensil is an accident that can seldom occur. All these good points, added to the lustre and beauty and lightness of the metal, which would in themselves atone for many faults, give aluminum an assurance of a brilliant future. It is not at all handicapped by its slightly greater cost, even in its rivalry with the common tin pan, for an aluminum pan will outlast a dozen tin ones. Tin pans are made of sheet iron, coated with tin, and every housekeeper knows what happens as soon as the thin tin coating is worn a little. You will never see rust on aluminum. Every article for table use which is made in silver is now duplicated in aluminum, and for table use the latter metal has every advantage of silver, except that it lacks the curious glamor of costliness. It is too early to say just what success the new metal will have in this field. The demand is large, and the physical superiority of the lighter, less tarnishable metal quite obvious. An aluminum spoon, for example, is only brightened by vinegar and salt, and the sulphurous yelk that blackens the silver spoon has no effect whatever on the other. Yet it is not expected that families that can afford silver will ever use aluminum on their tables. Campers, yachtsmen, tourists and people who cannot have solid silver and dislike plated articles, however, give aluminum a wide field in this regard.

For purposes where lightness is desired to the exclusion of considerations of great strength and cost, aluminum to-day has no competitor. In this great field it stands absolutely alone, and its presence there transforms into possibilities what were only idle dreams before its arrival.

It is a metal as beautiful as silver, almost as malleable as gold, almost as ductile as copper, as untarnishable as tin, lighter than any of these, and infinitely more abundant. It may be said with almost no departure from scientific accuracy, that aluminum possesses, or can be endowed with, all the properties of these metals that make them desirable to man, and surpasses them all on two other points.—*Ainslee's Magazine.*

Battle Between Spider and Wasp.

A fierce battle between a large spider and a wasp was witnessed one day last summer. The spider had spread his web in a corner of the fence and was patiently waiting for something to turn up. Suddenly a wasp flew into the web. He was firmly caught, but his desperate efforts to escape tore several holes in the flimsy network about him. Here the spider rushed out and rapidly began to repair the breaks. The wasp fought harder still and seemed to be trying to get a chance to sting his sly foe. In a minute or two the wasp lay perfectly still, as if dead. The spider rushed out and seized the body of his victim. The wasp, who had apparently been playing possum, suddenly became very much alive, and in a flash spider and wasp were clasped in a deathlock. There was a short, fierce struggle, and both insects fell from the dilapidated web to the ground. They lay there quite still, and on inspection it was found that both were dead.

Recently Dr. MacDonald, of Mombasa, East Africa, encountered a puff adder, which is one of the most deadly snakes. He discharged his rifle at it and killed it. He took the body to the hospital verandah, and, finding it to be a male, returned to the spot to search for the female, but without success. A few nights later, however, while sitting on his verandah, the doctor espied the snake he had been seeking, and fired at her. Afterward no fewer than ninety-one young adders were found scattered on the ground, and had all been killed by the shot fired at the mother.—*Scientific American.*

The largest producer of sulphur is Sicily. Its deposits occur in Miocene limestone, with unaltered beds of gypsum below, and it exported in 1903 475,509 tons.

The Caspian Sea.

One of the most remarkable physical features of the globe is the deep and wide depression in the hollow of which stands the Caspian Sea, and near to it the Sea of Aral.

The Caspian Sea lies at the southeast of Russia, between Europe and Asia. It is 700 miles long with an average width of 200 miles, and is therefore about the same area as the State of California. Its surface is 84 feet below the level of the Black Sea, while high mountain ranges nearly surround its shores. This sea is 600 feet deep near its southern end and 3,000 feet deep near the center, but its shores are very shallow. In some places it is not 3 feet deep 100 yards from the shore and in others does not attain a depth of 12 feet for several miles from the shore. Although so large a body of water it does not seem to be effected by tides.

The Sea of Aral is somewhat larger than the State of New York, and is very little over the sea level. Within recent geological times the vast expanse in which these lakes are found was one vast sea. Its floor has been gradually raised, and the waters filling the depressions are all that is left of an ancient Mediterranean.

A strange feature of both bodies of water is that, although they receive large rivers, especially the Caspian, into which the Volga, the Ural River and scores of streams from the Caucasus flow, both have for many years been getting shallower. Evaporation, for they have no outlet, exceeded the inflow. But, for some climatic reason probably, Lake Aral and its neighbor, Lake Balkhash, has since 1891 been increasing in depth. *Nature* reports that M. Berg visited Lake Balkhash last summer and found that the level was rising with comparative rapidity. Whereas the Caspian, like the Dead Sea, and Great Salt Lake of Utah, is very salt, owing to the rate of evaporation, Aral and Balkhash are brackish only.

These remnants of what was once a great sea opening into the ocean, as the Mediterranean does now, are still very prolific with marine fish and seals. Some of the latter survive in the Aral and Baikal Lakes, having gradually become fitted for their habitat, though it is no longer salt, but merely brackish, and in the case of Baikal actually fresh water.

A Four Years' Flea Hunt.

An unusual Arctic expedition has recently been concluded. Charles Rothchild of London fitted out a scientific expedition whose sole purpose was to make a collection of Arctic fleas.

After being gone four years it has returned, having penetrated well into Baffinland, and having collected fleas of strange and varied kinds, some from the hides of the polar bear and the musk-ox.

The largest species of serpent now living is the regal python (*Python reticulatus*) which attains a length of at least twenty-four feet. In captivity it prefers to feed on poultry, and will swallow several eight-pound fowls in full feather without difficulty and in a few days be ready for more.

RANDOM NOTES.

A variety of feldspar of blue color is found in Syria—the only known locality in the world where it is found of this color.

The length of a day on the moon is about two weeks, as measured by terrestial time, the length of the lunar night being, of course, equally long.

Star-fish possess to a very high degree the power to reproduce lost members. With but a single ray left they will reproduce the lost members and again become perfect star-fish.

Singular though it may seem, some species of turtles belonging to the genus *Emys* prey on insects, mollusks, aquatic reptiles, fishes and even birds and mammals which come within their reach. Their feet are expanded and webbed so that they swim with great facility.

In the Cumberland Mountains in Tennessee are many caves, some of them miles in extent, but they are mostly unexplored. Large deposits of fossil bones of extinct animals have been found in them, and impression of the feet of animals have been found in the limestone.

Not man only is fearfully and wonderfully made. The most insignificant insect is a marvelous creation, yet complete in all its faculties, though it be so small it cannot be seen with the naked eye. There are 400,000 scales on the wings of a silk-worm moth and each is as perfect as the lens of a telescope.

Not many years ago it was announced that 8,000 kinds of growing things were discovered and catalogued. Later this list of growing things had been increased to 80,000. Still later 100,000 different kinds of growing things have been found on the earth. No two growing things, not even two leaves, are precisely alike. The above includes plants only.

Bears are found in almost every portion of the world with two notable exceptions, namely, Africa and Australia. What is called the "Australian bear" is no bear at all but belongs to the family containing kangaroos, opossums, etc. While bears may yet be discovered in the vast continent of Africa, yet from the days of Pliny to the present time, no bears have been found there.

It is estimated that the river Rhine carries to the sea every day 145,980 cubic feet of sand or stone.

In less than one hundred years from the first white settlement in Tasmania the aboriginal population was totally extermined.

The leaves of the taliput palm are usually 18 feet long exclusive of the leaf-stalk, and 14 feet broad. The tree grows to the height of 100 feet.

There are above sixty genera of cleistogamous plants; that is, plants which possess two or more kinds of flowers, one set being self-fertilizing and others being cross-fertilized by insects or other methods.

Corundum showing flesh pink and dull blue color, but not of the gem quality has been found in the mountains of Tennessee. Sapphire is the bright colored, clear crystal of corundum of which blue is the true sapphire color.

Only one kind of tortoise (*Testudo Græca*) is found in all Europe, "and even in that continent," says the Rev. J. G. Wood, the well known British naturalist, "it is by no means widely spread, being confined to those countries which border on the Mediterranean."

The terrible plague of 1348, which continued during eight years, destroyed, it is believed, nearly two-thirds of the human race then existing. In London 50,000 bodies were buried in one grave-yard; in Venice the number of deaths is said to have been 100,000; in Lubeck, 90,000; in Spain the disease raged three years and carried off two-thirds of the people; in the East 20,000,000 perished in one year.

From seven diamonds—weighing from 2 to 21 carats—that have been picked up in Wisconsin and adjoining states, Prof. Wm. H. Hobbs traces the diamond fields of North America to the volcanic region of the Canadian wilderness, south of Hudson Bay. The only known matrix of the diamond is the black shale—or "blue ground"—around the necks of burned-out volcanoes. The loose stones found seem to have been transported by glaciers, and on following up the probable courses of these ancient ice rivers the lines converge in the barren territory stated.

The Amateur Naturalist.

"To him who in the love of Nature holds communion with her visible forms, she speaks a various language."

VOLUME 2.   BINGHAMTON, NEW YORK, MARCH, 1905.   NUMBER 2.

NOTES OF THE MELITEAS.

BY ADDISON ELLSWORTH.

IN A former treatise on butterflies we promised a further description of the genus *Melitea*, Fabricus, and more especially of "The Baltimore" or *Melitea Phæton*, Drury. The history of these insects is particularly interesting, though from their isolated haunts are little known, except to the collector after years of study and observation. Although its range extends over the whole Northern United States east of the Great Plains, and into Canada as far as New Brunswick and Nova Scotia, and southward to West Virginia and Kentucky, it is seldom seen and is often considered as among the most valuable specimens in a collection. The reason for this is that it is found only in boggy places or in moist meadows which are rarely visited by the entomologist and is often so limited in its range that it is scarcely ever taken a few rods from where it literally swarms. After collecting lepidoptera for several years among the hills and vales of Chenango County, in open fields and on wooded land, without taking a single example of this lovely insect, I almost despaired of ever finding it, when one day upon visiting a swamp in quest of wild flowers, I was greatly astonished and delighted at seeing them by the hundreds, the more so because I had visited the adjacent fields and forests many times. And here it may not be out of place to state for the benefit of those who are wont to seek specimens only on high and dry ground, that there are a number of rare and beautiful species of butterflies and moths that are found only in swamps and marshy lands. Among these, besides the one under consideration, are several *Phyciodes*, an allied genus, *Satyrodes canthus*, and a number of Hesperidæ.

Melitea Phæton is of medium size, expanding about two inches, with elongated wings, rounded at the margins, and are nearly black on both surfaces. It has a broad reddish margin preceeded by pale yellow lunules, and there are three (occasionally but two) curved rows of small pale yellow spots, while the base of the wings are marked by a rather confused intermixed mass of irregular yellow and red spots.

The variety *Streckeri, nobis*, was first described in the Entomological News from a specimen taken

MELITEA PHAETON.

at Vestal, N. Y., June 10, 1900. It is of a deep velvety black with a marginal row of bright orange-red spots on both fore and hind wings, much larger than in the normal form. This is followed by a single row of pale yellow spots, the third, fourth and fifth on primaries being geminate. A single faint and almost imperceptable red dash marks the center of the discal cell. On under side of primaries are two large brick-red spots and a slight indication of a second transverse band of yellow lunules. On secondaries are six large red spots promiscuously arranged and three or four light yellow dots near inner angle. In general appearance it differs materially from the parent form and is a much handsomer insect. As its name implies, it was dedicated to the late Dr. Herman Strecker, of Reading, Pa., the peer of American lepidopterists. Besides this, two other varieties have been described—*Superba*, by Mr. Strecker himself, and *Phætusa*, neither of which is the writer acquainted with in nature.

The flight of *Melitea Phæton* is slow and laborious, usually near to the ground, and it alights often on red clover and whiteweed blossoms, to feed on their juices or to rest. The eggs are subglobular and are laid in large irregular clusters, several layers deep upon the under side of the leaves of snakehead (*Chelone glabra*) which forms the principal food of the young caterpillar. Later it leaves this to feed on the *Lonicera* (flowers belonging to the honeysuckle family) and other caprifoliaceous plants. This is peculiar and a trait shared by but few other butterflies. A number of other species are also known to lay their eggs in clusters, but none where they are so large and heaped up as here. They hatch in about twenty days. In hatching the larva bites an opening around the summit of the egg, the lid thus formed is thrust off, and the caterpillar emerging, partially devours the deserted shell. It then moves briskly about with its companions, but before eating any of the leaf they prepare a small web as a base of operations. They feed in rows, those in each row moving the head and fore part of the body from side to side simultaneously with true military precision. As they grow older they wander about uneasily, sometimes entirely away from their food-plant but always return to their web at night. As they grow they enlarge their web, all working for the common good. If at any time the web is destroyed or injured they set about to repair it and do not rest, rain or shine, until it is completed. As the time for the third moulting approaches additions to the web are made until it is as large as a base ball and capable of resisting the severest storms, and even the vigors of winter. Into this "hibernaculum" they crowd about the last of August or first of September where they remain securely housed until the following spring. As cold weather comes on, however, the nest contracts until it is often less than one-fourth of its former size, and would scarcely attract attention.

But in the spring all is changed. They forsake their web and wander ceaselessly about, swarming over Lonicera and other plants and seek concealment during their moultings and in storms under leaves or other objects but at other times are always exposed to full view, when their bright colors and active movements render them very conspicuous. If frightened or disturbed they roll themselves up into a coil and drop to the ground and are then very hard to find.

The butterfly with us is single brooded, the caterpillar attaining its full growth in May and the chrysalids hang from fourteen to eigheeen days. They are on the wing from four to six weeks, and the eggs are usually laid after the third week, and after eclosion the caterpillar is of very slow growth when compared with other butterflies.

As stated previously, there are twenty-eight species of Meliteas found in the United States, most of which are found on the Pacific Slope, but, so far as they have been noted, their habits are nearly the same as those described, especially those found in the northern part of this section. Those found further south still await further observation before their history can be fully determined.

Binghamton, N. Y.

INSECT STINGS.

BY MARY-LEE VAN HOOK.

EARLY in the fall I was attracted by a certain willow (*Salix discolor*) which I then thought unlike any other of its kind, but as is usually the case when once one's attention is called to a thing, I have since noticed many willows which present the same peculiarity. The branches of this large shrub, for it was scarcely more than a shrub, were well covered with buds an inch long and nearly as wide, supported on stalks of their own. The more I looked the more I marvelled that a plain little pussy willow should make such a display, though I was not quite so much astonished as I might have been in the case of another individual, for this particular little tree had committed an indiscretion early in December, after an unusual warm spell, in transforming, three months too soon, some of its modest grey maltese pussies into handsome white angoras. However, I was sufficiently interested to appoint myself examiner-in-chief, and with a sharp knife I literally went to the heart of the matter. I cut the bud open. There within the overlapping scales ot the false bud lay the explanation—the yellow larva of the gall-fly. The bud then was an adventitious growth stimulated by the sting of the insect when her eggs were deposited. The willow, it seems to me, is much put upon since it must not only receive the eggs but is also aroused to provide suitable cradles for the young larvæ who enjoy a safe retreat until ready to emerge.

The whole willow and poplar family are particularly subject to the stings of insects and each species of tree is so characteristic in the abnormal growth produced that one can tell the variety by the peculiarity of the gall. Poplar trees in this region are covered with stiff, black galls which are the distorted leaves. Breaking one of these open one finds entombed the little silvery winged gall-flies which die after the eggs are deposited; a fact in nature which sounds like a romance in the Arabian Nights.

Oak trees are often curiously blistered or disturbed by the stings of insects; in their case it is usually a small wasp that does the mischief; that is, mischief from the oak's point of view. Some oak-galls are very pretty, looking like little rosy cheeked apples. It is thought by some that these galls may be the mythic mad apples, or apples of Sodom, which, when plucked, turn to dust and ashes. Not only trees but many plants are stung by insects. I have seen a field of asters, almost everyone of which was swollen at some point on the branch into a shapely habitation for young larvæ.

Lakeside, Ill.

⚹

THE MIGRATION OF BIRDS.

BIRD migration is a subject that has always excited the wonder of the thinking mind, but it is scarcely a hundred years since any systematic study of the problem has been made, and a much less time since there has resulted any definite progress towards a solution of the problem. The following facts about the migration of birds are taken from data compiled by Wells W. Cooke, Assistant of the Biological Survey and published in the Year-book of the United States Department of Agriculture for 1903:

For nearly twenty years the Biological Survey has been accumulating data on the migration of birds. Its own field naturalists, whose visits have extended over the North American Continent from Guatemala to the Arctic Circle, have furnished voluminous notes, besides which the assistance of ornithologists throughout the country has been enlisted, so that reports are received in the spring and fall of each year from hundreds of observers. These reports give, for each species, the date when the bird was first seen, when it became common, and when it disappeared. Light-house keepers also have supplied valuable information concerning the destruction of birds at their lights. The facts thus gathered from these various sources form the largest amount of material on bird migration ever collected in this country, and permit broader and safer generalizations than have heretofore been possible.

For more than two thousand years the phenomena of bird migration have been noted; but while the extent and course of the routes traversed have of late become better known, no conclusive answer has been found to the question, why do birds migrate? Some dismiss the subject with the statement that fall migration is caused by failure of the food supply, spring migration by love of home. All are familiar with the rush of waterfowl northward so early that they are often forced by storms to retrace their flight; and all know that robins, bluebirds and swallows, following closely in the rear, sometimes lose hundreds out of their flocks by cold and starvation. If strong home love causes these birds thus to hazard their lives, why do they desert that home at the earliest possible moment; and if fall migration is caused by lack of food, why does it commence when food is most abundant? Data recently collected at the Florida l ght-houses by the Biological Survey show that southward migration begins at least by the 10th, and probably by the 1st of July, insect-eating birds departing when their food supplies are most plentiful, and seed eaters just before the heyday of harvest.

HOW DO BIRDS FIND THEIR WAY?

How do birds find their way over the hundreds or thousands of miles between the winter and summer homes? Among day migrants sight is probably the principal guide, and it is noticeable that these seldom make the long single flights so common with night migrants. Sight undoubtedly plays a part in guiding the night journeys also; on clear nights, especially when the moon shines brightly, migrating birds fly high, and the ear can scarcely distinguish their faint twitterings; if clouds overspread the heavens, the passing flocks sink their course nearer to the earth, and their notes are much more distinctly heard; and on very dark nights one may even hear the flutter of vibrant wings but a few feet overhead. So far as known, birds never intentionally migrate above the clouds, and when suddenly formed vapor cuts them off from sight of the earth, they lower their flight until the friendly landscape is again visible. Nevertheless, something besides sight guides these travelers in the upper air. We recognize in ourselves the possession of some such sense, though imperfect and easily at fault.

Reports from light-houses in southern Florida show that birds leave Cuba on cloudy nights when they can not possibly see the Florida shores, and safely reach their destination, provided no change occurs in the weather. But if meantime the wind changes or a storm arises to throw them out of their reckoning, they become bewildered, lose their way, and fly toward the light-house beacon. Unless killed by striking the lantern, they hover near or alight on the balcony, to continue their flight when morning breaks, or, the storm ceasing, a clear sky allows them once more to determine the proper course.

Birds flying over the Gulf of Mexico to Louisiana, even if they ascended to the height of five miles, would still be unable to see a third of the way across. Nevertheless this trip is successfully made twice each year by countless thousands of the warblers of the Mississippi Valley.

In the fall thousands of birds reared in Indiana, Illinois and northwestward visit South Carolina and Georgia, cutting directly across the valley of the Ohio and the main chain of the Allegheny Mountains. Palm warblers from New England and others from the northern Mississippi Valley both pass in the fall through Georgia, but by courses approximately at right angles to each other; and the Connecticut warbler seeks variety by choosing different routes for the spring and fall, each course in part being at right angles to the other. The truth seems to be that birds pay little attention to natural physical highways, except when large bodies of water force them to deviate from the desired course.

DISTANCE OF MIGRATION.

The length of the migration journey varies enormously. Some birds do not migrate at all. Many a cardinal, Carolina wren, and bobwhite rounds out its whole contented life within ten miles of its birthplace. Other birds, for instance, the pine warbler and the blackheaded grosbeak, do not venture in winter south of the breeding range, so that with them fall migration is only a withdrawal from the northern and a concentration in the southern part of the summer home—the warbler in about a fourth and the grosbeak in less than an eighth of the summer area.

The next variation is illustrated by the robin, which occurs as a species in the middle districts of the United States throughout the year, in Canada only in summer, and along the Gulf of Mexico only in winter. Probably no individual robin is a continuous resident in any section; but the robin that nests, let us say, in southern Missouri, will spend the winter near the Gulf, while his hardy Canada-bred cousin will be the winter tenant of the abandoned summer home of the southern bird.

Most migrants entirely change their abode twice a year, and some of them travel immense distances. Of the land birds, the common eastern nighthawk seems to deserve first place among those whose winter homes are widely distant from their breeding grounds. Alaska and Patagonia, separated by 115 degrees of latitude, are the extremes of the summer and winter homes of the bird; and each spring many a nighthawk travels the 5,000 miles that lie between. But some of the shore birds are still more inveterate voyagers. These cover from 6,000 to 8,000 miles each way, and appear to make traveling their chief occupation.

ROUTE OF MIGRATION.

Birds often seem eccentric in choice of route, and many land birds do not take the shortest line. The fifty species from New England that winter in South America, instead of making the direct trip over the Atlantic, involving a flight of 2,000 miles, take a slightly longer route which follows the coast to Florida, and passes thence by island or mainland to South America. What would seem at first sight to be a natural and convenient migratory highway extends from Florida through the Bahamas or Cuba to Haiti, Porto Rico, and the Lesser Antilles, and thence to South America. The bird that travels by this route need never be out of sight of land; resting places may be had at convenient intervals, and the distance is but little longer than the water route. Yet, beyond Cuba, this highway is little used. About twenty-five species continue as far as Porto Rico and remain there through the winter. Only adventurers out of some six species gain the South American mainland by completing the island chain. The reason seems not far to seek—scarcity of food. The total area of all the West Indies east of Porto Rico is a little less than that of Rhode Island. Should a small proportion only of the feathered inhabitants of the eastern part of the United States select this route, not even the luxuriant fauna or flora of the Tropics could supply their needs.

A still more direct route, but one requiring longer single flights, stretches from Florida to South America via Cuba and Jamaica. The 150 miles between Florida and Cuba are crossed by tens of thousands of birds of some 60 different species. About half the species take the next flight of 90 miles to the beautiful Jamaican mountains. Here a 500-mile stretch of islandless ocean confronts them, and scarcely a third of their number leave the forest-clad hills for the unseen beyond. Chief among these dauntless voyagers is the bobolink, fresh from despoiling the Carolina rice fields, waxed fat from his gormandizing, and so surcharged with energy that the 500-mile flight to South America on the way to the waving pampas of southern Brazil seems a small hardship. Indeed, many bobolinks appear to scorn the Jamaican resting point and to compass in a single flight the 700 miles from Cuba to South America. With the bobolink is an incongruous company of traveling companions—a vireo, a king bird, and a nighthawk that summer in Florida; the queer chuck-will's-widow of the Gulf States; the two New England cuckoos; the trim Alice thrush from Quebec; the cosmopolitan bank swallow from frozen Labrador, and the black-poll warbler from far-off Alaska. But the bobolinks so far outnumber all the rest of the motley crew that the passage across the Caribbean Sea from Cuba to South America may with propriety be called the "bobolink route."

West of the Florida route the Gulf is crossed by migrating birds at its widest point, from Louisiana southward. Still farther west, the numerous species of Plains and Rocky Mountains birds choose Mexico and Central America for the winter, and make a land journey of short stages that extends over several weeks.

As already stated, the longest migration route is taken by some of the wading birds, especially the American golden plover, the Eskimo curlew, and the turnstone. The journey of the plover, which is typical, is wonderful enough to be given in detail. It the first week of June they arrive at their breeding grounds in the bleak, wind-swept "barren grounds" above the Arctic Circle, far beyond the tree line. Some even venture 1,000 miles farther north (Greely found them at latitude 81°). While the lakes are still icebound, they hurriedly fashion shabby little nests in the moss only a few inches above the frozen ground. By August they have hastened to Labrador, where, in company with curlews and turnstones; they enjoy a feast. Growing over the rocks and treeless slopes of this inhospitable coast is a kind of heather, the crowberry, bearing in profusion a juicy black fruit. The extravagant fondness shown for the berry by the birds, among which the curlew, owing to its greater numbers, is most conspicuous, causes it to be known by the natives as the "curlew berry." The whole body of the curlew becomes so saturated with the dark purple juice that birds whose flesh was still stained with the color have been shot one thousand miles south of Labrador.

After a few weeks of such feasting, the plovers become excessively fat and ready for their great flight. They have reared their young under the midnight sun, and now they seek the Southern Hemisphere. After gaining the coast of Nova Scotia they strike straight out to sea, and take a direct course for the eastermost islands of the West Indies. *Eighteen hundred miles of ocean waste lie between the last land of Nova Scotia and the first of the Antilles, and yet six hundred more to the eastern mainland of South America, their objective point.* The only land along the route is the Bermuda Islands, eight hundred miles from Nova Scotia. In fair weather the birds fly past the Bermudas without stopping; indeed, they are often seen by vessels four hundred miles or more east of these islands. When they sight the first land of the Antilles the flocks often do not pause, but keep on to the larger islands and sometimes even to the mainland of South America. Sometimes a storm drives them off the main track, when they seek the nearest land, appearing not infrequently at Cape Cod and Long Island.

A few short stops may be made in the main flight, for the plover swims lightly and easily and has been seen resting on the surface of the ocean; and shore birds have been found busily feeding five hundred miles south of Bermuda and one thousand miles east of Florida, in the Atlantic, in that area known as the Sargasso Sea, where thousands of square miles of seaweed teem with marine life.

Though feathered balls of fat when they leave Labrador and still plump when they pass the Bermudas, the plovers alight lean and hungry in the Antilles. Only the first, though the hardest, half of the journey is over. How many days it has occupied may never be known. Most migrants either fly at night and rest in the day or vice versa, but the plover flies both night and day.

After a short stop of three or four weeks in the Antilles and on the northeastern coast of South America, the flocks disappear, the later their arrival is noted at the same time in southern Brazil and the whole prairie region of Argentina almost to Patagonia. Here they remain from September to March (the summer of the Southern Hemisphere), free from the responsibilities of the Northern summer they have left. The native birds of Argentina are at the time engrossed in family cares; *but no wayfarer from the north nests in the south.*

After a six-months' vacation the plovers resume the serious affairs of life and start back toward the Arctic, but not by the same course. *Their full northward route is a problem still unsolved.* They disappear from Argentina and shun the whole Atlantic coast from Brazil to Labrador. In March they appear in Guatemala and Texas; April finds their long lines trailing across the prairies of the Mississippi Valley; the first of May sees them crossing our northern boundary; and by the first week in June they reappear at their breeding grounds in the frozen North. What a journey! Eight thousand miles of latitude separates the extremes of their elliptical course, and 3,000 miles of longitude constitutes the shorter diameter, and all for the sake of spending ten weeks on an Arctic coast!

ARE BIRDS EXHAUSTED BY A LONG FLIGHT?

During the spring migration of 1903 two skilled ornithologists spent the entire season near the coast of northwestern Florida, visiting every sort of bird haunt. They were eminently successful in the long list of species identified, but their enumeration is still more remarkable for what it does not contain. About twenty-five species of the smaller land birds of the eastern part of the United States, including a dozen common species, were not seen. Among these were the chat, the redstart, and the indigo bunting, three species that are abundant throughout the whole region to the northward. The explanation of this seems to be that these birds, on crossing the Gulf of Mexico, flew far inland before alighting, and thus passed over the observers. It would thus seem that the popular idea that birds find the ocean flight excessively wearisome, and that after laboring with tired pinions across the seemingly endless wastes they sink exhausted on reaching terra firma, is not in accordance with the facts. The truth seems to lie in almost the opposite direction. Endowed by nature with wonderful powers of aerial locomotion, under normal conditions many birds not only cross the Gulf of Mexico at its widest point, but may even pass without pause over the low, swampy coastal plain to the higher territory beyond. So little averse are birds to an ocean voyage that many fly from eastern Texas to the coast of southern Mexico, though this four hundred miles of water journey hardly shortens the distance of travel by an hour's flight. Thus, the birds avoid the hot, treeless plains and scant provender of southern Texas by a direct flight from the moist, insect-teeming forests of northern Texas to similar country in southern Mexico. Under favorable conditions, birds can fly practically where, when, and how they please; consequently their choice of route and the distance covered at a single flight are principally governed by the food supply.

SPRING MIGRATION.

Spring migration has its own special features. No such synchronous movement occurs in the spring as has been described as "normal migration" in the fall. With many birds, possibly the majority of land birds, the first individuals of a species to appear in spring at a given locality are supposed to be old birds that nested there the previous year. The supposition is that these birds are followed by those that nested in the region just to the north; and that later, those of still more northern homes pass by; and that the last to appear will be those whose homes are in the most northern part of the breeding range.

Still later in the spring another transposal occurs. The northern birds pass across the southern portion of the breeding range, where the southernmost birds are already busy with their domestic duties. Spring migration seems to be therefore for some species a game of leapfrog—the southern birds first passing the northern, and the northern passing them in turn.

RELATION OF MIGRATION AND TEMPERATURE.

A popular notion exists that birds push northward to their summer homes as soon as weather conditions permit. This may be true of a few species, but certainly birds in general have no such habit. Some summer warblers that return to the Great Slave Lake region to breed, after spending the winter in Central and South America, arrive at their nesting grounds when the average daily temperature is about 47° F. According to the notion mentioned, these birds might be expected to move up the Mississippi Valley and on to their summer homes at the same time as the northward-moving temperature of 47° F. But were this so, they would never leave the United States, for the average of the coldest month of the year at New Orleans is 54° F. As a matter of fact, the summer warblers of Great Slave Lake are probably too well content with the warm, humid, insect-laden air of the South to brave the arctic blasts before necessity compels. They linger in the Tropics so late that when they reach New Orleans, April 5, an average temperature of 65° F. awaits them. They now hasten; traveling north much faster than the spring does, they cover 1,000 miles in a month, and find in southern Minnesota a temperature of 55° F. In central Manitoba the average temperature they meet is 52° F., and when they arrive late in May at Great Slave Lake they have gained 5° more on the season. Thus, during the whole trip of 2,500 miles from New Orleans to Great Slave Lake, these birds are continually meeting colder weather. In fact, so fast do they migrate that in the fifteen days from May 11 to 25 they traverse a district that spring requires thirty-five days to cross. This outstripping of spring is habitual with all species that leave the United States for the winter, and also with most of the northern birds that winter in the Gulf States. Careful examination of the migration records of each species of the Mississippi Valley shows only six exceptions—Canada goose, mallard, pintail, common crow, red-winged blackbird, and robin.

The robin as a species migrates north more slowly than the opening of the season; it occupies seventy-eight days for its trip of 3,000 miles from Iowa to Alaska, while spring covers the distance in sixty-eight days. But it does not follow that any individual bird moves northward at this leisurely pace. The first robins that reach a given locality in the spring are likely to remain there to nest, and the advance of the migration line must await the arrival of other birds from still farther south.

THE UNKNOWN.

Marvelous tales of the spring and fall movements of birds were spun by early observers, yet hardly less incredible are the ascertained facts. Much remains to be learned of migration; and it may be of interest to note a few of the mysteries which still occupy attention.

The chimney swift is one of the most abundant and best-known birds of the eastern part of the United States. With troops of fledglings, catching their winged prey as they go, and lodging by night in some tall chimney, the flocks drift slowly south, joining with other bands until on the northern coast of the Gulf of Mexico they become an innumerable host. Then they disappear. Did they drop into the water and hibernate in the mud, as was believed of old, their obliteration could not be more complete. In the last week in March a joyful twittering far overhead announces their return to the Gulf coast, but the intervening five months is still the swift's secret.

The mouse-colored bank swallows are almost cosmopolitan, and enliven even the shores of the Arctic Ocean with their graceful aerial evolutions. Those that nest in Labrador allow a scant two months for building a home and raising a brood, and by the first of August are headed southward. Six weeks later they are swarming in the vicinity of Chesapeake Bay, and then they, too, pass out of the range of our knowledge. In April they appear in northern South America, moving north, but not a hint do they give of how they came there. The rest of the species, those that nest to the south or west, may be traced farther south, but they, too, fail to give any clew as to where they spend the five winter months.

The familiar cliff swallow, which swarms over the western plains and breeds from Mexico to Alaska, spends the winter in Brazil and Argentina. The earliest records of the bird's appearance in spring come from northern central California, where it becomes common before the first arrivals are usually noted in Texas or Florida. The route the species takes from Brazil to California is one of the yet unsolved migration puzzles.

The red-eyed vireo, the commonest and best known of its tuneful family, winters in Central America, from Guatemala to Panama. The advent of the species in spring at the mouth of the Mississippi and its even-paced passage at 20 miles per day for six weeks to the headwaters of the river are well attested by numerous records. But just about the time northern Nebraska is reached, and before they have appeared in any of the intervening country, red-eyed vireos are noted in southern British Columbia, 1,000 miles to the northwest. Is the presence of the red-eye in British Columbia to be explained by the theory that it suddenly flies 1,000 miles in a single night? It is such problems as these that continually vex and fascinate the investigator.

The Amateur Naturalist.

A Journal for those who Study Nature from a love of it

ISSUED BI-MONTHLY.

Entered as Second-Class matter October 6, 1904, at the post office at Binghamton, N Y.

SUBSCRIPTION, 50 CENTS PER YEAR.   SINGLE COPIES, 10 CENTS
ADVERTISING RATES ON APPLICATION.

————————EDITED AND PUBLISHED BY————————
CHARLES D. PENDELL,
85-87 STATE STREET,   -   -   -   BINGHAMTON, N. Y.

We give place in this issue to an article on bird migration, and though longer than the usual average of contributions, its timeliness and absorbing interest seemed to warrant giving it place.

The columns of THE AMATEUR NATURALIST are open to any of our readers for the publication of any article that comes within the scope of its purpose,—articles on any branch of natural science that are accurate in fact and interesting in narrative. Of course, we cannot promise in advance to use all that may be received, but will give all a careful reading and if in accord with the plan and purpose of this journal will gladly give them place.

The contributors of any periodical are no doubt anxious to know the scope of readers reached by the journal publishing their articles, and it is but fair that they should know. THE AMATEUR NATURALIST has been peculiarly fortunate in the excellent character of its contributed articles, and also in their wide spread welcome by that portion of the public interested in nature study. Entering the lists but a little over one year ago in the character of a free lance, as it were, disclaiming the specialty hobby, but catering to all who are interested in the study of nature in any of its various and varied forms and manifestations, the welcome has been wide spread and cordial, which speaks well alike for the purpose and scope of the magazine, and for the excellent character of the articles which have made this success possible. It now numbers subscribers in a majority of the states of the Union, and a large number in Canada as well, covering a field from Nova Scotia to British Columbia. It goes to our island possessions including the far off Philippines, to Mexico, and crossing the Atlantic has readers in England and Germany. Complete files are also on the reading tables in the libraries of the Smithsonian Institution and the United States National Museum, in Washington. Contributors therefore may rest assured that their articles will be read by a wide circle of intelligent and appreciative readers. While this fact may not bring particular fame or distinction, the writer will naturally be gratified to know the facts and feel assured that his effort is not being "wasted on desert air."

Hunting with a camera will become a leading pastime from now on as the season advances and can be made a means of adding to our knowledge as well as affording much pleasure.

While societies of one kind or another are making demand for public recognition it is a pleasure to note the increased growth of the Audubon Societies. Among the objects of this society are stated the following: "To disseminate information respecting the economic value of birds to agriculture, and their importance to the welfare of man; to discourage the purchase or use of feathers of any birds for ornamentation except those of the ostrich and domesticated fowls; to discourage the destruction of wild birds and their eggs," and others. The organization is now established in nearly every state of the Union, and is one that can do much good.

While most of our subscribers were very prompt to renew with the new year, there are some who have as yet failed to do so. Believing that none would like to have their file broken we have continued their names on our list, but would ask that the matter be given prompt attention. To such as may feel personally inclined to assist in increasing our subscription list we would suggest that they send us the names of two new subscribers, inclosing one dollar, and we will in payment for the favor extend their subscription one year. We also extend this offer to any not now subscribers,—send us two names with your own and we will send THE AMATEUR NATURALIST to all three for one year for one dollar.

The Journal of the Maine Ornithological Society is a rather lengthy name of an excellent publication, but the longitudinal dimensions of its titular caption almost deterred us from giving it the commendation it deserves for the March number. A frontispiece representing in natural colors five North American warblers is followed by thirty-two pages of text of great interest to bird students, and the typography is faultless. The notes on "The Warblers found in Maine," by J. Merton Swain, will afford a good basis for study and companion. This and a history of the society make the *Journal* of unusual interest. But the journals published as organs of different societies have, as a rule, names too long for convenient reference. Although there are several exceptions, one will illustrate our point. The organ of The Wild Flower Preservation Society of America, under the euphonious and appropriate title of *The Plant World* takes its place among the leading botanical periodicals of the day. Perhaps a little too technical for the general reader, yet it contains much of popular interest and is well illustrated. *The Fern Bulletin* is another such. Although the official organ of The Linnæan Fern Chapter of the Agassiz Association, as a publication devoted to ferns, it is known and taken by fern students in all parts of the world.

MY DREAM OF THE BIRDS.

BY HATTIE WASHBURN.

At eve along the vast, crowded street
Echoed the trend of numberless feet.
The peal of church bells fell on the air
Summoning all to the house of prayer;
And irresistably borne along
I joined the devote and silent throng.
And in the house of peace and rest
Sat among the ladies richly dressed,
Where in defiance to mercy's law,
Birds upon many a hat I saw.
I thought of the songs the world had lost,
Of the melody false pride had cost.
I thought of the woods with songsters filled,
Of those beauties so ruthlessly killed,
And as the hymn from the organ rolled
Closed my eyes on their forms still and cold.
Then from those victims' small, feathered
  throats
Came a changing flood of wild, sweet notes.
Wilder and sweeter the music grew
And many a well loved song I knew.
In calm dignity each lady sat
Unmindful of the music in her hat.
All lost to me were the preacher's words,
I heeded naught but the songs of birds;
Perchance he taught to the cultured mind
To each of God's creatures to be kind,
And each listener with herself content
Ne'er thought for her was the lesson meant.
Voices of man and bird were blended,
The music ceased—my dream was ended.
And stately ladies with queenly smiles
Bore the slain in triumph down the aisles.

Goodwin, S. D.

New Use for Clam Shells.

BY W. N. C.

IT is reported that our common bull-frog is now protected by law in certain states. Had anyone suggested a few years ago that a time would come when it would be unlawful to catch frogs except at certain seasons, he would doubtless have been laughed at, but the progress of time changes many of our ideas. When any species of animal or plant becomes commercially important, there seems to be no reason why law should not be enacted looking toward its preservation.

It may be suggested, therefore, that the time may come when our stolid and unpalatable fresh-water mussel may need the protection of the law for its existence. Until recently it has been left much to its own devices and has spent its days in tranquilty, rooting in the mud at the bottoms of ponds and streams, its principal enemy, now that the Indian is gone, being the muskrat. But since the white man discovered that its shell makes excellent pearl buttons, a new danger threatens its very existence. Every time it opens its shell there is a chance that one of the fingers of a crowfoot dredge, slowly dragging along the river bottom, may be inserted into its anatomy and, of course, the more it then tries to withdraw into its shell the firmer becomes its grip upon the dredge and in this predicament it is drawn aboard a boat and carried off to the button factory.

A single factory in Iowa makes from ten thousand to fifteen thousand gross of buttons a week from these shells and it is said the mussels in that vicinity are growing very scarce in consequence. We may even be obliged to set up hatcheries to keep up the supply. This, however, will not be as easy a matter as it was in establishing fish hatcheries for the reason that the young mussels are retained in their mother's gills until they are of some size and for a time thereafter they are reputed to attach themselves to fishes and other aquatic fauna, living as parasites. It would seem that in addition to hatching the young we shall have to supply them with nurses from the fishes; but doubtless the ingenuity of the button makers will be equal to the task.

Joliet, Ill.

Some Disappearing Fauna.

BY STANLEY WATERLOO.

TO the park commissioners of the United States has, by accident, been relegated the duty of preserving types of our wild creatures in danger of absolute extinction.

The buffalo, or rather the bison, the direct descendent, or at least the cousin, of aurochs of paleolithic times—and even now existing in a certain district in Lithuanian Russia —has practically disappeared, and is kept existent only by a few specula-tors or by one set of park commis-sioners or another.

The wild pigeon, whose vast flight all men of middle age must bear in mind, has also gone. The remnant of the wonderful migrants are now doubtless feeding and breeding in the comparatively uninhabited parts of South America.

There is another inhabitant of the United States which is also in danger of extinction and which should be preserved. It is the black squirrel, formerly numerous in Illinois, Michi-gan and the Canadian forests of Ontario, and scattered elsewhere throughout the United States, but now almost extinct in the United States and abundant only in portions of Canada. Park Commissioners have put squirrels in their parks, and

a wonderful addition they are to the natural effect of the attempt to imi-tate Nature, but the commissioners seemingly get only the fox squirrel and the gray squirrel. Why not also have the black squirrel? The black squirrel becomes easily acclimated and almost semi-domesticated as do the other squirrels, though it is liable elsewhere to extirpation as the forests disappear. In parks, with a little care, it would readily acclimate and accommodate itself.

There is another creature that park commissioners should consider. It is the wolverine, that trade-mark of one of the great states of the Union, an animal remarkable in the fact that he has not changed from the time of the woolly rhinoceros or the great cave tiger. His bones have been found with their bones in ancient caves. He, the so-called glutton of Northern Europe and Asia, is one of the most interesting and curious animals in existence. He is still abundant in the northern fringe of the Northern States, and in British-America and Alaska. Why is he, a creature so distinguished, not on view in the animal houses of any park of any note in the United States?

Bort, the Real Black Diamond.

Carbon, carbonado and black diamond are terms expressive of practically the same product—bort— which is marketed in America to the extent of something like $800,000 annually, and pays no duty. This valuation, it should be stated to avoid confusion, does not include the imports of small uncut diamonds used by miners, glaziers and engravers, which are included with gems in the returns.

Bort is an opaque, massive mineral with a crystalline, sometimes granular or compact structure, resinous to adamantine luster, and hardness equal to or slightly in excess of the gem diamond. It is also very brittle and will not stand a shock or blow, but friction does not affect it.

The black diamond occurs in commercial quantity only in Brazil. There it is found associated with the more precious stone, in river beds beneath the slit and on top of the stratum of clay, on mountain sides, and elsewhere, particularly in the provinces of Bahia and Minas Geraes. The diamond-bearing fields in Brazil are owned and leased by the state, which also taxes exports at 13 per cent. ad valorem. The black diamond is not found in South Africa, notwithstanding the extensive diamantiferous deposits that are being exploited there.

In Brazil the bort recovered varies in size, and on several occasions some very large stones have been found. Perhaps the largest ever discovered was in 1895, when a stone weighing 3,075 carats was marketed abroad at an extraordinarily high price. To be of commerical value, however, these large stones must be broken to sizes weighing from 1 to 3 carats—a rather expensive operation, as there is always a loss, since they have no cleavage planes. Bort, weighing from 1 to 3 carats (a carat is equivalent to 4 grains) is worth in New York at the present time $10, $13, $15 and $18 per carat, the prices varying with the size of stone required.

The uses to which bort may be put are many, as it will stand the severest test for mechanical purposes without apparent wear, especially where there is considerable friction and when the hardest steel cutter will not hold an edge.

Bort is especially well adapted for drilling, sawing, reaming, planing, turning, shaping, carving, engraving and dressing various stones, wheels, paper calendar rolls, screw tops, and numerous other purposes.

Perhaps the most important of all its uses is in diamond drilling, a branch of industry that has been particularly active in recent years. For this class of work bort, round and hard, is most serviceable. Usually from six to eight stones are set in the bit of a drill, and, when the rock is extremely hard, two more are added, being set on the outside of the bit directly opposite each other. The Turf Club bore-hole at Johannesburg, 4,800 feet deep, was accomplished with Brazilian carbons that were worth about £9 per carat.

Other uses for bort that show expansion are in wire-drawing, in which a flat stone is preferred, and in stone-sawing, employing angular shapes. Each one has its preference for an individual shape and size of stone.—*The Mineral Collector.*

Drawing in Plant Study.

What plant do any of us really know? The systematist may tell you its name and the physiological botanist may have an idea of the tissues that compose it, but each knows only a part—and a very small part at that—of its life history. But when one has drawn all parts of a plant and watched it long enough to obtain all its phases, he cannot fail to have a very intimate knowledge of it. Especial stress is to be laid upon the drawing. It is not enough to carefully examine the plant even with a microscope, for one may easily overlook important points, but in drawing he must see everything and its relation to all else. Educators have recently found this out, hence the great importance now attached to drawing in laboratory work. There are doubtless many who will be inclined to say that they cannot draw; but it should be remembered that botanical drawing is not primarily to make a pretty picture, though this also is desirable. Accuracy is the first requirement and this can be attained by all who care to try for it.—*The American Botanist*

Buried Treasures of Herculaneum.

It is more than probable that the long buried secrets of Herculaneum will be surrendered to the twentieth century. The excavations which brought to light the wonders of Pompeii are comparatively recent. The city of Herculaneum, as is well known, was destroyed by the same eruption of Mt. Vesuvius, A. D. 79. Pompeii is thought to have been a commercial city, though influenced by Greek culture, where as the results of the excavations of Herculaneum tend to show that it was a center of Greek culture. In one villa were found 1,750 papyrus manuscripts, while not one has yet been discovered at Pompeii, where the excavations have been most exhaustive. From such evidence as this, which the few excavations so far made have produced, it is thought that the city contains great treasures of literature and art, and it may be that some of the important lost books of antiquity may yet be unearthed. It is probable that the excavations will be made under international auspices.

Referring to the intrinsic differences between the two cities, Dr. Charles Waldstein, of Cambridge University, says:

" Pompeii, standing on an eminence, was destroyed, but not completely covered, by hot ashes, cinders and pumice stone. The objects of art as a result have either been modified, damaged or destroyed. As the tops of the houses were visible after the eruption, the inhabitants of the surrounding country returned to dig after treasures. Herculaneum, on the other hand, was covered by a torrent of liquid mud, a mixture of ashes and cinders with water. Almost instantaneously it was completely buried, and to a depth so great that its ancient works remained untouched. It is a widespread misapprehension, wholly without foundation, that Herculaneum is covered by solid lava. Geologists and archeologists are now agreed that the so-called lava fungosa is a friable material which can be worked by the excavator, and something that preserves exceptionally well the objects buried in it. The marble is not calcined, the wood not burned, the glass not melted and the manuscripts not destroyed."

Adventures of a Grosbeak Family.

BY J. L. SLOANAKER.

THE beautiful rose-breasted grosbeak is a common summer resident of and a well known and favorite bird in Jasper County, Iowa. I have found them nesting in fruit trees, in climbing grape-vines, and in osage hedges, but more often in box-elder trees at from six to thirty feet from the ground. Their nests are very frail structures and the complement of eggs three, sometimes four.

A pair of grosbeaks have nested for the last three years in a box-elder tree in our backyard, hardly twenty feet from the door. Last spring they arrived from their winter resort on May 5th and very soon after commenced nest building. We watched their frail nest grow from day to day until it contained three eggs. After careful brooding by both parents, at the end of two weeks, three tiny chips off the old block were safely ushered into bird-dom. About this time a spying bluejay thought that something similar to veal would suit him for breakfast. Happening near, he soon changed his mind, and decided that a brisk walk (or rather a fly) would benefit his appetite and constitution. For the male grosbeak assisted by two screeching robins, which he had called to his aid, soon made him hike out of sight on the overland route.

One bright day near the first of June, we observed the three youngsters perched at different heights in the tree, uttering at regular intervals their mournful little cry. They eventually reached the ground, where the children caught and patted them, placing them time and again in the nearby trees and a lilac bush, where they would stoutly cling and climb as high as they could towards the end of the limb. They would allow us to approach at any time and stroke their heads, at which they would open their mouths at us as if expecting food. The mother would fearlessly come to feed them while I stood only three feet away, but the father would never come out of the trees.

At last after several days two of them disappeared, but the third a little male, stayed several days longer. He, a funny little fuzzy miniature of his illustrious father, was still covered with yellow down, as when he left the nest, and would always be seen hopping or taking three-yard flights along the ground. One morning while I was eating breakfast, I was startled by the excited calls of birds in our front yard. I rushed out to find the mother grosbeak flitting excitedly from tree to tree, while at the foot of an oak a woodpecker was waging war against her offspring. I ran toward them, firing a club at the red-headed rascal as I went, and picking up the poor young adventurer, found he had been severely pecked about the head and mouth by the stout sharp bill of the woodpecker, who was now exulting over his victory from the top of a neighboring telephone pole. The sides of the young bird's mouth were badly torn and his throat was so filled with blood that he could not peep. After washing his mouth out with warm water and rubbing his wounds with cosmoline, I placed him in the sun on our wide front porch, from which on the following day he followed his mother off into the wide world somewhere, apparently none the worse of his exciting adventure.—*Oologist.*

Gold Production of the World.

The gold production of the world for the past four hundred and ten years is estimated to have been $10,693,236,302. The United States production is placed at $2,507,010,-492, of which $507,010,492 comes from the mountainous country west of the Denver meridian.

California and Colorado are the states credited with the heaviest production, but the western portion of the United States is actually credited with 23.5 per cent., or nearly one-fourth, of the total gold production of the world for four hundred and ten years.—*The Mineral Collector*

An Ancient Tree.

While the "Big Trees" of California hold the palm for age in things vegetable, occasionally we meet with others that, considered on their own merits, are certainly remarkable. Charles E. Bessey of the University of Nebraska writes to *Science* of a cedar which he claims to be over one thousand years old, as follows: "In the Garden of the Gods, near Pike's Peak, Colorado, there are many large specimens of the brown cedar (*Juniperus monosperma*), and in a recent visit to that place it occurred to the writer that these trees must be very old. He was fortunate enough to find the stump of a recently-cut tree, on which it was easy to distinguish the annual growth-rings. There

were counted for a section of the trunk, care being taken to select a portion in which the rings were of average thickness, and on this basis the number of the whole stump was calculated. In this way it was found that this particular tree was between eight hundred and one thousand years old. In other words, this tree was a seedling some time between the years 900 and 1100 A. D."

Fighting Lizards.

The ring necked lizard of the Arizona desert is not a mere devourer of weaklings. He is always ready to fight, whether he is challenged by another or cornered by a man. When brought to bay in some hole, he opens his jaws and dashes bravely out, snapping at everything which opposes him, and so fierce and sudden is his rush that it is impossible to face it without flinching. By holding two of these lizards loosely by the small of the back and allowing their heads to clash as they struggle to escape, one may be able to induce combats such as must occur every day in the desperate lizard world.

Forgetting that they were captives, they would seize upon each other and vent their thwarted rage to the utmost in a fight which, but for timely interference, would doubtless lead to the death of one or the other. Such bull-dog pugnacity is rather unlooked for in lizards, but a student of character could easily read in the set jaw and pouched throat of this species the signs of fighting blood. — *Country Life in America.*

RANDOM NOTES.

None of the remains of many in the so-called stone age indicate a race inferior to some races that now exist.

Greater New York City has a total of 6,862 acres in public parks. The city of London, England, has about the same.

There are probably five thousand species of ants in existence. More than two thousand species have been described and classified.

Owing to the difference in the force of gravity a body weighing 1,000 pounds on the earth would weigh but 163 pounds on the moon.

Excepting the musk-ox of the subarctic regions, the "buffalo" (*Bos bison*) is the only species of the ox family indigenous to the American continent.

Although not now found anywhere on the Eastern Continent, fossil remains of the musk-ox have been found in Siberia, England, Denmark and Germany.

Some seventeen diamonds have been found mostly in the beds of streams between Chicago and Milwaukee, having an average weight of a little more than 8 carats. The largest weighed 21¼ carats.

While single nuggets of gold have been found weighing as high as 140 pounds, the largest single mass of platinum ever found weighed but 21 pounds. It was found in the Ural Mountains, from which region most of the world's supply is taken.

The spectroscope reveals a great number of the substances in the sun which compose our planet, viz.: sodium, magnesium, calcium, iron, zinc. nickel, chromium, hydrogen, and others; but neither gold, silver, platinum. mercury, tin nor lead have as yet been found in it.

Anent animal life in deep sea, it may be mentioned that the pelican fish has been captured at a depth of 7,080 feet near the Canary Islands. Other fish have been captured at a depth of 9,000 feet. As these fish have well developed eyes it would seem that light penetrates further into the ocean depths than theory has figured. The color of these fish is a deep black hue, which also adds another feature to the light problem.

The bulk of the sun is 600 times greater than the bulk of all the planets known, together.

The vine of the morning glory invariably twines in a direction opposite the sun; the hop vine always with the sun.

The cave animals of North America comprise one hundred and seventy-two species of blind creatures, nearly all of which are mostly white in color.

The Black Sea with an area of 172,000 square miles contains but one island, and that a small one. This sea drains nearly one-fourth of Europe and 100,000 square miles of Asia.

Thibet is said to have the highest spot inhabited by human beings of any place on this earth. This is the Buddhist cloister of Hanie, where twenty-one monks live at an altitude of 16,000 feet.

In parts of Australia, where the average rainfall is not more then ten inches, a square mile of land will support only eight or nine sheep. In Buenos Ayres, the same area, with 34 inches of rain, supports 2,560 sheep.

An iceberg was found by Captain Ross grounded in Baffin's Bay, 20 miles from land and in 61 fathoms. It was 4169 yards long by 3869 yards wide by 51 yards high and its estimated weight was 1,292,397,673 tons. Even larger have been found.

The ...... (......rus), once numerous in ...... time supposed to be ...... in Wallachia, Lithunia and Caucasus. Heros numbering about eight hundred roam through the great forests of Bialoweiza, in Lithunia, being under the special protection of the Czar of Russia.

Probably the largest geode ever known was one found a few years ago in Brazil, a portion of which is now in the American Museum of Natural History, New York City. The geode measured 33 feet in length by 16 feet 5 inches in width and was 10 feet in height. Its estimated weight was 35 tons. It was lined with quartz, colorless near the outside but gradually passing into richly colored purple amethyst crystals, some of them as large as a man's hand, and having brilliant lustrous faces as though polished by a lapidary.

The Amateur Naturalist.

"To him who in the love of Nature holds communion with her visible forms, she speaks a various language."

| VOLUME 2. | BINGHAMTON, NEW YORK, MAY, 1905. | NUMBER 3. |

WHEN MARCH GOES OUT LIKE A LAMB.
BY GERTRUDE S. BURLINGHAM.

THIS year *Barbara* has missed her *fifth season* and her books must remain undusted until July, because spring having come there will be no cessation in the unfolding life before then. And even in July, one can afford to remain indoors only rainy days. For once March has made herself agreeable. One day, half as if to show its protective care and half its sternness, winter wrapped tree and shrub and earth in snowy embrace, then passed off like an eclipse, leaving the filmy haze of an Indian Summer day mingling with and softening the air of spring.

And thus by the middle of the month the call of the robin echoed from tree to tree. Although the bluebird is accredited with being the first to arrive, the larger size of the robin together with his louder imperative call and that fearless friendly spirit which brings him close to us in the lawn, usually makes him the first herald of spring. What a difference there is in the character of birds! Who ever approached near enough a bluebird and kept him in close range long enough to gaze to heart's content at his matchless blue coat with vest of just the right shade of rusty red? But perhaps his coloring has developed in him the modesty due to shyness, and his soft plaintive warble has been born of a protective instinct. It is difficult to think of the robin and bluebird as belonging to the same family, but the robin is the odd one in the family, and the bluebird seems to be the connecting link between him and the thrushes. By the twenty-fifth of the month both the male and female bluebirds had arrived, but except for an occasional one, they keep on the outskirts of the city around farm houses, or in villages.

The day after the robins came, the song-sparrow's joyous song burst from the tops of the willows along the river and the next day they had invaded the gardens in the city and were calling from the pear trees and the apple trees whose brown bark and skeleton twigs successfully hid the songster. *Yes, yes, yes, spring is here, is here, here, here. O!* How he trills now on *spring*, now on *here* toward the end of the song, and with what abandon he sings. But a solo is nothing compared to a concert of voices. It was not until the last week of March that I could attend an opening concert of these little songsters. At about ten o'clock Monday morning in a small swamp covered with a second growth of willows and aspens, I found the chorus at its height. At least one hundred song-sparrows were vieing to sing the sweetest and loudest, and roundelay followed roundelay till it seemed as though there must be twenty-five different varieties of songsters. But every bird I sighted was a song-sparrow. He is a great vocalist. Even as I watch one he sings three decidedly different songs while the repetition of any one of them is slightly varied. In order to identify the song-sparrow from his singing one must learn to recognize the tone and quality of the voice, for it requires years to become familiar with his repertoire of songs.

Animal life responds to the spring influences sooner then does plant life. But by the time the song-sparrows are here in force, the reddish mottled hood of the skunk's-cabbage blossoms is peeping through the ground in the swamps. I was not disappointed in my search for it here. This may be called a cold blooded plant because while the frost is yet in the ground it awakens and sends up its spadix of blossoms carefully protected by a stiff oblong hooded spathe mottled with red and yellow. Enclosing the base may be a spear-like leaf, little resembling the broad ribbed leaf of the plant two months later when it may cradle a nest of Maryland yellowthroats.

In a meadow bordering the swamp I heard the whistle of the meadow-lark and soon discovered first here, then there, one of the birds stalking along, his gray and brown stripped head projecting above the brown grass and stubble with which the color of his back blended perfectly. When the clear, confident, persuasive whistle of the meadow-lark comes up from the meadow, then we feel sure that winter has lost its grip—it is indeed, "Spring o' the year," even though it be the twenty-fifth of March.

I saw nothing of the red winged blackbirds, but on Tuesday along a little stream bordered with a grove of elms, maples and evergreens we found them and heard their liquid call *coop-er-dee*. Here the grackles were so numerous that their squeaky shrill call nearly drowned the fainter bird notes. Their vocal organs seem to be in a chronic *change of voice* period. Up from the stream in a sunny spot a flock of goldfinches were twittering and warbling their song which seems to have no set beginning or end. But they seemed very shy and not until another day was I able to get near enough to them to find out whether they had donned their spring suit of black and yellow. Close view revealed them clad in brown. Hidden among the foliage of an evergreen I came upon another flock of birds. Out from the mysteries depths of the tree came half warbled, half murmured songs, whisperings such as birds give in their sleep, intermingled with occasional chirps and muffled calls, like the smacking of lips over some dainty morsel. Not until it flew was it possible to catch sight of the bird. Then its fan-like tail with white feathers on either side alone made it conspicuous. Once sighted it is not difficult to make out the coloring of the junco. Although called the snowbird, its white tail feathers and extreme under parts together with its yellowish white bill are the only portions of its body which suggest contact with the snow. Its bill looks as though it might have been worn clean picking seeds out of the snow! When the various notes of the junco are fixed in mind, it is surprising how many of the birds may be discovered in the trees or picking up seeds on the ground. Their spring song is very gentle as though they were afraid lest they awaken prematurely some slumbering wild thing.

From the evergreens, too, came the faint *zee* of the golden crowned kinglet. But his is so small and so restless that unless fortune intervene, you may follow a flock for half a morning without catching a glimpse of a bird sufficient to see his golden crown.

Occasionally I heard the quick energetic song of the phœbe, and on coming back again to the stream I saw one in the top of a small tree standing now, in flood time, in the midst of water. As the phœbe sits quietly on a branch, one would not imagine that the next moment he could dash off so suddenly after a passing insect. What a clear eye and unerring aim the bird has. The coming of the phœbe announces the awakening of insect life. The insects have not been noticeable before, but from now on their minute bodies may be detected glistening in the light, especially along the streams. Often during the day the mourning-cloak butterfly fluttered out from among the dry leaves before me.

On Wednesday, March twenty-ninth, I went again to this place hoping to see some other of the sparrows or perhaps the purple finch, but found no new birds. On both days, of course, I saw the white-breasted nuthatch and either the downy or hairy woodpecker. But from the bog just beyond came the chorus of the hylas or peeping frogs. They had found their voices since the day before. The pussy willows, too, had reached their maltese angora stage, and the alders were covered with the staminate catkins from which the yellowish golden pollen shakes in quantities.

These signs led me to choose for the next days' tramps, an open woody ravine running north and south so that one slope was protected from the cold winds and at the same time exposed to the sun. Here I searched for the first hepaticas. Finally at the base of a tree in the valley between the slopes, I found two flowers nearly open. How tenderly the first hepaticas are gathered! But best of all, close by a bed of wintergreens far up the sides of the ravine, I discovered a cluster of arbutus buds well out of their winter condition, showing pink petals snugly folded around each other. A week of warm temperature, culminating in two days when the thermometer registered 75° Fahrenheit and 80° Fahrenheit at four o'clock, had begun to tell on the life stored up in root and stem and bud.

There is a double advantage in beginning bird study in March. Not only can we welcome the spring birds one by one as they come, but we can renew our acquaintance with the winter birds and bid goodspeed to those which are leaving us for farther north. The cold and snow have successfully kept us from the haunts of the winter birds and only now and then a

chickadee or a nuthatch or a downy woodpecker or a junco has deigned to
come to our lawns, and oftener the English sparrow has reigned supreme.
Now ground and skies and air favor us and we invade their precincts. The
sight of a redpoll or a kinglet is as great an event as the sight of the first
phœbe. As the spring birds come, some of our winter birds go farther
north. Soon the juncos, the kinglet, the redpoll and the brown creeper will
leave us for the Catskills or the northern part of the state. Each time now
that I see the brown creeper I shall say goodbye for he may be gone before
I can see him again. Five times this month have I seen the little fellow.
His streaked and mottled brown and gray back makes him most unnotice-
able as he creeps zigzag up a tree, hunting for spiders' eggs which though
stowed away under the loose edge of some piece of bark he is sure to reach
with his long slightly curved bill. The voice of the brown creeper is most
befitting to him. It is more gentle and delicate than the note of the cedar
bird which it slightly resembles. Sometimes as he makes his way up the
tree he utters a soft contented *tsee* between each mouthful. Then again he
trills the note, and the other day I heard a little snatch of the warble which
is his love song.

March has gone out like a lamb, and the first of April has come in with
a touch of March wind; but in my tramp to-day I was glad to find the
hermit thrush here exactly on time, and I shall also record that I saw a
pair of brown creepers.

Binghamton, N. Y.

*VISIT TO A ZIRCON MINE.
BY GEORGE MIDDLETON.

I WILL take you with me first to Saluda, N. C., and then on a six mile
tramp to the Zircon Hill, across the beautiful Green River on the trestle
—a short stop to enjoy the rare scenery; then the walk onward with
the eyes in every direction at once, looking, looking, side to side; closely scaning the railroad cuts for "outcrops."

Ah! the lovely, ever-changing Blue Ridge, what a stupendous and
grand monument to that nature that can delicately paint the lilies' throat
or crush the land until high mountains are thrown into the air, and their
stony hearts melted by the fierce heat which that pressure engenders!

But on we go, and finally reach the foot of the hill; our spirits rise
higher and higher as we ascend. Do you notice the absence of vegetation,
only a few trees and little grass here, while all around the herbage is

---

*Zircon is a tetragonal crystal of silica and zirconia, varying in color, sometimes colorless
like quartz, but usually brown or gray. A red variety, called hyacinth, is used as a gem.
There are only two other sources of zirconia besides the locality in North Carolina here
described, one being in Ceylon and the other a district in the Ural Mountains.—[ED.

luxurious? I've figured it out, after "tasting" the soil, that there's too much soda present from the decomposition of the rocks, mostly feldspathic and the alteration products of other minerals.

This mine, at Zirconia, N. C., is situated in the crystalline belt of the Appalachain Chain, and granite and gneiss are the predominating rocks.

The depth of degradation must be considerable, for at the mines above spoken of, the quartz originally deposited in veins in the feldspar shows signs of change, some I noticed being well on the way to "graveldom"

The jeffersite here, I think an alteration, product of Muscovite, is crumpled, contorted and twisted into every conceivable shape, forming huge veins. It has no stability, coming out easily in chunks and about as easily falling to pieces, until dry, when in the absence of water it seems to gather strength but even then a finger rubbed on its edges demonstrates its friability. The feldspar is, of course, kaolinized to a degree, and only in isolated patches does it show its distinctive cleavage plane and other characteristics. The kaolin is very friable and stained with ferrugineous oxides; at one center of concentration was found a "bunch" of cellular hematite which would have weighed six pounds or thereabout. This is a specimen worth studying.

The titanite shows itself in the peculiar wedge-shaped sphenoids; the crystals of a greenish-gray tint, somewhat mottled and scattered singly and in groups through the feldspar. When altered, as a great deal and by far the largest part is, they are of a yellow color. Sometimes we find a zircon perched upon a titanite or a titanite on a zircon, a literal reconciling of the true assertion is possible in one sense, but with us it resolves itself into the problem of which was first formed? As the zircon is usually embedded or rather penetrates the titanite crystal, when thus associated I have concluded that the last named was the first to separate from the combination of which it had been a part.

One gem zircon was found, though milky or cloudy. Several groups of two and three individuals were uncovered, but invariably became detached. The zircons, themselves, are in a very bad state, as a rule, and easily crack and crumble. Long continued exposure to the everlasting chemical change taking place will alter the hardest stone, and the zircon, though up in the scale of hardness, usually, here would sink quite low.

I have a specimen of jeffersite about 2½ by 4 with several zircons embedded therein, and I detached a large, unaltered but flattened one from a slice of the vermiculite.

Strange to say no titanites were observed with jeffersite as the matrix, and I doubt if any can be found, though I have not given that idea much thought (and no study) on which to base a conclusion. I did no investigating on this line while there because the query has but just suggested itself to me. Had such an idea occurred me while on the grounds, a thorough search would surely have been made.

The absence of hornblende struck me forcibly, being in a granitic country; only a little being observed. Why the feldspar should have been concentrated at this point with its lens of muscovite, and without the usual accompaniment of accessory minerals of the granitic type, is hard to understand, and I must confess that I have no theory to offer.

Magnetite is abundant thereabout, mostly in small grains, though several good sized pieces were collected. The mustard-seed size is especially noticeable in the brooks and this also points to the breaking down of a rock of the granite type.

Pseudos of hematite after pyrite and other undefinable minerals, also came to me from these mines; and other nondescript specimens, which are interesting as showing the transition of one mineral to another.

The amphibole is of a grass-green color for the most part and is found in several forms, the alteration of which gives a fibrous structure, but with no tensile strength, and it is easily crushed to powder.

No terminated quartz crystals were procured, but the prisms of several showed up in crevices, both ends out of view and they are now in my collection.

In one of the tunnels there is a ochreous mass of a plastic consistency in which the zircons are freely disseminated, but they, like the matrix itself, have lost almost all cohesiveness and in the absence of water easily crumble away. A great pity, truly, because I *had* several groups and large crystals from that point which now are *non est*—but a regretted memory.

Queer looking are a few specimens of cellular chalcedony, the structural details of which resemble rude efforts at castle-building. One about 3 by 4 by 4 is a beauty. The crystals around which it was formed have long since gone to join their affinities, but their impress remains and gives a fair idea of what they were like.

It is all intensely interesting and shows that the tragedies of life are not confined to breathing creatures but that even the solid stone lives and dies; and sometimes, overcome by disaster like its breathing prototype, it is snuffed into vapor and forms other combinations.

What an endless cycle is it all—life, death and then re-incarnation and on forever! While life may end for our personality, it cannot for the constituents of our bodies and each atom, seeking its fellow and their affinities, goes on and on exercising its peculiar functions.

Savannah, Ga.

THE COLORS OF NORTHERN FLOWERS.
BY JOHN H. LOVELL.

IN northeastern America north of Tennessee and east of the Rocky Mountains there have been described some 4,020 flowering plants. The distribution of coloration in our flora is a question of much interest, but one which up to the present time seems to have received no attention. Recently I have tabulated the above species according to the predominant colors of their flowers. I find that in the area named there are 1,244 green, 956 white, 801 yellow, 260 red, 434 purple, and 325 blue flowers. White flowers, as is certainly very fitting after the snowy months of winter, are most common in early spring. Yellow flowers are common throughout the entire season, though perhaps rather more abundant in fall than midsummer. Red and blue are rarest in spring, but gradually increase as the months pass until they reach their maximum in autumn.

By far the larger part of the 1,244 green flowers are pollinated through the agency of the wind. A very familiar illustration of wind-pollination is maize or Indian corn. No one who has walked through a field of newly spindled corn can have failed to notice that bright clouds of yellow pollen are borne away on the wings of every breeze. I place the wind-pollinated plants in the Northern States and Canada at about 1,048. They include the great company of grasses, sedges and rushes, and such homely weeds as the nettles, pigweeds, amaranths, spurges, plantains and ragweed. Among the shrubs and trees, which produce wind flowers, are the alders, the earliest plants to bloom in northern New England, and the birches, poplars, beeches and elms. These trees all blossom before or with the appearance of their leaves, and many people never know that they bloom at all. It is not difficult to understand why they flower so early, for the leaves later in the season would intercept the flight of the pollen.

Wind-pollinated plants have small and inconspicuous flowers which are green or dull-colored. Usually they flower and fruit entirely unnoticed. It would be of no advantage for them to produce bright colors or sweet odors, for the wind bloweth where it listeth regardless of all such attractions. The birches, however, have golden and greenish yellow aments and the blossoms of the elm are purplish. The glumés of grasses and the perianth of rushes are also often purplish or reddish. So conspicuous are the flowers of some rushes in Europe that they even attract a few insects. The sorrels sometimes have the entire plant red-colored, and in the Alps Muller saw a butterfly examining a plant for honey. The plantains are midway between wind-fertilization and insect-fertilization. Some odoriferous species display several hues and attract not a few insects. But as a whole wind-pollinated plants have small greenish flowers.

Setting aside the great company of dull-colored wind flowers there remain in northeastern America 2,972 species, which are pollinated by insects or are self-pollinated. Of this number 223 have green, 955 white, 790 yellow, 257 red, 422 purple and 325 blue flowers. Most of these 223 green flowers are small or even minute, and many of them have no petals. They are attractive chiefly to flies and the smaller bees, as in the smilax and sumac families. But the green pendulous flowers of the garden asparagus are favorites of the honeybee. In the grape family the petals never expand, but fall away by separating at the base and coiling spirally upward. The fragrance which resembles that of mignonette can be perceived at a long distance. Kerner relates that in a journey up the Danube he found the whole valley of the Wachan so filled with the scent of the vine flowers that it seemed impossible that they could be far off, yet the nearest vines were 300 yards from the boat. The honeybee and many beetles have been collected on the flowers. Various exotic species of the nightshade family and some Brazilian orchids possess large green flowers. They are strongly scented in the evening and are attractive to moths.

There are 790 yellow flowers in northeastern America, which vary greatly in size and form. Usually they are wheel-shaped as in the buttercups and five-fingers; but not infrequently they are very irregular in form, as in the pea and figwort families where the corolla bears a more or less fancied resemblance to butterflies and the heads of reptiles. As a whole, however, they are much less specialized than red or blue flowers. Highly modified yellow flowers usually exhibit great persistency of the primitive yellow, and little tendency to vary in color. In the goldenrods the individual flowers are very small and conspicuousness is gained by their aggregation in dense clusters. The bright yellow color of the flowers render them visible in the evening as well as by day, and as the temperature of the inflorescence at night is several degrees above the surrounding air they sometimes serve as a refuge for insects.

White flowers are most common in our flora as well as in that of Europe. Many of the 955 white flowers in the territory under consideration belong to shrubs and trees. There is nothing more beautiful in the temperate zone than an apple orchard in bloom with its billowing banks of innumerable white blossoms, tinged with rose and flecked with the vivid green of the newly unfolding leaf buds. The cornels and viburnums are justly ranked among our handsomest shrubs. They produce large clusters of white flowers in such boundless profusion that the entire shrub is transformed into a huge bouquet. Small densely clustered white flowers are also common in the mustard, saxifrage and carrot families. Nocturnal flowers are also usually white.

Any bright colored flower may occasionally revert to white. Whatever impairs the vigor and vitality of the plant, as cold, impoverished soil, injury to the roots, or continued self-fertilization, will cause the floral hues to become paler or change to white. I once transplanted a scarlet poppy when in bud and the flowers became much smaller and changed to pure white. On the other hand whatever stimulates the growth of a plant, as bright sunlight, strong manures, or crossing, increases the brilliancy of the flowers. From this point of view we can understand why white flowers are most common in nature, and why they are truest to name under cultivation. Naturally florists find that they can develop any desired color variety from a white flower more easily than from one already containing pigments. Individual white flowers not infrequently change to yellow, as in *Lantana*, or to red, as in *Dianthus* and *Hibiscus mutabilis*.

There are only 257 red flowers in our northern flora. They are most abundant in the pink family, or Caryophyllaceæ, which contains 22 species. The pinks exhibit a wonderful variety of red shades varying through rose, pink and deep red to scarlet and crimson. The petals may be dotted or marbled with white, and they are often notched or fringed, and surmounted with a corona of scales. The scent is aromatic and the honey lies at the bottom of a long slender tube, where it is inaccessible to a great number of insects. The flowers are great favorites with butterflies. Red flowers are also very common in the rose family, but there are no species which are adapted to butterflies. They are also numerous in the pea, mallow and heath families. Undoubtedly the two handsomest North American shrubs belong to the heath family. They are *Rhododendron maximum* and *Kalmia latifolia* or the mountain laurel. Asa Gray says that in North Carolina they adorn the valleys and mountains in immense abundance and profuse blossoming of every hue from deep rose to white. In the brilliancy of its coloring the cardinal flower is unsurpassed by any other red flower.

The purple flowers number 422. This group contains both red-purple and blue-purple flowers, as well as a few brown, green and yellow-purple flowers. It presents evidently a much greater variety of hues than any one of the preceeding groups. Red-purple flowers are common in the orchid and geranium families, while blue-purple are numerous in the pea and mint families. The flowers of *Aristolochia*, or birthroot, are lurid purple. In the Dutchman's pipe of cultivation (*A. sipho*) the calyx is prolonged into a tube, with a contracted throat either straight or shaped like the letter S, which is set on the inside with reflexed hairs. Flies can creep inside easily, but the hairs prevent their escape. As soon as the anthers have ripened, the hairs wither and the imprisoned insects, now more or less covered with pollen, are set free. These flowers should be compared with the pitcher-like leaves of *Sarracenia* and the spathes of *Arum*, as all three serve as traps for small flies and are lurid purple, a color which is thought by some to be attractive to these insects.

The 325 northern blue flowers are most common in the pea, violet, gentian, mint and figwort families. They are often very irregular in form, with the honey deeply concealed and accessible only to the long-tongued bees.

The red and blue coloring found in the leaves, flowers and fruits of many plants is due to a soluble pigment called anthocyan. It does not occur in grains like the green and yellow pigments, but is dissolved in the cell sap. When its condition is acid the color of the flower is red, but when it is alkaline the color of the flower is blue. In the rose family there are no blue flowers because the cell sap is strongly acid. For the same reason there is but a single blue flowered species known among the orchids.—*The American Botanist.*

The Amateur Naturalist.

A Journal for those who Study Nature from a love of it

ISSUED BI-MONTHLY.

Entered as Second-Class matter October 6, 1904, at the post office at Binghamton, N. Y.

SUBSCRIPTION, 50 CENTS PER YEAR.   SINGLE COPIES, 10 CENTS

ADVERTISING RATES ON APPLICATION.

————EDITED AND PUBLISHED BY————

CHARLES D. PENDELL,

85-87 STATE STREET,   -   -   -   BINGHAMTON, N. Y.

The increasing value of the back numbers of a magazine should be borne in mind by all who desire a complete file of THE AMATEUR NATURALIST. Once out of print it is seldom indeed that a new edition of any magazine is reprinted, and as the number of subscribers increases there is a demand on the part of many for complete files. This is evidenced in the case of one of our contemporaries, a recent advertisement appearing in its columns offering $15.00 for a complete file. The periodical in question was, when started and for a number of years thereafter, but a four-page leaflet and its price nominal. To-day it is the representative journal of its class and the early numbers are eagerly sought. At present the first volume of THE AMATEUR NATURALIST can be supplied at the regular subscription price of 50 cents, but it is evident that this price will eventually have to be increased. Fully one-half of the subscriptions received during the past month have begun with Vol. I, No. 1. We would therefore suggest that those who have not already the first volume, complete their file while they may. The price of single copies is ten cents; the volume, fifty cents.

One of the greatest needs of the amateur paleontologist is a manual on the subject, descriptive and fully illustrated. Gray's Manual will help out the student of botany, Clute's Our Ferns in Their Haunts will enable one to identify almost any fern, Dana's Mineralogy will assist the student in minerals, but so far as the writer knows there is no book on fossils at all commensurate with the needs of the subject, and we suggest to our readers that here is an open and untrodden field awaiting development and offering the reward that comes to those who are first to take advantage of opportunities. School text books and various government reports seem at present to be the sources of information mostly sought, but utterly inadequate. In almost every locality fossil shells may be found in abundance, but from any ordinary book of reference most of these must be unknown and unnamed to the beginner. The long technical names may be undesirable to some but the average collector wants to know them whether he makes frequent use of them or not. A few fossil coral, a half a dozen trilobites, some spirifer and a few others scattered through the text comprise the list of most of the illustrations usually found. The best book we have seen on the subject is "Our Common British Fossils," by J. E. Taylor, F.G. S. (London, England: Chatto & Windus.) This volume contains 331 illustrations and the text is interestingly written, though as the author says his desire has "been to whet the appetite rather than to satisfy it." A similar though more comprehensive book especially adapted to American students is much needed.

Another subject for which the popular demand has never been supplied is a book on the fern allies. Of fern books there are several good ones, as well as books representing other specialized departments of botany; but such plants as the scouring rushes, horsetails, running pine, club mosses and others known as fern allies have never been treated collectively in detail. We are glad to note, therefore, the announcement of a new book which will treat on this subject. "The Fern Allies of North America" is the comprehensive title of the book written by Mr. Willard N. Clute, which will be issued early in July. Mr. Clute is so well known as an authority and writer on botanical subjects that the announcement of the publication of such a book by him will be sufficient to secure for it a large advance sale. For price and combination offers see last page of cover.

"Does botany pay?" is a question treated at some length in the April *American Botanist*, arriving at the conclusion that from a financial standpoint the botanist receives less pay than those engaged in other occupations. If this be so, and we doubt it not, may it not be because the botanist heretofore has not made his calling of equal practical value as the other sciences? Has it not, like a trip to the North Pole, been a matter of speculative research rather than a science producing results applicable to commercial needs? But with the botanist now carrying on his researches in plant pathology, plant physiology, soil bacterialogy, and other branches of botany, and bringing to the farmer knowledge that will enable him to realize the difference between 100 per cent. and 1,000 per cent. in his crops, his work has an applied value and practical botanists will have their worth recognized and receive the increased renumeration that is their just due. The work in the past has not been without value, but has been preliminary to the greater work yet to come.

There is no denying that the typewriter has become a force in modern business methods and one of the necessary adjuncts of this hustling age. In this instrument the genius of the inventor and the skill of the mechanic have united. Mr. A. E. Wilbur, whose advertisement occurs in this issue has made the study of typewriters a business for 20 years and puts the results of his experience into his work, and anybody desiring to purchase a typewriter would find it to their advantage to write him for his list.

MAYFLOWER.

BY CHARLES E. JENNEY.

Reared in adversity,—
(A harsh New England Spring means such):
Proud of her poverty,—
(Her tattered cloak would tell as much),
There dwells among the whispering pines,
  Whose hearts for her are ever sighing,
A maid to whom mine own inclines,—
  A maid whose worth is past denying.

Tells of thy pureness,
The glorious tintings of that dainty blush;
Reveals demureness,
Thy half shy peeping from the underbrush.
The lily and the rose I leave
  To those whose pampered tastes dispute
    us ;
My pledge of faith, I pray, receive
  My heart to thee, my sweet Arbutus.

Fresno, Calif.

In the Coteaus.

BY HATTIE WASHBURN.

RUFFLING for a distance the surface of Dakota's level prairie, near the eastern border, extends a range of low grass-grown, rock bound hills called the "Coteaus."

There may one travel for miles seeing no sign of human habitation save some settler's shanty perched upon a desolate hill and surrounded by low outbuildings, straying cattle and small fields nestling in the fertile valleys or skirting the hills; miles and miles of wire fencing and the lone herdsman with his faithful dog and pony upon a sunny bank while about him his well fed charges crop the mesquite or buffalo grass on the hills or stand full knee deep in the rank growth of the bottom lands. Among these hills, thickly interspersed with treeless lakes and impassable marshes, the hunter finds an endless resource of employment for there are the homes of the mal-lard, teal, shoveler, redhead, canvas back, pintail, gadwell and others of their tribe. Great flocks of wild geese wander there in early spring and late in Autumn while at all seasons the prairie chicken is found in vast numbers, and at frequent intervals starts from the rank wild grass in its sudden, whirring flight, and should the sportsman deign to kill so small a prey the Jack snipe, quail and prairie plover become his easy victims. Many a gravelly bank is the home of the cyote who despite the price upon his head rarely falls before the hunter's rifle.

Such is the game in the Coteaus to-day, but less than two score of years ago there roamed innumerable buffaloes who left their traces mingled with those of their pursurers, the war-like Souix. Within the memory of the oldest settler the skeletons of the buffalo were found entire, but now only fragments of horn and bone are seen as are the spearheads, arrow points and stone hammers of the Indians. The buffalo rings are still plainly visible for the sod must be several times turned by the plowshare before the vegetation ceases to grow ranker upon this strangely formed circle, and with equal prominance on the summit of a hill shows the Indian grave, a grass-grown mound in which large stones lie thickly imbedded.

Goodwin, S. D.

Butte, Montana, produces more copper than any other district in the world. No shaft there has ever been sunk to a depth of 300 feet without yielding ore; and no bottom has yet been found to the great ore shoots.

Powerful Acids.

CHEMISTRY affords means for many interesting and fascinating experiments, and withal many that are dangerous to the novice and from which the expert is not wholly exempt. Hydrochloric acid is a colorless, irrespirable, intensely acid gas. Water, at a temperature of 60° F., will absorb over 450 times its volume of the gas which is then commercially known as "muriatic acid." Hydrochloric acid is formed of the two gases, hydrogen and chlorine. These may be mixed in the dark and will remain together without any action on each other. But if brought into the sunlight will unite with a loud explosion. When in the liquid form if mixed with nitric acid it forms "aqua-regia," in which gold is as thoroughly dissolved as is sugar in hot water.

Prussic acid (hydrocyanic acid), one of the most deadly poisons, is readily distilled from the kernels of peach stones, bitter almonds or horse-chestnuts, and from other plants. It boils at a temperature of about 80° F. and solidifies into a crystalline mass at 5°. It is so volatile that if a drop be allowed to fall on a piece of glass part of the acid becomes frozen by the cold produced by its own evaporation.

Fluorine is the only element that will not unite with oxygen. United with hydrogen it becomes hydrofluoric acid. When the most concentrated form is required it must be kept in a platinum bottle as any other kind would be rapidly coroded. A bottle of glass would be thoroughly dissolved in a very short time.

When it is desired to keep it for some time the acid is generally mixed with water and may then be kept in a bottle of gold, lead or gutta percha. It is colorless, like water, but so caustic that it would eat right through one's hand, and its inhalation is sure death. It is volatile and hence a paraffine covered stopper must be used over the bottle's mouth. Nor must the temperature of the room rise over 60° F. or even the platinum bottle may burst. This acid is used in glass etching, and is probably the most dangerous thing in the world to work with. The etching on thermometers and other similar work is done with it.

The Saw of the Mosquito.

The bill of the mosquito is a complex institution. It has a blunt fork at the head and is apparently grooved. Working through the groove and projecting from the angle of the fork is a lance of perfect form, sharpened with a fine bevel. Beside it the most perfect lance looks like a hand saw. On either side of the lance two saws are arranged, with the points fine and sharp, and the teeth well defined and keen. The backs of these saws play against the lance. When the mosquito alights, with its peculiar hum, it thrusts its keen lance and then enlarges the aperture with the two saws, which play beside the lance until the forked bill with its capillary arrangement for pumping the blood can be inserted. The sawing process is what grates upon the nerves of the victim and causes him to strike wildly at the sawyer.

Bird Slaughter.

One day, armed with a rifle of very small caliber, I was shooting at a mark, when a man standing near by pointed to a bird which was perched on the top of a pole a long distance from where he stood, and dared me to try my marksmanship, says *New Thought Magazine*. I aimed, although the distance was such that it seemed impossible that I could hit the bird, but when I fired the fluttering thing fell to the ground. I walked to the spot, exulting at my skill, and enjoying the praise and wonder of the man who had dared me. When I reached the bird I found the poor creature struggling in its death agony, mangled and torn. Looking closer, I saw in its bill a bit of food which it was evidently carrying to its nestlings far away, it having rested on the pole on its long journey home to its little ones. The bird's eyes looked into mine with a strangely human, pitiful gaze. It may have been imagination, but it seemed to me that I saw the mother-look in the eyes of that poor dying thing, and I felt like a murderer—and I feel so yet. The thought of those little nestlings waiting for the mother who would never return to them haunted me for many days, and the memory is with me still.

African Hippopotamus Hunters.

Dr. Livingston, the celebrated explorer of Africa in his "Last Journals," gives the following interesting account of the hunting of hippopotamus:—"At the Longwa of Zumbo we came to a party of heredity hippopotamus hunters, called *makomb-we* or *akombwe*. They follow no other occupation, but when their game is getting scanty at one spot they remove to some other part of Loangwa Zambesi, or Shire, and build temporary huts on an island, where their women cultivate patches; the flesh of the animals they kill is eagerly exchanged by the more settled people for grain. They are not stingy, but are everywhere welcome guests. I never heard of any fraud in dealing, or that they had been guilt of an outrage on the poorest; their chief characteristic is their courage. Their hunting is the bravest thing I ever saw. Each canoe is manned by two men; they are long light craft, scarcely half an inch in thickness, about eighteen to twenty feet long. They are formed for speed, and shaped somewhat like our racing boats. Each man uses a broad, short paddle, and as they guide the canoe slowly down the stream to a sleeping hippopotamus, not a single ripple is raised on the surface of the smooth water; they look as if holding their breath, and communicate by signs only. As they come near their prey the harpooner in the bow lays down his paddle and rises slowly up, and there he stands erect, motionless, and eager, with the long-handled weapon raised at arm's length above his head, till coming close to the beast, he plunges it with all his might towards the heart. During this exciting feat he has to keep his balance exactly. His neighbor in the stern at once backs his paddle, the harpooner sits down, seizes his paddle, and backs too, to escape; the animal, surprised and wounded, seldom returns the attack at this stage of the hunt. The next stage, however, is full of danger. The barbed blade of the harpoon is secured by a long and very strong rope wound around the handle. It is intended to come out of its socket, and while the iron head is firmly fixed in the animal's body, the rope unwinds and the handle floats on the surface. The hunter next goes to the handle and hauls on the rope till he knows that he is right above the beast; when he feels the line suddenly slacken he is prepared to deliver another harpoon at the instant when hippo's enormous jaws appear with a terrible grunt above the water. The backing of the paddles is again repeated, but hippo often assults the canoe, crushes it with his great jaws as easily as a pig would a bunch of asparagus, or shivers it with a kick of his hind foot. Deprived of their canoe, the gallant comrades instantly dive and swim to the shore under water; they say that the infuriated beast looks for them on the surface of the water, and being below they escape his sight. When caught by many harpoons the crews of several canoes seize the handles and drag him hither and thither, till weakened by loss of blood, he succumbs."

Scientific View of Beer Drinking.

For some years a decided inclination has been apparent all over the country to give up the use of whiskey and other strong alcohol, using as a substitute beer and other compound. This is evidently founded on the idea that beer is not harmful, and contains a large amount of nutriment; also that bitters may have some medicinal quality which will neutralize the alcohol it conceals.

These theories are without confirmation in the observation of physicians. The use of beer is found to produce a species of degeneration of all the organs; profound and deceptive fatty deposits, diminished circulation, conditions of congestion, and preservation of functional activities, local inflammations of both the liver and kidneys, are constantly present.

Intellectually, a stupor, amounting almost to a paralysis, arrests the reason, changing all the higher faculties into a mere animalism, sensual, selfish, sluggish, varied only with paroxysms of anger that are senseless and brutal.

In appearance the beer drinker may be the picture of health, but in reality he is most incapable of resisting disease. A slight injury, a severe cold, or a shock to the body or mind will commonly provoke acute disease, ending fatally. Compared with inebriates who use different kinds of alcohol, he is more incurable and more generally diseased.

The constant use of beer every day gives the system no recuperation, but steadily lowers the vital forces. It is our observation that beer drinking in this country produces the very lowest kind of inebriety, closely allied to criminal insanity. The most dangerous ruffians in our large cities are beer drinkers. Recourse to beer as a substitute for other forms of alcohol merely increases the danger and fatality.— *Scientific American.*

Seeking the Pole.

According to *The New York Tribune*, the Duke of Orleans has been trying, without success, to purchase the Fram, the ship in which Nansen sought the vicinity of the Pole. Why the negotiations failed does not appear, but it is not impossible that Sverdrup, who was Nansen's sailing master and who is probably able to control the sale of the vessel, wants to retain it for some venture of his own. Futile as was the endeavor of the French prince, however, it is noteworthy for the purpose which it reveals. Men of influence who have not hitherto engaged in such enterprises are eager if not actually to reach the Pole at least to surpass the performance of those who have won fame in trying to do so.

The honor of attaining latitude 86:33 and of beating Nansen's record by sixteen miles is claimed by Capt. Cagni, who sustained the same relation to the Duke of the Abruzzi that Sverdrup did to the great Swedish explorer. The spirit of international rivalry, a perfectly legitimate motive, is evidently one of the forces which impel the Duke of Orleans to brave the perils of the Arctic Seas; and if his ambition is realized France will rob Italy of the distinction which the latter now enjoys. Americans, appreciating the value of experience in such undertakings, expect Peary to win the greatest glory attainable in this field of activity. They have no reason, therefore, for wanting the Frenchman to abandon his attempt.

Having failed to get the Fram, the Duke of Orleans will doubtless endeavor to buy or borrow another ship that has had a similar experience. The Gauss, built for the German Antarctic expedition of 1902-03, is beyond his reach, having been sold to Canada. The Terra Nova, one of the ships sent to the south of New Zealand to find the British Antarctic expedition, has been bought by M. Ziegler, and will be used in northern waters next summer; but the Discovery, which has been further south than any other craft yet built, and the vessels which carried the recent Swedish and Scottish Antarctic expeditions ought to be available, and if none of them can be secured it is not impossible to build an entirely new ship, as Peary has done.

The grasses of North America include more than 1,300 species. At the beginning of the nineteenth century barely 100 species were known. The National Herbarium at Washington contains 35,000 sheets of mounted specimens, more than 25,000 having been acquired since 1894.

Cyclone, Tornado, Hurricane.

The ordinary land cyclone is usually quite harmless, and it is only by a mistaken use of the term that it has become associated with those terrifying storms, known as tornadoes, peculiar to our country. Cyclones have a bad reputation because they are commonly associated with other more harmful storms. Instead of being dangerous and destructive, they are the chief source of rain in spring and autumn, and supply the snow which adds so much to the pleasure of our northern winter. They cover a large extent of territory at one time, and on an average follow one another across the country from west to east at intervals of about three days.

A tornado often does great damage. It is known by its funnel-shaped cloud, which bounds and bounces along, now high in the air and again touching the ground. Where it skims along the ground the havoc is the greatest. Here the mightiest structures of men are crushed in an instant before the avalanches of wind let loose from every direction. The air seems to have an explosive force, buildings falling outward instead of inward, as one might think. In such a storm no place is safe, but the southwest corner of a cellar affords the best protection obtainable. If in the open, lie flat on the ground. During a tornado, which lasts but a few minutes, the sky is covered by clouds of inky blackness, which here and there take on a livid greenish hue. The surface winds rush spirally upward into the funnel-shaped cloud, carrying with them many articles which are afterward dropped some distance beyond. The danger zone is confined to a path less than half a mile in width, and one hundred miles in length. These storms occur only on land.

The true hurricane is ocean-born. On the high seas of the tropics it marshals its forces of wind and wave, before which the stoutest ship is helpless and the fairest islands are laid waste. Even the sturdy mainland trembles under its awful casti-

gation. These ocean storms last much longer than tornadoes, cover more territory, and cause more damage. The hurricane which overwhelmed Galvaston destroyed several thousand lives and millions of dollars' worth of property. The West India Islands are frequently scourged by these awful visitations, and our own Atlantic coast sometimes feels the lash of these dreaded storms.

But the hurricane and tornado are rare. The former seldom extends far inland, and usually occurs in the late summer or fall. Tornadoes are products of the south and west, and are mostly confined to the spring and early summer months. The cyclone is a universal storm which travels over land and sea, in season and out of season, in spring or in winter. It is an old friend, but one much abused.

Historic Forest Fires.

When all the conditions are favorable, forest fires sometimes reach gigantic proportions. A few such fires have attained historic importance. One of these is the Miramichi fire of 1825. It began its greatest destruction about 1 o'clock in the afternoon of October 7 at a place about 60 miles above the town of Newcastle, on the Miramichi River in New Brunswick. Before 10 o'clock at night it was 20 miles below Newcastle. In nine hours it had destroyed a belt of forest 80 miles long and 25 miles wide. Over more than two and a half million acres almost every living thing was killed. Even the fish were afterward found dead in heaps along the river banks. Five hundred and ninety buildings were burned, and a number of towns, including Newcastle, Chatham and Douglastown, were destroyed. One hundred and sixty persons perished, and nearly a thousand head of stock. The loss from Miramichi fire is estimated at $300,000, not including the value of the timber.

In the majority of such forest fires as this the destruction of the timber is a more serious loss by far than that of the cattle and buildings, for it carries with it the impoverishment of a whole region for tens and even hundreds of years afterward. The loss of the stumpage value of the timber at the time of the fire is but a small part of the damage to the neighborhood. The wages that would have been earned in lumbering, added to the value of the produce that would have been purchased to supply the lumber camps and the taxes that would have been devoted to roads and other public improvements, furnish a much truer measure of how much, sooner or later, it costs a region when its forests are destroyed by fire.

The Peshtigo fire of October, 1871, was still more severe than the Miramichi. It covers an area of over 2,000 square miles in Wisconsin, and involved a loss in timber and other property of many millions of dollars. Between 1,200 and 1,500 persons perished, including nearly half the population of Peshtigo, at that time a town of 2,000 inhabitants. Other fires of about the same time were most destructive in Michigan. A strip about 40 miles wide and 180 miles long, extending across the central part of the State from Lake Michigan to Lake Huron, was devastated. The estimated loss in timber was about 4,000,000,000 feet board measure, and in money over $10,000,000. Several hundred persons perished.

In the early part of September, 1881, great fires covered more than 1,800 square miles in various parts of Michigan. The estimated loss in property, in addition to many hundred thousand acres of valuable timber, was more than $2,300,000. Over 5,000 persons were made destitute, and the number of lives lost is variously estimated at from 150 to 500.

The most destructive fire of more recent years was that which started near Hinckley, Minn., September 1, 1894. While the area burned over was less than in some other great fires, the loss of life and property was very heavy. Hinckley and six other towns were destroyed, about 500 lives were lost, more than 2,000 persons were left destitute, and the estimated loss in property of various kinds was $25,000,000. Except for the heroic conduct of locomotive engineers and other railroad men, the loss of life would have been far greater.

This fire was all the more deplorable because it was wholly unnecessary. For many days before the high wind came and drove it into uncontrollable fury, it was burning slowly close to the town of Hinckley and could have been put out.—*Farmers' Bulletin.*

Siberian Libraries and Museums.

In the surprisingly short time of seventy years from Yermak's entrance to the valley of the Obi, Russian pioneers had reached the Pacific Ocean, and penetrated to the mouth of the Lena, and established important centers of civilization at numerous points which have continued to increase to the present day. Tobolsk, Omsk, Tomsk, Krasnoyarsk, Minusinsk, Irkutsk, Yakutsk, Verkhne Udinsk and Nertchinsk have behind them as long a history as Salem and Boston.

While they have not developed in size like those early New England settlements, they can render an excuse for not so doing by pointing to the limiting conditions which have surrounded them, which even yet are only partially removed. But at Tomsk one will now find a university which will compare favorably with any in the United States fifty years ago. At Krasnoyarsk he will find a library of a wealthy Siberian, filled with many treasures which any European library would covet, but could not obtain.

At Minusinsk, three hundred miles away from the Siberian railroad, is a museum which is the admiration of the world, where from the local collections the transition from the stone to the bronze and the iron age is more perfectly shown than anywhere else. In this collection are sixty thousand specimens well housed in a two-story brick building and arranged and classified after the most approved methods, with an equally commodious library building adjoining it. All this has been accomplished by private subscription.

And this is only a specimen of what is to be found in nearly every Siberian town of more than ten thousand inhabitants. The country abounds in museums and in people who are interested in them. Minusinsk has but fifteen thousand people, but in the larger cities of Irkutsk and Khabarovsk, where branches of the Royal Geographical Society exist, the museums, though not so much specialized as this one at Minusinsk, are built and organized on a larger plan.

Irkutsk nearly four thousand miles east of St. Petersburg, though containing only about sixty thousand inhabitants, has, besides its large museum, an elegant opera house, vying, in proportions and fullness of equipment, with anything found in America outside of New York City. It has a public reading-room and a library containing books and magazines in all the leading languages of Europe.

At Blagovyeschensk, on the Amur River, fourteen hundred miles farther east, in a city of thirty thousand, one will find, in addition to a well-equipped hospital and library and museum, a community of such high musical culture that a local society renders with ease and in most creditable style such choruses as those of Saint-Saens' "Sampson and Delilah."—*Review of Reviews.*

Bright polished surfaces radiate less heat than the same surfaces that are rough or colored, hence retain heat much longer.

RANDOM NOTES.

Tourmaline of an emerald green color is more valuable than a genuine emerald.

Rain water contains ammonia to the extent of about one grain of ammonia to fourteen gallons of rain water.

The cockroach family date from a very remote ancestry, the type being a very persistent one. Insects of this family existed in geological times prior to the tertiary. They are found in carboniferous rocks and one form has been found in Silurian sandstone.

Lettuce, according to Herodotus, was used as a salad in 550 B. C. and has ever since been cultivated as a garden vegetable, but not until 1895 was it discovered that it was possessed of remarkable polarity when allowed to flower, or "go to seed," the surface of its lower leaves facing east and west and the edges to the north and south.

In records for sixty-one years, a warm summer has been followed by a severe winter in 9 cases, and by a mild one in 19; a cold summer, by a severe winter in 17 cases, and by a mild one in 12. Of summers both wet and cold, the mean temperature being below 60.5 degrees Fahrenheit, 9 were followed by severe winters and only 3 by mild winters.

Alaska has the biggest bear, the biggest moose, the biggest mountain sheep and the biggest salmon and grayling in the world, and the biggest mountain on the North American continent. Moreover, it has been found to be anything but an uninhabited and uninhabitable country. It is without doubt the greatest game country on the globe to-day, because it is the newest, and the conditions are right for the maintenance of game animals and birds.

A primitive chart prepared by the Polynesians to assist them in their travels from island to island has been acquired by the British Museum. The chart in question refers to the Marshall Islands, and was prepared by the natives. Routes, currents, and prevailing winds are represented by pieces of split cane, straight or bent according to the chart-makers' knowledge of the facts of the case, while the islands are indicated by univalve shells attached to the canes.—*Scientific American.*

The males in all the blood-sucking families of flies, including mosquitoes, are harmless, their proboscis not being adapted for piercing the skin of mammals.

Paladium is a metal found in the ore of platinum. It combines with gold, and when it forms 20 per cent. renders the alloy brittle and white. Alloyed with silver and polished it makes the best reflecting surface known, and will not tarnish from atmospheric causes.

An iron mine in Sweden, according to a recent survey by that Government, contains 235,000,000 tons of iron ore above sea level, and drilling tests show that there are 400,-000,000 tons within a depth of 400 feet below the sea-level, with unknown quantities at still greater depth.

By means of the hydroscope, objects have been recovered from the bottom of the sea where they have been submerged for 2,000 years. These were found off the Grecian coast and include some valuable creations of Greek art. The hydroscope is a recent invention and is likely to prove an important one.

It has been the custom lately to fasten wire ropes and chains at perilous places on the Alps to assist climbers. But last summer's experiences have indicated an unforeseen peril arising in unsettled weather from the wires and chains themselves. A number of tourists were severely shocked and stunned by charges of electricity passing through the safety guards, which act as lightning conductors. Any one can easily understand how a shock of that kind, experienced at certain points, might, without being severe enough in itself to produce fatal results, cause a terrible disaster.

In 1882, during the progress of some excavations on the estate of Lord Normanton, near Crowland, Peterborough, Eng., workmen exposed a subterranean forest some ten feet below the surface and about three acres in extent. Some of the trees were in an admirable state of preservation, and one large oak measured fifty-four feet in length. Although buried for unknown ages, the trees were found in such state of preservation that the different kinds of wood could easily be determined. A kind of fir tree was most abundant. The surrounding clay contains quantities of remains of lower animal life.

The Amateur Naturalist.

"To him who in the love of Nature holds commun on with her visible forms, she speaks a various language."

| VOLUME 2. | BINGHAMTON, NEW YORK, JULY, 1905. | NUMBER 4. |

THE HUMOROUS SIDE OF NATURE.

BY NORMAN FOERSTER.

"THE comedies and tragedies of Nature" is a familiar phrase nowadays. But it is doubtful whether the application of the term "comedy" is justifiable. Nature has her tragedies—a countless host of them—but we may well question whether a light, a farcical, mood is ever attained. If we test the pith of the matter we will soon be impressed with the fact that the humor is chiefly in ourselves. The participants in what we are pleased to regard as an amusing incident or a funny performance may be entirely oblivious of the humorous side of it. Perhaps I can recall a few illustrative incidents.

Last winter, one cold day of dazzling brilliance with a cloudless sky and immaculate snow, I took a stroll up a wooded valley through which a half-frozen stream flowed with its life at low ebb. The snowfall had been of recent occurrence and the transparent pellicle of ice that had formed beneath it on the creek had a sloshy covering of semi-melted snow. But this a deep mantle of fluffy crystals ensconced completely, so that the whereabouts of the creek could be told only by the occasional gurgling, muffled sounds that issued from it.

I was engaged in the fanciful occupation of following a gray squirrel's track, where the agile little animal scampered along a log, or down a declivity at an angle, or up a tree, when to my surprise the quaint footprints headed straight for the bank of the creek at a point where the channel had cut into the ground sharply to the depth of six or eight feet. Here the tracks, hitherto regular, suddenly became confused. At the brink of the little cliff the layer of snow was much disturbed. There were similar signs in the stream below. Poor, cold, wet squirrel, I almost laughed at his mishap. Intent on crossing the stream he had ventured to the edge of the bank to reconnoiter and had tumbled over. Perhaps as he fell a faint hope coursed through his brain that the ground was not yet granite-frozen and the downy snow would cushion him, or perhaps he knew that the creek was below. At any rate, down he went, descending without a jar, indeed, into the soft snow and disagreeable slosh and the crackling ice-crust and the frigid water. Ugh! . . . . Terror-stricken the poor beast clambered out from his icy bath, onto the lower bank, and horrified at the thought that the water might become congealed and eventually congeal him, he scurried off at a great rate.

Another incident, less serious to the concerned, occurs to me: It was well on in March when I was leisurely climbing up a hillside covered with thin woods. There was considerable brush at places, and a confused mat of dead leaves was strewn broadcast. A party of half a dozen robins were marching about in their dignified manner, enjoying a tasty supper of big angleworms, so deeply engrossed in this occupation that they seemed oblivious of the whole world. Suddenly there was a clatter of brush and dead leaves, and a brownish form with a white beacon dashed from the cover directly among the alarmed robins. Consternation reigned in their ranks as the hair dashed among them, almost striking one or two. He seemed to enjoy the sport, charging through the array of the robins at its widest part; and I vow that as he stopped beside a log some distance away I could see his abdomen rapidly heaving as if he were splitting his sides with laughter. At the same time, the frightened robins, breathless with alarm, hopped about as if exchanging comments on the freakish act of that mild-looking cotton-tail calmly gazing from behind his log shelter.

On another occasion a squirrel was observed within an ace of coming in contact with a slate-colored junco. This is one respect in which protective coloration is an obvious disadvantage. Had the Quaker-like junco been adorned like a Baltimore oriole I doubt if the squirrel would have so narrowly averted a collision.

The vagrant sparrow in the street wins his mate by a constant fluttering of his wings as if his soul were in an agony of love; the male ruffed grouse drums until some coy female has come to see the fine performer, when he in turn becomes inquisitive; and so on, each species with its peculiar type of love-making. But the yellow-eyed thrasher with his "face to face talks on matrimonial subjects" is among the most curious. The general appearance of this bird at any time is rather foolish and uncanny—strange words to couple but applicable, nevertheless. With his long, cumbersome tail, awkward gait, and yellow eyes, there is ample reason for inspiring both of these impressions. But when the courtship ardor has released the full flow of emotion, then he is most amusing.

The pair are observed together in a field near a favorite haunt of a wooded valley with dense undergrowth. The male is following the female sedulously, humbly grunting his amours to her, but pursuing so closely that she turns about sharply. For a moment or two they glare at each other, bill almost touching bill. Then she goes on again as before, perhaps feeling that he is cowed. But, his ardor more aroused than ever by this delightful proximity, he follows as before. Of course she turns about again at the proper moment, and so it goes on till she is assured that his protestations of devotion are true, and the two are united by an Unseen Hand.

It was on a cold day last April, a day that called forth unusual activity among the winter birds, that I witnessed an amusing mishap that befell a downy woodpecker. He announced his presence with a steely "peek," and on looking up I saw him mounting a dead tree trunk in a most dignified manner. Chickadees were disporting in the branches nearby, but he did not regard them with the slightest condescension. Perhaps he was in training for courtship, endeavoring to attain an extra primness and a certain manly gruffness. Be this as it may, I never saw Downy more sober and business-like. Well, he went up the dead tree trunk until he arrived at a smaller bare branch extending perpendicularly. Out on this he went to the very end, when snap! crack! the branch severed its connection with the mother tree and plunged earthward, striking numerous objects on the way. The frightened woodpecker quickly recovered himself, however, and calling his clear "peek, peek" with greater emphasis, paused to survey the scene of the disaster. The chickadees, meanwhile, were in a state of great excitement, which did not cool down for a considerable time.

During April I witnessed another "Lepus" incident. Four boys discovered a hare in the extreme end of a hollow with a macadamized roadway almost surrounding it, somewhat as the horseshoe surrounds the space within it, the open part corresponding to the widening of the valley. The boys were in the bottom of the valley following a little creek when they saw Lepus just a short distance up the hill to their left. Hastily arming with stones, they rushed after him in hot pursuit, regardless of brush or rocks. Arriving at a cliff where they had last seen the hare, they carefully examined every nook and cranny where the shy animal might be in hiding. For a long time they kept up this fruitless search and at length, somewhat disappointed and disgusted, went their way.

Sly Lepus, meanwhile, had scampered up the hill at his utmost speed when pursued, directly past the cliff until he reached the roadway. Here he rested, looking down the hill at his troublesome foes with a degree of contempt. Then he skirted the hill for a short distance and by stages reached the spot he had started from, now behind the boys, while the latter were looking for him under the cliff in full confidence of rousing him. I thought they looked at me rather sheepishly when they saw I had been watching them, but to this day they do not know how miserably they were duped by a creature they considered far inferior in intelligence.

This ruse the hare uses with great success. I have seen it effective even when a dog had taken up the scent. . . . . I was walking along the road, with a brush-covered depression to my right, and a wooded knoll rising at an obtuse angle to the road before me on the other side. A man and two boys and a dog were in great excitement, evidently led by the dog, going along the hill from me, he of the canine tribe barking vociferously. Suddenly a little reddish-brown beast dashed down the knoll directly toward me, crossed the road only a few feet ahead, and entered the dense brush of the hollow. At the same moment a dog with a good nose but little brain and two boys and a man with good brains but no scent power, were all hotly pursuing him in the opposite direction!

A serio-comic quarrel in the bird world came to my notice in June. A chunky, square-shouldered little pewee was chattering angrily and making desperate sallies at a brilliantly-uniformed bully, a red-winged blackbird, whose spotless, unsullied black was in marked contrast with his fiery red epaulets. Determined to uphold his reputation—I don't mean as a bully, but as a redoubtable fellow who should be feared by his inferiors and respected by his peers—he made a savage dart at the little flycatcher. But the quick-witted fellow, flashing a look of Japanese hatred at the bully, almost turned a somersault, and left the blackbird nothing but a barbed wire fence to grasp! Then, after chanting a few defiant "pee-a-wees," mingling a flavor of pugnacity in their dreamy cadence, he perched on the same fence on which the blackbird, a few feet away, was glaring at him. Here the encounter ended suddenly. The combatants seemed to understand each other. The plucky fellow of small stature had once more shown the big bully that he was not to be meddled with. The red-wing saw his own helplessness and joined his jeering comrades who had gathered to see the fun; the pewee unconcernedly recommenced his endless fly chase.

Pittsburgh, Pa.

ल ज

THE NATURALIST AND THE MICROSCOPE.

BY WILLIAM B. DAVIS.

A GREAT many people, and not a few naturalists, have an idea that the purchase of a good working compound microscope means the expenditure of considerable money. An instrument that will fulfill all the requirements of an amateur can now be purchased from the makers as low as $10, and better yet, if one is smart—a first class microscope, which probably cost new say $50 to $75, can often be picked up second hand for a trifle. Nearly all the dealers keep a list of second hand instruments for sale.

For a number of years the writer has obtained great and increasing pleasure, particularly during the long winter evenings, from the views of the hidden world which the microscope reveals. To give an idea of the wonders to be thus found, one only has to consult the many books written on the subject. Every public library, as a rule, contains some—sufficient to say that there is hardly an object, no matter how insignificant, that does not become doubly interesting when sufficiently magnified and its true structure brought out.

Take a walk some summer day with a microscopist of some experience and you will be greatly astonished at his observations of the minute things in this world of ours—things that heretofore have entirely escaped your notice—but none the less important for being small. It was from watching a friend one spring afternoon collecting material for the succeeding winter's study that caused at least one person to become an enthusiastic microscopist. That walk still stands out fresh in my memory, although taken years ago. We had not proceeded far into the woods when my companion reached down and picked up a small twig; this, when examined with a hand-lens, disclosed the presence of any number of little fungi, closely resembling minute mushrooms or toadstools and known as the myxomycetes. If the appearance of the various members of this family is curious, what can we say of their life history? At one stage moving about, every micron an animal, and at another surely a vegetable.

A little further into the woods, and the practiced eye of my friend detected the filiments of Nitella in a small stream of water. When the stems of this plant are examined under the moderate power of a compound microscope, we see the protoplasm in each elongated cell (sometimes the cell over an inch in length) flowing majestically up one side, making a graceful turn at the end and flowing down the other side, and carrying along in its current the starch and other granules. The small piece of Nitella, which was carried home in the folds of a newspaper upon this occasion, was placed in a Mason fruit jar filled with water and lived and flourished without a change of water the entire fall and winter, and furnished amusement and instruction upon many occasions. The same fruit jar becomes the home in turn of countless beings—each with an interesting life history.

One piece of good advice in closing—let the prospective purchaser of a microscope perfect himself in the use of the lower powers before attempting the use of the high power objectives. Adherence to this will avoid many disappointments and much confusion.

Philadelphia, Pa.

જ ટ

THE SHOVELLER DUCK.

BY HATTIE WASHBURN.

THE snow had not yet left the gentle northern slopes nor the ice the sluggish streams, small treeless lakes and grass grown sloughs, when the shoveller led his long, wavering, V-shaped flock northward to Dakota's prairie and slowly circled downward to the pond near which he was reared. A noisy and happy throng they were as they swam gracefully over the chilly waters or walked awkwardly upon the ice which bound the margin of the pond, the bright orange of their great newly-washed feet contrasting beautifully with the melting snow.

As the spring advanced he chose his mate, and though the other members of his flock were scattered far and wide, he and his mate were daily seen upon his favorite pond, the somber brown and black plumage of the female contrasting strongly with his own bright colors, his glossy dark green head and neck, snow white breast shading into rich chestnut and the brilliant green, blue, brown and white of his wings and back. Truly Mistress Shoveller has reason to be proud of her lord resplendent in his wedding garments, for few of their tribe are more gaily dressed than he.

The ice and snow having disappeared, they frequented the edge of the pond where the soft rich mud beneath the shallow water furnished them with food which was obtained by stretching their necks downward and shovelling in the mud in that manner peculiar to themselves which gives them the name of "shoveller" as does the queer shape of the large black bill give them the other and perhaps more common name of "spoonbill." The upper mandible of this organ broadens from the base and curving downward at the sides assumes a shape not unlike an ordinary spoon. Beneath a thick clump of low bushes near the pond in due time a nest was made by scraping together the prairie grass and weeds with which each egg was covered until a setting of nine was completed when uncovering them the female began incubation and each day the dusky feathers from her breast added to the warmth and beauty of her nest.

The ducks were very trustful and swam placidly about the pond, even though the barnyard being near, it was frequented by cattle and human pedestrians and one need to approach very near before the male would utter his peculiar warning note and arise, closely followed by his obedient mate. Trustful they were and I grieve to state that their trust was shaken not by human agency but by a four-footed prowler of the night, who approached so stealthily that the setter narrowly escaped with her life while her grayish green treasures were destroyed, her nest torn asunder and a number of the broken though but partially emptied shells buried in the soft loam of a near-by field. The would be parents, saddened but hopeful, sought a new nesting site and this time being undisturbed one bright day the proud mother led ten downy ducklings from the nest toward the pond.

Now it chanced that a road led near the pond, a road furrowed by countless wheels and washed by the rains of many seasons until so deep in places that the mother, having led her offspring into this thoroughfare that fewer obstacles might impede their course, was forced to stretch her graceful neck upward to watch for danger upon either side. There no danger threatened but from the rear, for a team suddenly drove up and the ducklings were unable to escape from this trap their overly solicitous mother had led them into. Limping badly and with both wings dragging and apparently useless she hurried onward and they following in frightened haste turned repeated summersaults, displaying their downy yellow breasts and extremely short legs, until the driver becoming aware of their distress turned from the road and they reached the pond without farther adventure where they found their sire grandly breasting the waves to watch with pride their maiden voyage along the margin.

He passed the summer among familiar haunts, the head of this numerous and happy family, and in Autumn led them to a lake surrounded by trees and dotted with small wooded isles—one of those beautiful spots which breaks at intervals, the monotony of Dakota's level, grass-grown and treeless prairie. Save the presence of hunters this was the wild duck's paradise, but alas, their name was legion and empty cartridges lay like pebbles along the rocky margin or among the reeds and coarse, rank grasses. The shoveller and his family soon lost all confidence in mankind and passed most of the day afar from shore or close among the rushes, visiting their feeding grounds only in the early morning and at evening. In spite of these precautions their number was reduced, but this seemed not to grieve the father. Perhaps he was unable to count to ten or his children, having grown so like others of their kind, could not be identified. One morning while shoveling delightedly along a stretch of muddy shore a shot was unexpectedly fired among them and leaving one of their number flopping piteously in the shallow water, they flew toward the middle of the lake crossing in their path a narrow neck of land overgrown with low willows and rank grasses. As they crossed above this innocent looking spot a shot rang out and the shoveller with a despairing quack slowly settled downward while a hunter arose from among the grasses to view the victim at his feet whose life blood crimsoned the snowy breast and stained the withered rushes.

Goodwin, S. D.

USEFULNESS OF THE AMERICAN TOAD.

[Abridged from Bulletin 196 prepared by A. S. KIRKLAND, M. S., United States Department of Agriculture.]

THE heavy tax levied by insects on nearly all agricultural crops is well known to farmers. While the value of birds as destroyers of noxious insects is now becoming generally recognized, the common toad (*Bufo lentiginosus Americanus* Le. C.), nocturnal, of quiet habit and appearance, renders notable service to farmers and gardeners throughout the entire growing season; yet to many its worth is unknown, while to others it is even an object of disgust, if not of fear. Yet, judged by the standard of good works, the toad does not suffer by comparison with any of the lower animals.

To the nature lover there are few more interesting subjects than the development and habits of the toad. In New England toads do not bestir themselves until April or May, but in more southern latitudes March finds them wakening from their winter's sleep and beginning their annual migration towards the breeding ponds. The number of toads which migrate even to a small pond is remarkable. The writer once counted 356 toads on the shores of a pond containing scarcely half an acre. Mating is commenced as soon as the water is reached, or even before. The tiny black eggs, with their gelatinous covering, are laid in long "ropes," the envelope swelling to a notable degree as soon as it comes in contact with the water, thus forming a mass many times larger than the body of the parent toad. In two weeks, or even sooner if the water is warm, the eggs hatch and the young tadpoles feed greedily upon the gelatinous envelope. Next the slimy deposits common to ponds are attacked. The tadpoles grow rapidly, until by June or July the legs develop, the tail is absorbed, and the young toads leave the pond which has sheltered them, never to return except for brief visits at the mating season.

The little toads are very sensitive to heat and secrete themselves under leaves, rubbish, stones, etc., during the day; but let a vigorous shower descend and frequently walks, roads, and gardens at once become peopled with these thirsty leaping creatures. So sudden is their appearance under these conditions as to lead to the popular belief that they rain down. The inability of toads to endure heat serves as an indirect protection for them at this stage. They are delectable morsels to many birds, and, were it not for the fact that they are obliged to seek shelter by day, large numbers would be destroyed. As it is, many are devoured by the predaceous birds and mammals which prowl at night.

It seems probable that the toad does not begin to reproduce until the fourth year. The number of eggs laid by a full-grown female toad is remarkable. It is a rule of nature that where the chance for a species reaching maturity is small the fecundity is large, and this rule is well illustrated in the case of the animal under discussion. The writer once removed 1,279 eggs from a female toad which had already commenced laying. The total egg production is better indicated by the record of 7,587 and 11,545 eggs obtained from two toads by Dr. C. F. Hodge, Clark University, Worcester, Mass., as recorded in his book entitled "Nature Study and Life."

Many stories are extant concerning the longevity of the toad. These animals are said to have been found embedded in rocks, trees, masonry, etc., thus indicating that it was possible for them to exist in dormant condition for many years. The writer has gone to some trouble to investigate statements of this kind coming to his attention without finding a single case where there was conclusive evidence of such a prolonged dormant state. On the other hand, we have the experiment of M. Herrisant, who in 1777 embedded three toads in plaster and placed them in the archives of the French Academy of Sciences. At the end of eighteen months two of the toads were still alive. In 1817 Doctor Edwards repeated this experiment, but submerged the plaster blocks in water, with the result that all of the toads died. Buckland buried toads in cavities in sandstone and limestone and found that all the toads in sandstone were dead in thirteen months, while those in limestone survived for nearly two years.

The toad has a strong "homing" instinct, and lives year after year in the same locality. Convincing evidence has been furnished the writer of two toads that have occupied dooryards in two different towns for twelve and twenty-three years, respectively. In view of these facts, there can be little doubt that the toad attains to a considerable age.

The belief that the toad is venomous probably arises from its habit, when disturbed or roughly handled, of ejecting through the skin a certain milky acrid fluid. No harm attends contact with the fluid on the hands, but dogs attempting to bite toads show signs of discomfort, and even distress, due to this acrid skin secretion. That the fluid is not objectionable to all animals is shown by the avidity with which certain hawks and owls capture and eat toads.

Though living alone through the summer, it is not an uncommon thing to find a dozen or more toads hibernating in a colony under some convenient rock or board. Winter quarters are sought quite early in the fall beneath rocks, leaves, or rubbish, or in other places where the action of the frost will not be severely felt. Figuier states that these animals freeze without being killed, and it is not unusual to find toads in winter apparently frozen stiff some distance below the surface of the soil.

Soon after sundown, or even before on cool evenings, the toad emerges from its shelter and sallies forth in search of food. In country districts it nightly patrols over roadsides, gardens, cultivated and new-mown fields—in short, all places where insect life abounds and long grass or herbage does not obstruct its travel. In cities and villages the spots beneath electric lights are particularly favored, while lawns and walks also receive attention.

The toad is of direct service to man by reason of the noxious insects which it destroys. The writer a few years ago collected and examined 149 toads' stomachs, particular effort being made to secure representatives from different sections and from a wide range of places, i.e., gardens, fields, hills, woodlands, city streets, etc., during every month of the feeding season. From examination of these stomachs it was shown that at least 98 per cent. of the toads' food is of insect and, arranged in the order of quantity found, consisted of ants, cutworms, thousand-legged worms, tent caterpillars, ground beetles and allies, wire worm beetles and allies, weevils, grasshoppers and crickets, spiders, sow-bugs, potato bugs and a large number of miscellaneous character. The amount of food consumed by the toad is remarkable. Records have been given of the finding of 77 thousand-legged worms in one stomach, 37 tent caterpillars in another, 65 gypsy moth caterpillars in a third and 55 army worms in a fourth. The amount of food consumed by a toad is equivalent to four times its stomach capacity every twenty-four hours. In three months (June, July and August) a toad would destroy at the same ratio 9,720 injurious insects. The toad's worth is an established fact. Should it not receive protection?

The Amateur Naturalist.

A Journal for those who Study Nature from a love of it

ISSUED BI-MONTHLY.

Entered as Second-Class matter October 6, 1904, at the post office at Binghamton, N. Y.

SUBSCRIPTION, 50 CENTS PER YEAR.　　SINGLE COPIES, 10 CENTS

ADVERTISING RATES ON APPLICATION.

————————EDITED AND PUBLISHED BY————————

CHARLES D. PENDELL,

85-87 STATE STREET,　　-　-　-　　BINGHAMTON, N. Y.

On July 26 Commander Peary sailed in "The Roosevelt" for the frozen Arctic world. His destination is the North Pole. He expects to reach latitude 83 north off the most northerly point of Grant Land by September 15. The winter will be spent in preparation for the final "dash for the Pole" which is expected to start early in next February. The final stage of the journey will be made with twenty-five sledges, each in charge of an Eskimo and drawn by a team of six dogs. No effort has been spared that would contribute to the success of the expedition. Commander Peary is backed by plenty of experience, this being his nineth journey to the far north. It seems doubtful, however, if he or any other man ever reaches the Pole by the route outlined. A careful study of the explorations of the past in this direction would make it seem that other routes would hold out better opportunities for success, though the experience of Peary should lend weight to his judgment in matters pertaining to Arctic exploration.

A tornado in an interesting phenomenon, but not especially desirable. Binghamton was visited by one of these terrific wind storms shortly after 10 o'clock on the night of June 5th, which was the worst that has ever been known to have occurred in this section of the country. The track of the tornado was about two miles in length and possibly two hundred or more feet wide. Eight houses were completely demolished and upwards of one hundred were badly damaged. Big trees were torn up by the roots, twisted and torn and the fragments scattered like straw. Though several were injured, providentially there were no fatalities. Such in brief is the news report of what to many was a disastrous catastrophe. The tornado furnished an opportunity for viewing many curious features of this kind of storm, one of these being the numerous instances in which the most serious damage was wrought on what may be termed the leeward side of the wrecked buildings, roofs being frequently torn off and windows blown outward, and in one case the whole front of a large residence being laid flat on the ground on the side opposite to that from which the wind came, instead of being crushed in by the force of the elements as might more naturally be expected, though this latter feature was also often in evidence. A study of these features corroborates this summary of tornadoes in general: It is a funnel-shaped tube a half mile high, 6,000 feet in diameter at the top, 100 or more feet in diameter at the bottom. It travels with a forward motion, covering fifty to eighty miles an hour. The outer edge of the top revolves at a comparatively moderate rate; the rim near the bottom of the vortex at approximately 200 miles an hour. In the lower tube is thus produced tremendous contrifugal force, a partial vacuum causing objects in its path to explode and producing a low temperature. This cold generates the sheath of vapor that makes the funnel visible in the form of a cloud and causes a condensation, producing electric discharges, just as in thunderstorms on a large scale. The tornado's duration may vary from a few minutes to several hours. (In the one above mentioned not to exceed five minutes.) The wind's great velocity prostrates every obstacle in its path, its effect not only to hurling objects before it and to produce an explosive action in its vacuum, but also lifting bodies in a vertical direction, and hurling them about promiscuously.

The field for archæological research seems almost as unlimited as any branch of natural science, and if "the proper study of mankind is man," there is an abundance of material for study along the lines preceeding the dawn of history—or we might say of undiscovered history. New discoveries are constantly being made of the evidences of man's civilization and development, some of them in places remote from modern centers of enlightenment. Archæological remains are being exhumed in Siberia, and even in central Africa in what is known as the Umtali district, besides the better known localities of Egypt, the Arabian peninsula, Chaldea, Nineveh, Palestine, Asia Minor, the Druidical remains of France and England, those even more remote in time in Ireland and Switzerland, and the later but still unknown civilizations of America, Mexico, Central America, and Peru, with probably other localities as yet unknown. The study is one of absorbing interest. Nearly every collector has among his curios some Indian arrowheads, possibly a celt and some ancient coins. The mere collection and possession of these has a certain interest, but an analytical study of the habits, character and history of the races who have left to us these evidences of their existences is more so, but sometimes misleads the student into erroneous conclusions in regard to the chronology, the tendency being to give a date to the time when these people lived far antedating reason. An instance of this occurred in the finding of a piece of burnt timber under some sixty feet of silt in the lower Mississippi Valley. "Expert" scientists ascribed to it an age of at least 60,000 years, but subsequently a more careful comparison proved it to be without question a part of a river steamer and its age not more than 30 years! the changing of the bed, filling in of old channels and making of new being a yearly occurrence with the "Father of Waters."

A FIELD FANCY.

BY ROSCOE BRUMBAUGH.

We choose the grass-grown upland way
  And talk of days gone by;
We drink the scent of new-mown hay,
  The warm breath of the sky.

The bob white calls his mate to him,
  The vesper carols low;
Along the wood in shadows dim
  The night-hawks come and go.

So peaceful now this sea of green,
  The world is all at ease;
The hour so quiet and serene,
  No wind-song stirs the trees.

This is the rich land of our birth,
  And though we've wandered far,—
No sweeter spot in all the earth,
  No brighter bedtime star.

Wilkinsburg, Pa.

Bird Conditions in Western Pennsylvania for July.

BY C. LEON BRUMBAUGH.

JULY is the high noon of the year. The high tide of June has ebbed, leaving but faint traces of the swelling bird life and activity on the beach of the summer. It may be said, however, that the tidal waves still occasionally beat until about the 15th, when the lake birds and the tree swallows gather for migration.

All our birds but the goldfinch and the cedar wax-wing have already had at least one brood, and you may chance upon an occasional nest with eggs or unfledged young of the phœbe, wood thrush, golden-winged woodpecker, black-billed cuckoo, scarlet tanager, ovenbird, cardinal, vesper sparrow, indigo bunting, hairbird, and house wren— the second brood—early in the month. I have even found young in the nest of the wood thrush and car-

dinal on the 15th of August, but this is not usual. You will be almost certain to find young in any hummingbird's nest you may discover, for their young remain in the nest for three weeks after incubation. The nidologist finds occasional freaks in this matter of nest building and altricial young, due frequently to sickness of the female about nesting time, and to the fact that some birds, notably the golden-wing, the sparrows, the cardinal, wood thrush, quail, and the phœbe will build nests and deposit eggs as many as five times, if their former attempts are all abortive through accident.

July is the month of faithless identification afield. You will see a "new" bird on a fence, in the bushes or on the trees, and a sudden eagerness possesses you to pursue it for the purpose of making its acquaintance. You may chase it for half a mile, over swamp, and through tangle in the hope of fixing your field glass upon it long enough to catch the peculiar and unfamiliar markings. It may be days before you fall in with another—all your bird books having failed to help you out in the classification—when lo! some day you meet several of the same species in company with two familiar and well-known friends, and the secret is out—you have been observing immature young! It may be said that the young of few birds resemble the male, and many times little similarity is borne to the female, until after the first and in some species, the second and even the third year. This fact is puzzling, but extremely fascinating to the bird-student and bird-lover. It puts a wire edge on your wits.

Have all bird songs died out in the initial heat-tide of the year? Much of it has undoubtedly become but the memory of the ecstasy of June, not so much by reason of the languor of these days of the zenith-sun, perhaps, as because of the passing of the ardor of courtship and the common places following the brief "honeymoon," combined with the domestic cares—and they are tremendous to any bird—imposed by the addition of a number of hungry and helpless members of the household circle.

It is true that many songs are now to be heard only from dawn to nine and from sunset to twilight in the deeper woods, but the scarlet tanager, wood thrush, cardinal, golden-wing, chickadee, cuckoo, ovenbird, black-and-white creeping warbler, Carolina wren and the catbird may break forth in a dreamy song at any time throughout the entire day. The wood pewee, black-throated, blue-back and the vireos are constant in song in the woods, while in hot, brambly places the tireless indigo bunting, bush sparrows, Maryland yellow-throat, yellow-breasted chat—that Punchinello of the brambles—and an occasional chewink will greet you any sunny hour, golden plover and the meadow lark still pour out their charms. Thoreau sings:

Upon the lofty elm tree sprays
  The vireo rings, the changes meet
During these trivial summer days,
  Striving to lift our thoughts above the
    street.

In fact, the July woods and fields possess a strange fascination to the bird-lover, even though the bird melody has become, like the insect songs, a little stridulent and languorous, in keeping with the weather; and by some cool brook where, in fancy at least, the wood nymphs still are straying, he may see almost a procession of our entire summer residents, feathered Psyches at their bath. And the soul is glad of these things.

WOODLAND VOICES.
Lyrics of the golden time,
Ballads of the olden time,
  Troubadours from every tree
  All in tuneful harmony,
    Bring me in the glooming.

Fancies out from dreamland sent,
Idyls from their leafy tent,
  Wood-sprites whisper dreamily
  With such tireless constancy,
    I forget my moaning.

Wilkinsburg, Pa.

Siberian Archæology.

Excavations have recently been made in the Kurgans, or old turtle-back burying mounds, near Tomsk, in Siberia. Some of these, dating before the Russian conquest, contain beads, earrings, knives with artistically carved bone handles, copper kettles, rings, bracelets and ornaments of silver. The oldest mound was five or six centuries old. Those of more recent date showed evidence of a much deteriorated stage of civilization, very few metal objects being found, and the arrow heads and knife blades being made of bone. Discoveries made in Manchuria show a similar and perhaps cotemporaneous civilization. The researches are being continued.

MY BOTANY FRIENDS.

BY ALICE B. WAITE.

Along country way they study wild plant life,
Where flowers, ferns and brambles run rife.
They pluck rare blossoms to common weed,
From purple-thistle with its downy seed
To cinquefoil, chickweed, dandelion blow,
Yellow buttercup, daisy, bluets low,
Mossy wild-pink, feathery meadow rue,
Roadside chicory of azure hue,
Butterfly weeds growing tall and rank,
Blue-bells swinging from overhanging bank,
Partridge-vines twining o'er mossy bed,
Whip-poor-will shoe, marshy turtle head,
Jewel-weed, deer-grass, Indian-pipe;
Plucking bud, full flower, seeds when ripe

Thus roaming field, lane, and forest-walk,
Digging up bulb, corm and deep root-stalk,
Finding choice orchis beside the brook,
Pressing them flat 'neath heavy book;
Seeking the hardy rock-saxifrage,
Seeking it again on Botany's page;
Classifying flowers of field and wood—
Wild-rose, fire-lily and frail monk's-hood.

Studying "Gray's Manual" to refresh their
wits,
Dessecting blossoms to ragged bits,
Counting petals 'round a glowing heart,
Pulling off stamens, cutting style apart,
Studying cross-fertilization of plants—
How carried on by bees and ants
By brushing stamens as they lightly sup
In seeking nectar from flowery cup;
Thus carrying pollen from flower to flower
Through sunny field and woodland bower.

But do they see spiritual beauty when the
lilies unfold,
Spiritual beauty in their hearts of gold?
Do they read Love's message in the rose's
heart,
God's loving message that the flowers impart?
Can they solve their fragrant charm, their
magic power,
The quickening life force of each perfect flower?

South Lyme, Conn.

A Message From the Hills.

BY KATE A. JONES.

SUNSET, a cloudless sky, and the great hills all aglow: mingling with the rich green of the pines and spruces, which clothe their giant sides, are the white birches which gleam like frosted silver as the sunlight falls upon them. On every hand one sees the delicate greens of beech and poplar, the glow of red maples, and the white blossoms of sugar plum and hobble bush. Road sides and meadows have been golden with the graceful bells of the adder's-tongue—made even more attractive by the rich, mottled foliage.

The last of April we went in search of trailing arbutus. Hidden safely away under the leaves we found the fragrant blossoms, some pure white, others deep pink, and all of them very large. In a grove of pines we found some beautiful fern-like mosses, while the ground was red with the berries of the wintergreen. A field through which I often pass is really blue with the dainty blossoms of the blue-eyed grass.

May 29th we took a walk through the pine woods. The sky was cloudless, and the silence unbroken save by the faint sounds of insect life, and the songs of shy woodland birds. In the deeply shaded spots we found the painted trillium, dwarf gensing, spring beauty, bellwort, Jack-in-the-pulpit, star flowers, bluets, blue and white violets, the delicate foam flowers, and Solomon's seal. Many plants of wood sorrel, *Maianthemum Canadense* and *Clintonia borealis* were just ready to burst into bloom. A tiny brook was murmuring softly over the stones. Along its mossy banks we found the ferns—maiden hair, ternate grape fern, and Christmas fern, while the rocks were covered with the cheerful little polypody. It is Nature's resurrection time, and if we listen to her voice what lessons she will teach us through every fern leaf, every wayside flower, every bird song, and grand old mountain, we find grace and perfection in the ferns, beauty and sweetness in the flowers, faith and joy in the bird songs, and strength in the hills.

Grantham, N. H.

A Night Hawk's Courage.

BY WILLIAM B. DAVIS.

THE writer witnessed an exhibition of bravery on the part of a night hawk during the month of May that was truly marvelous. A party of us while on a geological excursion in Chester County, Pa., frightened one from her nest, if the bare ground can be so termed. The gentleman walking in advance of the others almost stepped upon the bird before she arose. It then flew to an adjoining rock say five feet away and occasionally hissed at us. Noting carefully the location of the eggs, we moved off and waited for her to return, and then moved up cautiously to the place again, although making no attempt at concealment and not without considerable noise. The mimicry was perfect, the plumage being in exact keeping with the surroundings, so much so that one of the party was unable to locate the bird, although within two feet and looking right straight at it. A gentleman present pointing his finger to within two or three inches of its beak exclaimed "Now do you see it?." The entire party of six or seven then passed by in single file within two feet of the bird, making considerable noise by the breaking of twigs under foot and talking all the while. During all this time the hawk never moved a muscle, deeming, no doubt, and very wisely, that she was better protected in her mimicry than she would be in flight. It is hardly necessary to add that either course was a safe one for her to pursue that day.

Philadelphia, Pa.

The Solitaire.

THE Solitaire (*Pezophaps solitaria*) is an extinct species of bird formerly abundant on the island of Rodriguez, mention of which was made in the article "Exterminated by Man," in Vol. I, No. 1, of THE AMATEUR NATURALIST. Probably the name of the original discoverer of this bird will never be known, and it might have been better for the birds had man not discovered them, as not fifty years elapsed after their discovery ere they had become numbered among the extinct species. M. Leguat visited the island in the year of the first recorded date of their discovery (1691) and to him we are indebted for what knowledge we have of this singular bird. His publication issued in 1708 gives the following account of its habits:

"Of all the birds in the island the most remarkable is that which goes by the name of the Solitaire, because it is very seldom seen in companies, though there are abundance of them. The feathers of the males are of a brown-grey color; the feet and beak are like a turkey's, but a little more crooked. They have scarcely any tail, but their hind part covered with feathers is roundish, like the crupper of a horse; they are taller than turkeys; the neck is straight, and a little longer in proportion than a turkey's, when it lifts up its head; its eye is black and lively, and its head without comb or cop. They never fly, their wings are too little to support the weight of their bodies; they serve only to beat themselves, and flutter when they call to one another. They will whirl about for twenty or thirty times together on the same side, during the space of four to five minutes. The motion of their wings makes then a noise very like a rattle, and one may hear it two hundred paces off. The bone of their wing grows greater towards the extremity and forms a little round mass under the feathers, as big as a musket ball. That and its beak are the chief defence of this bird. 'Tis very hard to catch it in the woods, but easy in open places, because we run faster than they, and sometimes we approach them without much trouble. From March to September they are extremely fat, and taste admirably well, especially while they are young. Some of the males weigh forty-five pounds. Though these birds will sometimes very familiarly come up near enough to one when we do not run after them, yet they will never grow tame. As soon as they are caught, they shed tears without crying, and refuse all manner of sustenance till they die. When these birds build their nests, they choose a clean place, gather together some palm leaves for that purpose, and heap them up a foot-and-a-half high from the ground, on which they sit. They never lay but one egg, which is much bigger than that of a goose. The male and female both cover it in their turns, and the young, which is not able to provide for itself in several months, is not hatched till at seven weeks' end. All the while they are sitting upon it they will not suffer any other bird of their species to come within two hundred yards round of the place; but what is very singular is, the males will never drive away the females, only when he perceives one he makes a noise with his wings to call the female, and she drives the unwelcome stranger away, not leaving it till 'tis without her bounds. The female does the same as to the males, and he drives them away. We have observed this several times, and I affirm it to be true. The combats between them on this occasion sometimes last pretty long, because the stranger only turns about, and does not fly [run] directly from the nest. However, the others do not forsake it till they have quite driven it out of their limits. After these birds have raised their young one, and left it to itself, they are always together, which the other birds are not, and though they happen to mingle with other birds of the same species, these two companions never disunite.

We have often remarked that some days after the young one leaves the nest a company of thirty or forty brings another young one to it, and the newly-fledged bird, with its father and mother joining in the band, march to some bye-place. We frequently followed them, and found that afterwards the old ones went each their way alone, or in couples, and left the two young ones together, which we called a marriage. This peculiarity has something in it which looks a little fabulous, nevertheless what I say is sincere truth, and what I have more than once observed with care and pleasure."

Extermination of the White Heron.

THE recent history of the white herons is pathetic in the extreme, as it is a tale of persecution and rapid extermination. It was a sad day when fashion decreed that the nuptial plumes of these birds should be worn as millinery ornaments. Feathers and scalps, rapine and blood are the accompaniments of savage life, but better things are expected of civilization—especially of civilized women. It is hardly possible that any women of the present day are unacquainted with all the horrible details of plume-hunting. The following pen picture of the horrors of the plume trade, drawn by Prof. T. Gilbert Pearson, secretary of the North Carolina Audubon Society, shows the work in all its bloody reality:

"In the tall bushes, growing in a secluded pond in a swamp, a small colony of herons had their nesting home. I accompanied a squirrel hunter one day to the spot, and the scene which met our eyes was not a pleasant one. I had expected to see some of the beautiful herons about their nests, or standing on the trees near by, but not a living one could be found, while here and there in the mud lay the lifeless forms of eight of the birds. They had been shot down and the skin bearing the plumes stripped from their backs. Flies were busily at work, and they swarmed up with hideous buzzings as we approached each spot where a victim lay. This was not the worst; in four of the nests young orphan birds could be seen who were clamoring piteously for food which their dead parents could never again bring to them. A little one was discovered lying with its head and neck hanging out of the nest, happily now past suffering. On higher ground the embers of a fire gave evidence of the plume hunters' camp.

"The next spring I visited this nesting site, but found only the old nests fast falling to decay.

"When man comes, slaughters and exterminates, nature does not restore."

This story of a single Florida colony is the story of what has happened in all of Florida, the Gulf coast of the United States, along the Mexican and Central American coast, both on the Atlantic and Pacific sides, and has extended into South America. From the enormous number of heron's plumes that are annually sold in the London feather market there is no doubt that plume hunters are at work wherever the white herons are found.

The Sun.

GREAT as may be the apparent size of the sun, and vivid as may be its light, it still is only one of those myriads of stars which form the Milky Way. But for us it is the center of a system or family of globes, and is the luminary whose invisible power upholds in space all the planets with their satellites, directs their regulated course and disseminates everywhere movement and life. Without it eternal night would envelope the earth, all created things upon it would perish, and a mantel of ice would cover its surface. Astronomy has weighed and measured the sun long ago, and in our days chemistry aided by physics makes an analysis of it. Prof. C. A. Young in an article in *Harper's Weekly* upon this point writes as follows:

The sun is a typical star, the nearest one, and not so far away as to prevent us from studying it in detail, and yet presenting conditions so different from those we can obtain in our laboratories that to a considerable extent it defies our reasonings and renders our conclusions merely conjectural.

We know, however, that its mean distance from the earth is very closely 93,000,000 miles; that its diameter is about 866,500 miles, or 109½ times that of the earth, and its bulk about 1,300,000 as great.

We know also that its mass is about 330,000 that of the earth and that consequently gravity upon its surface is about 27½ times as powerful as here. A man who here weighs 150 pounds would weigh more than two tons upon the sun, and there a squirrel would not be able to jump any more friskily than an elephant here.

Experiments with burning glasses make it certain that the effective temperature of the sun's surface taken as a whole (doubtless the actual temperature varies widely at different points) is much above any which we can produce by artificial means. Not even the electric furnace can rival it. Carried to the sun and kept there for a few hours only, the earth would melt and pass into vapor. The estimated temperature is about 12,000 degrees F., but cannot be regarded as exact.

The Life of a Seed.

Some interesting experiments are being made by the United States Department of Agriculture for the purpose of determining the extreme vitality of seeds. Over a hundred species of plants have been packed in a soil consisting of dry clay enclosed in pots, and buried at varying depths underground—eight sets at a depth of six inches, twelve at a depth of twenty, and a third set of twelve at a depth of three and a half feet. At the end of one, two, three, five, seven, ten, fifteen, twenty, twenty-five, thirty, forty and fifty years, a set from each depth will be exhumed and tested. The results of the experiment are likely to be of extraordinary value to agriculturists, both commercially and scientifically. Incidentally, it may be recalled that authentic cases are on record which prove that certain seeds have the power of sprouting after having been buried for long periods of time, reliable tests having shown that twelve out of twenty-one species have the power of germinating after twenty years.

Losses From Destructive Insects.

Insects are such insignificant things that, even when we know them to.be injurious, we rarely comprehend the extent of damage they do and the amount of loss they cause us. Dr. H. C. McCook in an article in *Harper's Weekly* gives some figures in this matter that are startling to one who has never studied it. The chinch bug, he says, caused a loss of $30,000,000 in 1871, upwards of $100,000,000 in 1874 and $80,000,000 in 1877. The Rocky Mountain locust in 1874 destroyed $100,000,000 of the crops in Kansas, Missouri, Nebraska and Iowa. The cotton caterpillar causes an average loss of $15,000,000 in the southern states, while in 1868 and 1873 this loss was doubled. The grain weevil inflicts an annual loss on us of $40,-000,000 and the codling moth destroys from $30,000,000 to $40,-000,000 of our fruit annually. These are but a few of the destructive insects which are working in our crops, and, if it were possible to compute the damage done by all, the figures given above would appear insignificant. It is a fortunate thing that for most of our destructive insects nature has provided enemies that keep them in check.

Earthquakes.

According to Prof. John Milne, who is generally regarded as authority on matters pertaining to earthquakes, about fifty earthquakes disturb the world throughout its mass, yearly. Between Jan. 1, 1899, and Jan.1,1902, the world-shaking earthquakes numbered 196, of which 25

originated west and south of Alaska, 14 west of Central America, 16 west of the Antilles, 12 west of the Andes, 29 east of North Japan, 41 south and east of Java, 17 north of Mauritius, 22 on the east side of the North Atlantic, 3 on the west side of the North Atlantic, 3 in the North Atlantic, and 14 in the Balkan, Caucasian and Himalayan regions. These sources are near the base of the steepest flexures, are all submarine except the last three, and their boundary ridges are mostly lined with volcanic peaks. Both on land and under the sea, the great earthquakes seem to be accompanied by a deepening of the furrows and an elevation of the flanking ridges. The elevation may reopen long-sealed volcanoes, as in the eruptions in the Antilles in 1692, 1718, 1766, 1797, 1802, 1812, 1836, and 1902. The small earthquakes — of which 10,000 a year are recorded in the world—have no sensible connection with volcanoes.

Ruins of Great City in Mexico.

The ruins of a large city have been discovered in a remote part of the State of Puebla, Mexico, by Francisco Rodriguez, an archæologist, who has just made a report of his find to the Mexican Government. The city contains large pyramids and extensive fortifications. It is situated in the midst of a dense forest, and a large amount of excavation will be necessary to learn its true extent and importance. The Mexican government has appointed a commission to thoroughly explore the ruins.

RANDOM NOTES.

The silk spider, found on the sea islands of South Carolina, produces two kinds of silk, yellow and white, having a continuous length of two miles.

Among the elevated lakes of the world may be mentioned Sevier Lake, in Utah, having an elevation of 4,600 feet. It is 120 miles south of Great Salt Lake, the altitude of which is 968 feet lower. It has no outlet and no trees grow upon its shores. By analysis its waters are found to contain in 1,000 parts 62.3 of chloride of sodium, 13.4 of sulphate of soda, 10.3 of chloride of magnesium, and 0.4 of sulphate of lime.

An interesting find of subterranean dwellings of primitive man has been made in County Antrim, Ireland, thus, in all probability, establishing the presence at one time in that part of Ireland of a race which occupied a great part of the European continent before the appearance of the earliest Celt. It is held by some that the Lapps are the living representatives of the early race to which these underground dwellings are ascribed.

The island of Make' is the largest of the Seychelles Islands, situated nearly in the center of the Indian Ocean. It is 18 miles long by 3 to 5 miles wide and has one mountain peak rising 3,000 feet above sea level. Its peculiar feature is the rapidly forming coral banks with which the island is surrounded so that coral is universally used for building the residences even of the poor. Near Fort Victoria is a large and beautiful church built of this substance.

The upper portions of our atmosphere are intensely cold, though on a bright warm day one might suppose that the sun would heat the air very warm at a distance of several miles above the earth. Small balloons, carrying only apparatus for automatically measuring and registering altitude, and arranged to make very high ascensions and then drop the apparatus by parachute or smaller balloon, have been employed to investigate the temperature at great heights. On November 26, last year, apparatus carried by one such balloon showed a temperature of 76 degrees below zero at a height of six and one-fourth miles.

The amount of blood in the human body is one-thirteenth of the body's weight.

The supply of radium, notwithstanding its great cost, falls far short of the demand for it.

The continent of Africa has about 480 species of land mammals peculiar to that continent, of which 95 species belong to the monkey family and 50 to the antelope family.

Certain species of animalcules have been suddenly changed from a freezing apparatus at a temperature 40° below zero to an oven 176° above—216°—and with no apparent harm.

Probably the highest temperature yet attained consists in concentrating sunlight. In experiments conducted in St. Louis 6,000 silvered glass mirrors were used to throw the rays on a single point. It is said that by this means heat is produced that will readily volitize every known substance.

The Minnesota Geological Survey places the number of lakes within the boundaries of that State at over 10,000, though not more than ten or twelve of this number can be called large. The water area of the State exceeds that of any other state, being more than 5,600 square miles, exclusive of Lake Superior. The general elevation is from 1,200 to 1,700 feet above sea level.

An English horticultural journal gives as the average age of trees of that country the following: oak, 1,600; lime, 583; yew, 3,000; pear, 269; apple, 80 to 175; ash, 400; ivy, 600; Scotch fir, 90 to 120. The average longevity of other trees are as follows: plane, 1,200; Spanish chestnut, 700; Cedar of Lebanon, 800; larch, 270; and the juniper, 380.

Among the Cascade Mountains in Oregon are many natural curiosities. One is Rogue River Falls which are one hundred and ninety-six feet high. Another is the Mystic or Sunken Lake. The lake is forty or fifty miles around and is like a hole sunken in the ground; near the center of it there is an island with a crater in it. In the crater is a beautiful blue sheet of water without a ripple on it. It is as much as a thousand feet down to the water of the crater and is inaccessible except in one place and there it is almost so.

The Amateur Naturalist.

"To him who in the love of Nature holds commun on with her visible forms, she speaks a various language."

VOLUME 2.   BINGHAMTON, NEW YORK, SEPTEMBER, 1905.   NUMBER 5.

SOME VEGETABLE IMMIGRANTS.

BY WILLARD N. CLUTE.

THOSE who have not considered the matter are likely to think that the flora of a region is fixed and unchanging. So long as the salient features of the plant covering, the trees and shrubs, continue the same from year to year, it does not occur to them that there may be a constant struggle for very existence going on among the lesser denizens of the region. The fact is, however, that not only is the vegetation of a region constantly changing but it often proceeds so rapidly as to be visible to the casual observer. Each change, it may be added, marks the termination of a struggle in which, since the ground is already fully populated, one species must recede as another advances. Sometimes man himself is unintentionally the ally of one or another plant as when he cuts down a forest and allows the weeds to crowd in, or drains a swamp to the detriment of the sedges and the delight of dry ground species. Usually, however, the struggle, silent though deadly, is waged between species that must depend upon themselves alone, and which triumph or go down to defeat, accordingly as they are equipped for such encounters.

It is not meant that the plants actually grapple with one another, hacking and thrusting like doughty knights of old; no, indeed. When one looks at a wayside bank smiling in the rays of the morning sun, or surveys a broad expanse of flower-decked meadow, all appears serene. No signs of a struggle are visible for the plants settle their difficulties by quieter methods which might be likened to the siege of a city. Theirs is a policy of starving out the enemy and they follow it with cold-blooded persistance. There is not room for all, therefore the weakest must die. How relentlessly the dandelions and plantains on the lawn crowded the gentler grasses, spreading their leaves about, shutting out the light and eventually occupying the soil, if unmolested. All many plants ask is a foot-hold; they will attend to the rest themselves.

When these pushing, vigorous species begin to crowd our proteges of the plant world a new war is waged, with man and all his artifices on one side. And strange as it may seem it is not always the man's side that wins. Everyone who has ever tried to get the better of pigweed, or toadflax, or the multitudinous other foes of the farmer, knows this to be true. Plant your garden and neglect it and immediately the alien hordes appear. The black bindweed reaches through the palings, the sheep-sorrel creeps under the fence, and the toadflax makes unnoticed forays underground. Only valiant work with hoe, rake and trowel will save the crops now. Did anyone ever hear of a garden that got beyond bounds and choked out the weeds in the neighboring vacant lots? Never! And the reason appears to be that we have cultivated our food-plants so long, protecting them from their enemies, that they have in a measure lost the power of protecting themselves. The pigweed, the purslane, and the rest, on the other hand, have had to look out for their own interests and they do it with a facility that would excite only our admiration were their operations confined to other people's gardens.

We call these ubiquitous and irrepressible species, weeds, for they conform to all the requirements of the definition that says that a weed is a plant out of place. Many of them bear handsome flowers and first entered our fields by way of the flower garden. That almost ineradicable plant, the toadflax or butter and eggs, is said to have first been cultivated in this country for its flowers, just as many a near relative is cultivated to this day, for it comes of a noble plant family. Considered with an eye to beauty only, it, too, is a handsome plant. Its sole defect is its vigorous manner of taking the best of everything. Possibly it tried to usurp the entire flower-garden; in any event it has long been under sentence of banishment, though no means have yet been found to carry out the sentence to the letter. The various species of mallow have doubtless escaped to our meadows and roadsides from the garden and with them have gone live-forever, bouncing Bet, rocket, various pinks and many another.

The flower-garden, however, is not responsible for all our weeds. The vegetable garden has contributed its share, for there are exceptions to the general rule that our garden plants cannot take care of themselves. The carrot, parsnip, caraway, tansy, chickory and water cresses have shown no lack of ability in the art of self-defence. It may be noted that few of these are noxious weeds. That the tansy has spread to an occasional retired fence corner, or that the water cress has found new ditches and streams to its liking, should not be charged too strictly against the list of garden plants.

When we come to inquire into the nativity of our worst weeds we find that their family lines nearly all run back to European countries. Nor can we say so much against them when we remember that we, too, like the burdock, the thistle and the butter-cup, came from the Old World to supplant another species with better claims to the soil. That so many plants from Europe and Asia should thrive so amazingly in a new world seems due to the fact that American plants have not been subjected to quite the same stress as those of the Old World. The immigrants thus appear among our plants like practiced soldiers among raw troops. But just as the raw troops may occasionally furnish a soldier of unusual talents, so have American plants supplied a few instances in which the tables have been turned. We must not forget the career of the prickly pear in Australia or that of the ditch-moss in England.

How the advance guard of these conquering hosts reached our shores would make a long and interesting story if it could be written. Some stole in as stowaways in grain and fodder; others, as the burdock, doubtless clung to the fleece of sheep or cattle coming to the New World; still others, persuing the independent course that has characterized their actions among us reached shipboard on parachute or wings of their own and landed by the same means at the end of the voyage. Many more may have first reached American fields as impurities among the seeds of farm and garden.

If the weeds may be considered the black sheep of the vegetable world, then some of the plant families are entitled to great credit for several of them have not produced a single bad weed. The orchids and heaths may be cited as conspicuous examples and the rose family is due for nearly as much commendation. The composites, on the other hand, have produced a large number. This is to be expected since the composites are the most specialized of plants which argues an ability to conquer their full share of the world. To their ranks belong the burdock, daisy, elecampane, thistle, chickory, goat's-beard, dandelion, orange hawkweed and prickly lettuce from abroad and the cockle-bur, tick-seeds, rag-weed and various others from native sources. The borage family has fewer noxious species, but makes up for the lack in number by viciousness of individuals. The hound's-tongue, gromwell and viper's bugloss are enough to cite. The qualities of the last may be inferred from the common name of blue devils. The weeds show a curious tendency to group about the dicotyledonous plant families. In the plants with but a single cotyledon or seed leaf there are no bad weeds if we except a few coarse grasses.

As our country has become settled, the changes wrought in the plant covering by man has produced a few weeds from among our native plants; that is, some species finding territory to their liking where man has disturbed the balance of nature have pushed in and taken possession. But the majority of the plant foes that trouble farmer and gardener are from the ranks of the vegetable immigrants. Accustomed to shift for themselves in a flora where competition is keen, they find the task of conquering new territory an easy one and thrive in spite of other plants and their ally, man.

Binghamton, N. Y.

❁ ❧

As far as our present knowledge can determine, some, at least, of the meteors once belonged to a globe developed in true geological epochs, which has since been shattered into fragments by agencies with which we are not acquainted. The existence of organic remains in some has been proven.

THE SPONGE.

BY GEORGE MIDDLETON.

THE sponge is the horny skeleton or framework which was made by and supported the living parts. These living parts are protoplasmic in constituency, and are next to the diatoms the lowest form of life, the latest "radiomicrobes" in my opinion being merely a chemical and not an organic formation.

The living parts of the sponge are found both in the interior and on its surface. The opening or canals through the sponge are lined with this matter, whether found in the "canals" of the sponge themselves or imbedded in the substance; the living sponge particles are represented each by a semi-independent mass of protoplasm.

The sponge is a colony and not a single unit—not having been differentiated, and in fact incapable of those higher functions. In other words it is composed of aggregated masses of living particles, budding out one from the other, and while doing so manufacture the "body" which supports it, and this is what we know as "sponge."

The microscope shows these living units in various guises. Some are formless; that is having no distinctive form, ever altering as size increases, resembling somewhat the amœba.

The members of the sponge colony wander about through the meshes of their home seizing food and grow. As the colony becomes opulent the home grows too, and in time when quarters seem to grow somewhat restricted, the sponge "papas" and "mamas," in a way not understood by the most learned oologist, reproduce their kind. Whether by eggs or by divisions I do not know. But whatever means are taken to perpetuate their kind, it is effective.*

I think I said the sponge is a simple illustration of protoplasmic life, but I must retract that statement in a measure, because what seems to us a very simple matter, may really be of great complexity, when viewed by "science's piercing gaze."

How characteristic are certain units of this living sponge colony which claim the lining membrane of the canal as their home? Again, other units people the inner lining.

The nourishment for these diverse individuals is obtained from the water which circulates through the canals.

The water enters at the large apertures (pores) and by the time that it has passed out again through the oscula the food matter needful to the sponge organization has been absorbed. Thus there is a perpetual current

---

* According to excellent authority sponges of some species propogate "by budding or gemmation, a process involving cell-fission or ordinary division of cells." Other species also reproduce sexually by ova and spermatozoa.—[ED.

swept in at the pores and out at the oscula which furnishes sustenance to the living organism, and incidentally to the size of the home.

In the sides of the sponge passages are little chambers or recesses. Lining the chambers we see living sponge units of a type different from the shapeless specks which occur in the meshes of the sponge skeleton. In these recesses are living particles whose free extremities are raised into a kind of collar from which project filaments known as flagellum. These wave to and fro in the water and, acting as a brush, sweep water into the pores, the current thus created carrying it through the canals and finally through the oscula. This circulation serves the purpose of nutrition and also furnishes the oxygen gas which is a necessity of sponge life, the same as in all life; and when the current finally passes from the sponge it is laden with the waste matter, inevitable to all living organisms, and to dead matter, too, in fact, because the gradual disintegration after life has departed is in a direct ratio to the expulsion of effete matter from the living protoplasm (used in a general sense).

The sponge skeleton is very tenacious and I have seen it perpetuated in limestone passages, large and small; even the texture being clearly reproduced. Like all other pseudomorphs, though, it had lost its individuality, and was as much limestone as the surrounding matrix.

It has been said, but never proved to my knowledge, that the sponge harbors parasites, in common with all other living substances. But the question is, where is it all to end? If the sponge has parasites, and those have their guests, and so on, will we ever land where we can say, "We know it all, now"? I doubt this continued multiplication of life. There must surely be a limit, and to be told that a flea had a parasite would surely open the way to a very big doubt. However, in the case of the sponge I am not prepared to say.

In these days of scientific attainment those of us who make a pretense of studying the varying processes of nature are likely to give thought to almost any proposition which bears in the remotest degree on the evolution of life, and while the chasm between protoplasmic and human life as we know it—as we understand it—seems very great, still in the final analysis it may not be so, as all life is founded on the one principle, to deviate from which means death and annihilation—not at a loss to nature, however, because there is no loss—simply a separating of the different constituents into their primal form, and a recombination with certain elements that form an entirely distinct individuality. Thus, in the case of the sponge, after its usefulness as a home for the living protoplasm is over, though its form be perpetuated in the stone that has formed about it, its principles of life have departed from it in their earlier forms, and though still locked up in its stony heart, yet its texture and substance has departed somewhere somehow; and now, unrecognizable as a sponge, still shows the outside structure of its earlier form. I have seen on Tybee Island, a certain form of sea weed (of a red color) almost entirely covered with this protoplasmic matter, not necessarily that which makes the "sponge" possible, but surely a substance which resembles the sponge host, and gives off a fetid odor— apparently dying the same as other organisms, and "smelling" some, too.

This seems a lower form than the "jelly fish" (of which there are hundreds cast up on Tybee's beach monthly) but from observation I am inclined to believe there is some family connection between them, though I have not been able to demonstrate a solid foundation for this belief, as yet.

No matter from what point of view, or from whatever standpoint of scientific attainment the subject is approached, the "thinkers" are filled with an awe of the sublime conceptions that made possible the knowledge up to this day attained in the wonderful field of nature.

Savannah, Ga.

ભ ℔

THE CANADA JAY.

THE range of the Canada jay (*Perisoreus Canadensis*) covers all the northern United States from New England west to the Rocky Mountains and all of southeastern Canada. In length the bird is about eleven and one half inches. In color its back, wings and tail are smoky gray, its throat white shading into gray on the under part; its forehead is a buff white shading to black. *American Ornithology* gives the following interesting description of its habits:

From the name by which this bird is commonly known, such as "Whisky Jack," "Moose Bird," "Camp Robber" and scores of others, the character of these jays can well be imagined. They have all the bad traits common to our well known blue jay, and, like him, have no redeeming virtues except their beauty, vivacity, audacity and sense of humor. I believe no bird has the sense of humor so keenly developed as the jay and his relative, the crow. They like to play tricks on anybody or anything, and will cackle with glee when anything particularly pleases them, but when the joke is on them they usually show their appreciation in squawks of anger. Living as they do, in sparsely settled regions, the Canada jay are very tame as compared to ours; consequently their actions are more often noted and commented upon.

They are thieves of the first order, and their knavery is not confined to the theft of eatables but they will take anything that they can lay their hands, or rather their bill upon. If there is anything in sight that is especially valuable to mankind and absolutely worthless to them, they will exercise their wits to acquire it. They are the constant companions of hunters, trappers and lumbermen in the northern woodland and watching them at their antics is one of the chief sources of amusement of these men. They will enter a camp, go right inside the tents and carry off everything, edible

or not, and what is too large they will tear to pieces and carry off in
sections. They will work like beavers carrying articles away and storing
them in crevices under the bark of trees or even under leaves, and, from my
observations of jays, I think they remember the location of everything they
conceal and dig it up at some future date. They eat carasses, pelts and
skins, and frequently annoy trappers by taking the bait from their traps or
damaging the skins of animals that they have caught. Their food consists
largely of flesh when it can be obtained and, like the blue jay, they rob the
nests of other birds of their young and eggs. At other seasons of the year
they eat berries, acorns, buds and seeds of all kinds. They are practically
resident wherever they are found and usually commence nesting long before
the snow is off the ground.

ᚼ ᚼ

THE PAPAW.
Asimina triloba.

BARK gray, smooth; young shoots dark pubescent; leaves obovate, acute, cuneate at
base; petioles short; flowers appearing with the leaves; sepals three; petals six,
dull red, the outer set larger: stamens many, in a globose mass; pistils several,
distinct, but few ripening; fruit a fleshy pod-like structure, containing several large
flattish seeds.—A shrub or small tree in rich moist soil ranging from western New York,
Michigan and Nebraska southward to the Gulf.

Although the papaw extends northward in the Mississippi Valley nearly
to the Canadian border, and spreads eastward under the salubrious influence of the Great Lakes until it crosses this border into Ontario, it is essentially a southern species and is at its best nearer the Gulf. The northern
botanist coming upon a papaw thicket for the first time is likely to be
impressed with the tropical appearance of the plant and is not surprised
upon being told that this is the most northern member of the great custard-
apple family which in the tropics numbers nearly five hundred species. The
large leaves, for the most part borne near the extremities of the slender
branches, give our tree an individuality that prevents its ever being confused with any of the other plants that affect the same habitat.

In other ways the tree shows its southern kinship. The leaf-buds are
not encased in scales during the winter as they are in strictly northern
plants, but hang from the bare branches, naked save for their coating of
dark brown hairs. In appearance they strongly suggest the leaf-buds of
the witch-hazel. Nor do they develop with the first warm days of spring
as the naked buds might lead one to expect. On the contrary the leaves are
not fully spread in the States north of the Ohio River until the last week in
May—near the end of the season for the early spring flowers, and some
time after the other trees have donned their summer foliage.

The flower-buds appear to be formed in autumn and to pass the winter
in wrappings similar to those of the leaf-buds. The flowers are as deliberate

in opening as are the leaves and when they do bloom present a singular appearance strung along the nearly naked branches as represented in our illustration. At a little distance, a papaw thicket at flowering time looks like a thicket through which a forest fire has recently passed.

FLOWERING BRANCH OF THE PAPAW—Asimina triloba.

The flowers approach globose in form and hang downward from the axils of the leaves. The sepals are rather short, but the six petals are quite large, often twice as large as those in the illustration, and increase in size for some time after the flower has opened. Although the flower is constructed upon what appears to be the plan of three, it is really a dicotyledon. As floral relationships go, however, it is not very high in development and it is noticeable that it belongs to the group which includes the barberry, magnolia, mandrake, water-lily, calycanthus and other plants whose flowers have not yet settled down into the usual five-parted type of the dicotyledons. The color of the petals may be described as dull red, though Gray calls them dull purple and others describe them as brown. Careful observation will show that red and brown colors predominate. The flowers are apparently adapted for cross-pollination for the stigmas, though ripening at about the same time as the stamens, project beyond them and so are not easily self-pollinated. The two sets of thick, veiny petals alternate with each other and enclose the essential organs except for a triangular opening which resembles the entrance to the flower of Canada ginger. The smaller inner petals secrete an abundance of nectar on the inner side near the base, and here the color is paler, serving as an efficient "honey-guide." The flowers have a heavy, yeasty, rather disagreeable odor with just a hint of the smell of the ripe fruit in it. The flowers are overrun with ants and small beetles that should prove most effective agents in pollination if the pistils could be affected by the pollen in the same flower. The plant, however, rarely produces much fruit in the northern parts of its range, though the flowers are usually abundant and each contains several pistils. The larvæ of an interesting butterfly, the zebra swallow-tail (*Iphiclides ajax*), feeds upon the papaw and it is suggested that the adult insect is the species likeliest to affect cross-pollination. This insect, like the tree itself, is rather southern in its distribution, and its rarity may account for the scarcity of fruits in the Northern States. It may be queried in passing how the ants discover so quickly that the papaws are in bloom. In flowers nearer the ground their presence is not so surprising, but in papaw flowers twenty feet or more in the air one might expect to find them absent.

Late in autumn the banana-like fruit ripens. At maturity it is four inches or more long, a third as broad, and reddish yellow with a thick rind that encloses a soft fragrant pulp in which are embedded a half a dozen or more large smooth seeds. The pulp is edible and has a flavor that at once brings to mind the flavor of the tropical fruits of this family if one has ever eaten them. To many palates the flavor is too strong to be agreeable, but there is enough demand for the fruit in some sections to cause it to be sent to market in some quantity. The leaves remain on the tree until late in the autumn and before falling turn to a rich clear yellow that lights up the thickets for some days.—*The American Botanist*.

The Amateur Naturalist.

A Journal for those who Study Nature from a love of it

ISSUED BI-MONTHLY.

Entered as Second-Class matter October 6, 1904, at the post office at Binghamton, N Y.

SUBSCRIPTION, 50 CENTS PER YEAR.   SINGLE COPIES, 10 CENTS

ADVERTISING RATES ON APPLICATION.

————————EDITED AND PUBLISHED BY——————

CHARLES D. PENDELL,

85-87 STATE STREET, - - - BINGHAMTON, N. Y.

The idea has been conceived by a few that our "Random Notes" department is merely a place where we fill in a lot of little "clippings," and one of our valued exchanges, with this idea evidently in mind, makes frequent use of the department for "fillers" for his own magazine, and so far without giving credit. It will not be amiss therefore to say that the idea is wholly erroneous, that department involving as much original investigation and study on the part of the editor as any part of this magazine. Clippings are used very infrequently, and when used credit is given. No item appears in those columns that has not been verified on what seems to be good authority.

With the coming of the long evenings of fall and winter there will doubtless be formed in many localities clubs or social societies for the purpose of literary and scientific entertainment, and that such organizations can be productive of much good there can be no doubt. There is no magazine that we know of that will so well meet the needs of such a society as THE AMATEUR NATURALIST. Many and varied forms of questions will naturally be suggested, and the whole realm of nature study will from time to time be brought up for discussion, and magazines devoted to some specialized branch of natural science will have their place. But in this magazine there can hardly be a meeting but that some articles will be found that will be pertinent to the subject that may be under consideration. THE AMATEUR NATURALIST is not seeking to become the "official organ" of any such society, having already received that honor from the Binghamton Academy of Science; but nevertheless we are confident that good use could be made of its pages by all such, and will make special rates to clubs for that purpose. Our subscribers might well take the initiative in the forming of such societies for the long evenings before us. A half a dozen to ten would form a good nucleus to commence with, and after a few meetings in which original or selected papers were read and followed by informal discussion, the interest would cause a natural and spontaneous growth. Such societies should not be too scientific or too formal, but held informally as parlor meetings in different neighborhoods would bring out much latent talent and prove a profitable and interesting form of sociability.

In response to the suggestion made by several that we open an "ex-change department," we would say that any who are subscribers may send in their exchange notice and they will be given a place gratis. Should the number of such exchange notices be sufficient the "department" will natu-rally result. But in giving opportunity for exchange, subscribers must bear in mind that advertisements of goods for sale cannot be classed as exchanges.

Vacations are mostly over for this year and many of our subscribers have enjoyed a portion of their time in closer and more intimate contact with nature. In many instances their observations or experiences are such as would interest others, and we would suggest that they write them up and give their fellow-naturalists the benefit. The mutual interchange of ideas and experiences can hardly fail to be helpful no less to the writer than to the reader, and the columns of this magazine are open. Let us hear from you.

Mr. O. W. Barrett, who has for some time held the important position as Entomologist and Botanist at the Porto Rico Experiment Station, Mayaguez, Porto Rico, has resigned that position to accept the position of Plant Introducer with the Bureau of Plant Industry, Washington, D. C. We understand that the distribution of the tropical and sub-tropical plant stock, as well as the inspection of incoming and outgoing shipments of such stock, will be in his charge. Several articles by Mr. Barrett have interested the readers of THE AMATEUR NATURALIST. The change is in the nature of a promotion and involves much responsibility. We trust, however, that Mr. Barrett will find leisure to favor our readers with other contributions at no distant date.

Aerial navigation has been a matter of experiment for a long time, and has not yet passed the experimental stage; but the successful trial trip recently made in New York City by Mr. A. Roy Knabenshue, of Ohio, marks the beginning of a new era in the matter of air-flight. Mr. Knabenshue's machine is a combination of balloon and flying machine, a gas bag 62 feet long and containing 7,000 cubic feet of hydrogen gas, gives it bouyancy. The frame work 38 feet long supports the apparatus, including a ten horse-power engine, and weighs, engine included, but 210 pounds. By means of a screw propeller in the Toledo II, as the airship is named, the inventor rose from the ground to a height of 1,000 feet and navigated against the wind at a speed varying from 6 to 15 miles an hour, and after going from Central Park to the Battery returned to his starting place. Mr. Knabenshue him-self says he has not solved the problem of aerial navigation, but a successful start has been made and its further perfection is simply a matter of experi-ment and development.

THE BROWN THRASHER AT DAY-BREAK.

BY INA LORD MC DAVITT.

I felt the leaves rustle,
    I heard the birds sing,
I felt, far above me,
    The spell of a wing.

Singer of the morning;
    This is what he sings,
Something high and fragile
    Above the ken of kings.

Magic song from No Man's Land,
    Fairy princes wooing,
Sweeter music ne'er was sung
    For the soul's undoing!

Singer of the morning;
    Listen while he sings
Something high and fragile
    Above the ken of kings!

Vineland, N. J.

Glimpses.

BY KATE A. JONES.

SITTING on the lawn of this pretty farm home, beneath the shade of a giant maple, there is much to study and enjoy. On every side rise the great hills bathed in brilliant sunlight. White cloud ships freighted with dreams are sailing lazily across the blue. Nature's gardens (the broad intervals) are glorious with buttercups, white daisies with "hearts of gold," and black-eyed Susans,—"beautiful wild country girls with striking brunette faces, and gowns of yellow and black, which fairly make the meadows dance with life and gaiety."

Almost at my feet is a sparrow so small he seems hardly more than a pinch of feathers. Across the road on a fence post is a catbird evidently expressing his opinion of me in very emphatic bird language, while trying to persuade me into the belief he is a cat in feathers. As I watch a ruby throated humming bird darting about among the columbines, I am reminded of our Father's care of even the smallest creature.

A goldfinch resplendant in black and gold is balancing himself on a slender flower stalk; a downy woodpecker is tapping on the limb of a tree, and a black-capped chickadee is calling merrily to his mate. Swallows and robins are every where busy with their family cares.

A bed of white phlox is alive with beautiful butterflies; some velvety black, their wings edged with cream color, and dotted with blue; others are pale yellow while a few are richly gowned in brown and gold. A saucy red squirrel is running along the stone wall on mischief bent, while "like trains of cars on tracks of plush I hear the level bee." Some distance away is a pretty lake, the surface of which is white with water lilies; along the shore we find pink pogonia, turtle-head and the large purple-fringed orchis.

We follow a brook which winds through the meadow to hide itself in the deep woods. Here we find new ferns and mosses, rattlesnake plantain with its dainty white blossoms, the ghostly Indian pipe and curious fungus growths, some richly shaded brown ones take the form of morning glories, pure white ones resemble sea mosses, while others are brilliantly colored in pink, orange, purple, and red.

Tired with our wanderings we paused to rest and watch the sun set in a "cloistered spot where golden lilies tinkled, thrushes sang, and every leaf breathed peace."

Gantham, N. H.

Big Trees and the Forestry Building at Portland.

BY WILLIS S. EDSON.

IT makes one feel small to see the tremendous scale on which nature has laid out her landscape here. One almost feels lost in the fastnesses of some limitless forest as he speeds hour after hour through the big timber. And so you feel easier as you roll into the station, and realize that towering trees are no longer frowning down upon you, and that the forests on either hand are not pressing in upon you as though to overwhelm you and make you a prisoner for life. Yes, you were interested, nay, captivated, by the giant monarchs of the forests. You would not have missed the sight for anything. The overpowering sense of the bigness of things has made its lasting impression upon us and we realize as never before that it all has to be seen to be appreciated and understood.

We were more than ever anxious to see the Forestry building, the fame of which has gone out into the world wherever tidings of the Lewis and Clark Centennial Exposition has spread.

The first glimpse of the building was gained as we came up through the charming bit of natural park which adjoins the building on one side and which is one of the attractive features of the fair grounds.

Through the vista of large trees there loomed before me the biggest log house I have ever seen, or expect to see. I guess that the base logs are four or five feet in diameter—measurements are hard to make with the eye under such conditions—and then I step up beside one of them and find that it is considerably above my head. Six feet through and fifty-two feet long. I try to picture the tree as it stood on its native heath down along the mighty Columbia River. Fifty-two feet and more straight up towards heaven's blue before a single branch breaks forth. I pass through a colonnade of six-foot logs, thirty feet high which supports a gallery over the main entrance, and I find on the other side a similar colonnade of giant logs. Inside the building as I pass through its length, I count fifty-two columns of fir and cedar trees forty feet high which support the roof.

As I contemplate the impressive sight, my thoughts go back to the journey through the miles and miles of giant timber, and I think: Well the trees didn't look quite so big around when I sped past them as they do here. At that moment I overheard the words of a young woman standing near me, and I am startled at what she says:

"Why, papa," she exclaims, addressing a gentleman standing at her side, "these are not big trees. Why, we have seen plenty of them in the forest and are larger in diameter than any logs in this building. And the evident disappointment in face and voice tell me that the Forestry building has not come up to her expectations, and that there are plenty of bigger logs still uncut in the forest. I find they are residents of the place, and every season take their camping outfit and revel in the heart of the woods and find trees that for size put the logs in the Forestry building to shame. It sets me to thinking, and I begin to realize that even the splendid Forestry building, made up of its six-foot logs, fifty-two feet long, cannot tell all the story of the wonderful forests of Washington and Oregon.

Of the 94,560 square miles comprised in the state of Oregon, over 54,000, it is estimated, are covered with timber, nearly one-sixth of the total amount of standing merchantable timber in the United States. This means that there are over 3,000,000,000,000 feet of standing timber, which, when cut and sawed into lumber, will make piles of lumber which figures are inadequate to express. And Washington has a larger percentage of her area wooded than has Oregon, being 70 per cent., or 47,000 square miles. Idaho, which was part of the original Oregon country, discovered by Lewis and Clark, has an area of woodland which is estimated at 35,000 square miles, or 42 per cent. of the total area of the state.

The fir, hemlock, cedar and the spruce are the trees found in the greatest abundance, while the larch, pine, ash, maple, alder, cherry, juniper, cypress, mountain mahogany and cottonwood are also plentiful. But the red, yellow and silver firs are the most valuable commercially. The introduction of western hemlock to the market as a building material has met with many obstacles. A strong prejudice has been aroused by the name of hemlock, owing to the quality of the eastern species of the same name. So great is this prejudice even now that, although large quantities of the timber are cut and sold, it is sold under false or fictitious names, such as Alaska pine, and Washington pine, spruce or fir. Western hemlock, as such, has no market standing.

Last year Oregon cut approximately 1,405,000,000 feet of lumber, valued at $12,650,000. The mills of the Columbia River basin produced 600,000,000 feet, and the Portland mills 413,559,285 feet, and the Astoria mills 71,358,480 feet. The cargo trade from the Columbia River aggregated 164,564,015 feet. Foreign shipments showed a gain of 12,607,161 feet, and domestic shipments an increase of 24,313,653 feet. In addition to this there were over 10,000,000 lath cut.

Washington last year shipped 480,889,911 feet of lumber to domestic points, including Hawaii, Alaska and Manila. Her foreign shipments to China and Japan, South Africa, Peru, Chili and other South American ports; Mexico, the United Kingdom and Europe totaled 186,144,995 feet. The rail shipments amounted to nearly as much more as the total cargo shipment, being 658,290,000 feet of lumber, and 5,759,640,000 pieces of shingles. Washington has over 80,000 men employed in the lumbering industry, and over $47,000,000 are paid them annually in wages, so it can readily be seen how large and important is the lumbering industry to that state, and Oregon can tell even a bigger story in the matter of men employed and wages paid.

Tacoma is the largest lumber manufacturing center of Washington, and for that matter of the Pacific coast. Of the total lumber cut of Washington the mills of Tacoma cut nearly a sixth. Tacoma claims to be the largest lumber center west of Minneapolis, and the largest lumber exporting port in the world. The largest cargo ever loaded was taken on board the United States transport Dix at Tacoma and comprised 3,800,000 feet.

For the first three months of the present year the Pacific Coast Lumber Manufacturers' Association reports an aggregate of 259,276,222 feet of lumber, 7,481,781 feet of lath, 554,615 feet of pickets and 18,775,-325 shingles in foreign and domestic cargo shipments from the two states.

Underground Water Supply.

BY CHARLES D. PENDELL.

THE development and study of the water supply in the region of the great Central Plains has afforded excellent opportunity for the observation of the geological formation of the territory involved and has led to some remarkably deep borings which are described by N. H. Darton in his report on the geology and underground water sources of the great plains. More than 1,000 deep

wells have been sunk in South Dakota east of the Missouri River, most of which are from 500 to 1,000 feet deep, though in rare instances the depth exceeds 2,500 feet. The aggregate flow from these wells is estimated to be about 7,000,000 gallons daily. The source of this water is believed to be in the Black Hills and in the Rocky Mountains and permeates the entire formation of Dakota sandstone which underlies the whole state, or nearly so. Over sixty artesian wells are reported in Brule County, most of them between 800 and 1,000 feet deep. They nearly all furnish large flows of excellent water, which is much used for irrigation. Many of the towns, however, derive their water supply from these artesian wells, Pierre and Yankton being among those thus supplied. Several of the wells are reported to have a flow of 3,000 gallons per minute. The average flow of a six inch well is about 500 gallons. One of the wells in Chamberlain has a pressure of 100 pounds to the square inch and develops 10 horsepower.

In numerous instances the water power developed from these wells is utilized to run flour mills, and other machinery. A well at Springfield, though its pressure is not so great as that of many others in the state, has a flow of 3,292 gallons per minute, and furnishes power for a 60-barrel flour mill by day and for an electric light plant by night. At Woonsocket, South Dakota, is a well which throws a stream of three inches to the height of 97 feet. All the sandstones contain water, but the volume and pressure usually is greater in the lower beds.

A careful study of the underground water supply is also being carried on in Nebraska and Kansas. Lincoln, Neb., and other large places are thus supplied with water. A well at Deerfield, 7 miles west of Omaha, is 1430 feet deep, 10 inches in diameter, has a pressure of 15 pounds to the square inch and is said to flow over a million gallons a day.

In a deep boring at Lincoln, Neb., says Mr. Darton, the Carboniferous beds are reported to have been entered at a depth of 269 feet, and distinctive fossils were obtained as low as 1,090 feet. Below this depth magnesian limestones were reported to a depth of 1,813 feet, presumably in part, at least, of Mississippian age. They were underlain by rocks believed to represent the Trenton, St. Peter, lower magnesian, and Potsdam to 2,192⅔ feet, where supposed Sioux quartzite was entered and continued to the bottom of the well at 2,463 feet.

Osmium is a bluish-white metal with a violet luster, discovered nearly a century ago in the residue from dissolved platinum ores. Its specific gravity is three times that of iron and twice that of lead. It is also the most infusible of metals, even the electric arc, which causes most other metals to melt and flow like water, produces only the faintest traces of fusion on osmium. Alloyed with iridium, which defies acids, nothing better has been found with which to tip gold pens.

THE BLACKBIRD CHORUS.

BY HATTIE WASHBURN.

They come like a swiftly floating cloud
    Of sable forms with flame decked wings,
And the wood is filled with music loud
    For sweet the blackbird chorus sings.

'Tis a song of hope and happiness
    In which a thousand voices ring,
And far beyond human words express
    The hopeful spirit of the spring.

A song of promise and kindly cheer;
    Promise of what the summer bring:
A joy to all who but lend an ear
    When loud the blackbird chorus sings.

Goodwin, S. D.

A Nest for Mites (Acarina).

BY DR. ALFRED C. STOKES.

THERE is no fruit that grows in the temperate regions of the world quite so satisfying as a good apple, and I am not ashamed to confess that up to a recent time I have generally devoured my supply by putting it, blossom-end and all, where it would "do the most good." But hereafter—well, any way, that blossom-end deserves a better fate, and it shall be carefully removed and reserved for another purpose.

It occurred to me, not long ago, that there might be some interesting things microscopical in the depression over which the remains of the blossom stand guard in the mature fruit, as it seemed a likely place for floating fungi or fungous spores to lodge and to develop, or for floating particles of various kinds, and after gently scraping out the contents of the hollow into a little water, I examined them with a one-fifth inch objective. I was not disappointed. Bacilli were numerous. Fungous spores were there by the myriad; vegetable hairs, dried and shrivelled but with the hollow pre-empted by the mycelial threads of fungi; fragments of the dried parts of the flower were coated with fungous spores and with bacteria; wrinkled grains of pollen, brown and brittle, increased the list. It was all interesting until a wriggling, sprawling, clawing mite, lively as any creature of the kind can be on smooth glass, suddenly came into the field. A flat, oval Arachnid, with eight legs vainly striving for a foot-hold on the slippery surface, the pointed head almost sunk into the body, which is not differentiated into thorax and abdomen, it struggled as if it realized that it had forever left a warm and snug home in that blossom-end of the apple, and had fallen into a cold world and a wet one. Living mites, really living spiders of a low form, had not been in my pre-arranged programme, and dead ones were simply out of the question. Dead mites? Why I am afraid to tell how many dead bodies I found in the blossom-end of a single apple, and the apple was not a big one either, and the fruit had just come into my home from the city dealer. Would you believe me if I should put the number at six? Make the examination for yourself, and you will feel as I do, that the blossom-end of an apple deserves to be removed and laid aside, gently but firmly. I can swallow fungi, and pollen, and bacilli, and hairs, and spores and dust, without permanently losing my mental poise, but living mites, and dead mites, and mites' shrivelled up skins, and mites' excrement—would you?

Value of Insect Remedies.

Investigations made by the United States Department of Agriculture have clearly shown that from the depredations of insects the loss to orchard, garden and farm crops frequently amounts to from 15 to 75 per cent. of the entire product, and innumerable instances could be pointed out where such loss has been sustained year after year, while now by the adoption of remedial measures, large yields are regularly secured with an insignificant expenditure for treatment.

It has been established that in the case of the apple crop spraying will protect from 50 to 75 per cent. of the fruit which would otherwise be wormy, and that in actual marketing experience the price has been enhanced from $1 to $2.50 per barrel, and this at a cost of only about 10 cents per tree for labor and material. This is especially true of regions where the codling moth has but one fall brood annually.

In the case of one orchard in Virginia, only one-third of which was sprayed, the result was an increase in the yield of sound fruit in the portion treated of nearly 50 per cent., and an increase of the value of this fruit over the rest of 100 per cent. The loss from not having treated the other two-thirds was estimated at $2,500.

The saving to the plum crop and other small fruits frequently amounts to the securing of a perfect crop where otherwise no yield whatever of sound fruit could be secured.

A Philippine Volcano.

Sixty kilometers, or about thirty miles due south of Manilla, is one of the most active and vicious volcanoes in the world. Scientific men have said that the damage done by volcanoes is not in proportion to their height, but that the lower ones often do the most damage.

Vesuvius and Mount Pelee are both about 3,000 feet in height and have both made a great deal of trouble for people living in their neighborhood. Taal Volcano, our neighbor, is less than 500 feet in height, and is loctaed on a small island in the middle of a lake fourteen miles long by ten wide. History records many destructive eruptions of Taal, often occurring at intervals of about six years; but the volcano is never entirely idle.

A column of steam is constantly rising from the crater, and on clear mornings this can be seen from Manilla, rising over a range of low mountains in Cavite Province.

Last June these clouds of steam could be seen very plainly, every morning, continuing until the sky became cloudy, toward noon, thereby cutting off the view. At that time people living in the neighborhood of the volcano expected an eruption, but beyond throwing out a little lava and a great deal of steam, accompanied by rumblings and explosions, and changing the interior arrangement of the crater, nothing happened, and in three or four weeks every thing had quieted down.

Although the mountain is only a few hundred feet high, the crater is almost a mile in diameter, and the floor is about on a level with the lake that surrounds the island.

Inside the crater are three lakes, one in the center, of boiling hot water of a bright sulphur-yellow color, that fills a crater that one of my companions said was the active crater when he visited the place a few months before; another lake, right at our feet as we stood on the south rim of the crater, was of red water, of the color of iron rust, and on the left side of the crater was a long lake of green water.

On the extreme south of the main crater was a hole about a hundred feet in diameter, out of which a column of steam was rising, with a churning and clugging sound, and occasionally a dull booming explosion away down deep underground, and every few seconds a stream of jet black mud, boiling hot, was spurting up, often to a height of five hundred feet, and as it went up, a popping noise like fire-crackers came from the stream of mud. Sometimes the mud would hiss like a rocket as it went up; and, as the jet fell back, a cloud of dazzling white steam would disengage from the mud, and float off over the rim.

The water of the lake has a distinct taste of sulphur. They say that when the lake is smooth the towers of an old church, and the ruins of the old Spanish city of Taal may be seen deep in the waters of the lake, where they sank many years ago, during an earthquake and an eruption of the volcano. However this may be, there is a ruined city on the shore of the lake, that is also known by the name of Taal, and another city of the same name has been built at a little safer distance, no doubt profiting by the experience of the older towns.

It is several years since Taal has been active, to the extent of throwing out rocks, but people living in the neighborhood say that it may go off at any day. Although the volcano is over thirty miles in a straight line from Manilla, its eruptions have been violent enough to throw stones weighing half a pound each to such a height that they have fallen in the streets of Manilla, and the clouds of dust and cinders have obscured the sun, making lights necessary in the daytime, even at greater distance.—*Mineral Collector.*

Largest Flowers in the World.

The flowers of the rafflesia (*R. Arnoldi*), which expand more than thirty inches, are easily the largest flowers in the world. If our measurements were merely from the tip of one petal to the tip of another, however, a South American orchid (*Cypripedium caudatum*) would lead for the lateral petals, from which the plant gets its scientific name, grow to the enormous length of twenty-eight inches, according to Kerner. The same author states that one of the tropical aristolochias, with whose relatives, the Dutchman's pipe and Canada ginger, we are all familiar, often grows to be fifteen inches long and somewhat wider. Children use them for caps in play and are able to draw them down

over their ears. The largest flower growing on a tree is said by Kerner to be a species of magnolia (*M. Campbelli*). The petals are bright red and spread nearly ten inches. Other large flowers are, the lotus, various water lilies, cacti, and the opium poppy, which reach diameters of from eight to fifteen inches.—*The American Botanist.*

Singular Fences.

Rider Haggard has written of a fence in Africa built entirely of elephants' tusks, and though regarded by some as highly improbable is not necessarily so. What might seem even more singular does exist. A Maine newspaper relates that a member of the Life Saving Station at Small Point has gathered enough swords of the swordfish so that he has constructed of them a picket fence forty feet in length.

It is a well known fact that the elk drops his horns in the colder season of the year, and that the casual hunter traveling over the country often will find several of them in the course of a day's journey. A man living at Livingston, Mont., has his house and lot entirely enclosed by a fence made of elks' horns. The owner started in with a small collection of these horns but soon conceived the idea of making a fence of them and took advantage of every opportunity to add to his collection. They are stood upon end and fastened together by a railing, making a strong but singular looking fence. One hundred and sixty-eight pairs of antlers are used in its construction.

RANDOM NOTES.

A list of over 200 insects that damage corn at various stages has been compiled, yet as a garden crop sweet corn is remarkably free from troubles.

The largest block of granite ever quarried, exceeding considerably the famous "Cleopatras Needle," was quarried at Redstone, N. H. It is 145 feet long, 35 feet wide and 28 feet deep. The blast took 300 pounds of powder, and the concussion shook the entire village. The cleavage was absolutely perfect, as it split like a block of wood.

The Dakota sandstone is a formation of the upper Cretaceous age, and contains abundant plant and molluscan remains in its outcroppings. The mollusca remains are fresh water forms which occur in considerable variety. Many of the wells driven attain great depth, and in wells near Esmond, South Dakota, fresh water mollusks are found in considerable numbers at a depth of 785 feet, and plant impressions were found in a well near Hitchcock.

American Machinist has figured out the weight of the earth on this wise: A cubic foot of earth weighs about five and a half times as much as a cubic foot of water. A cubic mile of earth then weighs 25,649,300,000 tons. The volume of the earth is 259,880,-000,000 cubic miles. The weight of the world without its atmosphere is 6,666,250,000,-000,000,000,000 tons. If we add to this the weight of the atmosphere given above we get a grand total—6,666,255,819,600,000,-000,000 tons.

In the limestone regions of Tennessee are numerous caves, mostly unexplored. Several in the Cumberland Mountains are 100 feet deep and miles in extent. A considerable river has been discovered in one at a depth of 400 feet; another opening perpendicularly into a mountain has never been fathomed. In some of these caves are large deposits of fossil bones of extinct animals. In some places are seen impressions of the feet of animals in lime stone. Tracts of several acres have sunk into caverns 100 feet deep. In many places are interesting remains and fortifications, similar to those found in Ohio.

The peat bogs of Ireland are estimated to have a fuel value of 5,000,000 tons of coal.

In ancient times many of the mountains of Palestine were terraced, and some of these terraces still remain.

The remains of sixty mastodons have been found in New York State. All have been discovered in what was evidently old river banks—their ancient feeding grounds.

Radium only exists as a chloride or bromide. It is never isolated because it would be immediately oxidized by the air, whereas as a chloride or bromide it undergoes no change.

The Island of Hogolen, in the Polynesia, is an immense coral atoll, 130 miles in circumference, having four entrance passages. On the reef and within it are seventy islands.

The Arsinoitherium, a fossil monster of Egypt, had a head nearly a yard long, with a pair of small horns near the eyes and an enormous double long horn on the nasal region. If differed, however, from the rhinoceros and was probably more nearly related to the early elephants.

Pointing out the need of protecting egrets, or white herons, attention has been called to the possibilities of egret-farming. This has been successfully established at Tunis, and as egret-plumes are worth more than their weight in gold, the profits from cutting the feathers from the birds should be large.

As the result of 29 years of experiments, it is shown that in the winter months more than half of the amount of moisture (snow and rain) that falls penetrates into the soil and becomes available for the supply of springs, while in the summer only one-quarter of the rainfall is absorbed by the soil. The maximum quantity of water in the soil is at a depth of about 40 inches.

The sensation of seeing for the first time is difficult to imagine. A man of thirty, blind from birth, who was successfully operated on, on being told to look, his ears directed him to the source of the sound, when his recollection of what he had felt upon himself showed him that he must be looking upon a mouth and a face—those of the surgeon. The first sight of yellow made him feel very sick, but red gave him pleasure.

The Amateur Naturalist.

A MAGAZINE FOR ALL STUDENTS OF NATURE.

VOLUME III.   ASHLAND MAINE, JANUARY, 1906.   NUMBER 1.

SOME NOTABLE SOUTHERN PLANTS.

BY GEORGE MIDDLETON.

AMONG the wonders of plant life, the sensitive plant (*Mimosa*) which is a native of this section, has some sensitive nerves, which will effect the plant at the slightest touch.

The elongated tube of the "Pitcher Plant" (side-saddle family, order Sarraceniaceæ), the yellow trumpets, and the spotted varieties, common in bogs of this locality, have no odor, but I have seen them with all kinds of insects drowned within their cups, probably filled by rain. Some are not as tightly drawn as others, and cannot hold water. Whether or not they absorb the juices of their victims, I know not of my own knowledge, though there is little doubt in my mind that they do so.

The low-growing nettle, with its pure white, star-like blossoms, produces more discomfort to the sixteenth part of an inch than almost any other of our common plants, unless it is the common cactus (*Opuntia vulgaris*) which with its countless, almost microscopic spines, makes misery for all who pick their fruit. This last is also armed with spines which in themselves are no mean antagonists. But the small ones are the limit, like the nettle. Though caused by no super-sensitiveness of the plant, they will be readily recognized as an effective means of defence. In the *Opuntia*, though the leaves of the common varieties are palatable and succulent, no animal will try more than once to eat it. Now that the wizard of the vegetable (or floral) world, Luther Burbank, has perfected a spineless and thornless cactus from the Opuntia, it will in time form one of the most important of food plants.

Among flowering trees there is none that measures up to our Southern laurel (*Magnolia grandiflora*), which in this section attains noble proportions. The large, fleshy white flowers, with their superb fragrance, set in a background of dark, shiny green leaves is as perfect a picture of purity as the mind can conceive of. A perfect tree is a grand sight; symetrical, its evergreen leaves, and in summer the lovely flowers—it is one that lasts with memory. It well deserves a high place in the tree kingdom, and in the hearts of all lovers of the higher thoughts of life; having none of those baneful qualities which have given to others an unenviable reputation, it certainly deserves high rank.

The laurel has long been symbolic of heroism, and here in the South, as elsewhere, where attainable, on memorial days, a wreath formed of its leaves is reverently placed upon the graves of our departed heroes—those of the gray; those of the blue.

None other can rise to the height of its fame, as typifying the love and veneration of us all to our heroes who have passed away. A relic of antiquity, it is to-day as then, one of the brightest memories of mankind.

At this season of the year, (autumn) with the dew-berry, blackberry, huckle berry, whortle berry and others of summer all gone, the persimmon, chinquapin, and hickory and walnuts are in full fruitage. The persimmon, however, is the more satisfying, and after frost falls they are at their best. But don't make the mistake of biting into an unripe one, as they are extremely astringent when green. This tree is a member of the ebony family of the order Ebonaceæ. This is a small family and the *Diospyros Virginiana* is the only species which deserves notice.

The persimmon and the pickaniny are now almost inseperable, and what with the "woody" chinquapin, the little darkeys in all the glory of a voracious appetite and multi-colored rags, finds ready diversion in the woods. Then there are the nuts, but as they usually require a certain amount of labor to reach the meat, are not quite so popular with them.

The leaves, red and yellow, and the *Opuntia vulgaris*, or prickly pear, before mentioned, as it is known locally, are also fall products enjoyed by them.

Among the shrubs which attract the most attention is the crepe myrtle which is extensively grown in Savannah. The flowers of this shrub almost completely cover the plant, and at a distance is a solid mass of color on the perfect shrub.

We have transplanted here from the islands round about the palm, or palmetto tree, and an avenue in Colonial Park lends a distinctive sub-tropical air to the landscape, heightened by others with almost equal individuality.

This park is an old colonial cemetery, in which are buried the ancestors of many of Savannah's prominent families, heroes and representative men in their days. Here was discovered the remains of Gen. Nathaniel Green, which were subsequently re-interred with full honors under the monument to his memory in Green

Square, at Savannah. Thus after 100 years had past, the deeds of our hero were honored as if of yesterday.

The giant of the palmetto family, of which I have spoken, is very numerous along the southern coast, and is the principal figure on the seal of our sister state, South Carolina.

The most important tree of our southern forests, in a commercial sense, is the long leaf pine, which furnishes rosin, turpentine and other by-products, to the uses of humanity. It furnishes the principal parts of our dwellings, and is an important factor in our everyday life.

Forty feet below the surface, whilst drilling an artesian well, a tree trunk that had been laid low in a lagoon and subsequently covered by the wash of ages with deposits of marl, quicksand, etc., was found. This proves, (if no other proof were available), its antiquity: though analogous forms have been found in Jura-Trias deposits in the coal measures. The time necessary to cover this fallen giant with such an almost inconceivable amount of earth is beyond computation. No one knows accurately the values to allow for the subsidence and elevation of land areas, and its subsequent erosion by the sea. Tybee is eighteen miles away with an altitude of about six feet at its highest, while at Savannah it is about eighteen feet. The age of the stratas are inconceivable to the lay mind, and at best it requires an inordinate stretch of imagination to even approximate it. Who would believe it anyway, when the scientists all differ?

Among the vines distinctly southern, the "Southern smilax" is the most popular for decorative purposes; with its glossy green leaves and red berries, it lends itself with a wonderful effect to any decorative scheme that could be suggested.

The yellow jessamine is a sight to behold in the spring with its abundance of fragrant canary-yellow blossoms, though the essence is poisonous. But no one cares to eat flowers anyway. To see them with a backing of Spanish moss, and twining over trees and bushes, is something never to be forgotten.

The Passion flower (or May pap) is a most wonderful flower to look at, though too fragile to gain popular favor.

Among the grasses, the cat-tails, wild rice, marsh and allied plants are attractive at flowering time, which is in August. Those growing on the sand dunes of Tybee are lovely, and as ornaments for a vase, have a never dying beauty, even though their lively green has given place to the sere.

But the chief glory of the fall is the golden-rod which grows here in riotous profusion, the September fields and woods being ablaze with their rich color. And well named they are, too, but the weedy smell of their foliage makes much handling disagreeable.

There are so many beautiful plants of the low-growing habit that even to enumerate them would be to lengthen out this article to undue proportions. At another time I shall endeavor to describe them fully.

Savannah, Ga.

SPRING MOODS.

BY MARY-LEE VAN HOOK.

"I dreamed that as I wandered by the way,
Bare winter suddenly was changed to spring."

A STRONG wind blew from the east and it was cold although April was far spent. White caps on the grey and somber lake were like the billows of snow that so lately had rested upon its frozen surface. A woman walked the lonely beach, back and forth, where the sand was smoothest. Slowly she walked and looked long at the water and watched the white crests come in and lap the sand. Sometimes she stooped down and wrote something in the wet sand and waited for a wave to come and blot it out. Then she wrote again —always the same thing. Again she walked, now where the stones were heaped, left there by waves which had brought them from the far north. She pulled her coat closely about her but the wind pierced through and struck her chill. It blew her hair about and beat against her cheek. Bitter drops overflowed her eyes and her heart was heavy as the great mass of ice that but a short time ago had fallen from the pier. The lake knew of hearts too heavy, of burdens too great, and utter loneliness, but to the woman it told nothing; it only wiped out what she had written. So again she walked back and forth and her heart was bitter cold.

The regular tap of the flicker on the limb of a dead oak resounded in the still air. In the distance a song sparrow sang his sweet note ending in an abrupt trill that left the ear unsatisfied until it was repeated again and again. The woman's heart bounded as she wandered in the woods. She stood and looked at the bright glory of the budding maple and at the silver bloom of the willow. Now a breeze blew the dead oak leaves about and one leaf flew past her quickly; no, it was a little kinglet, its gold crown glittering in the sunlight. Up and down the ravine she climbed aud did not care if sometimes she fell, for the earth was sweet and odorous. Hepatica leaves were pink, and purple, and red, and there were some fresh green ones. The pure blossoms springing from a mass of downy buds seemed full of the earth message as they looked up at her. She gathered some and buried her face in their fragrance. Other flowers she found; spring beauties, and wind-flowers that swayed with the slightest breeze, and bloodroot, each bud of which was folded about with leaf of tender green, and slightly pink as if with a faint memory of the bloodroot stock from which it sprang. The woman felt her heart grow warm with the promise of life, hope and joy, and a song came to her lips again and again—always the same song, and there was spring in her heart.

Chicago. Ill.

NATURAL HISTORY CLUBS.

BY WM. B. DAVIS

WHEN "one touch of Nature makes the whole world kin" was written, Shakespeare hardly had in mind its applicability to Natural History Clubs, and yet there is something about the nature studies that has this effect. The result of the popular Natural History Clubs that are being formed all over the country are underestimated in their importance. In the first place there can be no more entertaining study for man than man and his environment, and the tendency to form small societies which have for their aim the special studies that Nature affords are good signs of the times. It is rather difficult in fact to find a town of any pretension that does not have its amateur organization formed for the purpose of investigation along these lines—if not boasting of an actual scientific society. The many good popular books that are being written upon these subjects and which are in such active demand, have all had a tendency for good and have made their influence felt. The writer asked the librarian of a large public library which books, after fiction, were in the greatest demand and was surprised to hear that just at that particular season (the spring) that those pertaining to nature studies had an extensive call.

Were we to put aside entirely the material benefit to be derived by an increased knowledge of our surroundings, surely societies of the kind referred to only attract the better thinking of the community. The collection of individuals that can once in a while forget our ever increasing commercialism and frivolity and actually enjoy the influence of nature, is to say the least refreshing.

Philadelphia, Pa.

THE BATTLE: A WINTER SKECTH.

BY NORMAN O. FOERSTER.

THE spectacular splendor of autumn is of short duration. In one short week the trees are almost bared, the myriad leaves swarm to their dead congeners on the earth. The firm grasp of frost manifests the power of the approaching cold weather.

Yet, after all, winter comes upon us furtively. A brief respite—the golden haze of Indian Summer—disarms all thought of the inevitable siege; the contending forces of summer and winter become languid under the temporary sway of the milder season.

But with what unrelenting cruelty—ferocity in its suddenness—the boreal wind heralds the coming sovereign; a plenipotentiary that voices the savagery of his nation! The dismal wind that before with its vituperative howling made us shudder, no longer sweeps with its unseen, stinging ammunition, but, its strength exhausted, drives the unresisting flaky battalions to destruction. The warm earth swallows them up eagerly, but as usual, persistance and resources prevail. True, there is no diminution in the avidity with which the flurry is absorbed, but the constantly pouring hordes, by their very infinity of number, gradually gain a foothold. Then, not mollified by this victory, the countless invaders stream in.

In the morning when we gaze upon the battlefield of this nocturnal conflict, the flaky struggle is over, and the potentates themselves are in combat, in comparison with which the strife of the snowy crystals was but the prelusive skirmish. The long arms of a powerful foe hold a tenacious grasp on the bare limbs of the trees, despite a frantic expostulation against the smother-weight. Finally they tremble beneath the burden and the invader plunges headlong into that division of his forces which holds the earth in subjection. The white puffs that sweep from the powdery ranks occasionally gather in great clouds which, rising over the field of carnage, muffle the noises of the struggling elements. The very frigidity of the irresistible foe, congealing all, prevents the crimson discoloration that would otherwise make the scene hideous.

"The combat deepens," and now the overlord of the combatants, enraged by his struggling vassals, sweeps his whole force against the two enemies. The north wind, rushing into battle, dislodges the level lines of snow on the trees. Array after array of the snowy ranks is plunged to destruction below. But even while the freed limbs are exulting, they are forced to bow before their new master.

The opposing forces beneath are molded by the plastic art of the wind into a marvellous architecture. The military power of the wind has been evinced, and now his æsthetic capabilities are manifested by the most exquisitely perfect conceptions. Now a vast, level sea is formed, illimitable and monotonous, suddenly changed to a grassy prairie, rolling with fruitfulness. Again a medieval castle rises up, with well worn moats and forbidding battlements, a leaf flag bravely flaunting on a weed pole. As a memorial of a forgotten age are the mounds that denote the burial-place of an unfamiliar people, mounds clothed in sepulchral whiteness.

Evening brings an end to the strife. The fatigued opponents fall into a deep slumber, the wind is at last appeased, the sullen gray of the sky gives place to the steely, star-lit cope of the heavens. A muffled feeling, a vague stupor, pervades the air; the snow mantle rests inert, passive; and overhead stretches that unsolved, unfathomable mystery, the sky—the stars of its galaxy clustered like a snow flurry.

Pittsburg, Pa.

Spain was not always a bad ruler. Hardly had Spain occupied the Americas when she sent across the Atlantic to these shores scientific explorers, botanists, scholars, and engineers: she established schools of the higher learning, and many of her viceroys, in Mexico as well as in South America, were men enlightened and progressive. Her explorers were stout hearted men, whose exploits, told in quaint old chronicles, compel the admiration of all impartial readers.

A WORD FOR MOSSES.

BY DR WM. WHITMAN BAILEY.

AFTER all the wild flowers have gone; when we can no longer, after diligent search, find even the spider-like yellow blossom of witch-hazel in the woods, or "butter and eggs" in the meadows, we turn for consolation to the mosses. These, like the poor, we have always with us. The more one examines them the more fascinating become these delicate creatures. To study them properly one needs both a dissecting and a compound microscope, the first for the gross examination of preparations, which are afterwards removed to the more powerful instrument. The beginner without directions, is so apt to begin wrong end to. High power lenses are for very small objects; for general study the low-powers are much the more useful. Moreover, it takes skill and instruction to use the compound microscope to advantage. How many persons have I set right who were using right instruments wrongly, and thus wasting precious time.

The parts of mosses upon which we depend for indentification are extremely small. Everyone will recall the pedicels, bearing capsules or urns at their summits. These in a general way only, may be called the female flowers, though flowers as we know them, mosses have not. We can, in the same restricted way, call them the fruit, though they are but slightly analogous even to that. Reproductive organs it is perfectly correct to call them. This is not the place to enter upon the modern view or interpretation of the productive process in mosses; it presupposes other knowledge. I confine myself here simply to what one sees. A capsule, *theca*, or urn, then has generally a ring obout its mouth, called the *annulus*, upon which a series of teeth, always a multiple of 4, is supported. These processes are collectively called *peristone*, and may or may not be accompanied by additional *cilia* and *ciliotae*. The whole opening is generally covered by a lid, which assumes many beautiful forms, and is known as the *operculum*. This, in its turn, has a hood-like or mitre-like cap which is usually deciduous, and is called the *calvptra*. The so-called fruit may be borne on the axis, either terminally or laterally, and upon this fact hinges the classification of mosses. It is not always easy at first to determine this. When the fruit is terminal the main stem may be continued by so-called "innovations"—axillary shoots arrising below but over-topping the stem by vertical growth. We have often been perplexed by these.

Indeed, anyone who takes up the study of mosses must be pre_ pared for hard work; every step in advance, however, is delight. ful, so exquisite are the objects examined.

Why should these almost invisible parts be so marvelously fashioned? The little scales on a butter-fly's wing are more gorgeous in pattern and color than any Japanese fan. The ornamentation of a diatom more intricate than any design of man. The lines on the last are so minute as to require the highest power of our best microscopes to resolve. Why this exquisite finish? We find it throughout nature. Sometimes it would seem as if nothing were devoid of beauty—as if, indeed, beauty was the key note to the whole great mystery.

Besides the fruit of mosses so diverse, the leaves are charming; they are extremely varied in outline and margin, now broad and pellucid; again narrow, curve pointed, serrate and of finer texture. The colors, too, are far from uniform; moreover, the veining (*areolation*) is distinctive, at least of genera. Like ferns, mosses lead their votaries to most entrancing localities. The very odor of a moss, an odor which it seems always to exhale when moistened, will carry one in imagination to shaded rills, to dashing cascades and to high alpine summits, riven and split by the wild contests of time and storm. At any season there are some mosses in condition to study, hence they offer numerous attractions to the botanist.

Our country has produced some very distinguished students of mosses, among these Dr. W. L. Sullivant occupied a prominent place. Then there are the great names of those only lately among us—Tuckerman, James, Austin, Lesqueraux. Among our living students of merit are Prof. C. R. Barnes of Chicago, Mrs. Elizabeth G. Britton of New York, Prof. J. Franklin Collins of Brown University and Dr. Kennedy of Milton, Mass. The man or woman who knows mosses may be relied upon to possess a vast deal of other useful botanical knowledge.—*American Botanist*.

ASTRONOMY.

SELECTED.

IT IS a regrettable fact that so few of the younger generation know very little concerning the planets and fixed stars and stars and meteors and comets that are moving in the depths of space which surround this earth on every side. Though the more startling discoveries in starland were made long ago—

by Kelper and Galileo and the Herschels—the fact remains that so far as definite knowledge regarding the make-up and movements of these same stars, more is learned in a year now than could be gained in a century prior to the time America was discovered. About all the old astronomers did was to name the stars. Newton and LaPlace told us the reason for their movements and enabled us to predict eclipses with accuracy for many years ahead. Our own Bowditch rectified the computations of LaPlace and LaGrange, and enabled us to detect errors in computations. For the past century or more the labors have been specialized. One class of men has been mapping the heavens with delicate cameras Another set has been analyzing individual suns and stars with the spectoscope. Still another set has been looking into the nature of nebula and double stars and comets. Though the wisest astronamer in the world is still standing at the entrance to the temple of knowledge, enough is known to enable mankind to follow out the investigations with certainty of arriving at accurate results.

For example, though we have the best telescopes and the most accurate measuring instruments the world has ever seen, as yet we are unable to say within a trillion of miles how far away most of the stars are from us. Perhaps we can come approximately near to determining how far away 25 or 50 of the fixed stars are from us, but what is the knowledge of 50 stars compared with the more than ten millions of what we know absolutely nothing! But we are learning new facts every day. Two of the best telescopes on earth are in America—the Lick telescope in California and the great Yerkes glass belonging to Chicago University. Professor Lowell has the glass of greatest penetration mounted in the clear mountain air of Flagstaff, Arizona. The number of smaller glasses that are trained upon the heavens every night in this country can be counted by hundreds.

And every observer is learning new facts or verifying facts that have been learned by others. Every bit of information from those far off worlds is made public at once. Whenever a new comet heaves in sight from the depths of space, its appearance is announced by dozens and scores of watchers almost simultaneously. Never before were the starry portals which guard our globe so faithfully watched. No matter what happens in the depths of the great realm of space, as quickly as it manifests itself to earth, it is noted and studied by scores of trained men. The latest maps of the moon are more accurate than any map of

Maine in existance. The so-called canals of Mars have been photographed and charted to scale scores of times. We know more about the rings of Saturn and the belts of Jupiter than we do concerning the interior of Labrador. Though a star may be so far away from us that it takes light 500 years to travel from that star to the earth, the spectroscope tells us whether that particular star is coming in our direction or going away, and also tells us how many miles it is traveling in a minute.

Until his death some 20 years ago, Richard A. Procter performed an inestimable service for mankind by traveling from place to place and delivering popular lectures on astronomy. We thought then and think now that he had the faculty of making the science more interesting than any other man. His lectures were inspiring poems. Since his death we have read his books many times, and the charm still holds. Sir Robert Ball, an Irish astronomer, is also interesting, though more ponderous than Procter. For the others, few rise above the commonplace. Men who are capable of putting astronomical facts into picturesque words are needed badly on the lecture platform today. They should visit every high school in Maine at least once in a term and give informal talks on this most delightful subject.

In a sense astronomy is of small practical use to such of us as must work for a living. We are not dealing with suns and stars at present, and hope we may not be called to visit them for some years to come. For this reason few study astronomy in school, as indeed, there seems small need of such study. But for a winter's reading or for a lecture topic there is no more delightful study in existence. It opens one's mind to the immensity of the universe. It arouses one to understand his own insignificance.

ANTS AND THEIR WAYS.

THE *Scientific American* recently had a profusely illustrated article illustrating the physical power of the ant, from which we glean the following facts.

The ant, despite its biblical reputation for industry, has characteristics which are not altogether admirable, and which prevent it from posing as a general good example for sluggards to follow. For instance, it is well known that certain species of ants are most determined and ferocious slave hunters and slave keepers, and that they make destructive attacks on neighboring and less powerful colonies, for the sole purpose of carrying off the infant members of these into bondage. It is true that the slaves are afterward both well treated and protected, though it is doubtful whether this is done because of their value as chattels, or because the masters recognize the ethical iniquity of the situation and thus try to ameliorate it. Besides this, ants are not merely warlike, they are positively "spoiling for a fight," and often support in their communities armies of idle and otherwise useless fighters, not only for defense, but for the purpose of depredatory incrusions upon their neighbors as well.

The strength and activity of these insects is often astounding. In one experiment for instance an ant held on to a pair of forceps with one leg, holding in its jaws a small globe weighing 800 times as much as itself. To understand completely what this would mean if a man were to attempt a feat comparatively similar, we must imagine him suspended from a height by one leg and holding in his jaws a weight of nearly 130,000 pounds, or, say, a 75-ton locomotive, if we assume that the man weighs 160 pounds. The mere contemplation of what such strength represents renders comment unnecessary, and it enables us to comprehend how these little creatures can perform such marvels of labor in the building of their great communistic dwellings and colonies.

In two other views an ant is shown first grasping a coin with its jaws, and then holding it while hanging from a pair of micro-forceps. The remarkable strength of the jaws is well illustrated by this performance, for the coin weighs over five hundred times as much as the insect itself. It is said that the natives of Colombia, South America, use the jaws of a certain species of indigenous ants for closing wounds. They induce the insects to bit the two lips of the wound, and thereupon sever the bodies from the heads, which then serve as a suture.

In another engraving there is shown an ant displaying its pulling power by dragging a little silver coach toward the nest. This coach has a weight some thirteen hundred times that of the insect, and if it were possible for a man to pull a hundred-ton railroad train, his labor would be commensurate with that of the ant. In dragging the weight up an incline, the ant wisely eases its toil by moving from side to side like a horse going up hill.

Ants are undoubtedly to be numbered among the fiercest fighters, not only of the insect world, but of all living creatures as well. So strong is their fighting instinct and tenacity of purpose, that if two of the soldiers have grappled, the hold is not re-

leased till one has succumbed, One of the illustrations shows a
number of ants attacking and destroying two caterpillars. The
caterpillar is often able to put up a stiff fight, and not infrequently a number of its little adversaries are killed, though in the end
the caterpillar is invariably slaughtered and triumphantly dragged to the nest. Another of the engravings depicts a portion of a
battlefield upon which the armies of two ant colonies are shown
in mortal combat. The engagement has degenerated into a series
of sanguinary individual fights, and large numbers of dead and
wounded are shown scattered about the scene of action. The
other of the larger illustrations does not show a similar battle,
but is merely illustrative of the swarming of a number of ants
upon a bit of honey, of which they are inordinately fond. Sweets
in general are highly prized by these insects, and it is known that
certain species of ants keep *Aphides* (small louse-like insects) in
their colonies, and milk these of a sweet fluid which they secrete.
In other words, ants keep cows.

The "agricultural ant" myth has apparently been in part exploded, for it has been shown that ants do not plant seeds or
"ant-rice" for a harvest. It is probable that the error was due
to the fact that the sprouted seeds stored up, and thus form a
partial circle of tall grass around the nest. It has, however, been
recently shown that certain South American species of *Atta* cut
and bring pieces of leaves into their cellars and comminute these
till they form a pulp, which is heaped up and soon becomes invaded by a fungus which is carefully cultivated and used as food.

The Dandelion.—From time immemorial "greens" and the
salad plants have been held in high esteem because of the excellent
medicinal effect which they exercise upon the functions of digestion. Among all the various kinds of vegetables which are used
for these purposes, not one is of more value than the common
dandelion (*Taraxacum officinale*). Although indigenous to America the dandelions grow in all parts of the civilized world. Growing wild in almost every field, lifting its golden face to the sun
along the country roadsides, and decorating every dooryard in
which there is a bit of fertile soil, it may be had for the picking.
To be enjoyed in all its glory it should be taken fresh from the soil,
just so short a time before eating that it may have no opportunity to lose any of its natural good qualities.

The Amateur Naturalist

......ISSUED MONTHLY.......

Subscription, 50 Cents per Year. Single Copies, 5 Cents.
ADVERTISING RATES ON APPLICATION.

————EDITED AND PUBLISHED BY————

CHARLES D. PENDELL, - - ASHLAND, MAINE.

WITH Volume III, THE AMATEUR NATURALIST becomes a monthly magazine. With this change there is also some change in make-up, which was decided upon as a result of a desire to avoid raising the subscription price. While the magazine contains but 16 pages instead of 20 it comes twice as often and therefore is virtually 32 pages to the 20 in the old form. Some among our subscribers have critized the long lines formerly used as being difficult to follow with the eye. While shortened some, the amount is not sufficient to interfere greatly with the amount of reading matter, as those typographically inclined can figure out for themselves. On the whole we trust our readers will like the change.

IN our advertising pages will be found some special offers which we trust may be taken advantage of. It is not our purpose to give special advantages to new subscribers which are not open also to those who have helped the magazine during its first two years, and any subscriber renewing may have his subscription extended three years from the time already paid to by sending $1.00 with the renewal.

WHILE not desiring to pose as the official organ of any society, preferring rather the free lance role, the idea has occurred to us that in several places where we have a large number of subscribers, it would not be a bad plan to form some kind of of a naturalists club among themselves. Their ideas evidently would be in harmony, and THE AMATEUR NATURALIST is ready to publish the results of the doings of any such club that may be organized upon this suggestion.

ALMOST everybody at sometime or other has been a collector. We will not digress upon the various kinds possible, but have in mind a collection made by a friend, which while perhaps not strictly scientific, is interesting and has scientific possibilities. This is a collection of pressed leaves. Regular herbarium size sheets would be the best size to select, Commence in the spring and get two leaves from the trees, for instance, and as the season progresses get another set, and with autum get the third. Have them pressed and mounted, the two showing obverse and reverse sides at each period of growth. It is surprising the amount of interest it would afford; and astonishing too, to see how many people would fail to recognize even the most common leaves when not on the tree. Of course each sheet should be properly labled. "The Making of An Herbarium" shows proper form for labels and would be an aid to the collector in many other ways.

THE possibilities of new discoveries are not yet exhausted even in our very door yards. A correspondent writes that last summer he collected twenty new species of blackberry (*Rubus*) at Kennebunk, Me. He has also discovered and described others of this genus elsewhere. It is by acquiring the habit of close observation that we learn new truths in nature

BOOK NOTICES.

If when one goes for a ramble he could always have a companion that knew every land bird east of the Rocky Mountains, was always ready and willing to give this information, and never obtruded his thoughts or opinions on other matters—well, it is ideal, isn't it? Yet that is just what Bird Guide, Part 2, will do. Every bird is illustrated, properly colored to make indentification easy. A brief but succinct description of the bird, its note or song, nest and range; the common name and scientific name are both given. The book is especially adapted to being taken into the field for ready use, being 5½ x 3½ inches in size. (Price 50c. Chas. K. Reed, Worcester, Mass.)

One of the most desirable books for all interested in plant life, and especially those who wish to make a collection that will have a permanent value, is "The Making of An Herbarium." No treatise that we have seen is its equal. The price is only 25c. and may be had of the publisher of this magazine. To all renewing subscribers or others who send another subscription with their own ($1.00 in all) we will send a copy free. This is the best premium ever offered for so little effort.

Random Notes.

The deepest gold mine in the world is at Bendigo, Australia. Its shaft is down 3,900 feet, or only 60 feet short of three quarters of a mile. The heat at that depth is 108 degrees.

Only four meteorites are recorded as having fallen in Ireland, the last, which fell Dec. 13, 1902, and weighed ten pounds, is now in the British Museum. Only two are recorded as having fallen in Scotland, the last fall having occurred near Perth. May 30, 1830.

In his revised book of altitudes, the geographer of the Geological Survey gives the height of Mount Hood as 11,225 feet, in place of the old measurement of 11,-932 feet. Shasta is set down as 14,880 feet high, and Rainier at 11,363. California has twelve peaks over 14,000 feet, twenty-three over 13,000, and fifty-five over 12,000.

The production of gold in the United States in 1905, the director of the mint reports, showed a total of about $75,000,000, and of silver about $45,000,000. Both showed heavy increases over the year before. The Klondike is constantly falling off in production, but western Alaska is increasing, her contribution being nearly $15,000,000 last year.

Although fossil lizards of the earliest geological periods and of large size of the order *Rhynchocephala* are found widely distributed, but one living representative is known and that the hatteria, which is found in Australia, where so many other singular animals exist. It is about 16 inches in length. Its anatomical structure differs from all other living species.

Since astronomy became an exact science we are apt to overlook the fact that inaccuracy once characterized what is now a fixed measurement of time. The year 46 B. C. was the longest year on record. By order of Julius Cæsar it contained four hundred and forty-five days. The additional days were put in to make the seasons conform as nearly as possible with the solar year.

An interesting story is told about a Kansas cement mill. For years near Mulvane there used to be a large tract of "smoking prairie." It was good grazing ground, but during and after a rain it smoked, and no one knew the cause until a stranger quietly bought the tract one day and announced that he had a fortune. The cement lies near the surface and in great quantities, and there is a ready sale for all produced.

Sir Frederick Treves the great English physician states that in the march of the 30,000 British soldiers who went to the relief of Ladysmith during the Boer war "those who were first to fall out were not the fat or the thin, the young or the old, or the short or the tall, but those who drank. So well marked was this fact that the drinkers could have been no more clearly distinguished if they had worn placards on their backs."

The ganoidei were very numerous in early geological times and some of them of large size. They are represented by but few living species, and in some the bony scales are so enlarged as to form a coat of mail. The sturgeon is perhaps the best known example. The lepidosiren, or doko, is an eel-shaped ganoid fish of the order Dipnoi which inhabits the rivers of South America, grows to a length of 4 to 6 feet and what is especially remarkable is that it has both gills and lungs.

The Amateur Naturalist.

A MAGAZINE FOR ALL STUDENTS OF NATURE.

VOLUME III.   ASHLAND MAINE, MARCH–APRIL, 1906.   NUMBER 2.

NOTES ON LEAVES.

BY GEORGE MIDDLETON.

ONE of the most fascinating divisions of the study of botany is that which pertains to the leaves; mode of indentification, the essential part that they play in the plant's life, and the various characteristics, such as scent, power to move, the secretion of acid and sweetish juices, the carrying of defensive weapons, and of tendrils for support. From the swelling of the leaf buds in early spring, the birth of the young leaves, their maturity and finally, death, the subject possesses a peculiar interest, even to the philosopher, typifying as it does, the plan of nature as applied to all of its processes in living, sentient beings.

The functions of the leaf are now well understood as forming a most important part of the plant's eternal economy.

Taking up carbonic acid gas, (so hurtful to human beings) through its pores, the element carbon, one of its constituents, is utilized in the forming of plant food, while oxygen, the other element that goes into the composition of the gas (in the proportion of 1 of carbon to 6 of oxygen) is expired as pure air. Hence it is said that the presence of living plants in the sleeping room is healthful as purifying the air.

Leaves exhibit an almost endless variety of forms which afford easy marks for differentiating the families, though plants of the same species may bear leaves apparently widely differing from each other. Botanists can thus easily place a plant where it belongs by analyzing a leaf.

In every locality a collection is easily obtainable, showing the structure, veining, rib, etc., and will prove interesting and profitable, as a study of leaves cannot but induce a most intense desire to know more of the science.

The ideal leaf is formed of a blade, footstalk and two stipules, though some leaves are without stipules or blade, and others devoid of footstalk as in the Trillium. They may be simple, as when the blade is all in one piece; compound when several leaflets grow on one petiole. Decompound, when a pinnate leaf is again divided, or has its leave twice compounded. Intermediate between them are the binate and ternate, terms which explain themselves.

All leaves are composed of the same kind of materials for the stems, viz: wood or fiber and cellular tissue. The skeleton or framework, the woody or fibrous part, gives the leaf strength and stability, and is left after the cellular tissue has decayed. This tissue is protected in the living leaf by the epidermis, through which the plant absorbs moisture and air, and is the laboratory from which the plant draws its supply of prepared nourishment. Under the leaves especially, are myriads of pores which open into the passages of the pulp, through which the air circulates, analogus to our breathing and having somewhat the same effect, and, too, giving off a small amount of carbonic acid gas, which is again absorbed, however.

Some may have the idea that the crude sap flows in a stream through special tubes to the leaves, but this is not so. The stem is made up of cells, each partitioned from its fellows, and with no direct opening thereto. In some way not well understood, the fluid rises from one cell to another through the dividing membrane. After its passage through all this system of cells, the crude sap is conveyed to the laboratory, where, distributed through the leaves, it is subjected to the influence of light and air. The water no longer needed in its work is evaporated and returned to the atmosphere in the form of vapor, through the breathing pores.

It is a well known fact that the leaves of grass and other vegetation radiate heat very freely, and that rough, wooly leaves like those of the hollyhock, etc., more so than those of the hard and polished leaves of the laurel, camelia, and others like them. The processes at work after the crude sap reaches the leaf change mineral into vegetable matter; and heat and light are absolute necessities at this time, because in their absence, the progress of the plant is checked, and it soon perishes.

Bulbs and tubers may commence their growth in the dark, but the sprouts are weak and spindly, and will die so soon as the plant food stored up therein is utilized in their functions.

The product of the above-mentioned processes is now in the form of a thin mucilaginous compound which is conveyed to the growing parts or stored away for future use. In the latter case it is deposited mostly as a starchy material, the little grains of which may again be rendered into their first form as needed. It is used in the production of flower, fruit and seed, and in the latter it is stored up as a nutrient for the young plant until it becomes self-supporting from root and branch.

This compound is not retained in the leaf itself, except in some fleshy-leaf plants, but is distributed through the plant to aid in all of its various functions, as already formulated.

The ash left after burning any part of a plant is from earthy matter which has been dissolved out of the soil by the radicules, conveyed and deposited through the plant by the sap; it not being assimilable by the juices.

Fleshy leaves like those of some cactus are reservoirs in themselves, of plant food, and are partial to hot, dry weather, retaining their vitality for a remarkably long time.

The apparently dried up leaves of *Opuntia vulgaris* during a drowth, regain their fleshy appearance after a rain, and almost immediately put forth new sprouts, utilizing the compound which is so rapidly generated therein. In the cactus the underground stem is a reservoir, and in Mexico it has an ideal development, travelers in need of water find sufficient for their needs stored therein. These stems are sometimes as large as a barrel and hold a considerable quantity. This plant being so well provided with minute spines makes its study a doubtful pleasure except to the enthusiast.

The wizard of horticulture, Burbank, has produced a spineless cactus, but the true botanist abhors the products of the crossing of species; though the commercial aspect of the results of this selecting may look good to those interested. The spines are, however, the only protection the plant has against extermination, for all animals are partial to the juicy, palatable leaves; but they speak a warning not to be neglected.

Leaves are renewed every year; even the so-called evergreens produce new ones annually, though the old ones may not fall for a year or two. As soon as the working functions cease and they have become useless to the tree or plant, they are dropped; and at last when decomposition has done its work, and they are again a part of the soil, the endless cycle of all nature makes them avail for further growth.

A peculiarity of leaves as illustrating the separate functions of either side is that a leaf placed with its upper surface on the water will wither very soon, but with the lower in the same position, will retain its vitality for a long time, comparatively speaking

Of course, theories have been advanced to account for the different forms and outlines of leaves. A writer in the London *Spectator* says "that the favorite theory is that the simple, large uncut forms are those which grow to a height, and lie nearest the sun. The elaborately cut leaves and leaflets (as ferns) belong in the main to plants of lower growth, and others intermediate.'' This is ingenious, but does not correspond to the facts. With some plants the size of their leaves are merely a matter of environment and nourishment, though the ideal leaf may be meant in the theory above-mentioned. But in nature one cannot base theories on the ideal leaf, for the reasons mentioned. The position of grasses in a hay field may in a measure carry out the premiss, but one would hesitate to apply such a theory to the flora in general.

Leaves have many characteristics other than their shape and texture; color ranging from near white, through the creams to browns, the various shades of green, red, and often combining the various colors in one leaf, as in some coleus, poinsettia. In the so-called foliage plants, a scheme of color is given as a rule, by the contrast in the tint of the ribs and veins of the leaves, with the tissues filling in the network so formed.

Scents, no less delicious than those distilled from flowers, are often given off by leaves. There are some who even think these odors from the leaves are far more delicate than those from flowers, though this is a matter of personal opinion. Certain it is that the odor of the lemon verbena, sweet-briar, wild ivy, myrtle, and the many species of cultivated geraniums are the most clean and refreshing in the list of sweet scents, all of which are made stronger and more penetrating by the simple expedient of crushing the leaves. Many deposit on their leaves and fruit a powdery substance which may easily be rubbed off. This is one of the waste products of the sap generation—an efflorescense, or glaucous, compound without function. There are many that secrete sweetish, and acid and spicy juices; or volatile oils that may be powerful poisons; the poison ivy and others of like power, secrete a juice that will poison on touch.

The power of contracting under some exciting cause is well illustrated in Mimosa or sensitive plant, which closes its leaves on touch; or as evening approaches, probably to protect the inner surface from too much moisture, as this plant prefers its leaves somewhat dry. There are others of the locust family having the same habit, though not sensitive to the touch.

Some leaves, as previously stated, simulate flower petals in a marked degree, while others, with their thorns and spines, are no mean antagonists; then, again, some are fitted up with tendrils, which with almost human intelligence, reach out and grasp supports for the growing vines.

There are others again which have the faculty of developing young plants from the notches and ribs therein, notable examples being some of the begonias. Others, like the cactus, when planted, will develop their kind from the base, or stem.

The leaves of most trees fall in the autumn because it would be poor economy to retain them, as the gales of the winter would soon render them useless, and they would present lodging places for ice and snow which would break the branches; and while these possibilities are rare with us in the South, still we do have them sometimes. Then, too, with so many open "sores" the vitality of the tree would be considerably lowered. And here, I think, is the real reason: because the leaves would prove a drain on the vitality at a time when their functions were dormant, and the "food" laid away would be rapidly depleted, and the tree set back in its renewed growth in springtime. Those that retain their foliage will be found to be those with tough, leathery leaves, with a varnished exterior, or the needle-like leaves, as of the pine, etc. Many trees cast their leaves off by an action somewhat in the nature of amputation, having previously, however, prepared for covering the scar with a veneer of cork that has the effect of stopping the bleeding and excluding hurtful influences from without, such as the effects of the weather, and of spores and germs. At this time, and before their fall they assume those most beautiful, gorgeous colorings which make autumn a season of never-ending charm even to those whose artistic sense and love of nature is but ill developed. There is implanted in every human soul this love of nature's lovely displays; often latent, perhaps, and yet, ready at the psychological moment, to break forth in pæns of praise.

Dr. Rolling W. Barton, of Johns Hopkins, some years ago gave it as his opinion:

"The strangest part of these yearly shows of brilliant foliage which nature offers is that it all seems to be without meaning; or, as the naturalists would put it, has no special biological significance: it is a mere incident in the later life and the death of the leaves. Color in flowers makes of them organs of allurement to insects, birds, and others, whose services are necessary for pollination, and to which a bait of honey is offered. Again, color in fruit makes it conspicuous and secures free transportation by sundry animals, which thus scatter the seed.

"But the hues of autumn foliage means little more in the lives of the plants than do the colors of precipitates in the test tubes of the chemist."

While the hues of the dying leaves may have no special significance in the life of the plant, it is evident that the "change of life" due to the changing season, and the fact that their usefulness to the erstwhile hosts is at an end, is the moving cause which prompts the plant to cut off the supply of sap from below by interposing an impenetrable barrier of cork.

As the nights grow chill, as autumn advances, and even before we ourselves note the change, the plant begins its preparations for the winter. Work in the laboratory of the leaves is gradually stopped; as the previously manufactured goods are drawn off—the chlorophyll, the starch and sugars, etc., are carried into the body of the plant. To do this they must be changed into a soluble substance and in this form removed to the storage. And this change while of so much benefit to the plant itself, (though we deplore the loss of the refreshing green, and the reminder of the approaching winter), has its compensation to us in the beautiful scenes of the autumn woods.

And accidents or unhealthy conditions may bring about the change, so that even in midsummer the most brilliant hectic colors may be displayed. This seems to bear out the theory that a weakened vitality, whether caused by disease, accident, or the sluggish flow of seasons, is the primal cause of the transfiguration.

Another theory that is accepted by some is that there is a considerable ferric compound left in the leaf, which forming a combination with the waste products left after the barrier between leaf and tree is put up, oxidizes and thus produces the brilliant effects; the quantity of iron present affecting the coloration in a marked degree. No one wonders when different trees produce different colors in their dying leaves, but it is something to wonder over that the same tree should produce so many diversified colorations. This has been variously attributed to differences of soil, amount of water, exposure, etc, which may or may not be true, but the more probable theory seems to be the oxidation of some chemical compound of the metals.

In accounting for the colors the same author says: "In this breaking up of the chlorophyll especially, new products arise, such as microscopic oil drops and certain fine granular bodies (probably a solidification of the compound). These refract the light and are the cause of the color in the leaves, together with other coloring matters dissolved in the cell sap. In a word, the colors of fall foliage is due to waste products at the times the leaves are being emptied of the valuable material preparatory to being cast off as dead tissue. The most brilliant display should be expected after a season of strong growth, as then the leaves are especially full.

The trees in the North are more brilliant than with us, the hot suns of summer seeming to burn the leaf, so that the vivid colorings are subdued by the soberer browns and russets.

But when the early autumn has faded into fall and that season borders on hoary winter; then it is the dead and dying leaves
are

"Filling the streets with their golden flood,
    Falling like painted snow
Are the leaves, but yesterday wrapped in the bud,
    Now hurled by the breath of breeze below
        To soften the paths of men.

But not in vain, O crimson flake,
    Was the life of that summer spent;
Of thy sheltering cool did all partake,
    And lustrous beauty to earth was lent
        To brighten the paths of men."

Savanah, Ga.

BACTERIA IN COAL FORMATION.

BY WM. B. DAVIS.

IN THE formation of coal in past geological ages, bacteria no
doubt played an important part. Coal, we know, is the accumulated vegetable matter of a past age and practically
represents carbonic dioxide which the plants then on the
earth extracted from the atmosphere. Under ordinary circumstances, however, and we have this illustrated in our woods to-
day, when the leaves and trees fall, a complete decomposition
takes place (entirely owing to the presence of bacteria) and the
entire vegetable substance with the carbon is lost and there is
practically very little residue. If the decaying vegetable mass is
covered over with water, and this appears to be the condition of
the fern and equiseta jungles of the coal forming period, the covering of water would prevent a free access of oxygen. This would
result in an increase of carbon and a decrease of hydrogen. We
have every reason to suppose that the decomposition under water
is caused by bacteria and it may be due to a special bacterium.
The process of decay is a slow one. A good illustration may be
seen in the peat bogs of Ireland and some of the more northern
countries. Here we have a distinct coal making process. Were
the peat beds not covered with water a complete oxidation would
take place and the vegetable material would be completely disap-
pated. The beds become denser at the bottom and the lower
stratas are found to have almost lost their woody structure. In
fact the lowest beds may be termed true lignite. No doubt, some

loss of carbon occurs as is evidenced by the presence of the gas on marshes popularly known as "will-o-the-wisps."

The difference between ordinary vegetable matter as it falls and true coal is the much higher percentage of carbon which the coal contains. We have here, therefore, one of nature's methods in which bacteria has no doubt taken a part. Without the decomposition of the vegetable mass, slowly and under water, there could have been no coal and without bacteria there could not have been the decomposition.

Philadephia, Pa.

THE OVENBIRD.

BY LAURA HOAG TYLER.

PERHAPS you would like to peep for a moment into the home life of a couple of ovenbirds that lived in the woods back of the parsonage. The vigorous disturbance of the leaves that you hear as you approach would incline you to think that something as large, at least, as a barnyard fowl was about to be discovered. As you draw nearer you will see some little object fluttering wildly in an agony of fright occasioned by your presence.

Sit down and he will become calm. After he has looked at you awhile he will so far recover his equlibrium as to begin walking about on the logs and fallen limbs that are strewn about his tree, his eye continually on you, and at intervals he will entertain you with his second best song which is "teacher—teacher." This he begins in a very low voice which increases in volume with each word till it seems to have reached the limit, reminding one of an insistant school boy.

His wife may be rustling around, out of sight, on the other side of the tree. Just as you have about decided that you must leave, feeling somewhat abused that she does not at least come in and speak to you, she comes in time to say good bye.

She is dressed with the same yellow olive as her husband with orange crown. Her cream front is striped and spotted with brown, while his is only striped—a little digression from the regulation style.

You will conclude that in her quiet domain she has never even heard of woman's rights. She takes a lower perch, watches her husband's manners, tries to sing when he does, failing when she is half way through, and in many ways shows she thinks him a superior fellow. He may come to have so much confidence in you that he will sit comfortably and stretch first one wing and then the other over his legs till you begin to feel quite a part of the company.

All the time you are wishing you knew what is in the underbrush on the other side of the tree. You hesitate to impose upon such courteous hospitality and go away planning to come again sometime and find upon the ground their nest. This looks like a bunch of leaves pushed upward by some starting plant underneath. It is a softly lined ball of earth resembling a dutch oven or a minature buggy top set on the ground with a nest under it.

If you next visit it a little later and in the evening you may possibly hear the "luxurious nuptial song" which only a few have heard. John Burroughs seems to have been the first to record it. He says "mounting by easy flight to the top of the tallest tree, the ovenbird launches into the air with a sort of hovering suspended flight like certain of the finches and burst into a perfect ecstasy of song, clear, ringing, copious, rivaling the goldfinch in vivacity and the purple finch in melody." Neltja Blanchan says it is a song to haunt the memory forever afterward.

Birdsall, N. Y.

HIBERNATION.

SELECTED.

THE sleep of hibernation is a very different matter from the sleep of repose. If it be complete, respiration can no longer be detected. A torpid bat when disturbed will heave a sigh or two when disturbed and being left alone, again to all appearances ceases to breathe.

Submerged in water of a temperature slightly higher than that of his own, the hedgehog not only continues to live but appears to suffer neither inconvenience nor harm. Inclosed in an air-tight receptacle, his atmosphere undergoes a change so slight that it cannot be imputed to breathing. But circulation does not cease. As respiration diminishes the irritability of the muscles of the heart increases, and thus, without the stimulus of oxygen, although much more slowly, the heart continues to beat. In the absence of the fresh air drawn into the lungs in times of activity, uncleansed and unrevigorated and venous blood passes on to fill the whole system of circulation.

A profound lethargy ensues, only distinguishable from death by the slight beating of the heart. The waste is very small. The fat accumulated during the plenty of summer and autumn supplies all expenditure until the coming of spring, when earlier or later the hibernating animal, having no capital in reserve, begins to suffer the pangs of hunger. In response to the demand respiration very slowly increases. His oxidized blood flows more quickly and his energy returns.

Then the bat flies forth once more from the hollow tree in the wood, to find the warm dusk teeming with insect life, and the hedgehog comes, it may be from the cavity under the gnarled roots below, to find beetles worms and slugs once more among the spring grass. Hibernation has saved him from starvation; but if his nook had not been snug and wisely chosen, it could not have preserved him from death from frost.

The hiding place also must be secret and free from intrusion, for the hibernating animal cannot bear to be suddenly roused. Even the little dormouse, which comes out at intervals to feed, when in a deep sleep does not survive too hasty an awakening. The heat of the hand gradually passing through the nest, or to be carried indoors to the warmer temperature of a room, is well enough.

He awakes refreshed, full of activity, and with a disposition speedily to become tame and make friends. But if you warm him suddenly back to life before he has gradually breathed the torpor out of his blood and established an equilibrium between his respiration and muscular irritability, his heart will beat at a tremendous rate, and in a few minutes he is dead.

THE FLOOD OF NOAH.

There are Biblical doubters who scoff at the idea that there ever was a great flood yet the testimony of the geologists, to say nothing of Ignatius Donnelly's theory of the submerged continent of Atlantis, proves that at one time the entire earth's surface was covered with water. Professor Wright of Oberlin, who has made geology a life study, in writing on the subject of the "Contributions of Geology to the Creditability of the Flood" states that the level of the land changes constantly. The highest mountains were once below the sea level, as is proven by the finding of sea-shells on the summit of the highest peaks. All of Central Asia was once covered by water and is now drying up. In fact the drying up process has been going on for thousands of years. The Turkestan and Siberian low-lands were once submerged, while evidence is shown that the Desert of Gobi was once a body of water equal to the Mediterranean in size and depth. The valley of the Jordan in ages back was covered with water to a depth of from 1,000 to 1,400 feet, while changes of level and climate in Asia seem to prove that the Deluge once passed over the entire country.

PUSSY WILLOW.

BY MILO LEON NORTON.

Thy silken, flossy banners fling,
First signal of approaching spring.
The rivulet sparkles at thy feet,
Clouds sail above thee, fair and fleet,
Casting their shadows as they go—
Wraiths of departed arctic snow;
Beyond upon the hill is seen
The graceful pine's perpetual green:
Then takest from the cloud its snow,
Lit by the golden sunset glow;
Then takest from the fragrant pine
Its hue and addest it to thine,
Till mingle in thy fluffy bloom
Softer than fruit of velvet loom,
The pine's soft green, the cloud's white spray,
The sunset's gold at close of day.
All hail to thee sweet harbinger
Of spring's returning. In thee stir
The pent-up forces which have slept
While o'er thee winter's letharge crept.
Beloved art thou: to me no flower
More welcome is in woodland bower,
Sweet cat-kin-tasseled willow, now,
At spring's return, to thee I bow;
My sweetest numbers to thee sing,
Thrice-welcome harbinger of spring.

South Lyme, Conn.

Notes and Gleanings.

Metals for Fuel.—Professor Roberts-Austen, in a recently delivered lecture in the Royal Institution in London, called attention to the fact that metals may be burnt for the sake of the light and heat they produce, just the same as ordinary fuels are burnt. There is one great difference, however, in that the products of combustion are not gaseous, but solid. The burning of aluminium, for instance, gives off sapphires and rubies. This metal is an especially valuable fuel for producing an intense heat to be used in welding. An instance of burning metal for the sake of light is furnished by the "magnesium star," a contrivance by which a shell packed with magnesium and attached to a parachute, is fired electrically, high in the air, thus producing an illumination of the ground beneath at night. This finds its use in warfare. Metallic fuel has assumed much industrial importance at Essen, Germany, where, it is said, metallurgy has entered on a new phase.

The Famous Asphalt Lake.—Asphalt is being dug out of the famous tar lake of Trinidad, the most notable existing source of the material in the world, at the rate of 80,000 tons per annum. There are still 4,500,000 tons in sight, but at this rate the supply could not last long were it not that the lake bitumen referred to is receiving a constant accretion from the bowels of the earth. This accretion is reckoned as amounting to about 20,000 tons yearly and would suffice to restore the lake to its original condition if it were allowed to remain undisturbed for a few years. This wonderful lake of pitch has an area of 114 acres, and recent soundings made in the middle of it have shown the depth to be 135 feet in that part. Near the center it is semiliquid and bubbling, but elsewhere it has so hard a surface that a man on horseback can ride over it without danger of breaking through the crust. Scattered over its surface are a number of small islands which have no proper roots in the earth, so to speak, but are composed merely of accumulations of soil, though trees of considerable size grow on some of them. These islands are not stationary, but are carried slowly from place to place by the movements of the lake. Now and then one of them is entirely engulfed.—*New York Post.*

New Stars.—It is suggested by Louis Rabourdin, a French writer, that in each of the new stars that blaze forth in the heavens from time to time we see the destruction of a celestial body by a volcanic cataclysm. At any rate, he says, if part of the earth's crust underlying the ocean should give way our earth would doubtless present in succession, to a distant observer, the same series of appearances that we witness in the case of "novæ" or "new stars." First there would be an outburst of blazing hydrogen from the sea-water, decomposed by the earth's internal heat, then fusion of the whole crust, reducing the globe again to a molten state, and the gradual extinction of its light, owing to cooling. As cooling would first take place locally, we should have a variable star, the darkened portions being periodically brought into view by the rotation of the globe.—*Success*.

Perfumes.—At a meeting of the Royal Institution, Dr. Adolph Liebmann gave a lecture on 'Perfumes: Natural and Artificial." Tracing the history of their manufacture, he said it was probable that the art of preparing them from flowers and sweet-scented spices by extraction and distillation was known to the Chinese, Hindus, Persians, Egyptians, and other ancient peoples. In the Middle Ages great progress in the art was made by the Moors; but the next stage in its history was reached when modern chemistry began to ascertain the components of the various essential oils that were obtained empirically and to discover the nature of the chemical compounds contained in them. As a result of this knowledge it became possible artificially to build up essential oils identical with the natural products, the component substances being obtained in the cheapest way—either from oils in which they naturally occurred or by synthetical means. Thus artificial Attar of roses, said to be equal in every respect to the distillate from rose petals, was now an ordinary product of commerce. Many chemical individuals were now being manufactured by synthetic processes; and this fact had proved a boon for many, particularly economic, reasons. Vanilline, for instance, in 1876 was worth about £150 per pound; in 1880 the price was reduced to about £25, and to-day it was only £1 10s. But chemistry had gone still further, and not content with simply reproducing the originals of the master-artist Nature, has produced aromatic compounds that were artificial in the full sense of the word. Examples were artificial musk and artificial violet, ionone and isomer of irone, the natural carrier of the violet aroma.—*Indian Planting and Gardening*.

The Amateur Naturalist

......ISSUED MONTHLY.......

Subscription, 50 Cents per Year.   Single Copies, 5 Cents.

ADVERTISING RATES ON APPLICATION.

————————————EDITED AND PUBLISHED BY————————————

CHARLES D. PENDELL,   -   -   ASHLAND, MAINE.

As announced in the November-December number the first two numbers of this year will cover the months of January-February and March-April. From now on the magazine will appear monthly.

EVERY person at all interested in natural history should have some magazine devoted to that subject. There are a number of good periodicals published, but generally too technical for the average reader. They are interesting to the professional nature student who desires technical descriptions and classifications, and nice distinctions. Such journals are useful—are necessary—but they do not appeal to the average nature student who is interested in all forms of nature, but though lack of time or force of circumstances cannot delve into the scientific lore and master its technical language and forms. Yet many desire interesting literature on various nature topics. There is another class of magazines that are more or less popular in style and the contents interestingly written, but they are for the hobbyist—the bird student, the botanist, the mineralogist. Most nature students who are not professionals are interested in all forms and phases of nature, and THE AMATEUR NATURALIST is the only magazine published that is devoted to just this class of readers.

MOST of the popular dollar magazines have occasional articles on various natural history subjects, but in the aggregate they form a very small part of the subject matter. THE AMATEUR NATURALIST this year will give its readers 160 pages of good timely matter relating to a large variety of subjects, all interesting, and while not of a technical nature will be scientifically accurate as to tacts stated. In no other magazine can so much matter on the subject be secured for the sum of 50 cents. Most of our contemporaries are $1.00 a year—and they are worth it. Were it not that the publisher of this magazine is himself in the printing and publishing business he also would be compelled to charge $1.00 per year. But the lower price has natarally tended to a larger number of subscribers. Those who desire to avail themselves of an exceptional opportunity should send one dollar for three year's subscription. This virtually is 500 pages of live and interesting reading by wide-awake and progressive nature students for a remarkably low sum—an offer that no other magazine published will duplicate. Just how long this offer will hold we cannot now say. But for the present it will apply to new subscribers who may begin with the current volume, or with Vol. 1, No. 1, or present subscribers may have their subscription extended for three years from the time to which they are now paid by sending one dollar. The offer will be withdrawn soon and we would suggest that all intending to renew, either now or at some future time, avail themselves of this exceptional offer.

THE balloon expedition of Walter Wellman is one to awaken interest, but whether success will attend the venture no one can at this time tell. The fate of Andree is still fresh in memory. But efforts to reach the Pole will not cease until the feat has been accomplished, and when once one has succeeded emulation will cause many more attempts. Andree did not succeed; Wellman may not. but each new attempt seems to make the next effort not quite so difficult as the one preceding. It is maintained by some that it is only by the balloon that the Pole can be reached. However that may be Mr. Wellman has our best wishes for a safe voyage, whether he reaches the Pole or not.

THERE have been in all ages some few who have studied nature's secrets, but until very recently only a few of each generation have given any thought to the subject, for its own sake. But within recent years an awakening has come and nature subjects are taught in the schools; popular books are being written; artists are making illustrations of forms of life that they themselves, a decade ago, scarcely dreamed existed. Summer schools are being founded and well patronized, too—in which nature is being studied as never before; and some colleges, too, are adding to the class room and text books, courses of field study. All this change is developing greater interest in the practical side of nature, leading to new discoveries, and not least is making a healthier and stronger generation, and a race of people with an energy and vitality never surpassed since civilization drawned.

Random Notes.

It is estimated that oat smut destroys each year in the United States over $20,000,000 worth of grain.

A ton of Atlantic water when evaporated, yields eighty-one pounds of salt; a ton of Pacific water, seventy-nine pounds; the water in the Dead Sea, more than twice as much—187 pounds to the ton.

It is said that on a visit to the island of Krakatoa, four years after the outburst of the volcano had destroyed every living thing there, a traveler found 246 species of plants that had already found a home there.

That a knowledge of crystallography is of the highest importance is evident from the fact that the most universal of all facts about minerals is that they are crystalline in their texture. Coal and opal and amber are the only minerals in which crystaline structure does not occur.

It is estimated that twenty-two acres of land are necessary to sustain one man on fresh meat. The same space of land, if devoted to wheat culture, would feed forty-two people; if to oats, 88; potatoes, Indian corn, and rice, 176, and if to the plantain or bread tree, over 6,000 people.

It is said that Florida has some 7,000,000 acres of swamp that can be reclaimed Illinois, 4,000,000; Michigan, 6,000,000; Iowa, 2,000,000; and Minnesota, 5,000,000. Virginia has her Great Dismal Swamp, Arkansas has a huge swamp area, and even New Jersey has many square miles now useless and practically worthless.

Meteorology owes its origin to Italy, which, as Dr. H. C. Bolton notes, produced the fundamental instruments now used in weather observations. The hygrometer was invented about 1450 by Nicolas de Cusa; anemometer, 1578, by Egnatio Dante; thermometer, 1595, by Galileo; raingauge, 1639, by Cartelli; barometer, 1643, by Torricelli.

The American opossum is one of the most curious animals living. It is the only animal outside of Australia and the adjacent islands that carries its young in a pouch like the kangaroo. It has hands resembling those of a human being. Its snout is like that of a hog, while its mouth is liberally furnished with teeth and its eyes are like those of a rat.

Standing side by side about three feet apart, near Pratts Junction railroad station at Sterling, Mass., are two venerable oak trees, each more than three feet in diameter. The peculiar feature about them is their "Siamese Twins" union, a large horizontal limb, itself a foot in diameter, having grown from one to the other and a perfect union having taken place, so that it is impossible to tell from which tree the limb was originally the offshoot.

Within the borders of the State of North Carolina are found every timber found east of the Rocky mountains; also within the same boundary have been found every mineral found in the world. What can be truthfully said in that line of North Carolina, can be almost as truthfully said of Rutherford county for within its confines is found every species of timber (with one exception only) which are found east of the Rocky mountains; and within the same territory has been found every mineral ever found in the world, from the precious diamond down.

The Amateur Naturalist.

A MAGAZINE FOR ALL STUDENTS OF NATURE.

VOLUME III.   ASHLAND MAINE, MAY, 1906.   NUMBER 3.

SOME RARE AND RECENTLY DISCOVERED MAMMALS.

BY WALTER L. HAHN.

CONSIDERING the rapid extension of our knowledge of zoology and geography in recent years it would seem that most species of the higher groups of animals should now be comparatively well known. Nevertheless there are still many gaps to be filled in our general knowledge in addition to the many purely technical questions which will ever vex the specialist.

One of the most striking species of large game animals was discovered as late as 1901. I refer to the Okapia, an ungulate most nearly related to the giraffe but having the form of a Nilghai, and the legs banded like a zebra. To be sure, this discovery was made in Africa, on the borders of the Congo Free State, but it seems incredible that an animal of such large size and striking appearance should have so long escaped the eyes of naturalists and sportsmen, even in the "Heart of the Dark Continent."

But apparently we do not have to go to Africa to find new and conspicuous species of large game. Only last year a white bear was described from British Columbia and it is needless to say that it is in no way related to the polar bear nor is it found within some hundreds of miles of the range of the latter species. It is supposed by some naturalists that it is an albino variety of the common black bear yet it is hardly possible that so large a number (20 or more) of albinos should be found within a very limited region when none are found elsewhere. The writer has also examined the skin of another bear which appears to him to represent an undescribed species, though from a single skin it can not be certainly determined that it is more than a freak. The animal was killed in the region of the St. Elias Alps, in Alaska. The under parts and legs are brown in color, while the sides and back are white so that when the skin is spread out in the usual manner for a rug it has a white center with a beautiful brown border.

When we remember that the blue or glacier bear of Alaska was not known till 1895 and the great Kadiak Island bear from the same territory, the largest of existing cornivorous animals, not till a year later, we may well pause and ask, "What does the great North-west still contain?" This question the next decade will answer so far as large animals are concerned.

Scarcely less astonishing than these recent discoveries are the species which first became known years ago but which have since nearly, or quite, eluded the collector's grasp. One of the largest members of the rodent order is the aguti-like *Dinomys braucki* of South America. The species was first described in 1873. The original specimen was found walking about in an orchard in the Peruvian Andes. It was unknown to the inhabitants of the region but fortunately fell into the hands of an European explorer and was described by the late Prof. Peters of Berlin as the type of a distinct zoological family. Collectors visited the region on subsequent occasions looking for additional specimens, but without success. Something over thirty years later the species turned up again in Brazil, perhaps a thousand miles away and in a country with totally different climate and vegetation.

Bats are probably the most uncertain and difficult of all animals to collect. They cannot be trapped nor can they be shot with any degree of success since their location is always uncertain and they are seldom active except in twilight or darkness when gunning is difficult. Sometimes, it is true, they may be captured in their roosting places in large numbers, but since most species are erratic in their choice of lodgings this is also an uncertain method.

In consideration of the above facts it is not surprising that some of the rarest of known species of animals belong to this order, nor that many novelties are still being found even in North America. One of the most conspicuous species, *Euderma Maculatum*, is known from but two specimens. The first of these was found sitting on a fence in Southern California in 1890. It is a good sized bat, black in color with conspicuous white spots over the shoulders, and enormous ears, larger in proportion than those of a jack-rabbit. During the next decade the region over which the species might be expected to occur was the scene of the most extensive and systematic collecting ever carried on in any similar area on the face of the earth, yet without bringing to light a second specimen. But thirteen years later another bat of this species obligingly flew into the Biological Laboratory of the New Mexico Agricultural College at Mesilla Park, New Mexico.

In 1901 a French collector obtained another species of bat in the same general region which is almost as remarkable because of the great size of its feet and claws. In addition to the three specimens secured at that time and now in Paris, the only other that has been reported was picked up dead on the beach in Sonora.

Many other rare species might be ennumerated but those given are sufficient to show the present incompleteness of our knowledge. Lay students of natural history, travelers and sportsmen can do much to close these gaps by preserving and sending to the large museums any interesting specimens or observations that may fall into their hands. In this way they can usually effect exchanges for publications or specimens which will be advantageous to themselves, and at the same time help to advance our knowledge in some of the yet unknown ways of Nature.

U. S. National Museum, Washington, D. C.

WINTER AMONG THE HILLS.

BY KATE A. JONES.

TO A NATURE LOVER winter among the great Northland hills is never dreary or uninteresting, there is so much to study and enjoy. The outlines of the trees are seen as they cannot be when summer wealth of foliage is upon them, and we are surprised at their grace and beauty. We look out some cloudless morning just at sunrise, to find that the Frost King has been busy during the night covering the trees with crystal, until every branch and twig gleams like frosted silver set with diamonds. After a light snow has fallen a sleighride along some woodland road gives one an opportunity to study the foot-prints, and trace the wanderings of mice, rabbits, and squirrels and sometimes larger game, while a rabbit is frequently seen, his fur coat as white as the snow. The cold weather in March formed a strong crust on the snow, which lasted for days: and such days! perfectly cloudless, the air pure and crisp, I spent hours in the fields and woods, looking out upon miles and miles of unbroken whiteness stretching away to the great hills. The mountain tops were clear white, shining in the sunlight against the blue sky; a vision it seemed, something not of this world. "Splendor immaculate, unearthly, unspeakable!" The woods were silent, save

the drumming of partridges, and the cheery notes of the chickadees. One saucy chickadee was balancing himself on the edge of a
last year's nest, singing merrily. I brought home branches of pine
loaded with lovely cones, and some dainty birds nests. As I
studied their wonderful workmanship I was reminded of the
thought given us by Hurdis:—

> "A birds nest: Mark it well, within, without;
> No tool had he that wrought, no knife to cut,
> No nail to fix, no bodkin to insert,
> No glue to join,—his little beak was all—
> And yet how neatly finished! What nice hand,
> With every implement and means of art,
> And twenty years apprenticeship to boot,
> Could make me such another?"

Looking from the window one afternoon I saw a deer walking down the village street; such a dainty graceful creature!
Something frightened him, and away he bounded across the fields

How much one has missed who has never seen the mountains
on a perfectly cloudless winter night, with the full moon shining
calmly down on their snow-covered summits. Then, the brilliancy of the stars on a cold night, and the glory of the Northern
Lights, I remember so well one evening when a bow, like a rainbow, only pure white, spanned the heavens, and lights like great
torches, some white, others rose-tinted, streamed far up into the
sky, constantly changing, bringing before us one weird picture
after another, while we were fascinated by visions of unearthly
splendor.

The morning of April 9th, 1906, dawned clear and bright, but
by afternoon leaden clouds had gathered, and it was snowing
steadily, the hills were hidden, and we were "shut in from all the
world without." John Burroughs gives us this description of
such a storm: "Out-of-doors you seem in a vast tent of snow;
the distance is shut out, near-by objects are hidden, there are
white screens about you, and you feel housed and secluded in
storm. Your friend leaves your door, and he is wrapped away
in white obscurity, caught up in a cloud, and his foot-steps are
obliterated. Travellers meet on the road, and do not see or hear
each other till they are face to face." When I looked from the
window next morning there was fifeeen inches of snow on a level,
with not even a foot-path to mar its whiteness. Birds were
singing in spite of the snow, and soon the lawn was alive with
chickadees, song sparrows, snow buntings, and blue-jays, eager
for the breakfast of crumbs I had provided for them.

To-day (April 13th) the snow is nearly gone, the air is soft and mild, blue-birds, robins, and song sparrows, are singing sweetly, and I saw a beautiful brown butterfly flying about in the sunshine. Soon the frogs will be making the twilight musical with their plaintive note, the pine woods will be fragrant with arbutus, and the roadside and fields golden with the graceful bells of the adders tongue.

Grantham, N. H.

COLLECTING BIRDS' EGGS.

BY GEORGE MIDDLETON.

A COLLECTION of birds' eggs, and their nests, is a prolific source of pleasure and profit: pleasure, because it stirs the æsthetic sense; the various shapes and arrangement of the nests, and the many colorings of the eggs, are pleasing to look upon—a pleasure which is felt in a more or less degrees by all of us when contemplating these visible workings of nature's laws.

The profit consists in the insight it gives one into the reproductive power of nature, as exemplified in bird life, leading, as it does to a higher conception of the ultimate purpose for which the eggs are produced; the perpetuation of species; and the species, one and all are of some material benefit to mankind, though the good may be veiled by some injurious qualities, it being our custom to magnify the evil and to belittle the good done by any of God's creatures.

It seems rather rough on the birds, themselves, that their efforts at reproduction should be thus rendered ineffective; but in the interest of science, for the advancement of human knowledge, all of which have really worked for their well-being and existence, it seems fair.

Were it not for fashion's decree our woods and cities would be crowded with bird life—the destruction by the scientists being infinitesimal.

To rob birds simply to have on exhibition a box of curios, or simply to pander to the inherent destructive proclivities of the human family is worse than reprehensible—it is a crime, and should not be tolerated anywhere.

A discriminating judgment should be shown, and not more than a single set of the eggs taken. Care should be aken to have a typical collection, and therefore it is far better to take the nest than to leave it, keeping each set in its own nest.

It is just as important to the proper enjoyment of the science to take a note book with one on a field trip as the collecting itself. It one nest of eggs is discovered and notes made in regard to parents, nest and its surroundings, number of eggs and anything else that may interest, we may feel richly repaid for an afternoon's outing.

There are problems which can only be solved in the field, and it is the close student who finds the answer.

Make it a point never to take a nest of eggs without the notes, because the pleasure and profit in their possession will soon fade away.

Following out these suggestions, in time one will be surprised at the readiness with which the reasons which actuate the birds can be understood, the rare discriminative sense which they display in the placing of their nests for the protection of their young.

Where one has no room for the nest, a kodak will be a pleasing adjunct to the collector's impedimenta, and where one becomes expert in its use, it gives an added pleasure.

The "Bird Book" should contain a complete list of specimens with species, family, and all else that is known, indexed. In this book could be pasted photos of birds and nests, that would lend additional interest.

Savannah, Ga.

HARDINESS OF THE DATE PALM.

IN an exhaustive bulletin treating on the date palm and its utilization in the Southwestern States, by Walter T. Swingle, issued by the United States Department of Agriculture, the following information concerning the hardiness of this well known palm is furnished:

Fortunately the date palm is able to endure much cold, it being one of the most hardy of the evergreen fruit trees. When in a dormant condition it is probable that it is seldom injured by temperatures above 20 degrees F., and is able to live in regions where the temperature occasionally falls as low as 12 degrees F. Commonly, however, date palms are severely injured by temperatures as low as this, sometimes losing many of their leaves. The amount of injury they suffer is partly dependent upon their condition at the time when they are exposed to the cold. If entirely dormant they are much less injured than if some of the leaves have only recently unfolded or are still growing. It should further be noted that young date palms are much more likely to be injured by cold than are old ones. This, no doubt, is in part because the young plants have fewer leaves and in consequence a growing point more exposed to cold, but doubtless largely because the growing leaves, with their inclosed bud, are much nearer ground on young trees, and would therefore be exposed to lower temperatures than on the tops of old palms far above the surface. Old and vigorous trees might perhaps occasionally weather cold snaps where the temperature fell below 10 degrees F., provided such were exceptional and occurred only at intervals of many years, In practice, then, four different limits below which palms would be injured by cold might be set: (1) young palms in active growth would be liable to injury if the temperature fell several degrees below freezing; (2) young plants not in active growth and old palms if nearly dormant would be severely injured only by temperatures falling below 15 degrees F.; (3) old and dormant trees would be severely injured only by temperatures below 12 degrees F.; (4) most date palms would be killed and all would be seriously injured by the temperature falling below 10 degrees F., and date culture would be impossible in regions where such temperatures occurred more than once in a decade. These considerations show that the date palm has about as much resistance to cold as the fig tree, for example, with this important difference—that a fig tree is able to recover and grow again the next year, even if it be frozen to the ground by severe cold in winter. With the date palm this is not possible, since, if the growing but of an old tree be killed, it is impossible for the trunk to sprout out again.

In the Salt River Valley, Arizona, the temperature not infrequently falls to 25 or 22 degrees F., and at rare intervals goes as low as 12 or 13 degrees F., which temperatures of course injure the date palm, but have not killed any of the many fine trees growing in the valley, though young offshoots recently transplanted have been frozen to death.

No temperature low enough to injure seriously even young date palms (below 18 degrees F.) are recorded from any of the stations in the Salton Basin, and if the first winter after the plants are set out is passed safely, no further danger from cold need be feared.

Speaking more generally of the date palm the following from *American Gardening* is quite appropos:

This tree furnishes the Arab not only with food and drink, but with shelter—the timber being used for the construction of houses—and with a thousand and one articles of daily use. It renders habitable many regions of the Sahara desert. Although it will hardly be called upon to perform such various functions in America, it may be found valuable in utilizing land that would otherwise be a trackless waste. For instance, the ill-famed Death Valley, of California, could be made, it is stated, an ideal habitat for the palm, thus not only redeeming this tract from arid sterility, but rendering it no longer a menace to the traveler in that region.

The date palm thrives under conditions that would be fatal to most plants—scorching heat, absence of rainfall, prevalance of dry winds. It has a remarkable power of resistance to alkali, and these characteristics especially fit it for use in sections that are so salty as to prevent the cultivation of other crops. Once the trees have attained maturity, their shade makes it possible to cultivate other fruit trees that could not so well withstand the direct rays of the sun—such as figs, almonds, olives, etc. Under these, again, vegetables can be grown, so that veritable oases are created in the deserts.

Upwards of 20,000,000 pounds of dates are imported into this country every year, and the market for a date of superior quality is practically unlimited. Besides California, regions in Nevada, Arizona, New Mexico and Texas are said to be excellently adapted to this culture. Tens of thousands of acres of alkali lands in the Southwest, it is declared, can be reclaimed and made profitable only by growing date palms.

AN ACCIDENTAL DISCOVERY IN ELECTRICITY.

A large number of the world's greatest inventions have been the result of some union of forces the nature of which the person who started them neither understood nor suspected. The working of dynamos at long distances apart was discovered by accident, an account of its discovery being as follows:

Soon after the opening of the Vienna exposition in 1873 a workman picked up the ends of a couple of wires which he found trailing along the ground. He fastened them in the terminals of a dynamo to which he thought they belonged, while they were really attached to another dynamo that was running in another part of the grounds. The dynamo to which he fastened the wires was not running, but as soon as the wires were placed in its terminals it revolved as if a steam engine were driving it. The workman was amazed. The engineers and electricians were astonished by the discovery that a dynamo electric machine (turned by steam, water or other power) would turn another similar machine a long distance away if properly connected to it by wires conducting the electricity. Thus originated one of the most revolutionary applications of electricity.

The fact that power can be transmitted for miles by electric wires is one of the most important factors in modern civil engineering achievements.

IN SYLVAN HAUNTS.

BY ALICE B. WAITE.

In the shadow of the forest,
   In the dusky thicket shade
Where the woodthrush sings her sweetest,
   Sweetest song of wildwood glade:
Where the wood-dove comes a wooing,
   Build aloft their piney nest,
Here doth come the sylvan maiden,
   Spray of wildrose on her breast.

Where the grasses of the lowlands
   Bend to winds that ripple free,
Over stretch of blueflag azure,
   All along the billowing lea,
Where the meadow-lark uprising
   Trills to mate in upper air—
Here doth come the sylvan maiden
   Spray of wildrose in her hair.

High among the rocky ledges
   Where the crags first flush at dawn,
Where the buck and doe feel safest
   'Mong the ferns with timid fawn;
Where the silver fox feels freest
   Tracking o'er the wild waste-land,
Here doth roam the sylvan maiden
   Spray of wildrose in her hand.

By the winding stream, half hidden
   By the rushes along the way,
Where the dragon-flies do gather,
   Skim and whirl through sunny day;
Where the wildrose by the brook side
   Bend o'er waves and fondly meet,
Here doth dream the sylvan maiden,
   Wildrose petals at her feet.

South Lyme, Conn.

Notes and Gleanings.

A New Dead Sea.—Central Asia is so completely a *terra incognita* that we hardly need be surprised at any discovery reported from there. The *Literary Digest* in a translation from *Revue Scientifique* tells of a very curious lake discovered in Tibet by the Swedish explorer Sven Hedin, which he describes as follows:—"It is a very large sheet of water, hitherto unkown—a new Dead Sea—almost as interesting as that of Palestine. It is one of the strangest sheets of water that I have ever seen, writes the learned traveller. It is of enormous extent, but not very deep. To sail on it you have to walk through it on foot for a kilometer [over half a mile] from the edge, to reach the boat: then the boat must be dragged another kilometer, so that a distance of two kilometers must be traversed from the shore before the boat with its equipment can be really floated. But the most curious and most remarkable feature of this inland sea is the incredible quantity of salt that it contains. The bottom is a compact mass of salt, on whose rough surface it is very disagreeable to walk, as one must do to reach the boat. The boat itself, our oars, our clothes, adds M. Hedin, were all as white as chalk, and when drops of water fell on the ground they left globules behind them as if they were sap from a candle. It is not remarkable that this sea and its neighborhood are as sterile as the Dead Sea of Palestine."

Arizona's Petrified Forest.—Situated in Apache County, Arizona Territory, and known as Chalcedony Park, there exists a marvelous deposit—nothing less than preserved sections of silicified trees. They are generally found projecting from volcanic ash and lava, which is covered with sandstone to the depth of twenty to thirty feet, and lie exposed in gulches and basins where water has worn away the sandstone. Many scientific men, whose study of geology has been all that years of toil and observation could embrace, have during the past few years visited this wonder of wonders, and all seem to be lost scientifically; their theories are like the pieces of silicified wood, NO TWO ALIKE. It is, however, generally conceded that this was a tropical wood, transformed in a pre-historic era from a living, growing forest to the present recumbent sections of interblended agate, jasper, jade, calcite, amethyst, etc. Although silicified wood is found in many localities, never before was seen such variety of coloring, with sound hearts of large trees, and sound bark. While the quantity of material is great, the sound sections are very limited, and after years of labor in selection of material fit for working, and the erection of costly machinery for cutting and polishing, it is and must ever remain a rare and costly article, since in hardness it is only three degrees from a diamond. Steel will not scratch it, nor can it be stained by ink. Microscopical examinations reveal a part of this wood to be the genus *Araucaria*, or the Norfolk Island pine of the Southern Pacific ocean. All the specimens examined show that the wood was undergoing decay before being filled with the various media which afterwards solidified. On some of the specimens traces of fungi *mucelium* causing decay, may be plainly seen. The process of petrifaction possibly resulted from the trees being submerged by hot geysers bearing silicon in solution, the rich oxides of Arizona intermixed with silicon and the cell tissues of the wood were substituted by the silicious solution and then solidified.

Oregon Trees in Austria.—A shipment of 750 pounds of the seeds of fir and spruce trees was recently made to replenish the depleted forests of Austria. About 600 sacks of cones were picked from young trees, from which the seeds were carefully taken. Between 200 and 300 pounds of seeds were sifted from the whole bulk that did not promise, only the very best being sent across the sea. Oregon fir and spruce are growing on thousands of acres of territory in Germany and Austria that had been denuded of trees.

In the Polar Night.—The power of the eye to adjust itself to varying intensities of light is illustrated by Dr. Nansen's account of his experience on his north polar expedition in the winter of 1895-96. He was determined to keep a continuous thermometric record during the months of darkness and and whenever the moon was above the horizon he and his assistants found no difficulty in reading the instruments, which were placed in the crow's nest of the ship's mast. But at the time of new moon they had only starlight, because they could not afford to use the oil needed for an outdoor lamp. Yet gradually their eyes became so well trained to see in the dark that they could read the figures on the thermometer scale even in the absence of the moon.

Thompson Seton as a Boy.—When any person achieves distinction it is always interesting to learn the incidents of his boyhood. County Treasurer Kay, one of the "old residents" up in Ernest Thompson Seton's early Manitoba home has this to say of the now distinguished naturalist: "This naturalist, Thompson Seton, used to work for my aunt, Mrs. Susie McCarthy, of Carberry, Manitoba. They called him 'that Thompson boy,' and the ranch hands despised him because they thought he was lazy. He was very careless of his looks, usually wore his hair long, and was a tattered, disreputable figure generally. His passion was nature. If a mouse ran out of a grain-stack and he was feeding the thrasher, everything must stop while that Thompson boy followed that mouse to its lair and studied it. Sometimes he took a dog and a gun and was gone for days among the hills, studying the birds and butterflies. After a while he met his wife, who was a New York artist, and he became more particular of his personal appearance. Then magazines and newspapers began to recognize the merit of his articles on nature, and success was assured.

The Planet Mercury.—Mercury is a body devoid, practically if not absolutely, of air, of water and of vegetation. Consequently it is incapable of supporting any of those higher organisms which we know as living beings. Its surface is a vast desert. It is rough rather than smooth. Whether this roughness be due to mountains proper or to craters we are too far away from it to be able yet to say. The latter is the more probable. Over the greater part of its surface change either diurnal or seasonal is unknown. Three-eighths of its surface is steeped in perpetual glare, three-eighths shrouded in perpetual gloom, while the remaining quarter slowly turns between the two. The planet itself, as a world, is dead. Whether it ever supported life upon its surface or not, the power to do so has now forever passed away. Like Venus and for like cause, it is now a dead world. And it was the first thus to reach the end of its evolutionary career, earlier to do so than Venus, inasmuch as tidal action was very much greater upon it than on Venus and consequently produced its effect more quickly. Mercury has long been dead. How long, measured by centuries we cannot say, but practically for a very long time. Venus must have become so comparatively recently. Both, however, now have finished their course and have in a most literal sense entered into their rest.

The Mantis.—This curious insect is, among other attributes, credited with an appreciation of musical sounds. In case any of our readers are prejudiced against this erie-looking insect, we quote the following from *American Gardening:* "An insect that is useful indoors as well as in the garden, that is interesting in its nature and its ways, and is not only harmless to man but rather likes his company is worth considering. Such is the mantis. It is rather formidable until one comes to know it, and as it turns its head on its slender neck without moving its body, as it alone of the insects can do, it has an eerie look one must get accustomed to, but which seems to place it near to the human side of the line, and to make it more companionable. Latterly the European variety *Mantis religiosa* (praying mantis) was imported in the egg on nursery stock to Central New York and of the Japanese variety, *Tenodero einensis,* by the same means was located in the Meehan nurseries near Philadelphia, Pa. In both instances the value of the foreigners as insect destroyers was so thoroughly disseminated among the school children and among growers that whenever seen they were recognized and protected, and as eggs and insects were given freely, so long as a surplus remained to whoever asked, new centers of dissemination were located not only in the two States but all over the country. So they are now quite common and correspondingly well known as helpful.

Huxley on Alcohol.—In a letter published in his "Life and Letters," in reply to a question as to what he thought of alcohol as a stimulant to the brain in mental work, Professor Huxley said: "Speaking for myself—and perhaps I may add for persons of my temperment—I can say without hesitation that I would just as soon take a dose of arsenic as I would of alcohol under such circumstances. Indeed, on the whole, I should think the arsenic safer, less likely to lead to physical and moral degradation. It will be better to die outright than to be alcoholized before death. If a man cannot do brain work without stimulants of any kind, he had better turn to hand work. It is an indication on nature's part that she did not mean him to be a head worker."

The Amateur Naturalist

..... ISSUED MONTHLY.......

Subscription, 50 Cents per Year. Single Copies, 5 Cents.

ADVERTISING RATES ON APPLICATION.

————EDITED AND PUBLISHED BY————

CHARLES D. PENDELL, - - ASHLAND, MAINE.

An Exchange not long since asked its subscribers for criticism and the one criticism that led all others was that it was "too technical." This criticism was as much a surprise to us as to the editor of the magazine in question, which is a publication devoted to botany, and edited in the most popular style of any reliable journal of its class we have seen. In treating any subject, botany or otherwise, where the aim is to instruct as well as interest use must be made of words peculiar to the subject, else how would apt descriptions be given—but what are dictionaries for? The mere looking up of a word will often fix its meaning in the mind and also cause one to better remember the article in which the word was found. Of course there are magazines that are technical in character—magazines intendedly technical. But, it is not a sign of progress to avoid everything that may have a technical look. It is better to get posted if one is not posted. It is better to advance in knowledge than to recede because of an occasional new word.

It seems a new theory of volcanoes is being developed. It used to be the theory that beneath a certain thickness of the crust of the earth (uncertain thickness, rather,) the whole interior was a molten mass. This still seems the most reasonable theory and the most susceptible of proof. The most recently accepted theory has been that there were certain localities where water percolating through the strata finally mingled with gas of some kind, or some sort of mineral substance and then formed a gas which exploded and produced volcanoes and earthquakes; the earthquake doubtless coming from a muffled explosion. The newest theory is that radium is the cause of all this terrestial disturbance. Just how it is done we don't know, and the discoverer (or shall we say inventor?) does not. But the heat producing energy of radium compressed in abundant masses is supposed to do the business. Now as astronomers are all agreed that the earth at one time was "without form and void" and even more remotely in creation perhaps only a nebulous mass of gas which has since cooled and hardened and through the lapse of æons of time assumed its present form, it seems more natural that the earth would follow the law of all cooling bodies and cool first on the outside forming a crust while the interior was still in a heated condition. The bent and contorted strata of geological formations clearly show that this at one time must have been the case, and it has not yet been very clearly shown that the same heated condition in a lesser degree does not still exist. When one reads of the recent eruption of Vesuvius hurling its ejecta to the height of 10,000 feet, of a volcano in Java throwing matter even 50,000 feet high, when one calls to mind the frightful eruption of Krakatoa in 1883, pictures to his mind the geysers of Iceland or the Yellowstone, or beholds the great seething crater of Kilauea, not to mention the many other volcanos in constant or occasional state of activity, it seems fairly evident to the average mind that the old theory most of us learned in our school days is still the nearest correct. We have read the objections to it, based upon unproven theories, but the newer theories offer still greater objections and the theory of a molten interior draws practically all the evidence needed right from the central source of supply.

ELECTRICITY was "known" to the ancients in about the same ratio as the inhabitants of Mars are known to the modern astronomer. The astronomer knows—or thinks he does—that conditions favorable for the maintenance of life exist on that planet: the ancients knew a few of the properties of electricity. Not until modern times was electricity made to serve man. It was not until 1856 that the practicability of the telegraph was demonstrated to the world, and twenty years after that before the first public demonstration of the telephone. Only during the present generation has electricity been sufficiently understood so as to be the great commercial factor it is to-day. The subject even now offers a vast and unexplored field for research.

GET SPECIMENS. In whatever branch of nature study one may indulge specimens should be procured of the subject. One can buy if preferred, but when one is studying a subject in true amateur spirit he will prefer to collect what he can for himself. One can read pages of description and no doubt be interested by the words of the writer, but if possible to get a specimen illustrative of the object described there is then an interest that can in no other way be attained, and specimens seen and known are not forgotten while words of description can never so aptly describe an object as a view of the object itself.

Random Notes.

The horn of a rhinoceros is not part of the bone of the head, but merely grows on the skin.

A diamond weighing 67 carats and worth about $15,000 was found on the Premier Johannesburg property the other day.

The condor keeps its young in the nest longer than any other bird. Fully 12 months elapse before the young condors can fly.

The highest mountain in the moon is thought to be at least 35,000 feet in height; that is, 6000 feet higher than Mt. Everest.

Malta is the most thickly populated island in the world. It has 1,360 people to the square mile. Barbados has 1,054 people to the square mile.

A homing pigeon in calm weather can attain a speed of 1,210 yards a minute. Travelling with a strong wind, some pigeons have made 1,980 yards a minute.

Vesta is the only one of the smaller planets which can be seen with the naked eye. Its diameter is only 300 miles and its whole surface but one-ninth that of Europe.

The gulf coast of Lower California has long been noted for its pearls and they are found there in greater variety of colors than any other known locality. Black gray, red, bluish-green and yellowish are among the principal colors found.

In high mountains there is no state to compare with Colorado. She can claim 407 peaks of at altitude of more than 10,000 feet, 395 of more than 11,000 feet, 233 of more than 12,000, 149 of more than 13,000 and 32 of more than 14,000.

The British museum has books written on bricks, tiles, oyster shells, bones and flat stones, together with manuscripts on bark, on leaves, on ivory, leather parchment, papyrus, lead, iron, copper and wood. It has three copies of the Bible written on the leaves of the fan palm.

The highest kite ascent is said to be that made not long since at Lindenburg, in Prussia. Popular Science Siftings says "21,100 were reached with six attached kites and 16,000 yards of wire. The temperature fell from 41 degrees at the surface to 13 degrees below zero; the wind, 18 miles at the surface. was fifty-six miles an hour at the highest point.

One of Maine's biggest old elms is in Bethel, so near the Androscroggin that its roots draw moisture directly from the river. Its circumference one foot above the ground is 26 feet, and five feet above the ground is 20 feet. Six feet above the ground the tree divides into two trunks which are nearly equal in size for about twenty-five feet. These trunks then divide and sub-divide into branches forming a tree of symetry and beauty 100 feet high.

A single mesquite seed, imported from the Southwest and planted in Honolulu in 1837, has propagated and spread until in the Hawaiian Islands to-day, says the Washington Post, there are 50,000 acres of the famous plant of alkali plains of Arizona and New Mexico. The most remarkable feature of the manner in which the desert growth has taken root on foreign and tropical soil lies in the fact that the mesquite has completely changed its character and is vastly different from the parent tree.

The Amateur Naturalist.

A MAGAZINE FOR ALL STUDENTS OF NATURE.

| Volume III. | ASHLAND MAINE, JUNE, 1906. | Number 4. |

COLLECTING MINERALS.

BY GEORGE MIDDLETON.

THERE is a rare, broadening influence in collecting natural objects, that can be found in no other hobby. The mere fact of collecting calls for an exercise of the mental faculties that can be aroused in no other way.

There is in every human breast a latent love for nature's works, and a desire to penetrate into her mysteries, which at the proper time, and under favorable circumstances, will seize the victim and hold fast until his mind is loaded down with facts and figures never to be unloaded; for one curious thing about the workings of the brain is that no matter how much we use it to enlighten others, nothing is taken away; and, in fact, the exercise of this faculty, induces new ideas, and new application of old ones leading on and on, but never attaining the *ultima thule* of its capacity.

Starting on the collection a few specimens of minerals, some years ago, merely out of curiosity at first, but which broadened out into passionate love, my collection grew slowly. At first content with small specimens I had quite a collection of that size the first year. Then I bought books on the subject and studied them faithfully until a glimpse of what the science really was began to dawn on my mental vision.

I realized that most of my specimens were inferior and scarcely typical—a non descript lot of rocks, and immediately set about improving the quality.

Several visits to localities in North Carolina on collecting trips produced a rare suite of zircons, single, double, in jefferisite and feldspar as the matrix; and also opened up to me a new field of thought—that of the occurence of the mineral, and of its relation to the country rocks. A quartz ledge produced specimens of that mineral, rather inferior, but here again I gained knowledge by observation that never could have been obtained from books.

Sillimanite, in situ; garnets that had been flattened by some dynamic force; magnetite lining cavities in quartz rock and filling what had been cracks, forming regular veins of the material; ilmenite lining pieces of rock; chalcedony in varying sized pieces, "floating" in the detritus from the eroded mountain; jefferisite in great banks twisted and screwed up as if put through a giant machine—and giant it was, and an irresistable one. This last, an alteration product of muscovite, was extremely interesting as a study of an advanced stage in the decomposition of that mineral.

While the specimens collected may not have applied to the "wealthy and blase'" collectors, or to those of the North who have unlimited possibilities at their doors, we might say, to me they were revelations; and some with whom I exchanged seemed to think my way too; while others—well, there are always "others" in all pastimes or lines of human endeavor, and we cannot hope to please everybody.

The chief thing in collecting is to please one's self; and not to become a rabid collector—one without thought of anything else—is the chief thing not to do. What comes between is simply incidental, and we should endeavor to make these incidentals conform to reason and common sense.

One should endeavor to procure good typical specimens of the common varieties first; the rarest kinds for the most part are either alteration products of the simple forms referred to, or are merely the same elements only in differing proportions and probably subjected to other influences whilst crystalizing.

Where the mineralogist does his own collecting, even if only occasional opportunities present themselves, he should study this mode of occurence before the specimens are taken and notes made of their relation to the surrounding rocks and the accompanying minerals.

It would seem superfluous to dwell on the necessity of this, as a proper study of locality, with the notes made as suggested, will conduce to a perfect understanding of their nature and lead to correct and interesting deduction; and will form a record to which one may turn at any time to subtantiate the theories which are bound to rise in one's mind, enhancing the subtle pleasure of the true collector and student, because of the accuracy to which it leads.

Even the cobblestones in the streets offer an interesting study when broken up—the roughest and commonest looking specimen, (even when the locality is not known), as the arrangement of the particles, and their wonderful beauty, the complexity of structure tenacity and hardness, all offer problems which give added pleasure in their solution.

A good magnifying glass is a necessary adjunct to the collector's impedimenta, to which may be added a horseshoe magnet for use in determining magnetic ores. A good book for the beginner is "Minerals and How to Study Them" by Dana, which can be procured of most dealers in minerals. It gives an insight into the science in easy stages and its accuracy cannot be questioned, and it is one which gives us a good understanding of nature's laws in the world of minerals.

Savannah, Ga.

ROUND LEAVED SUNDEW.

BY KATE A. JONES.

WHILE tramping through a bog one mid-summer afternoon I found for the first time this curious little plant with its white flowers. It was such a delight to see a number of fine specimens growing in their native soil; tiny plants almost hidden by the mosses that grew around them, and reminding one of pink rosettes covered with sparkling drops of dew. Many an insect has found these seeming dewdrops a delusion and a snare, for they are really "a glutinous expudation by means of which insects visiting the plant are first captured; the reddish bristles then close about them, and it is supposed that their juices are absorbed by the plant." I brought home some specimens and tried the experiment with small insects; it was rather a grusome task, and reminded one of some greedy creatures clutching at their prey:

"What's this I hear
About the new carnivora?
Can little plants
Eat bugs and ants
And gnats and flies?
A sort of retrograding:
Surely the fare
Of flowers in air,
Or sunshine sweet;
They shouldn't eat,
Or do aught so degrading."

Grantham, N. H.

KILAUEA, THE GREAT VOLCANO OF HAWAII.

MANY of the islands of the South Sea are of a calm and peaceful loveliness, such as we connect with the idea of the Pacific Ocean. Noislessly formed by the gradual rising of the coral from the water, they soon became clothed with vegetation, close to the water's edge, so that the spray of the ocean often fritters itself away over the fan-like leaves of the cocoa palms. They are truly "Isles of Eden," enchanted shores "where every prospect pleases and only man is vile." But there are other island groups in the Pacific which are centers of volcanic activity, wilder and more terrible than any that are in the older regions of the earth. In the Hawaiian Islands these volcanoes are especially grand. The greatest of all is the one known as Kilauea.

An American traveller, who unfortunately wrote anonymously, has given a vivid description of this volcano, a part of which we quote:

We stood on the high bank of an irregular lake of liquid fire, which was seething and rolling to and fro, glowing with exceeding great heat, and sending up vast columns of smoke. The bottom of the cliff was fringed with fire, and seemed ready to crumble into the lake beneath: the shore line of lava looked like blood compared with the black cliff above it. A cascade of fire was playing in the center of the lake, boiling up, rolling downward, bubbling, tossing up jets of molten lava, and scattering fiery spray all around it. Then for a few moments it subsided, and the lake cooled over on top, a thin crust of grey and black; but it soon heaved up slowly in the center and spouted up a fiery geyser, thirty or forty feet high, that played like a colossal fountain several minutes, flinging out showers and clots of lava, and dashing up red billows against the cliffs with a sound resembling surf on a rocky shore, only that it had something indescribably hellish and diabolical in it that filled me with an awful shudder. That swashing, self-conscious sound, now faint, now loud, was to me by far the most impressive part. I think I should go mad if I had to listen to it long, and realize that it was caused by the restless surging sea of fire that seemed the very lake of perdition. A large part of the cliff has fallen in lately, almost dividing the lake into two parts; and the southern part, that farthest from us seemed most active. Sometimes the wind shifted and sent the smoke right in our faces; it was just like the fumes of lighted matches, and set us coughing and strangling in a moment. We were at times almost suffocated, but dared not go farther on, for the edge of the cliff was seamed and scarred and scorched with fires, so that it hung together in crisp layers, with wide gaps between, whence issued volumes of smoke, and the peculiar glimmer and glow of great heat. The place on which we stood was so hot that we had to keep moving about lest our feet should burn; and I found by experiment that I could not hold my hand over a crevice more than a few seconds owing to the intense heat.

The scene below was never long the same; sometimes, when the lake had crusted over, a billow of red-hot lava would roll from under the cliff and break in the crust near the shore, roll again and break in more, all across the lake, till it was once more a mass of liquid fire, that boiled and bubbled in restless cascades, or spouted up jets with great force forty feet in the air. Remember, there was no flame or blaze about all this; it was liquid matter, heated to red or white heat, resembling exactly the molten iron seen in foundries.

Miss Isabella Bird in her book on "The Hawaiian Archepelago" gives the following graphic description of the same scene:

Kilauea is in a state of perpetual fury, ever changing, never resting, "raging forever with tossing and strength like the ocean." We think chiefly of the cones of a volcano, but here we have a flaming lake in a great abyss which opens on the flank of Mauna Loa, at a height of nearly 4,000 feet. The scene breaks suddenly upon the traveller, for "until you reach the terminal wall of the crater, it looks by daylight but a smoking pit in the midst of a dreary stretch of waste land." But such a pit! "It is nine miles in circumference, and its lowest area, which not long ago fell about 800 feet, just as ice on a pond falls when the water below it is withdrawn, covers six square miles. The depth of the crater varies from 800 to 1,000 feet in different years, according as the molten sea below is at flood or ebb." This lake, the Halemaumau, or House of Everlasting Fire, of the Hawaiian mythology, the reputed abode of the goddess Pele and her fiery companions, was the scene of the exploit of Kapiolani, the Christian heroine who defied their power. Following a lava flow for thirty miles up to the crater's brink, and a toilsome descent of three hours over recent lava, the glorious vision came in sight. Suddenly, just above and in front of us, gory drops were tossed in air, and springing forwards, we stood on the brink of Hale-mau-mau,

which was about thirty-five feet below us. I think we all scream-
ed, I know we all wept, but we were speechless, for a new glory
and terror had been added to the earth. It is the most unutter-
able of wonderful things. The words of common speech are quite
useless. It is unimaginable, indescribable, a sight to remember
forever, a sight which at once took possession of every faculty of
sense and soul, removing one altogether out of the range of ordinary life. Here was a real "bottomless pit"—the "fire which is not
quenched"—"the place of hell"—"the lake which burneth with fire
and brimstone"—the "everlasting burnings"—the fiery sea, whose
waves are never weary. There were groanings, rumblings and
detonations, rushings, hissings and splashings, and the crashing
sound of breakers on the coast; but it was the surging of fiery
waves upon a fiery shore. But what can I write? Such words
as jets, fountains, waves spray, convey some idea of order and
regularity, but here there was none. The inner lake, while we
stood there, formed a sort of crater within itself; the whole lava
sea rose about three feet; a blowing cone about eight feet high
was formed, it was never the same two minutes together. And
what we saw had no existence a month ago, and probably will
be changed in every essential feature a month hence.

What we did see was one irregularly-shaped lake, possibly
500 feet wide at its narrowest part, and nearly half a mile at its
broadest, almost divided into two by a low bank of lava, which
extended nearly across it where it was narrowest, and which was
raised visibly before our eyes. The sides of the nearest parts of
the lake were absolutely perpendicular, but nowhere more than
forty feet high; but opposite to us, on the far side of the larger
lake, they were bold and craggy, and probably not less than 150
feet high. On one side there was an expanse entirely occupied
with blowing cones and jets of steam or vapor. The lake has
been known to sink 400 feet, and it has overflowed its banks.
The prominent object was fire in motion; but the surface of the
double lake was continually skinning over for a second or two
with a cooled crust of lustrous grey white, like frosted silver,
broken by jagged cracks of a bright rose color. The movement
was nearly always from the sides to the center, but the movement of the center itself appeared independent, and always took a
southerly direction. Before each outburst of agitation there was
much hissing and a throbbing internal roaring as of imprisoned
gases. Now it seemed furious, demoniacal, as if no power on
earth could bind it, then playful and sportive, then for a second

languid, but only because it was accumulating fresh force. On our arrival eleven fire fountains were playing joyously round the lakes, and sometimes the six of the nearer lake ran together in the center to go wallowing down in one vortex, from which they re-appeared bulging upwards, till they formed a huge cone thirty feet high, which plunged downwards in a whirlpool only to re-appear in exactly the previous number of fountains in different parts of the lake, high leaping, raging, flinging themselves up-wards. Sometimes the whole lake, abandoning its usual centri-petal motion, as if impelled southwards, took the form of a mighty wave, and surging heavily against the partial barrier with a sound like the Pacific surf, lashed, tore, covered it, and threw it-self over it in clots of living fire. It was all confusion, commotion force, terror, glory, majesty, mystery, and even beauty. And the color! "Eye hath not seen" it! Molten metal has not that crimson gleam, nor blood that living light! Had I not seen this I should never have known that such a color was possible.

The crust perpetually wrinkled, folded over, and cracked, and great pieces were drawn downwards to be again thrown up on the crests of waves. The eleven fountains of gory fire played the greatest part of the time, dancing round the lake with a strength of joyousness which was absolute beauty. Indeed, after the first half hour of terror had gone by, the beauty of these jets made a profound impression upon me, and the sight of them must always remain one of the most fascinating recollections of my life. Dur-ing three hours the bank of lava which almost divided the lakes rose considerably, owing to the cooling of the spray as it dashed over it, and a cavern of considerable size was formed within it, the roof of which was hung with fiery stalacties more than a foot long. Nearly the whole time the surges of the farther lake, taking a southerly direction, broke with a tremendous noise on the bold craggy cliffs which are its southern boundary, throwing their gory spray to a height of fully forty feet. At times an overhang-ing crag fell in, creating a vast splash of fire and increased com-motion.

Almost close below us there was an intermittent jet of lava which kept cooling round what was possibly a blow-hole, form-ing a cone with an open top, which, when we first saw it, was about six feet high on its highest side, and about as many in dia-meter. Up this cone or chimney heavy jets of lava were thrown every second or two, and cooling as they fell over its edge, raised it rapidly before our eyes. Its fiery interior, and the singular sound with which the lava was vomited up, were very awful. There was no smoke rising from the lake, only a faint blue vapor, which the wind carried in the opposite direction. The heat was excessive. We were obliged to stand the whole time, and the soles of our boots were burned, and my ear and one side of my face were blistered. Although there was no smoke from the lake itself, there was an awful region to the westward of smoke and sound and rolling clouds of steam and vapor, whose phenomena it was not safe to investigate, where the blowing cones are, whose fires last night appeared stationary. We were able to stand quite near the margin, and look down into the lake, as you look into the sea from the deck of a ship, the only risk being that the fractured ledge might give way.

Before we came away a new impulse seized the lava. The fire was thrown to a great height; the fountains and jets all wallowed together; new ones appeared and danced joyously round the margin, then converging towards the center they merged into one glowing mass, which upheaved itself pyramidally and disappeared with a vast plunge. Then innumerable billows of fire dashed themselves into the air, crashing and lashing, and the lake dividing itself recoiled on either side, then hurling its fires together, and rising as if by upheavel from below, it surged over the temporary rim which it had formed, passing downwards in a slow majestic flow, leaving the central surface swaying and dashing in fruitless agony, as if sent on some errand it failed to accomplish.

THE WHITE EGRETS.

AS we look over the herons in North America, we find two that for pure loveliness stand alone,—the American Egret and the Snowy Heron.

The American Egret (*Herodius egretta*) is a large but slender built bird about 50 inches in length. His bill and eye are yellow and his legs are black; the entire plumage is snow white and in breeding season they are adorned with a beautiful train of about fifty long white aigrette plumes that grow from the center of the back and extend for six to ten inches beyond the end of the wings.

The Snowy Heron (*Egretta candidissima*), or Little White Egret is only about 24 inches in length. It has a black bill but the bare space about the eye is greenish yellow; the legs are black but the feet are yellowish in both adult and young birds, this distinguishing it positively from the young of the Little Blue Heron which is white, but has dark greenish legs. The plumage is snow white and during the breeding season it has a tuft of fine feathers on the back of the head and on the breast and about fifty recurved aigrette plumes from the middle of the back.

Both of these egrets were formerly very abundant in the southern states and occurred regularly north to Long Island and Oregon on the coast and to Illinois in the interior. The present range of the little egret is very uncertain; its center of existence is undoubtedly in Flordia and it is doubtful if half a dozen birds can be found in any other of the eastern states. The large egret is still found from North Carolina to Florida in insolated heronries. As late as 1895 there were many heronries in Florida containing thousands of both kinds of egrets, while now, especially in the case of the smaller bird, you will find only insolated pairs nesting with flocks of other kinds of herons. The nesting places of herons are always known as heronries; they often cover over extensive areas and are usually in swamps where none but birds, reptiles and insects can dwell. The larger white egrets often nest in the tops of quite tall trees, but the small ones were usually found in bushes or mangroves near the ground. Their nests are slight platforms of sticks, lined with smaller twigs; on these from three to five eggs are laid. The eggs are pale greenish blue, those of the American Egret averaging 2.30 x 1.50 inches, while those of the Snowy Heron measure about 1.80 x 1.20. Heronries are always interesting but filthy places; screams, croaks, squawks deafen you on the one hand while you feast your eyes on the beautiful birds sailing about or standing on the tops of the trees and the ungainly young standing on the edges of their homes, their long, skinny toes tightly grasping the twigs, for well they know if they once loose their hold and fall to the ground, their fate is sealed.

As these birds were once as abundant as Louisiana and Little Blue Herons, both of which can now be found in great numbers in their range, many wonder where they have gone to. Sacrificed for avarice and vanity. Many of the game birds have become scarce through the agency of man, but these plumage bearing herons, while killed by men, were destroyed because women made the market for their plumes. Their extermination is a disgrace to the human race. In spite of all the legislation that has been enacted, and knowledge that has been disseminated by the Audubon Societies, these plumes, under the names of "aigrettes" or "ospreys", are now being sold by nearly all milliners. A few days ago a lady told me she had always supposed that the plumes were secured from a living bird, the same as plumes from an ostrich, and that the bird was not injured. These herons bear these plumes only in the nesting season, and in order to get them the birds are shot in the heronries, the skin on the back with the plumes attached, is pulled off and the rest of the carcass is thrown away. Every two birds killed means the death by starvation of at least four young in the nest; at other times they are very shy and difficult to approach.—*American Ornithology*.

NUTRITIVE VALUE OF FRUITS.

CHEMICAL analysis would, according to scientific author-ity assign practically no nutritive value to the juicy fruits for they consist of little more than a collulose envelope containing a solution of sugar, the amount varying from 17 per cent. as with grapes, to about one-fourth per cent. as with lemons. The amount of water in fruit is considerable. In water melons it is no less than 95 per cent., in grapes 80 per cent., in or-anges 86 per cent., in lemons 90 per cent., in peaches 88 per cent., in apples 82 per cent., in pears 84 per cent., plums 80 per cent., in nectarines 83 per cent., and in strawberries 90 per cent., not a fruit in the whole category containing less than 80 per cent. The irresistible conclusion, considering these facts, is that fruit plays an important role in diet as a thirst-quencher. Certainly, when fruits are freely represented in the diet, less fluid requires to be consumed, and fruits would appear to be endowed with a subtle inimitable flavor which is ample inducement to imbibe fluid in this wholesome form. The question so prominent in most people's thoughts as to what to drink might, therefore, on sound physio-logical reasoning, be answered, eat sound, ripe, juicy fruit. It is noticeable that, as fruit enters into the diet, the indulgence in alcoholic drinks is diminished. The flavorings of fruits, although of little nutritive value, are undoubted stimulants to the appetite and aids to digestion. Moreover, the juice of fresh cut fruit is perfectly free from microbes, is as sterile as freshly drawn milk and the fruit acids tend to inhibit the power of those disease pro-ducing bacteria which flourish in neutral or alkaline media. The marked anti-scorbutic properties of fresh fruit, due to the vegeta-ble acids and their salts in the juice, are of great importance. For the most part these acids are combined with potash, and hence a free diet of fruit preserves a healthy alkaline condition of the blood, and there is consequently a reduced tendency to the depositing of acids in the tissues. Peaches, and that delicious and delicately flavored fruit, the nectarine, contain quite a small quantity of sugar, and this, coupled with the fact of the tenderness of their pulp, makes them suitable for the gouty and diabetic. —*Indian Planting and Gardening.*

Notes and Gleanings.

Great Caribou Herds.—The great caribou herds of Newfoundland migrate semi-annually, and no one but an actual witness of these migrations can form any adequate conception of the marvelous number of deer which the island contains. It is estimated that the number which crossed the Exploits river at one point during 10 days in the autumn of last year exceeded 4,000. This crossing ground is only one of scores of similar trails. Somewhere about the middle of September the migratory tide sets southward, the hinds with fawns forming the vanguard of the long procession. The lazy stags hang on the rear until some storm more severe than ordinary gives an unmistakable warning of the approach of winter. Then all alike hurry toward the sheltered districts in the south, taking a straight course, over bowlder strewn mountain heights, through tangled mountain torrents and immense lakes. During winters of unusual severity the animals often draw quite near to the settlements on the south coast; whereupon the settlers armed with fearsome firearms, such as sealers used some 50 years ago, straightway proceed to decimate the herds with volleys of buckshot. The foes of the caribou other than man are not numerous. Although the big gray wolf is still reported on the northern plains in considerable numbers, it is now seldom encountered in the interior. Having formerly existed in large packs, it is supposed that a migration must have occurred across the winter ice floes of the Belle Isle straits to the coast of Labrador.—*Empire Review.*

Effects of Altitude.—It was thought some years ago that no human animal could stand up and work, owing to the increased rarefication of the air, at a higher elevation than 23,000 feet above the sea. Since then a large amount of evidence has been collected as to the effects of altitude on the human frame. The British expedition that crossed the Himalayas to Lhassa not long ago proved that men may climb, carry loads on their backs, and even fight, at an elevation of 20,000 feet; and it is said that the Tibetans, fleeing before the advancing army, crossed snowfields at an elevation of 23,000 feet. It is matter for marvel that men have thus carried on their military campaigns at heights nearly as great as those to which balloons have ascended. There appears to be no doubt that existence can be maintained at a height greater than that of Mount Everest, for it is believed that Coxwell and Glaisher once reached in a balloon ascent an altitude of 30,000 feet, though they claimed an ascension of 37,000 feet. But there is always great danger in such ascents, particularly rapid balloon ascents, and the practice of essaying such aerial flights cannot be commended.

Gardening in Africa.—"The main trouble in a British West African diet is a lack of fresh green food," wrote the late Mary H. Kingsley, the African explorer, in *Climate*, and some of the difficulties in the way of supplying that defficiency she describes as below:—"Gardening in West Africa is nervous work. I have worked in gardens there, and know that even lifting a kalepot is not there, as it is here, a trifling act—because under the kale-pots you have there a chance of finding divers things that, if in spirits on the shelf of the British Museum reptile gallery, would give pleasure, but there, close to one's ankles, and not bottled and corked down, are merely exciting and unpleasant. Still, if the snakes go in the other direction, one has the satisfaction of having fresh vegetable. There are plenty of worse things than snakes connected with the West African gardening. In some places there are elephants, in others hippopotami. Specimens of either in a garden for a night are incompatible with success, for a season at least. Then, if you hire a man to sit up all night in the garden and ring a hand-bell to keep such intruders off, he keeps you awake also. If you take away the bell and set him up in business with a fire to scare game off, a leopard usually comes and takes him away, which distresses you very much. Gardening in West Africa is not to be undertaken light-heartedly by persons of a nervous or irritable disposition."

Trees Fighting One Another.—That nature is at perpetual war with itself is a fact which is generally known to students of its processes. Animal preys on animal, one form of life subsists on another, and man too often goes to war with his fellows. It is not so generally known that trees fight one another. In a paper read before the Boston Scientific Society by Arthur A. Shurtleff on "The Improvement of the Forests of the Metropolitan Park System"—a lecture illustrated throughout with artistic chalk pictures—it was pointed out that while a humane person could do no better deed than stoping a war between individuals, a great outcry will be raised if a single tree is cut down. It is one of the duties of the forester, Mr. Shurtleff holds, to stop the fights between trees, which represent conflicts between ephemeral trees and permanent ones, and which, if continued, can have no other result than serious injury to the permanent trees, while the ephemeral growths will be lost by natural processes within a few years, even if they survive the struggle with the longer-lived varieties. Of the seedlings which spring up in the forest probably over eighty per cent. die at an early age, but nevertheless they leave their mark on the more permanent trees. The birches make war on the slow-growing oaks, thus disfiguring trees that might be a joy to lovers of the woods for a century or two. Dead trees with their insect pests threaten and destroy the living trees, while "wolf trees" by their mass and shade destroy the seedlings, only to perish themselves after a time. The competent forester, therefore, by cutting down certain upstart trees, helps to preserve nobler varieties for the enjoyment of posterity.

Imported Insects.—Most of the insect pests which destroy vegetation in the United States are imported. The gypsy moth and the brown tail moth came from Europe in recent years. The Hessian fly was brought over by the British army during the War of Revolution. The chinch-bug is likewise an European importation. The San Jose scale came from Asia. The boll weevil came from Gautamala through Mexico. Congress has appropriated $100,000 to import bugs to eat up the gipsy moth and the experiment has been made of importing a species of ant to combat the boll weevil.

The Amateur Naturalist

......ISSUED MONTHLY.......

Subscription, 50 Cents per Year. Single Copies, 5 Cents,
ADVERTISING RATES ON APPLICATION.

————————EDITED AND PUBLISHED BY————————
CHARLES D. PENDELL, - - ASHLAND, MAINE.

JUST how to word an apology when it is made necessary by circumstances enforced by the acts of another is rather difficult. The lateness of this issue is due in part at least to that functionary of the United States government known as Third Assistant Postmaster General. Before the removal of this magazine to Ashland it had been entered at the postoffice at Binghamton, N. Y., as second class mail matter. We certainly anticipated the same classification here, and application was duly made for entry as such. It is said that the gentleman holding the third assistant's rank was at one time himself a publisher and is skilled in the knowledge of such things as will annoy and provoke other publishers. However that may be, the matter of securing such classification was delayed until we had already mailed three numbers on the postmaster's permit and then we were officially informed that in the office of the Third Assistant Postmaster General Edw. C. Madden the AMATEUR NATURALIST was not officially regarded as a publication entitled to such entry and the application was denied. We had an unexpectedly large postage bill in consequence and will hereafter have to pay one cent each for every copy mailed, whether subscriber or sample.

THIS will not interfere with the publication of this magazine but it does increase its cost very materially considering the low price at which it is published and will cause us to slightly change our plans. But only to this extent, for the present at least: we will follow the example of several of our esteemed contemporaries and take a vacation during July and August and issue again in September, after which time we hope to issue on time each month.

APPLICATION will again be made for second class rates and it is probable that they will eventually be granted. The publisher has had experience before, and in the case of the weekly newspaper which he is also publishing it was three months before the "powers that be" at Washington could officially make up their minds whether it was really a newspaper or not. So in the present case we are more annoyed than surprised.

CONTRIBUTIONS for this magazine from our readers are always available provided they are in conformity with its style and purpose. The more interest our subscribers take in it the better the magazine we can give them. We have used several selected articles and shall continue to do so, as there are many such that we consider worth a permanent place and which must be interesting to subscriber as well as editor. But it is after all the live and timely contributions from those in direct touch with the magazine that give it its standing, tone and animation. The editor regrets that his time is so fully occupied as to preclude the possibility at the present time of any such extended articles from his pen as appeared in the first two volumes. The 8-hour day may do for the laborer but the 16-hour day is nearer the length of the editor's working hours at the present time and the time for the recreation of magazine writing is thus precluded, and he must perforce rely somewhat on the generous inclinations of his subscribers.

KEEP a note book. We can hardly give more helpful advice to the amateur naturalist or collector than this. Most of us make collections of specimens in the line of our particular hobby, but fewer keep a note book which is almost equally helpful. We might almost say, keep two—one as a constant companion, the other as a place of more permanent record—a day book and ledger, as it were. In the first jot down *at the time*, such points of interest as may come under your observation. If collecting, record in this all your observations regarding time locality and other peculiarities and incidents that may relate to the specimen collected. Or, if simply on a trip of observation, make minute of the things seen that appeal to you as points of especial interest; describe localities or striking bits of scenery and note places that seem to merit further exploration. Record when reading, such words as are not thoroughly understood or places before unknown or things new and at first opportunity look them up further. Once such a note book is started, many occasions for its use will arise. To the other transfer such memoranda as may seem to have permanent value and record the result of investigation suggested by the jottings in the first. Try it for one year and you will have a record book you would not care to part with; you will have formed a habit that you will not care to give up and moreover you will have acquired an amount of useful information that will really be a surprise to you.

Random Notes.

Even though reputed to have "nine lives," cats cannot live at an elevation of 11,000 feet or more.

Ten species of "vegetable sponges" are cultivated in Asia and Africa, which are much used for toilet and domestic purposes.

Over 400 diamonds are known to have been recovered from the ruins of Babylon. Many are uncut, but most are polished on one or two sides only.

The bat has a larger ear in proportion to the size of his body than any other creature. In some varieties of bat the ear is one-third the size of the body.

Switzerland, to the million inhabitants, has 2,620 deaf mutes, the greatest proportion of any country. Next comes Austria with 980, then Germany with 770.

Cadmium used as a protective coating for iron is said to be much superior to zinc, the coat while having much the same appearance, being harder and much more adhesive.

A species of swallow has been observed flying over the Sargasso sea at a distance of 840 miles from the nearest land, but singularly enough no marine birds were met with.

The split hoof of animals of the cow kind is a great advantage in travelling over soft and marshy ground. On such ground a bull or buffalo can outgallop a horse. The split hoofs spread apart and do not sink into the mire as the horse's hoof does.

There is no doubt that Mars is very like the earth. Its days and nights, its summers and winters, differ only in their relative length from ours. It has land and oceans, continents and islands, mountain ranges and inland seas. Its polar regions are covered with snow, and it has an atmosphere and clouds, warm sunshine and gentle rains.

The vicinity of wires in a thunderstorm is apparently not extra hazardous as some imagine. Telephone wires seem to have an important influence in preventing lightning from striking, according to the investigations of the German telegraph department. Three hundred and forty towns with telephone systems and 560 towns without them were under observation. In the former the lightning struck three times for every hour of storm; in the latter five times. Moreover, the violence of the lightning was much less in the former cases.

The Sierra Nevada Mountains of California, "the largest and most interesting chain of mountains in the United States," is 600 miles long and from 75 to 100 miles wide, and covers an area equal to all New England excluding Maine. It contains the highest peak in America outside of Alaska (Mt. Whitney, 14,522 feet) from which to the bottom of Death Valley, some 200 feet below sea level, is nearly 17,000 feet. Within the range are 1,500 glacial lakes at an average altitude of 8,000 feet. The western slope of the range is gradual, averaging 100 feet to the mile, while the eastern slope is the steepest in all North America, being ten times as steep as the western. The State as a whole has 11 peaks exceeding 13,000 feet; 41 exceeding 10,000 and 120 exceeding 8,000.

The Amateur Naturalist.

A MAGAZINE FOR ALL STUDENTS OF NATURE.

VOLUME III. ASHLAND MAINE, SEPTEMBER, 1906. NUMBER 5.

AUTUMN: A SKETCH.

BY NORMAN FOERSTER.

WE anticipate the seasons, especially the fall. While the midsummer sun still shines with an unabated glare in the middle of August, we note a subtle change in the evening atmosphere, a restful, cooling property that is gradually infused. By September the breath of autumn is beyond doubt in the air. The mornings are likely to be chilly, with a thin fog pervading all. This is retained later in the day as a vague, uncertain mist. And yet, although presaged in this manner, the arrival of autumn is furtive. September brings a spell of midday heat that dispels all thought of cold weather. Asters and golden rod and ironweed bedeck the country as if the summer season had just begun. As the days grow colder again, we look about us for crimsoning trees and browning hedges. In spite of this alertness, we are sure to be surprised some morning to look beside the road and find a sugar maple a dome of rosy-gold.

Each day we note the increasing splendor of this herald of autumn, and, before long, skirmishers appear, lurking behind farmhouses, ensconced in the deep woods, with here and there a sentinel posted on a hillside. The stridulating insects no longer fill the air with an interminable sound; the cricket's chirp is silent, and the grasshopper's constant "bzwi-t't't'-bzwi" is forgotten. The birds, clad in fatigue uniform, are preparing for the journey southward. The milkweed fairies float into our houses.

But our chief almanac of the season is the coloring of the trees. The culmination of intensity and the turning point are reached a few days before the middle of October. Scarlet and gold, and orange, and brown, each rivals the other in alluring the eye. What can equal the rich creamy pink and gold of the maples, the immaculate saffron of the hickory, the mottled deep magenta and waxy green of the oaks, the massive golden-brown sprays of the elm? What dreaminess pervades these misty, mellow days! The sun's power is diminished by the succession of filmy clouds, that aimlessly wander across the sky, their motion so evading the eye that we can scarcely imagine them pausing to admire the beauties of the multi-colored landscape. The corn is in stock now, the shrivelled foliage rustling noisily as the hollow, mysterious October wind sweeps over the fields. The generous-faced pumpkins lie exposed in redolent confusion among the corn wigwams. Apples sprinkle the ground in lavish profusion. The yellow quinces reflect the pale hickory trees nearby. The luscious grapes hang in heavy clusters from the drying vine. It is the season of fruition, the result of constant labor through many vicissitudes.

Alas, the gay climax is all too quickly turned. In one short week the unsurpassed of all autumnal tints, the cream of her beauty, the rosy-gold of the maples, is neutralized to a dead brown; the oaks have lost their deep maroon; the hickories are brown; the buckeye and willow are less gay. Simultaneously the mornings and evenings become cooler, and the leaves are palsied and swarm to the ground. Each breeze carries before it a brown host, and although no breeze blows, there is no cessation; the sere leaves are loosed mysteriously and idle to the ground in a listless manner. Before we are aware of the fact, the trees are almost bare.

The merciless October winds have now decimated the once-legion leaves, and must needs have a muster. A fitful breeze whirls down the road, accompanied by a regiment of noisy leaves halts, wheels, and colliding with the clatering crowd, swirls them round and round with ever-increasing force until they ascend spirally. This gyration over, they descend rapidly and are at rest—for the time being—many feet from where they started. Helpless creatures of circumstance! Soon most of the leaves are stowed away in such prisons as depressions in the earth, cliff recesses, and narrow glens, where the winds will not touch them.

Now the frost king evinces his power. We look out some cold morning to find the world in his frigid grasp, a snowy whiteness covering all. One day it becomes quite warm. But this unwonted warmth augurs ill. By evening, low, torn, gray clouds rush overhead, a half gale is raging, at first pleasantly—tempered, but waxing cooler and cooler. A cold mizzles escapes the impending scud and is swept earthward with stinging force. We are lulled to sleep by the dismal howling of the wind, and the drizzle on the window-pane, and the cheerless pattering. A surprise is in store for us in the morning. The first snow of the season is falling,—great, soft flakes that leave no impression on the warm earth, and are seen only during their passage through the air. They fall thicker and faster, until a boreal wind suddenly rushes through the trees and drives the flury aslant, wrathful that the earth should thus receive her flaky heralds.

The first snow has fallen, the trees are bare, winter is once more sovereign, and the cold, leaden days of bleak November await us.

Pittsburg, Pa.

ECLIPSE OF THE MOON: OTHER MOONS.

BY GEORGE MIDDLETON.

AS is generally known a lunar eclipse is caused by the moon passing through the shadow cast by the earth and only occurs at full moon. This earth-shadow projected by the sun extends farther than three times the distance of the moon from us (238,818 miles). Sometimes the satellite as it travels in its monthly journey around the earth passes through this shadow and is partly, or even wholly hidden from our gaze; that is, while we still distinguish the outlines of the sphere we cannot distinguish any of its characteristics. Should the moon come between air, earth and sun, the moon-shadow falls upon the earth, resulting in a solar eclipse.

The moon revolves around the earth once in about 28 days. An eclipse of both sun and moon would take place every month if the plane of the moon's orbit were parallel to that of the earth's; but as it is inclined about 5 degrees to the earth's orbit so that the moon passes in the one case above and below the sun, and in the other above or below the shadow, thus preventing such occurrences. If the moon passes through the edge of the earth's shadow, it causes a partial, and when it plunges centrally through it, a total eclipse. The earth's shadow at the moon is about three times the diameter of that satellite.

The explanation of the appearance of the moon at total eclipse, a dull red disk, is that the rays of the sun passing through the atmosphere near the earth are, by well known physical causes deprived of their blue light, and, being deflected toward the axis of the earth's shadow, fall upon the moon and faintly illuminate its disk. Of course, this appearance is to a great extent dependent upon the condition of the atmosphere at the time of the eclipse. An exception noted by Prof. Ashmore was in the lunar eclipse of 1884 when the moon was for a time completely hidden from view.

Probably a half-hour before the moon reaches the shadow, its edge begins to be darkened by the penumbra, so that it is impossible to tell within a half minute when the first contact takes place.

Two eclipses of the moon cannot take place in two consecutive months. The greatest number that can occur in a year is seven, of which five are solar and two lunar; and the least number is two, both of the sun.

Some years ago there was quite a discussion in the *Illustrated American* as to whether or not the moon has a satellite. At that time scores of plates were exposed and developed, and though many suspicious objects were "unearthed," the final conclusion was reached that the moon is almost certainly unattended, unless, indeed, such a small one as to not be discernable "While it is certainly possible, no such body has ever been seen, nor has the moon of any other planet besides the earth ever been discovered with a satellite obedient to its gravitating force."

Such a satellite at its best, would shine only as a very faint star, and the full moon's light would wholly overpower it; while at other times, when moonlight is fainter, the light of the hypothetical satellite would be reduced at equal pace. This being true observations with the telescope would be negative. This led to the use of photography as mentioned, without any result as to the particular object sought, except in so far as determining to the satisfaction of the investigating scientists the absence of any body as satellite to our moon.

There are at least twenty moons in the solar system, and some are better than ours.

The moons of Mars were discovered by Prof. Asaph through the telescope at the naval observatory at Washington, in 1877.

Saturn is well supplied having eight, Titan being nearly twice as large as our moon. Jupiter has four, one of which, Ganymede, has a diameter of 3,480 miles to 2,160 through ours. Uranus has four little ones; Neptune has but one, and that small. Neither Murcury or Venus have any satellites.

Savannah, Ga.

THE SUNFLOWER.

BY WILLIAM WHITMAN BAILEY, LL. D.

IT is a very common belief among various nations that the sunflower (*Helianthus annuus*) always keeps its disk turned towards the sun. The scientific as well as common names prevailing bear reference to this supposed quality. It is even embodied in poetry. Thus Tom Moore says—I quote from memory—

"The sunflower turns on her god as he sets,
The same which she turned when he rose."

I remember, years ago, hearing E. L. Davenport, the well known actor, after singing this, remark, "Very pretty but all nonsense," and I fear it is,

Careful observation through many years has proved to my satisfaction that the flower in question shows no such heliotropism. I have, to be sure, seen a whole garden-full turned to the sun, but in the very next yard the heads might be directed all ways. If the Latin name has reference simply to a sun-like flower with rays, as does *Hetenium*, also, then it is an appropriate title.

A more interesting phenomenon, one which actually occurs in striking fashion, is the orientation or turning of leaves north and south in some species of Silphium and in the prickly lettuce, *Lactuca scariola*, a weed of European origin now common all over ths northern and mid-western states. Other plants like the two small wild cassia, show it in less degree.

Brown Utiversity, Providence, R. I.

HISTORIC VOLCANOES.

BY W. S. VALIANT.

DURING historic times, many volcanic eruptions have occurred, of which a few of the more important only can be mentioned at this time. Vesuvius, being best known, takes first place. An ancient book says: "Vesevus, a mountain of Campania, very fruitful and pleasant, till in the reign of Titus (79-S1 A. D.) a flame burst forth from the top of it and laid the country about it in ashes. Here the elder Pliny, prompted by his curiosity as to the cause of its burning, lost his life."

Many eruptions of Vesuvius occurred in early times, but that of 79 A. D. has been most fully described. The main body of this volcano is made of lava streams, with some layers of cinders; the large active one consisting at the top and outside of cinders; the small cone at the very top giving out vapors, or cinders alone, while the melted rock flows from crevices below the top cone, or over the edge of a lower and older crater.

In July, 1834, the whole height was about 4000 feet. Vesuvius is the center of much larger volcano of more ancient time, a remaining portion of which is known as Monte Somma. A part of Somma consists of fossiliferous rocks, but it is mostly lava. The earliest eruptions of Vesuvius were lost in remote antiquity, and no symptoms had been evinced within the memory of man, until A. D. 63, when an earthquake damaged some of the surrounding cities.

In 79 A. D. it began to show symptoms of activity, and immediately thereafter sent forth the terrible eruption which buried the cities of Herculaneum, Pompeii and Stabiæ. In this eruption the elder Pliny perished, and a graphical description of it is extant by the younger Pliny to Tacitus. A succession of eruptions followed, more especially in 203, 472, 512 and 993, but were not attended with any flow of lava, the ejected matter consisting of stones, ashes, and fragments of older lava. The first recorded discharge of liquid lava took place in 1036. Since then various eruptions, some of them extremely violent have occurred; especially those of 1770, 1793, 1834, 1838, 1847, and 1850, and eruptions of greater or less extent have taken place almost every year since.

The cities of Herculaneum, Pompeii and Stabiæ were buried in volcanic ashes and cinders, which were reduced to mud by the heavy rains, and no lava stream reached them at that time, though subsequently Herculaneum has been repeatedly overflowed with lava. The site of Herculaneum was discovered in 1713, and in 1848, while some peasants were cutting a ditch, Pompeii was found. About half of the latter city has been uncovered and everything seems to be in a state of extraordinary preservation. It appears that most of the inhabitants escaped. In 1631 an eruption destroyed Resina, a town that had been built over Herculaneum.

ETNA: An ancient description of this volcano says: "Ætna, a mountain of Sicily, which burneth continually and casteth out flames and ashes, and sometimes great stones, yet the adjacent valleys and plains are very fruitful and verdant, and the mountain itself, notwithstanding its continual fires, is generally covered with snow. Here Jupiter lodged the giants, after he had struck them with thunder." Etna—mountain of fire—has a height of 10,874 feet, and covers an area of about 90 miles in circumference. About 60 eruptions of Etna are recorded in history; the more remarkable ones of later periods are those of 1792, 1811, 1819, and 1832. The eruption of 1792 continued for a whole year. In that of 1832, in the midst of violent explosions and other convulsions, vast streams of lava issued; and, pouring down the declivity, overran cultivated fields and threatened the destruction of Bronte. At this time the stream of lava was 18 miles long, one mile wide, and 30 feet high. In 1669 one of these molten streams overtopped the ramparts of Catania, 60 feet in height, and fell in a fiery cascade into the city a part of which it destroyed. This lava stream overran 14 villages before it reached Cantania, whose walls had been raised to a height of 60 feet as a protection against the molten flood from this mountain. After destroying a part of the town, it flowed on in a stream 40 feet deep and 1800 feet broad, to the sea. This can still be seen curling over the ramparts of Catania like a cascade in the act of falling. Near the crater stands a small building called the English House, 9,770 feet above the sea, which is probably the highest habitation in Europe. This house is covered with snow till the middle of June, and fresh snow falls on it in August. In 1828 a large body of ice was found on Etna, lying beneath a current of lava. The ice had been covered by a shower of volcanic ashes, then by a stream of lava, the non-conducting ashes protecting the ice from the heat of the lava. This ice is used in the neighboring town, and is described by Lyell as being extremely hard and very pure. This is true fossil ice.

On Hawaii, Sandwich Islands, are the most remarkable volcanoes, perhaps, in the world. There are three of them: Mauna Kea, 13,950 feet, now extinct; Mauna Loa, 13,760 feet; and Kilauea, at the base of Loa, 3,970 feet in height. Eruptions are repeated from Kilueaa every few years. During an eruption in May and June 1840, the lava flowed through a subterranean passage for eight miles, when it reached the surface, and sweeping forest, hamlet, plantation and everything before it, rolled down to the sea, a distance of 32 miles, where leaping a precipice of 50 feet, the stream of half a mile wide and 20 feet thick poured in one vast cataract into the sea. The atmosphere for long distances was filled with ashes, spray and gases, the lava being shivered into fine particles as it fell into the water. The characteristic of the Hawaiian type of volcanoes is the comparatively perfect liquidity of the lavas, thus allowing them to flow long distances. In Vesuvius the lavas are so viscid that jets cannot rise freely over the surface; the vapors are therefore kept confined as bubbles until a collection of them burst, and fragments are sometimes thrown to a height of thousands of feet. The more important eruptions of Hawaii, after 1840, were in 1843, 1849 and 1852. All ot these were vast in extent, but were not accompanied by earthquakes, thus contrasting with the explosive eruptions of Vesuvius and Etna.

Jorullo, a volcano ot Mexico, has presented the most remarkable phenomenon in the memory of man, it having been wholly thrown up from a fertile plain to a height of 4265 feet above the sea, on September 28th and 29th, 1759.

Cotopaxi, near Quito, Ecuador, stands 18,875 feet ("19,660," Dana) above the sea. The upper 4,400 feet except a section around its very summit, is covered with snow. Its first recorded eruption occurred about the time of Pizarro's invasion of South America. In 1698 an eruption destroyed the city of Tacunga. In 1738 the "flames" (heated, or luminous, vapors) rose 3000 feet above the crater; and in 1743 the hot matter burst forth from several apertures near the summit, followed by profuse torrents of water, which flooded and desolated the whole plain below. Again in May, 1744, new passages were opened, and in April, 1768, the dust and ashes were so dense that the inhabitants were compelled to use lanterns almost the whole day. In 1803 another eruption occured, after a complete state of quiescence during 20 years. In January of that year the snow began to melt and the next day was all gone. At the port of Guayaquil, 130 miles distant, Humbolt heard, day and night, the roaring and explosions of this volcano, like continued explosions of artillery.

In the south polar region are two active volcanoes, on Victoria land: Mt. Erebus, 12,400 feet, and Mt. Terror, 10,900 feet above the sea. As this land is uninhabited, no recorded harm is done by eruptions, and the same may be said of Mt. Bridgeman, on one of the South Shetland islands. Deception Island, near the latter group, is volcanic, and consists ot alternate layers of volcanic ashes and ice, with a deep lake five miles in circumference, and hot springs, 140 deg. F.

At the other extremes is Hecla, in Iceland, 5,110 feet high. Since A. D. 900, 43 of its eruptions are on record, of which five have been nearly simultaneous with those of Vesuvius, four with Etna, and one with those of both. One eruption commenced September 2nd, 1845, and lasted until April 6th, 1846; on the 23rd of November the torrent of lava, two miles from the crater, was one mile in width and from 40 to 50 feet in depth. An eruption in 1783 continued for two years and destroyed 20 villages and 9,000 inhabitants. Imagine a river of molten rock, 90 miles long 7 to 12 broad, and 100 feet deep, and you have some idea of the amount of matter poured out at this time.

In 1815 a violent eruption took place on the Island of Umbawa, near Java. The lava flowed over the land and entered the sea. Whirlwinds swept over the island, tearing up trees and bearing off men, horses and cattle. Of 12,000 inhabitants only 26 survived the awful catastrophe. In 1883 an eruption from Krakatoa threw volcanic ashes 50,000 feet into the air, and it is supposed the fine ashes travelled around the globe, causing the red sunsets so noticeable at that time.

Volcanic eruptions occurred on the island of Martinique, Lesser Antilles, beginning May 6th, 1902, with tremendous explosions May 7th and 8th, which shattered the top of the volcano, Mt. Pelee, destroying the city of St. Pierre and about 30,000 people, shipping in the harbor, and devastating the entire north end of the island, and probably making it uninhabitable for years to come. Of all the people left in the city during the eruption, but one escaped, a negro confined in an underground dungeon for murder. This eruption saved his life, as there was no record of his crime left. The ejections continued for several days, with terrific explosions, which were called earthquakes by some, but they were probably only the usual accompaniments of volcanic action, but not true earthquakes. This eruption was followed a day or two later, by a similar outbreak from La Souffriere, a volcano on St. Vincent Island nearby. The eruption on St. Vincent was fully as destructive as at St Pierre, but the loss of life was much less, being only sparsely inhabited compared to St. Pierre. Mt. Pelee is 4,450 feet high, and there are six volcanoes of smaller size on Martinique, which are supposed to be extinct. Empress Josephine was born at St Pierre in 1763. Mt. Souffriere, on St. Vincent, is 3,090 feet high. A tremendous eruption occurred from this volcano in 1812, when volcanic ashes were carried to Barbadoes, 60 or 70 miles.

But volcanoes are not confined to the land. In 1783 volcano broke forth in the sea off the coast of Iceland, covering the water with pumice to a distance of 150 miles. At this place an island was formed which the Danish government called Nyoe; but it disappeared in less than a year, leaving a reef of rocks beneath the surface.

In 1811 an island, called Sabrina, was formed by a volcanic eruption, near the Azores, whose cone was 300 feet above the water; this was soon leveled down by the action of the sea. In 1831 a volcanic island arose off the south coast of Sicily, where a few years before was 600 feet of water; but this also disappeared in a few months.

Many cases might be cited of islands caused by volcanic action under the sea, many of which have been inhabited for centuries; and extinct volcanoes, or remains of them, are common the world over; some of them now represented by volcanic necks, others by thermal springs—and new ones may break out at any time, like Jorullo of Mexico.—*The Mineral Collector.*

MONSOON GARDENING.

In every part of India, without exception, the monsoon is looked forward to with an anxiety that must seem curious to people dwelling in temperate climes. All nature becomes "thirsty" after the three months of dry weather—*i. e.*, from about 15th March to 15th June, when the "hot wind," a veritable "Sirocco" blows almost continuously, licking up every drop of moisture from the surface soil, scorching up vegetation, and rendering life generally unbearable. Man, beast and plant feel its effects equally. Is it any wonder, then, that the life-giving rain is viewed with such feelings? After the first heavy downpour all nature seems to spring into life and rejoice, and the gardener realizes that it will be a busy time for him. He immediately sets about arrangements for propagating, layering, putting down cuttings, grafting inarching, "gooteeing," sowing seed, the preparation of beds and borders, and a hundred other operations of gardening are soon in full swing. The grass begins to grow with marvellous rapidity, and weeds appear in their thousands. On every side there are evidences of rank growth, and it takes the gardener all his time to keep it in check. The air is filled with the insect world, and caterpillars, grubs and worms are soon doing as much damage to plants as their short life will admit of. The atmosphere is humid, and when the wind lulls, and the sun comes out in all its fierceness, one feels like being in a Turkish bath.

The garden at this time is rich in its floral treasures. Ornamental foliaged plants are at their best. Many of our most beautiful trees and tree-shrubs are now in full beauty of bloom.

Here is the lovely *Magnolia fuscata* with its strongly perfumed purple flowers; there at the bend of a walk, a great clump of *Dombeya acutangula*, with its sweet-smelling cup-like flowers; over the plant-house is *Jateorhiza calumba*, with its small yellow flowers. Turn any side, and we see nothing but exuberant vegetation. Our annuals include the beautiful varieties of Balsam, Zinnia, Celosia, Amaranthus, etc., and beds and borders are a blaze of color, intensified by the hundreds of varieties of Cannas. On the Himalayas the hillsides are covered with an infinite variety of ferns intermixed with Foxglove, Columbine and Impatiens, and even Dahlias which have "escaped." Gardening during the Monsoon is a very fascinating pursuit.—*Indian Planting and Gardening*

Notes and Gleanings.

The Largest Described Snake.—Speke, in his narrative of the journey to the source of the Nile, describes the largest snake that has ever been seen by man. "I shuddered," he says, "as I looked upon the effect of his tremendous dying strength. For yards around where he lay, grass, bushes and saplings, in fact everything except full grown trees, were cut clean off, as if they had been trimmed with an immense scythe. The monster, when measured, was fifty-one feet two and a half inches in extreme length, while around the thickest portions of its body the girth was nearly three feet.

Mines of Mammoth Bones.—At some time in the distant past a remarkable state of affairs existed in what are now the bleak arctic regions of Siberia. At the time of which we speak the climate must have been comparatively mild, for thousands and hundreds of thousands of huge animals, mostly of the elephant type, roamed up and down the valleys of what are now frozen polar rivers. In the midst of their innocent happiness a sudden and awful change came. Some philosophers say that the earth "fell out of balance" and titled thousands of miles to the north. Whatever the cause, fierce winter almost instantly swept over the land of the mastodon and the mammoth and overwhelmed the great beasts in huge snowdrifts, from which they could not extricate themselves. In the course of time these huge banks of snow were transformed into great mountains of ice, and today specimens of the great hairy mammoth may be found that are as fresh as when they were frozen in, thousands of years ago. In some places along the Lena river the bluffs are perfect mines of mammoth's bones.

The Natural Bridge of Virginia, is 215 feet in height, 100 feet in width, with a span of 90 feet. Cedar Creek, the stream over which it stretches its arch, is clear as crystal. No photograph or painting can impress the mind with its immensity of grandeur, or geometrical proportions, or the rich coloring, or the picturesque surroundings. One must feast his eyes upon the mighty arch to realize its vastness. Under the arch are the outlines of an American Eagle, formed by moss and lichens. On one side is where George Washington, when a surveyor for Lord Fairfax, 150 years ago, carved his name in the rock. The ravages of time and exposure to the elements have nearly obliterated the name, but some of the letters are quite distinct. In the years gone by Henry Clay, Daniel Webster and many prominent statesmen before railroads were built, spent days of inconvenient travel to look upon this, one of the wonders of the world.

Gulliver's Astronomy.—Prophecy is a foreknowledge of events to come, so the following cannot strictly be called a prophecy, but to say the least is a singular foreknowledge of a discovery that did not come for many years after. A most remarkable account of the position of certain planets occurs in "Gulliver's Travels." This book, written somewhere about 1726 contains the following words: "They spend the greater part of their lives in observing the celestial bodies, which they do by the assistance of glasses far excelling ours in goodness. They have likewise discovered two lesser stars, or satellites, which revolve about Mars, whereof the innermost is distant from the center of the primary planet exactly three of his diameters and the outermost five. The former revolves in the space of 10 hours, and the latter in 21 1-2, so that the squares of their periodical times are very near in the same proportion with the cubes of their distance from the center of Mars." One hundred and fifty years before it was known that Mars had a satellite, when the theory that it had one would have been met with ridicule, or at least disbelief, the author of this remarkable book described the exact number of satellite sthat Mars possessed, told their location and unusual speed; also a peculiarity in the relation of the speed to the central orb, a peculiarity based upon no principles with which astronomers are familiar. A careful study of the statements made by many writers of marked ability will almost inevitably lead us to the conclusion that certain imaginative minds have the gift of prophecy, or, at all events, there may be flashes of divination possibly unsuspected by the writers themselves.

A Wonderful Cement.—Professor Alexander Winchell is credited with the invention of a cement that will stick to anything. Take two ounces of clear gum arabic, one and one-half ounces of fine starch and one-half ounce of white sugar. Pulverize the gum arabic, dissolve it in as much water as the laundress would use for the quantity of starch and sugar in the gum solution. Then cook the mixture in a vessel suspended in boiling water until the starch becomes clear. The cement should be as thick as tar and kept so. It can be kept from spoiling by dropping in a lump of gum camphor or a little oil of cloves or sassafras. This cement is very strong indeed and will stick perfectly to glazed surfaces and is good to repair broken rocks, minerals or fossils. The addition of a small amount of sulphate of aluminium will increase the effectiveness of the paste, besides helping to prevent decomposition.

Greatest Timber Area.—One billion dollars is the price tag on the standing timber in Washington, Idaho, Oregon, California and Montana. These timber lands are said to constitute the most important forest area in the world. In extent they are unapproachable, in the measure of production they are unequaled, and they surpass all other forests in the universal adaptability of their products. California has the fir, the western spruce and the red cedar. Eastern Washington has the yellow pine, which also is abundant in central and eastern Oregon and northern California, surpassing in size and equaling in quality the product of the pine belt of the great lakes. The amount of timber standing in the five states is placed at an aggregate of 700,000,000,000 feet.

The Amateur Naturalist

......ISSUED MONTHLY.......

Subscription, 50 Cents per Year.   Single Copies, 5 Cents.

ADVERTISING RATES ON APPLICATION.

————EDITED AND PUBLISHED BY————

CHARLES D. PENDELL,   -   -   ASHLAND, MAINE.

IN advocating the formation of local societies for nature study we have not intended to neglect the larger societies—those with a national reputation and prominence, or those which have some particular State as their special field. If they have apparently been overlooked it is because of the fact of their being already so prominently before the nature loving public that it has hardly seemed necessary. The Audobon Society, and the Wild Flower Preservation Society of America and others all provide for local branches, and this affiliation with a large body of specialists has many advantages. Probably the Maine Ornithological Society is the most prominent and influential organization of this kind in this State, a society which has had an existence of eleven years, during which time it has had a constant growth, and with its growth a decided influence upon legislation for the protection of our native birds. But whatever be the form of organization the benefit to the individual is great; new thoughts, increased knowledge and a widening vista of natures great field are sure to follow, and we would urge upon our readers the importance of membership in some such society, or the organization of local societies in which nature study shall form a prominent part. And to any such the files of the AMATEUR NATURALIST afford numerous selections which could be read with interest to all.

CIRCUMSTANCES or environment may modify but should never control the any human undertaking. Circumstances have modified the plans of the Amateur Naturalist and at times delayed the regularity of its issue, but it has come to stay and it is not the intention of its editor to allow any circumstance to interfere with this fact. No other magazine published gives so much matter of general interest and real worth as THE AMATEUR NATURALIST for the same price—only 50 cents a year, or the three volumes, I, II and III for $1.25 post paid. And subsequent volumes will be equally interesting.

IN THE May number we took occasion to refer editorially to those theories which attempt to explain volcanoes by ascribing them to some local disturbance. We maintained that the older theory of a molten interior of the eatrh was the more natural explanation and the more tenable. In part as a substantiation of our position and in part because the articles themselves are of such intense and general interest we published in the June number and in this issue two articles on the subject, giving the evidence of eye-witnesses and historical facts. The wide area covered by these disturbances, literally the whole earth, and the tremendous forces which produce them, seem to shatter any theory of mere local disturbance. And by the lesson of anology, considering that scientists generally admit that the great Desert of Sahara was once an ocean bed, may not the tradition of the former existence of the Island of Atlantis be a record of actual fact? Pliny regarded it as historically true, but the mists of time and the iconoclasm of the age have combined to characterize it as a myth. There does not seem much opportunity for real investigation at this late date, though Ignatius Donnelly has gone quite exhaustively into the matter; but the subject is one that at least deserves serious thought.

SOMEWHERE scattered among the 70 or 80 million people of America there are at least 7 or 8 thousand people to whom the AMATEUR NATURALIST would be a welcome visitor and who would gladly subscribe did they know of it. Will our readers help us reach them? Send us the names of your friends likely to be interested and we will mail them sample copies free and thank you for so doing. And in renewing your own subscription, why not send the names of two friends and $1.00 and we will give you a years subscription for your effort.

JUST as soon as time will allow we shall prepare an index to the AMATEUR NATURALIST which will be sent to all subscribers. We are in hopes to have it ready by the close of the current volume and include all the topics in the first three volumes.

Random Notes.

The largest mass of ice on earth has been accumulated in Greenland for thousands of years, and the immense block is supposed to average a mile and a half in thickness, its area being about 600,000 square miles.

A remarkable illustration of the force with which a swordfish strikes a blow has recently been reported. While repairing a ship recently which had completed a long voyage in Pacific waters, a sword was found which had successfully pierced a sheathing, one inch thick, a three inch plank and beyond that four and a half inches of firm timber.

It is calculated that a twelve horse-power touring car, built for moderate speed, requires more than five horse-power to overcome the resistance of the atmosphere—the wind of its own making—at thirty-two miles an hour, whereas the same automobile, if it could be driven at the speed of 114 miles an hour, would require 234 horse-power merely to offset the air resistance.

If Mars and Saturn reflected the same proportion of the light which falls upon their surfaces the smaller and much nearer planet would look three times as bright as the much more distant and much larger Saturn. As a matter of fact, there is no great difference between the two. It is inferred from this fact that the visible surface of Saturn consists of clouds, since no surface of land and water would reflect so much light as that planet gives.

The great planet Jupiter is not yet wholly cooled and is in a small degree self luminous. It is seen, therefore, that Jupiter has a greater or less resemblance to the sun in its physical constitution, a view which quite corresponds with its aspect in the telescope. A dull light is sent from parts of the planet's surface besides what it reflects, as though it were still feebly glowing like a nearly extinguished sun; and on the whole the main interest of these features lies in the presumption they create that the great planet is not yet fit to be the abode of life, but is more probably in a condition like that of the earth millions of years ago.

In the colbat mines of Ontario a vein has recently been uncovered and followed for 50 feet. It was about 13 inches wide where first discovered but gradually widened to 5 feet. One huge nugget of 800 lbs. weight was taken out, which contained 70 per cent. of silver. As a result of this find the price of colbat has dropped from $3. a pound to 37 cents. Colbat takes a long time to tarnish and when it does tarnish still presents an attractive appearance. It is white and harder and brighter than nickel, with about the same degree of malleability as iron. It is used extensively for electrical storage batteries and for plating material.

A great many people hesitate to handle plants with which they are not familiar for fear of being poisoned. There is a general impression that a large number of wild plants are poisonous to the touch, but as a matter of fact, not half a dozen in any one locality are really so. The number of plants that are poisonous when eaten is much larger. Several of these have poisonous roots as well, and some with poisonous roots have harmless or edible fruit. Among common plants with poisonous roots may be mentioned May-apple, Bloodroot, Poke, Elder, Indian Hemp, Hellebore, Lily-of-the-Valley, Bane-Berry, Bug-bane, Aconite, and various species of Iris, Solanum, Trillium, Euphorbia, Cicuta and Ipomea.—*American Botanist.*

The Amateur Naturalist.

A MAGAZINE FOR ALL STUDENTS OF NATURE.

VOLUME III.   ASHLAND MAINE, OCTOBER, 1906.   NUMBER 6.

NATURE STUDY IN THE MOUNTAINS.

EARL LYND JOHNSTON.

HAVING made three trips to the same region in the Rockies it occurred to me that it might be a good plan to tell of some of the things seen from the standpoint of one who is interested in nature study, in order that our less favored cousins of the East may know of the opportunities afforded Colorado people to see and study nature in nearly all its different phases.

This region of so much interest to me is Estes Park, Colo., a Park situated along the Thompson—a stream of clear, cool, and swiftly flowing water containing numerous rainbow trout, which seem to me to be the most beautiful of fishes. This valley also has overshadowing it a long expanse of snowy ranges, reaching up—up far into the clouds and from whose summits some of the grandest scenic wonders of this earth can be viewed,— a vista so grand that a very reverent minister was heard to say that it never could be duplicated this side of the New Jerusalem.

As we enter the Park we are encompassed with conflicting emotions, not knowing whether to laugh, cry, or keep silent, but, as a rule one is so impressed with the sublime scene that he feels as if it would be a sin to speak and mar the spell of enchantment. Then as we move forward into the Park we are impressed with the thought that it is nothing more than a dark green meadow from 10 to 12 miles in length and from 1 to 3 miles in breadth covered here and there with groves of pines, spruce and cedars in the uplands and birch, willow and cottonwoods along the streams. Then when our eyes are beginning to be opened we see bright and gay colored flowers with insects of dazzling brilliancy flitting from one to another of these blossoms and sometimes pausing as if to admire their own beauty; for it seems that at this altitude all life is arrayed in brilliant colors,—red or redish tinge being the most commonly found.

From the altitude of the Park (7,500 ft.) to that of the top of Long's Peak (14,276 ft.) we have a flora as varied as one would find on a trip from Boston to San Francisco or from Alaska to Florida, for Colorado boasts of more than three thousand described species of plants with new ones being added every year. Is it any wonder then that this region is, and has been, the camping ground for the summer of eminent eastern botanists and zoologists, in fact for scientists in all lines of scientific research? Now to get back, after a little digression, and say something more concerning the flora of this region. We find here as elsewhere that the Compositæ are greatly in the majority; in fact I shouldn't be surprised if some one were to to tell me that there were 500 members here, for everywhere you go—swamp, meadow, rocky slopes, timberline, yes, and far above timberline among the rocks one is greeted with one or more of this family in their many different blending of colors in the rays and disk flowers. To enumerate them all here would be too tedious and take too much space; however, I will give a few examples:—golden rod (*Solidago*) is found from the plains to far above timberline where of course they are modified in form and color, being of a very dark yellow and generally very small, some of them scarcely three inches long and so hid behind colossal rocks as to be entirely unnoticed by a casual observer as are many other of the beautiful plants of this region—beautiful because of the richness of coloring in the blossoms, the numerous and fantastic shapes found in many of the corollas and the extreme delicacy of some of the foliage of these alpine species, and to think that hundreds of persons pass them by every day unseen as though they were placed in a desert instead of in the most beautiful region of God's handiwork! How much then do we need Nature Study in our schools to train the eye and ear of the coming generations!

The asters and daisies (*Erigerons*) are to be found along with the golden rod and with as many adaptations, only of course they present a more beautiful contrast with the great variety of color in the rays and the length of the rays. Here also we will find the sage brush (*Artemisia*), a typical Colorado plant, at nearly all elevations. Besides this great division of the plant kingdom we find an extensive and varied flora, falling into about forty families, of very showy plants as, orchids, mariposa and tiger lilies, gentains from the rich meadows of the lowlands to the rocks of Boulder Field where little else but very small species of phloxes, alpine blue bells (*Mertensia*), little harebells (*Campanula*), saxifrages in abundance but just as small and as hard to find, Scrophulariaceae, a very prominent family consisting of paint brushes

(*Castilleja*), Pentstemons, Pedicularis, a queer looking plant and many others, with the Columbine, the prettiest of them all to break the monotony of this weird desolation of rocks, stones and an unlimited vision of high mountain peaks on three sides and a never ending view out over the plains to what seems to be infinity on the other—a scene beautiful because of its awfulness and sublimity causing a reverent attitude in one who would be unaffected wihh the ordinary surroundings of life.

But here I shall have to bring my general description of the Park to a close as I want to say something about some of the other phases of Nature Study found on the top of this mighty background to the plains of Eastern Colorado and also in the small depressions, canons and gorges formed in various ways. Here is a place for the geologist to search out and read the records of the past as they are written in the indistructible rocks and formations trom various causes for here are moraines, lateral, terminal and medial, showing the work of the ice age; one of these moraines according to Prof. Orton shows the record of two periods of ice activity. There are glaciers in the region of the Park and many more which have left their mark on the mountain sides. Why go to Switzerland and the Alps to see what can be seen and just as well here in our own land? Then with a little time we are able to visit craters of extinct volcanoes looming up as they do to tell of the formation of the earth's surface, how in the pre-historic past an unseen power was at work to form an inhabitable place for man.

Another avenue for the study of Nature is open for the enthusiastic zoologist where he would be in his element, for I saw in one day's tramp, fire-colored insects, of countless varieties, conies who make hay something after the fashion of man, ptarmigans which have four changes of raiment, one for each season of the year; they appear to be as proud as the "fairer sex" are of their seasonal change of apparel. Thrushes, grouse, campbirdslarks, with others are seen every day; then the beaver and his work is seen quite frequently. I might say here that recent authorities in forrestry give this little animal great credit in helping to conserve the water supply in the mountains of Colorado by making dams across the streams and thus preventing the unlimited flow of water; hence, the beaver is of an economic value to the Colorado farmer who has to depend upon water to irrigate his crops. Tracks of mountain sheep and the snow-shoe rabbit with the hind feet shaped like snowshoes are sometimes seen. Lynx, mountain lions, bears, coyotes, wolves, porcupines, and a long list of others inhabit this region giving us a fauna here in Colorado as extensive as any where else in the United States if not in the world.

One of Nature's most interesting places is Timberline for here we have the great struggle for existence graphically told, showing the survival of not what seems to be the fittest but the strongest. Here we have the line of battle between the winds and the woods. Trees all bow to or rather sway from this ever prevailing force on the barren sides of the mountains which is relentless with its power, for nine months in the year it blows filled with sleet, hail and snow and succeeds in dwarfing, bending and twisting the otherwise noble trees until they lose all appearance of the grandeur which their more favored brothers possess and are nothing but broken and flayed portions of what under favorable conditions might have been grand specimens of the forest. The desolation of this portion of the earth would be unbearable were it not for the countless myriads of living things, beautiful plants and dazzling butterflies and moths along with the scenic grandeur of a sunrise or a sunset from this spot or the long range of vision from the limit of the forest down over the moutains clothed in the rich dark green of a thick forest, with spots of blackened ruins to remind us of the devestation of forest fires, down to the mountain meadows, out over the foothills until our vision strikes the sunlight as it shimmers across the sandy plains and o'er the many lakes or reservoirs used for irrigation and then is lost in what seems to be an endless stretch of blue and gray, the place where the earth and sky seem to meet.

So taken as a whole we have within reach of any one in this land of ours a place where with eyes and ears opened one may enjoy a summer's vacation as they have never done before, seeing Nature from its æsthetic, moral, and scientific viewpoints and hence be a better educated individnal for having had one more avenue of life opened to them, so they may be better able to go back and take up the every day duties of life with the grand thought impressed on their mind that this world was made beautiful as well as useful. One person has spoken of it in this way: "I noted well on my trip up the trail all of my surroundings. As I was returning I began to think I was on a new trail for it seemed to me as if the Creator had been remodelling it all and making it more glorious than it was at first sight; then I remembered that such could not be the case and that I was mortal and that it must be my eyes which were being made new,—or rather opened, unfolding to my gaze a vision which will remain in my memory till the end of days." What a glorious image to think on as compared to that of the constant din of the city with the blacky murkiness of a never ending night of smoke and with its living pictures of squalor, wretchedness and vice; but why dwell upon this? We all know about it if not first handed by reading the papers! It serves only as a lesson to show us the wisdom of an omniscient Creator in giving us a world full of the Beautiful at whose fountain we are able to slack our thirst for beauty and satisfy our desire for something savoring of divinity.

Evans, Colo.

DROPPING NUTS.

BY WILLIAM WHITMAN BAILEY, LL. D.

FEW objects of vegetable nature are more beautiful than the horse-chestnut. The very seedling is a tree in miniature. It shows from the beginning a strong woody stem and spreads out its aggressive leaves as if foreshadowing its umbrageous manhood. Then, when the tree is mature, it bursts in June into a great candelabrum of white flowers spotted with pink and yellow. Then, in a moment, as it were, we note that some of the flowers, a few only, are rapidly developing a pistil, which will later mature into a fruit. The ovary is at first three celled, with several ovules. Something pre-destines one of these, with its contents, to take advantage of the others, He at once begins to take advantage of his brothers and crowd them to the wall. Finally the pod itself becomes one-celled instead of three, but frequently the shrivelled remains of other ovules and the original partitions may be seen.

In October, especially in a high wind, any nuts that survive the trail of the small boy, who from time immemorial has gathered them, come tumbling down, their old mahogany new polished and veined by the most skillful artist and cabinet maker. Each nut is wrapped too, in the finest kid as if put up by Tiffany, lest the surface should be dimmed. The valves of the pod are studded with spines, but these are, at least when fresh, weak and inoffensive; later they become more rigid.

Does any one know why boys like to amass such unreasonable quantities of thèse nuts? They are bitter and inedible, the plenteous starch being impregnated with a bitter if not noxious principle. So gorged is the seed with this albumen that the cotyledons never separate; they serve only as storehouses of food for the germinating plant. The line of cleavage is quite visible when one, with difficulty, peels off the seed-coats, as is also the caulicle coiled about the seed leaves and the plumule within.

Quite different things pass under the name of nuts. The nuts of horse-chesnuts are the seeds, but in the regular chestnut a prickly bur is found which is simply protective, commonly surrounding three, not seeds, but style tipped fruits. Each of these in turn originally possessed three cells and several ovules. All but one is rigorously suppressed. The acorn is in same case.

In the common hickory nut, butter nut, pig nut and black walnut, we have a kind of dry drupe, with a long shell containing a large fourlobed and straight seed without albumen. The fleshy and oily seedleaves are corrugated so that they resemble the hemispheres of the human brain, as is well seen in the English walnut. One of the very best of these nuts is the pecan.

To anyone born in New England and the central places of our Union, the memory of autumn days spent in nutting will always remain rubrical. Charming pictures of such childhood days are depicted in Beecher's "Star Papers" or in Miss Warner's "Queechy", They are redolent of the still hours of autumn, with the tonic odor of the new-fallen leaf and the purpling grape. Full of introspection are such times; in them one can only read poetry, the Arabian Knights or Idyls of the King.

Brown University, Providence, R. I.

BIRTH OF THE MOON.

MILLIONS of years ago the earth was not the land bound, sea swept globe so familiar to us, but a liquid mass on which floated crust some thirty-five miles thick. At that period, says the *Strand Magazine*, it turned on its axis at a constantly increasing speed that finally shortened the day to three hours. When that terrific velocity was obtained 5,000 cubic million miles of matter were hurled off by the enormous centrifugal force, and our moon was born. The cleaving of so large a body must have left some scar on the earth's surface. It has accordingly been suggested that the great basin now occupied by the Pacific ocean was once filled by what is now the moon. Yet our moon has the distinction of being the largest of all planetary satellites—so large, indeed, that to the inhabitants of Mars it must appear with the earth as a wonderfully beautiful twin planet.

Because the moon rotates on its axis in exactly the same time that it revolves around the earth we are destined to see little more than one hemisphere. So slow is this rotation that the lunar day is equal to fifteen of our days. For half a month the moon is exposed to the fierce heat of the sun; for half a month it spins through space in the densest gloom.

Smaller in mass than the earth is, the moon's attraction for bodies must be correspondingly less. A good terrestrial athlete could cover about 120 feet on the moon in a running broad jump, and leaping over a barn would be a very commonplace feat. A man in the moon could carry six times as much and run six times as fast as he could on the earth. Although separated from us by a distance that at times reaches 253,000 miles and is never less than 222,000 miles, we know more of the physical formation of the single pallid face that the moon ever turns toward us than we know of certain parts of Asia and the heart of Africa. Powerful telescopes have brought our satellite within a distance of forty miles of the earth. Physicists have mathematically weighed it and fixed its mass at one-eighth of the earth, or 73,000,000,000,-000 tons.

The moon presents aspects without any terrestrial parallel. Rent by fires long since dead, its honeycombed crust seems like a great globe of chilled slag. Craters are not uncommon on the earth, but in number, size and structure they bear for the most part little resemblence to those of the moon. A lunar crater is not the mouth of a volcano having a diameter of a few hundred feet, but a great circular plain twenty, fifty, even a hundred miles in diameter, surrounded by a precipice rising to a height of 5,000 or 10,000 feet, with a central hill or two about half as high.

Water cannot possibly exist as a liquid, for the temperature of the moon's surface during the long lunar night is probably not far from 460 degrees below the zero mark of a Fahrenheit thermometer, and the atmospheric pressure is so low that a gas under pressure would solidify as it escaped. Ice and snow are the forms then, which lunar water must assume. Because of the present paucity of water the moon's atmosphere is so exceedingly rare that startling effects are produced. Perhaps the most striking is that of the sunrise. Dawn and the soft golden glow that ushers in terrestrial day there cannot be. The sun leaps from the horizon a flaming sickle, and the loftier peaks immediately flash into light. There is no azure sky to relieve the monotonous effects of inky black shadows and dazzling white expanses. The sun gleams in fierce splendor, with no clouds to diffuse its blinding light. All day long it is accompanied by the weird zodiacal light that we behold at rare intervals. Even in midday the heavens are pitch black, so that, despite the sunlight, the stars and planets gleam with a brightness that they never exhibit to us even on the clearest of moonless nights at sea. They shine steadily, too, for it is the earth's atmosphere that causes them to twinkle to our eyes. In the line of sight it is impossible to estimate distances, for there is no such phenomenon as ærial perspective. Objects are seen only when the rays of the sun strike them.

At times there may be observed spots which darken after sunrise and gradually disappear toward sunset. They cannot be caused by shadows, for shadows would be least visible when the sun is directly overhead. They appear most quickly at the equator and invade the higher altitudes after a lapse of a few days. In the polar regions they have never been seen. What are they? Organic life resembling vegetation, answers Professor Pickering of Harvard University; vegetation that flourishes luxuriantly while the sun shines and withers at night. A single day, it may be urged, is not sufficiently long for the development and decay of vegetation, but sixteen hours on the moon is little more than half an hour on the earth; a day lasts half a month and may be regarded as a miniature season.

PECULIARITIES OF PURSLANE.

BY BYRON D. HALSTED.

THERE are some things that are peculiar concerning *Portulaca oleracea* L., commonly known as purslane or in contempt by the gardeners as "pusley."

In the first place its appearance is striking, and were it not so common, would attract much attention. Growing prostrate upon the soil, it forms a carpet of succulent herbage with its brittle stems and plump, ovate, spatulate leaves.

A second point of special interest is its fondness for the sun. Shade acts almost as poison to this obese herb. In my experiments with half-shade made by using lath and shutting off one-half of the sun, it was noted that under the lath the purslane failed to grow, except at a very feeble pace, while alongside in the full blaze of the sun, it was rampant.

PURSLANE.—*Portulaca oleracea.**

The purslane flower is inconspicuous, but of a bright yellow as it holds itself to the morning sun and closes long before the day is finished. Looked at closely, these blossoms are found to have their stamens sensitive, and when some tiny insect comes for the pollen, the filaments will bend toward the center and bring the anthers close to the pistil.

---

* Purslane was introduced from Asia, coming originally from India, and has spread over all Europe except the extreme north, and is common over all the older settled portions of the United States. In the cut a part of the stems are placed upright for the purpose of illustration, but in nature the stems are always recumbent upon the ground.—[ED.

The purslane dies with the coming of the autumn frosts and· beneath the blackened network of herbage there falls a crop of seed that in the ratio of multiplication would startle a Matthus. A single seed produces a plant that, if not crowded by its neighbors or overturned in its growth by the hoe, will thrive and ripen a million offspring as an inheritance of evil to the negligent gardener.

It is surprising how rapidly form these minute black seeds, shaped somewhat like some sea shells and rougher than most of them. Only a single week is needed from the time of pollination to the maturing of the green oval pod with its contents of a hundred shining seeds.

To the collector the purslane is a wonder, as it defies the desicating effects of weights and dryness, and even grows after it has been placed in press, and is a veritable "live-forever" without the name.

The Portulaca is remarkable for the lack of a long list of fungi; in fact there is but one usually met with and that is the white mould, *Cysyopus Portulacæ* (DC.), which is frequently a destructive enemy.

In connection with this parasite there is one fact of special interest, namely, the tendency of the Cystopustized stems to grow upright. A plant may have all of its five or six main branches flat upon the ground except one, which with its smaller stem and dwarfed, crumpled leaves, may rise bolt upright from the prostrate branch to the height of several inches. It would seem as if there was a design in this, for these stems are more apt to be hit by any passing object and the spores thereby distributed. A microspic examination of the stems show sthat the diseased stems have a larger percentage of starch than in the healthy ones. In the latter it is quite closely confined to the sheath of cells just outside of the wood, but in the infested stems it is widespread through the soft cellular tissue.—*Plant World*.

A remarkable botanical specimen of Japan is a hollow tree-trunk 65 feet in circumference containing a living tree 9 feet in circumference. The older tree was destroyed about 120 years ago, leaving 30 feet of trunk, and the inner tree is about 110 years old. The editor has several times seen this kind of double growth, but but on nothing like so large a scale.

Notes and Gleanings.

Numbering the Stars.—Nineteen years ago a congress of astronomers from all parts of the world met in Paris and parted the heavens among the observers of 17 countries for the co-operative production of an astrographic catalogue. Each observatory was allotted a definite zone of the heavens and made responsible for making a photographic map of its stellar territory. At that time the number of catalogued stars was 342,000. In a recent address before the Royal Society of England, Prof. Schuster reported that this international survey, now approaching completion, had resulted in the identification and mapping of 4,500,000 stars. One star differs from another in glory from the first down to the 14th magnitude, though only the first 11 magnitudes are to be catalogued.

Druidical Astronomy.—Astronomy, that science of illimitable marvels, seems, even in its most familiar phases, far remote from man's everyday life, observes *Collier's Weekly*. Yet the English astronomer, Sir Norman Lockyer, has recently established a fundamental date in human history by a simple and facinating application of this branch of science. Stonehenge's wonderful rock architecture, he has determined, was built as a sort of primative sacred observatory. Therein the priests of the sun worshipped, publishing to their wild congregations the changes of the seasons. More than mere priests and builders were they, for their edifices were so designed that on the longest day of the year the midsummer sun flashed the first ray of its rising direct upon the central altar. But in the slow procession of the ages the celestial pole sweeps around a great circle, and the midsummer day's sun veers by a minute fraction of a degree at each year's rising. So, the beam that illumined the solemn array of the astronomer-priests in that dim twilight of history, now falls nearly a degree aslant of the ancient altar. To estimate the time represented in the variation is simple. It establishes the building of Stonehenge at approximately 1680 B. C. Something of the wonder of the eternal ages is in this determination; something, too, of pride in the might of the human atom, since the very orb of day stands to the mind not so changeless as the massive and mystic handiwork of the first Britons.

Voracity of Fishes.—All the deep sea fishes are enormous eaters, says John C. Van Dyke, in "The Opal Sea." There being nothing to eat but the life about them, they live upon one another. They follow the prey like packs of wolves, and in turn are followed, band succeeding bands, increasing in size as they decrease in numbers. The herring eat the smaller fish, even their own young; they are harried by the blue fishes, until a trail of blood stains the water, while following the blue fish comes the insatiate porpoise. The cetaceans especially, Mr. Van Dyke says, are wonderfully equipped for the consumption of small sea life en masse—one rorqual perhaps swallowing thousands of herring at a single gulp. The seal's appetite is also phenomenal, in captivity fifty or more pounds of fish being required daily at a single meal. After gorging himself he goes to sleep, floating on his back with floppers folded, his head bobbing up and down upon the waves as peacefully as upon a bed of roses.

Eucalyptus, Tree of the Desert.—That phenomenal tree of the Australian deserts, the Eucalyptus, has been planted for forty years in the dry soil of our own Southwest, where it is commonly known as the blue-gum, or red-gum. Although of foreign origin, the Eucalyptus seems especially fitted to the dry country of Arizona, New Mexico, southern California and western Texas, where its value would be hard to overestimate. Its drought-resisting powers enable it to flourish where no large American tree will grow. It yields oil, gum, nectar for honey-bees, furnishes shade for the ranch house, wind-breaks for field crops, and firewood for localities where fuel is scarce. But its chief value lies in the possibilities it holds for the reforestation of the bare, dry mountain-sides of the desert country, and for the protection of irrigating-streams. It is especially adapted for such purposes by reason of its rapidity of growth in arid soil. No native American species can equal the extraordinary development of this exotic from remote Australia. On the ranch of Elwood Cooper, near Santa Barbara, Cal., there are Eucalpyts twenty-five years old as great in girth as oaks of three hundred years. And time and time again the species called blue-gum has, when cut to the ground, sent up sprouts from the stump which in eight years have reached a height of one hundred feet. Nor does this rapidity of growth shorten the life of the tree, for the Eucalyptus in its Australian home reaches a great age and is the only tree that rivals in size the giant redwoods and the big trees of California.

Erratic Boulders are rounded masses of rock that have been transported from their native locality by the action of ice. Usually they are strewn over surfaces that seem to have been scraped comparatively smooth, and from a good point of view they are impressive objects as they dot the landscape. For the greater part they are half burried, but in many instances they stand almost wholly uncovered. Erratic boulders are found all over the New England states, eastern New York, England the Scandanavian peninsula and hundreds of other localities. One near Mount Vernon, N. Y., weighs about 2,500 tons. It split along a cleaverage plane, and a butternut tree that for forty years has been growing in the cleft has wedged the halves three feet apart at the top. Erratic boulders are sometimes lodged on the top of dykes or other large masses of rock in such a manner that they tip back and forth. These are the famous rocking-stones.

NATURE'S LEGACY.

BY HATTIE WASHBURN.

I am an heiress though but plainly gowned,
Though my hands by toil are roughened and browned.
No miser with his hordes, nor millionaire,
Boasts of a fortune with mine to compare.
Yet none are unhappy, starving or cold,
Because of the boundless wealth that I hold.
Nature, my benefactor, does bestow
On me the wealth her loving children know.
The sunset sky where countless beauties shine,
The morning's burst of glory, too, is mine;
The gentle murmur of the winds that pass,
Changing shadows moving upon the grass;
The butterflies, like stemless floating flowers,
Fairy creatures of summer's fleeting hours;
Melodious carols the wild birds sing,
The peace and joy that to my soul they bring;
Moonbeams sleeping upon the waters fair,
Sunlight glory, the fresh and perfumed air,
The music the breeze in the tree-top plays,
Far reaching prairies, mine whereon to gaze;
The bright blossoms that at the wayside grow—
All countless are the riches that I know.
Nor would I hold them for myself alone,
The more wealth I bestow, the more I own.

Goodwin, S. D.

The Amateur Naturalist

......ISSUED MONTHLY.......

Subsoription, 50 Cents per Year.   Single Copies, 5 Cents.

ADVERTISING RATES ON APPLICATION.

————————EDITED AND PUBLISHED BY————————
CHARLES D. PENDELL,   -   -   ASHLAND, MAINE.

ONE of the most regretable instances of the autocratic power weilded by the third assistant Postmaster General, and from whose decision under the present administration there is no appeal, has occurred in connection with one of our most valued exchanges *American Ornithology*. The publishers of that magazine desired to change from monthly to bi-monthly in order that certain tain improvements in the make-up of the magazine might be added that were not feasible in its monthly form. But although it already was entered at second class rates as a monthly the third assistant has for reasons unknown refused the magazine entry under second class rates. The publishers have consequently suspended publication. We shall greatly miss it from among our exchanges. We regret, too, that the publishers felt the necessity of discontinuing. THE AMATEUR NATURALIST has likewise for no reason been denied second class rates but we shall not suspend on that account. A recollection of the parable of the unjust judge gives us courage to hope that sometime the autocrats of the postage stamp may relent, or perchance have successors, who can more readily distinguish what is a literary or scientific periodical from a purely advertising venture.

WAS ever more beautiful weather vouchsafed to humanity than the glorious days of autumn? From the dawning of the orb of day in the radiant horizon of the orient to the gleams of glory as it sinks in brilliant effulgence in the occident, the earth has seemed to possess the beauty and grandeur of some celestial realm. And this beauty is only intensified when the frost laid its withering hand upon foliage, forest and field, leaving here and there the deft colorings that no artist can rival. Photography has done much, but eternal fame awaits him who can give us a camera that can reproduce the beauties of an autumn landscape.

"SOMETIME, soon or late," says an exchange, "we are morally certain to have news from Peary." Now that is what we call encouraging, and we are inclined to believe the assertion. Commander Peary with an experience of twelve years in the Arctic regions, with an indomitable will and unquestioned courage, with the best equipped vessel ever sent to explore the frozen north: word was expected from him by October 1st, but it is not surprising that he has not been heard from, for all sorts of unexpected delays are liable to occur, or conditions exist that may make communication impracticable. Mr. Raven, Secretary of the American Geographical Society of New York, is quoted as saying: "We have every reason to believe that we shall hear from Commander Peary in some way or other soon. It is not improbable that the Danish government would in some way assist him to get into communication with this country. It is believed that his expedition is the best equipped which he has ever taken out and geographers everywhere think that he has a good opportunity to discover the north pole."

ANOTHER searcher for the Pole who has not been heard from, and who, it now seems probable, never will be, is Andree. His unique method of attempting his expedition in a baloon gives an added interest to any event concerning the navigation of the air. As a sport ballooning has received considerable impetus in the recent international contest for the James Gordon Bennett trophy. Seven different nations were represented—America, Great Britain, France, Germany, Italy, Belgium and Spain. The direction was of course decided by the wind and was north. Sixteen balloons were in the race but only seven crossed the channel. Lieut. Frank P. Lahn carried off the honors and brings the $2,500 silver art cup to America. He covered the greatest distance, 395 miles, in 22 hours and 28 minutes. The record distance, however, was made in 1900 by Count de la Vaulx. The wind on that occasion was from the west, taking him from Paris to Korostychew, in in Russia, a distance of 1,195 miles. On the present occasion none of the aeronauts cared to take an arctic voyage and so stopped when the North Sea was reached. Much experimenting must needs be done before the navigation of the air can be considered practical, but sometime it will be, and then the Pole will be reached; perhaps sooner.

Random Notes.

The highest clouds reach 10 miles above our heads. They are the white, feathery forms which we see on a clear day. Although apparently motionless, they often travel from 75 to 90 miles an hour.

Situated almost in the heart of the tropics, and regarded popularly, as a distinctly tropical country, Peru has such a peculiar configuration that every known climate is found within her borders, from the Arctic blasts that sweep across her snow capped peaks to the miasmic vapors of the Amazonian jungle.

Ptolemy Philopater, King of Egypt, was a broadminded shipbuilder for his times. He launched a vessel, which the chronicles of his reign says was 100 feet long, 56 feet wide and 80 feet high to the top of the poop. When fully manned it carried 2,820 marines, 400 cabin boys or servants, and 4,000 oarsmen. Its largest oars were 46 feet long.

Lake Superior is the deepest of the great lakes, showing by soundings 1,008 feet in at least one place. Michigan stands second with 100 feet less. Huron and Ontario are about 750 in the deepest parts, while Lake Erie is but 204. Vast areas of Lake Erie will not show a depth exceeding 80 feet. The bottom of Lake Michigan is 400 feet above sea level.

Monkeys are said to be indiguous to Southern Europe. However that may be they have lived in a wild state for many years in Southern Spain. It is now reported by the commandment at Gibraltar that the monkeys on the rock have for some reason dwindled in numbers, so that there are only five left, and these are all females. New blood from Morocco has been brought in, and there has been ill luck with these, through quarreling and murder—or at least suspicions of murder. But further importations were to be made, and this last lingering colony of real monkeys is to be saved anyhow.

The sapphire workings at Yoga Gulch, Montana, are being gradually developed into a great and permanent mining industry. Taken as a whole, the Yoga dike is perhaps the greatest gem mine in the world. It is about four miles long on the surface, and, being a true igneous dike, descends to an indefinite depth. It is estimated that the entire content of workable sapphire-bearing rock would approximate 10,000,000 cubic yards. A mining plant is now being erected there which will quadruple the previous output and make Montana sapphire mining a very important factor in American gem production.

Experiments have been made with other vegetable fibres than wood pulp for paper. The Lumberman reports that the Forest Service, in appreciation of the situation, has opened a labratory and begun a special investigation looking to the discovery of woods which may be acceptably substituted for spruce in paper manufacture. A mill at Orange, Texas, is making wrapping paper of yellow-pine shavings and refuse. Tupelo gum is also claimed to be a good material for the manufacture of some kinds of paper. And paper has been produced from waste cotton-stalks, the Manufacturers' Record claiming that paper thus made is of the best quality. It is reported that several mills for making paper from this product will be built in the South this year.

The Amateur Naturalist.

A MAGAZINE FOR ALL STUDENTS OF NATURE.

VOLUME III.   ASHLAND MAINE, NOVEMBER, 1906.   NUMBER 7.

THE MILKWEED AND INSECTS.

BY ADDISON ELLSWORTH.

IN an article bearing the striking title "Plants That Eat Meat," which appeared in one of our popular magazines some time ago from the pen of a well known writer, the author includes in his list the various species of Asclepias or Milkweed. Although, on various occasions, I have observed the remains of dead insects clinging to these plants, especially among the blossoms, I had grave doubts as to the conclusions set forth and determined to give the subject a more careful investigation. The result has been that after extended observations and study my covictions have only been strengthened.

However, the writer mentioned is not the only one to fall into the same error, if error it be, for a number of scientific investigators, including the illustrous Charles Darwin himself, have advanced the same idea.

Few flowers, wild or cultivated, hold out so enticing an invitation to insect visitors as do the milkweeds, and around none can be witnessed such vast swarms of bees, wasps, flies, beetles, butterflies and moths, as can be seen hovering the blossoms of these plants on any pleasant day in summer. Besides, the Milkweed forms the natural food for a half score of different caterpillars as well as the larvæ of numerous other insects. One of our largest butterflies, the *Danais plexippus*, already described at length in these columns*, is called the Milkweed Butterfly for this very reason.

Now if the Asclepias is carnivorous, and absorbs the juices from the various insects found "entangled in its meshes" to quote the writers words, they should be in sufficient numbers to make a showing, but I do not find this to be the case. During the past four years I have examined thousands of these plants,

*Volume 1, No. 6.

and the number of dead insects, or parts thereof, I have found upon them has been very few indeed, while in almost every instance their death could be tracable to some other cause.

As an example of the above, one day last August I carefully looked over some three hundred milkweed plants and found only seven dead insects on the whole lot. Of these three were grasshoppers which clearly had been killed by a fungus which annually destroys millions of them; two were flies, one a victim to the rapacity of a small spider, the other I could not account for; one bee that had succumbed to disentery, a disease often prevalent among these insects, while the last was a small caterpillar, the little round holes on the side indicating the work of ichneumons. During the same time and within the same range, I found twelve dead insects in the flower heads of the wild parsnip and three on the stalks, making fifteen in all; five on stalks of timothy and and eleven on other plants, giving a total of thirty one. Besides these there might be mentioned three others, two found on an old rail fence and one on the boll of a pine tree. And what was true on this occasion has been so on all others, excepting at times they have been a little more numerous; at others less. The greatest number I have succeeded in finding was nine on sixty-five plants, while on more than one occasion I have looked over large clumps of them without finding a single specimen. Surely, with its thousands of insect visitors every day, the above is a poor showing for Asclepius if he is the least bit meat hungry to say nothing about his being a carnivorous monster and "cannibal," as our friend would carry the idea. And, also, if the milkweed is carnivorous, the wild parsnip and timothy grass must likewise be as well as various other plants, to say nothing of the rail fence and pine trunk.

Quite a number of other plants are mentioned by the above writer, that draw their sustenance from the various insects they allure into traps set for them, and and some of these doubtless do to a limited extent, but how far I am at present unable to say. A careful, honest investigation would doubtless greatly reduce the number, if it did not wholly explode another pet theory. It is not scientific to jump at conclusions, and because dead insects are often found upon any one particular plant or shrub we are not justified in saying they are killed by that plant or shrub, until we take into consideration all other means by which they might have met their death. As already stated various diseases sometimes greatly decimate their number, and it is but natural to

suppose that they would be found more numerous on those plants
on which they have collected in swarms, while here too are found
the parasites that make them their victims, as well as the germs
of various fungi that frequently cause great havoc among them.
I would here say that I have in my collection a grasshopper from
whose thorax has sprouted two thread-like fungi more than two
inches in length.

Binghamton, N. Y.

THE FIRST SNOW.
BY EARL LYND JOHNSTON.

AS one looks out across the prairies and sees the remains of
a summer's verdure,—stalks of weeds, full of seeds for
the birds of winter when little else is available, trees with
a few fluttering leaves still clinging to the now almost
naked branches, the stacks of hay and grain, the shocks of corn,
the sky with a few suspicious clouds hanging near the horizon,
the atmosphere getting colder and with the wind in the north
east, he is likely to exclaim, "Its going to snow tonight!" Yes,
he is right for late in the afternoon the sun is obscured by the increasing clouds, the air is cooler, and here and there we see a few
scattering flakes of snow,—the first of the season. Little by
little more flakes appear until by dusk, when we have an apparent
never ending onrush of these small forerunners of winter. During
the night all is still—no wind, not a sound, but the snow is silent-
ly falling. In the morning you arise and look from your windows.
You see a beautiful sight: every thing is white and glistening
under the first rays of the rising sun; then you hear wonderful
music, little snow birds hopping over the snow and gathering the
seeds of the taller plants which keep them from starvation while
the seeds of the grasses and the innumerable smaller plant are
covered. You make your morning toilet and step out of doors to
see for yourself after a summer of hot and sweltering weather,
this wonderful carpet on mother earth. You are exhilerated. The
atmosphere feels bracing, everything is beautiful and you feel like
writing a poem or putting in words some grand thought, but
you remain in silent communion with self. After the first thrill
you pass around the house and there you see innumerable tracks
in the freshly fallen snow. The rabbits have been having their
share of enjoyment; the old habit forces itself you begin to look
for a track that leads out of this tangled network and follow it
up until, right before you a rabbit jumps up and scurries across
the plains.

You put in the day at your business with the thought of the first snow in your mind, you return home in the evening, it has grown colder, the snow crackles and sparkles under your feet, the air is filled with frost, you eat your supper and before you retire you go out once more. The moon is full and you look out over the country: the weeds, fences, trees and everything are covered with frost and show up grandly in the softening light of the moon and you are inspired again and perchance you will exclaim with the poet:

> "The trees bear spectral blossoms
> In the moonshine blurred and cold."

Evans, Colo.

AUTUMN IN THE SOUTH.

BY GEORGE MIDDLETON.

THE wild flowers of autumn in this section are mostly of a yellow color, easily leading of which is the golden rod, their long feathery plumes lending a bright dash of color to the somber hues of field and and fen. In some particularly prolific fields and when swayed by the breeze a continuous wave of the golden yellow greets the eye.

Now the leaves are beginning to take on fall tones, the beginning of their death and decay, the trees, in making ready for winter, withdrawing their support gradually so that all vulnerable points may be eliminated before the advent of the chilling winds of the cold season. The frost of October this year being the earliest known, hastened the process, and, therefore the change is further advanced than is usually the case.

Grasses and seeds rustle in the breeze, their russet tinge lending a decided fall tone to the landscape.

Chinquepins, walnuts, haws, persimmons, hickory nuts and others indigenous to the southern woods, are now ready for the lover of wild products of nature and parties of young people find pleasant and invigorating exercise in hunting for them. Among their most persistent seekers, however are the little darkies, and the most successful, too, for they know the whereabouts of all these delectable dainties.

Among the cultivated flowers none are more prominent than the chrysanthemums, and during November they brook no rival, . Numerous flower shows are held at which this beautiful flower

·holds chief sway. And yet the roses are with us still and will be for some time yet. Roses on Christmas day in the open gardens are seen and not until February do they cease their efforts, and then but for a short time.

The brilliant birds of the summer time have betaken them to summer climes, those species which remain with us the year through being of more sedate colorings. An exception, however is the "cardinal bird," whose bright red plumage is conspicuous in the edge of the woods.

Savannah, Ga.

THE FLIGHT OF AUTUMN.

BY HATTIE WASHBURN,

Ah, swift is the flight of autumn.
We scarcely miss the summer's green
Ere with her robes of brightest hues,
Autumn make beautiful the scene.

Beautiful for a few brief days,
Beautiful in her garments of gold,
Of russet, of crimson and brown,
So soon to grow withered and old.

The landscape must lose its brightness
The harvest field its golden sheaves,
The trees must yield their wealth of fruits
And gently shed their dying leaves.

Thick they lie along each pathway
And rustle 'neath the passing tread,
While sadly the winds are moaning
In the bare branches overhead.

There shows the songsters' empty nests
To the curious eye revealed,
Where in the flush of summer time
Their priceless treasures lay concealed.

There lonely sways the naked bough
Where they pour forth each merry lay;
There weaves the tree tops bleak and high
Where they heralded the coming day.

The aster and the golden rod
Are gone, the last of summer's train;
Within the woods the birds no more
Wake echoes with their sweet refrain.

Goodwin, S. D.

ARMORED NESTS.

BY CHAS. F. HOLDER.

IN the countries where cactus is common, numbers of animals evidently recognize the availability of this armed plant as a retreat from danger. In San Gabriel, California, the old mission fathers planted a hedge of prickly pear or tuna about their property as a protection from marauding Indians, disconnected patches of which still stand—interesting relics of the past. Such a group of spine-covered plants would seem to be the last place to be selected as a refuge, yet this cheveaux de frise constitutes the home of many rabbits that choose it as such, digging their burrows under its branches and roots, knowing that they are safe from the pursuit of owls, coyotes, hawks, and hounds, their enemies.

Almost every cactus in California will be found to afford similar protection, and the average hunter will invariably forego the game rather than engage the array of javelins. The various cacti, especially the variety which grows in clumps, serve as a protection particularly to birds. The writer has chased the road-runner on horseback, the bird refusing to fly, finally seeking refuge in an extensive cactus patch, where it dodges slowly in and out, apparently knowing that it was safe from pursuit. The nest of a roadrunner has been found in the cactus, and the writer has seen the nest of the California quail deftly concealed beneath the broad overhanging leaves with their spiney armament. One of the most interesting nests discovered in cactus was seen in a giant candle cactus, a typical form on the New Mexico desert and in old Mexico. The nest was indicated by the dark broken places half way up the trunk, which were made by the Gila woodpecker (*Centurus uropygialis*), an interesting bird discovered by Dr. Kennerly many years ago, when on his expedition along the 35th parallel, and first described by Professor Spencer A. Baird in 1854. The bird is, comparatively speaking, rare, not often seen; its strange and peculiar notes being seldon heard, even by those who frequent the great deserts of the Southwest, where it is found. Sometimes it is seen among the mesquite trees, rising, when observed, with a loud note of alarm, calling to mind, according to Dr. Cooper, that of *Phaenopepla nitens*. During the nesting season the woodpecker clings to the cactus and soon forms an opening, which by persistent pecking it gradually enlarges until it reaches the interior of the column, when it begins to work in the pith in a downward direction, finally completing a hollow, into which it takes leaves and the soft material from seeds, these constituting the nest, which being 12 or even 30 feet from the ground, in the heart of a column whose surface is a mass of needles, may be considered impregnable. The huge nests or the columns are among the picturesque features of the arid regions; and few, if not familiar with the habits of the Gila woodpecker, would suspect that the black on the surface are openings of nests of this interesting and clever bird, which in this manner hides its eyrie and young from the intense heat of the sun and from all pursuers.

A great mass of cacti is a veritable city. On the ground floor or in the cellar dwell the cottontails, kangaroo rats, and on the edge of one patch found by the writer, heaped up against the cactus, was the enormous nest of the wood rat, while, near at hand, was the burrow of a kangaroo rat; numerous gopher holes in the vicinity suggested the proximity of these pests. In the upper story were various kinds of nests—mocking-birds, finches, and a humming-bird, with several others which could not be determined, at least by the finder. Gorgeous spiders weave their webs from one great leaf to another. Various lizards claim the patch as their home, sunning themselves along the branches on warm days retreating at night to the ground, where their burrows lead in every direction. All these varied forms—and many beetles and several other mammals could be added—find perfect shelter in the cactus, protected by the array of spines which pierce and rend the inquisitive enemy.—*Scientific American.*

THE GIANT BAOBAB TREE.

THERE may be many who have never seen this truly remarkable vegetable product, but very few who have not read something concerning the gigantic proportions of this world-famous tree. For centuries it was acknowledged to be the largest tree known, and only in comparatively recent times has this distinction been contested by travellers, who have seen the enormous trees of Sequoia growing in the forests of California, or the colossal demensions of the Eucalypti of Australia; but there will be some doubt whether the two last mentioned ought to hold the first place, except it be for loftiness, and in this respect they undoubtedly excel all others.

The very peculiar conditions of growth exhibited in the trunk of a baobab have been remarked on by all who have seen the tree growing in its wild state, and in this country we may see for ourselves this extraordinary development. In most trees the trunks thicken uniformly as they increase in height, but in the baobab we get a swollen gout-like stem for a distance of 12 or 14 feet, and then branches quite out of proportion to the base of the tree. This swollen appearance is attributed to disease by some authorities, but by others it is considered to be due to the soft nature of the bark and wood.

The botanical name of the baobab is *Adansonia digitata*. The first, or generic part of the name, commemorates Michael Adanson, a distinguished French botanist and traveller, who explored the region of Senegal and other parts of Africa, and the author of valuable works on plants. The second part of the name refers to the finger-like arrangement of the leaflets.

M. Adanson tells us himself how he measured several trees which ranged from 65 to 78 feet in circumference, but as is usually the case, very low in proportion, the trunks of these two trees were from 12 to 15 feet high before they divided into many horizontal branches, which touched the ground at their extremities, each branch being equal to a monstrous tree.. The same traveler gives an account of a calculation he made to show that one of the trees, 30 feet in diameter, was 5,150 years old; and again mentions trees upon the bark of which were cut the names of Europeans, two of these being dated, the one in the 14th and the and the other in the 15th century. M. Thevet, another French traveller, who visited the same parts in the year 1555, mentions having seen these trees. Humboldt has been led to speak of it as the "oldest organic monument of our planet."

The baobab grows exceedingy well in some parts of India and Ceylon, and attains a large size of the trees already mentioned. In the Calcutta Royal Botanic Gardens are to be seen many specimens of *Adansonia digitata* in a perfectly healthy condition, and sufficiently developed to show the truly wonderful characteristics of the tree. July is a good time to visit the gardens and see for oneself the baobab at its best, for then it is in full leaf and flower, and very interesting ought the visit to be to any one with a fondness for plants, especially for the giants of the vegetable kingdom. The largest of the trees growing in the garden is from 50 to 60 feet in height, with a trunk measuring 13 feet in circumference at 3 feet from the ground, and 12 feet at 6 feet from the base. The trunk branches at about 13 or 14 feet from the earth these branches being thick at their bases, but suddenly attenuating and appearing like any ordinary branch of a tree. The trunk is perfectly sound and shows no signs of decay or attack from insects or fungi. The bark of the tree is very soft, and is said to furnish a fibre which is made into ropes, and in Senegal woven into cloth, and has the reputation of being very strong.

The flowers are extremely interesting and so unlike most other flowers. *Adansonia digitata* belongs to a sub-tribe of the Order *Malvaceæ*, called *Bambaceæ*, a class of plant that must be well known to most gardeners. The *Adansonia* bears very large white flowers, having a strong perfume, closely resembling that of an over-ripe orange. These are borne on the ends of the branches on pedicles a foot or more in length, usually singly, but sometimes in pairs. The flower is from 8 to 9 inchrs across, the companulate calyx being five lobed; and as the flower expands, these the lobes split down almost to the base of the calyx. The outside color is light green and inside a dull white, both sides being covered with a hairy down, but more pronounced on the inside, which has a velvety feel to the touch. The beautiful white petals are united at their bases, are broadly obovate in shape, 4 inches long and 3 inches broad, with crinkled margin. The strangest part of the flower lies in the stamens, these being united into a pitcher-shaped tube 2 inches long, and the same color as the petals. At the top of the tube the filaments spread out and form a mop-like head, each filament being surrounded by another conspicuous dark brown filament. Taken altogether, the flower of *Adansonia digitata* is one of the most extraordinary in the flower world, as it also is one of the largest. The leaves of the baobab are deciduous in the cold weather; palmately digitate (hand-shaped) and almost identical in shape with those of the horse chestnut(*Æsculus hippocastanum*). On the Eastern coast of Africa the leaves are reduced to a powder and constitute "halo" or "lalo," which the natives mix with their food for the purpose of diminishing the excessive perspiration ocassioned by the heat of that climate, and to keep the blood in a cool state.

The fruit of the baobab resembles closely a bottle gourd. From trees growing in this garden I have measured fruits 8 inches to a foot in length, containing a hard outer shell which is covered with a brown tomentum, or down. The seeds are imbedded in a mass of pulp, this latter having the reputation as a specific in cases of putrid or pestilential fevers, and owing to this circumstance it forms an article of commerce. The ashes of the fruit and bark boiled in rancid palm oil is said to be used as a soap by the negroes.

Adansonia digitata is a native of many parts of Africa, more especially in Senegal and Abyssinia. It is also cultivated in most tropical countries, and in India it is well represented. The village Italcha, near the celebrated old city of Mandoo, in the Deccan, is famous for its baobab trees.

Besides being called Baobab, the tree rejoices in other names such as monkey-bread, sour-gourd, mowana, and in Egypt bahabab, while in this country the natives call it Bilatee Imlee.

Another species of *Adansonia* also grows in this garden, it being a native of the sandy plains of Northern Australia, where it is known as the "cream of tartar tree." This is *Adansonia Gregorii*, and although only a small tree here, it is said to grow to even greater dimensions than the only other species of *Adansonia*, viz., *A. digitata*, the largest tree on record, being one seen in Gregory's expedition, measured 85 feet in girth 2 feet from the ground. The general habit, including trunk, leaves and bark, is similar in the young state in both *A. digitata* and *A. Gregorii*, the only difference being that the leaves are smaller and narrower in the latter.—*Indian Gardening and Planting*.

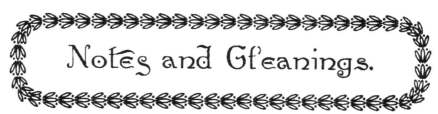

Notes and Gleanings.

Reading The Tree.—The forester reads the history of a tree in great detail, says the *American Magazine*. After taking out a few "borings" to the center of the tree at different heights and counting the rings on them he may regale you with a history of the tree's record something like this: "This tree is 150 years old (150 rings at the base). During the first five years it grew only seven inches (145 rings, seven inches from the base). Evidently it then began to touch crowns with other saplings, for it took a spurt and put on fifteen inches a year steadily till it was forty years old (forty rings forty-four and one-half feet above the ground). It was not growing as fast as its neighbors, however, for at this point it began to be over shadowed, and its growth declined for the next ten years to as little as four inches a year (forty-five rings at forty-eight feet and fifty at fifty feet.) Just in time to save its life something happened to its big neighbors, presumably a wind-storm, and it resumed a steady growth of about six inches a year, having passed its fastest growing time. Its growth in thickness doesn't seem to have varied much, about an inch every three years. But it grew faster and faster in volume, of course, as its height increased—a little over a cubic foot a year in its prime of life, I should judge. About thirty years ago it reached maturity and stopped growing in height (thirty rings at the top of the main stem), and now it is approaching old age (the last rings are pretty thin). Hold on a minute—here's a false ring, twenty, forty, forty-six years back; two very thin rings—see—instead of one thick one; means that something interrupted the growing season, probably a late frost."

The Earth as seen from Mars—In examining the earth then, as we have examined Mars, the Martian would find large yellow and reddish areas, extensive greenish areas, and, besides, large regions of varying shades of blue, possibly occupying three-fourths of the earth's surface. The yellow areas he would interpret as desert land, the greenish areas he might consider vegetation, but what would he make out of the larger regions of blue? These would certainly puzzle him, because, unfamiliar with oceans, he could not believe that such vast tracts could really be water. He would easily interpret the polar snowcaps and the waters at their edges, but the oceans would be impossible to solve. The suggestion by some audacious interpreter, that this vast blue area was water would be answered by showing that these so-called bodies of water, bordered vast tracts of sandy desert, with no canals running into them for irrigation or navigation purposes. Even the polar snowcaps would be doubted, because they seem to extend far down into temperate latitudes; and on their recedence in summer there would be seen no dark bordering seas as the result of their melting. The vegetation, instead of unfolding at the North and gradually extending southward, would unfold in a contrary direction, appearing first in south temperate latitudes and developing northward. The perennial character of the vegetation in the tropics would puzzle him. Even if he recognized oases in the deserts of America and Africa, the result of artesian wells or springs, he could not believe them to be vegetation; for he could detect no irrigating canals running into them. He would come to the conclusion that no creature could possibly exist on the earth, as the tremendous force of gravitation, with great atmospheric pressure, would forbid the existence of any organic forms.—*Prof. E. W. Morse's book.*

Labrador Barren.—One finds himself peopling the regions and dotting their hills, valleys and wild shores with human inhabitants, but a second thought, and a mournful one it is, tells that no men toil in the fields away there, no women keep the home off there, no children play by the brooks or shout around the country schoolhouse, no bees come home to the hive, no smoke curls from the farmhouse chimney, no orchard blooms, no bleating sheep flock the mountain side with whiteness and no heifer lows in the twilight of bleak, desolate Labrador. There is nobody there, there never were but a miserable and scattered few, and there never will be. It is a great and terrible wilderness, thousands of miles in extent and lonesome to the very wild animals and birds. Left to the still visitation of the light from the sun, moon and stars, and the auroral fires, it is only fit to look upon and then be given over to its primeval solitariness.

Age of Animals.—The following figures have been compiled by good authority and the ages given are those generally accepted as correct: Elephants live 100 years and upward, rhinocerous twenty, camel 100, lion twenty-five to seventy, tigers, leopards, jaguars and hyenas (in confinement) about twenty-five, beaver fifty, deer twenty, wolf twenty, fox fourteen to sixteen, llamas fifteen, chamois twenty-five, monkeys and baboons sixteen to eighteen, hare eight, squirrel seven, rabbit seven, swine twenty-five, stag under thirty, horse thirty, ass thirty, sheep under ten, cow twenty, ox thirty, swans, parrots and ravens 200, eagle 100, geese eighty, hens and pigeons, ten to sixteen, hawks thirty to forty, crane twenty-four, blackbird ten to twelve, peacock twenty; pelican forty to fifty, thrush eight to ten, wren two to three, nightingale fifteen, blackcap fifteen, linnet fourteen to twenty five, goldfinch twenty to twenty-four, redbreast ten to twelve, skylark ten to thirty-five, titlark five to six, chaffinch twenty to twenty-four, starling ten to twelve, pike thirty to forty, salmon sixteen, codfish fourteen to seventeen; eel ten, crocodile 100, tortoise 100 to 200, whale estimated 1,000; queen bees live four years, drones four months, worker bees six months.

Revised Altitudes.—In his revised book of altitudes, the geographer of the Geological Survey gives the height of Mount Hood as 11,225 feet, in place of the old measurement of 11,932 feet. Shasta is set down as 14,380 feet high, and Rainer at 11,363. California has twelve peaks over 14,000 feet, twenty-three over 13,000, and fifty-five over 12,000.

Victoria Falls.—Victoria Falls, in the heart of what was recently "darkest Africa" are about twice as broad and two and one-half times as high as Niagara Falls. The immense volume of water falls a distance of about 400 feet over a precipice more than a mile in breadth. There is only one small outlet about 100 yards wide to this awful chasm, and the roar of the waters as they rush into what is known as the Boiling Pot is terrific and awe inspiring. From the Boiling Pot the waters push their way between basaltic cliffs of great height, the Zambezi gorge extending with many zigzag windings for about forty miles. For 1,200 feet and often to a still greater height vast spray columns eternally rise from the canyon in front of the falls. It is only half a century since Livingstone discovered the falls, but now the traveler reaches the cataract on a train provided with dining cars, bedrooms, bathrooms and smoking parlors and on arriving at his destination is housed in a hotel lighted by electricity. The bridge over the Zambezi near the falls is the highest in the world.

Starlight Measured.—Various attempts have been made to estimate the light of the stars. In the northern hemisphere Argelander has registered 324,000 stars down to the 9½ magnitude, and, with the aid of the best photometric data, Agnes M. Clerk's new "System of the Stars" gives the sum of the light of these northern stars as equivalent to 1-440 of full moonlight, and the total light of all stars similarly enumerated in both hemispheres, to the number of about 900,000, is roughly placed at 1-180 of the lunar brightness. The scattered light of still fainter celestial bodies is difficult to calculate. By a photographic method Sir William Abney in 1896 rated the total starlight of both hemispheres at 1-100 of full moonlight, and Prof. Newcomb in 1901 from visual observations of diffused sky radiance, fixed the light power of all stars at just 728 times that of Capella, or 1-89 of the light of the full moon. It is not certain, however, that the sky would be totally dark if all stars were blotted out. Certain processes make the upper atmosphere strongly luminous at times and we never can be sure that this light is absent.

The Amateur Naturalist

......ISSUED MONTHLY.......

Subscription, 50 Cents per Year.   Single Copies, 5 Cents

ADVERTISING RATES ON APPLICATION.

————————EDITED AND PUBLISHED BY————————

CHARLES D. PENDELL,   -   -   ASHLAND, MAINE.

ONCE more we are under the necessity of offering an apology for being late. Just as we had got caught up and were in hopes of being on time with each issue several things happened that have overthrown the entire system of our business. The principal and most harassing inconvenience is the break down of our engine which furnishes the power to run our printing plant. For eight weeks it has been idle. We could have gotten a new engine, but the manufacturers of the one we have solemnly promised to make this right or put in a new one but up to date have done neither. We also publish the *Gazette*, a weekly newspaper, and the extra time required by hand work to issue that has compelled us to fall behind on all orders for job printing as well as on the AMATEUR NATURALIST. We have received numerous letters asking if we had suspended. To this we emphatically answer **no!** Suspension is the last resort and among the remotest of possibilities. This magazine has come to stay, and no plan or business proposition which involves its suspension will be considered. Of this our subscribers may rest assured. Among the many letters that have reached us are some containing words of praise for the magazine that are truly appreciated, and which we feel bound to share with our contributors who have done so much to give its columns the worth and value that places it on par with any magazine published. Late though we are, we shall do our utmost to catch up, and shall not try the expedient of skipping numbers to catch up. Every subscriber will receive just what he has paid for.

⁓

THE matter which appears in the AMATEUR NATURALIST has more than passing value—it is of permanent interest and worth, and though the delay is an inconvenience, to us as well as to our subscribers, if not even more so, yet the value of the contents is not lessened by age. This fact makes the back numbers as valuable now as the day they were issued. Those who have not as yet completed their files should do at once. Until the next number is issued we shall continue our special offer, sending Volumes I, II and III complete for only $1.00, post paid; but with the completion of this volume this offer will be withdrawn and the full price, $1.50, be charged.

FICTION of course has its place in literature, and from an examination of most of the current magazines it appears to have a very large place. But most of the current fiction is read and forgotten, while literature relating to Nature Study has a permanent value, and affords a genuine pleasure that time only enhances. One can spend a dollar each month and not obtain as much of real value pertaining to the natural sciences as is given each month in THE AMATEUR NATURALIST, and yet for the small sum of 50 cents may be had this magazine for a year; or for $1.00 we will enter your subscription for three years, this offer applying to new subscribers or to renewals. This is the price charged by most of our contemporaries for a single year's subscription. To those who are sufficiently interested and want to help increase our circulation we make this standing offer: Send us two subscriptions at 50 cents each, and we will send you the magazine one year gratis, and thank you besides.

AND now a few words about what our readers may expect for 1907. Perhaps the most important article will be the one entitled "Butterflies in Winter" which we expect to commence in the January number. This is from the pen of Mr. Addison Ellsworth, who has made a life study of these fascinating and beautiful insects, and whose private collection far surpasses both in number of species and numbea and value of specimens some of our best museums. Several articles by Mr. George Middleton, of Savannah, Ga., on Southern geology, flora and bird life will be among its valued features. Mr. Norman O. Foerster and Miss Kate A. Jones will also have articles of special interest. A number of articles on astronomy and descriptive geography are also in hand. Besides these we have a number of others promised, and shall continue from time to time to give such selected articles as seem to be worth preservation and of interest to our readers. Contributions from others of our readers are invited and no effort will be spared to make this magazine the best of its kind.

Random Notes.

An experiment has shown that 1000 tons of soot settle yearly on the 110 square miles of London's area.

Since the silver deposits of Potosi, Botovia, were discovered in 1546, that mountain alone, it is computed, has yielded 2,000,000,000 ounces of silver.

The deepest lake in the world is beleived to be Lake Baikal, in Siberia. Nine thousand square miles in area, or nearly as large as Lake Erie, it is 4,000 to 5,000 feet deep, so that it contains nearly as much water as Lake Superior.

It seems as if the day was not wholly profane in which we have given heed to some natural object......He who knows the most, he who knows the virtues that are in the ground, the waters, the plants, the heavens, and how to come at these enchantments, is the rich and royal man.—*Emerson.*

Man unaided can not cope with the countless number of insects that come into life every day. The birds are the only means through which insects can successfully be destroyed. Most every bird plays some part in the work, some destroy the eggs, some the caterpillars, some the chrysalis and some the full grown insects. Birds do not increase as rapidly as insects and we can never have too many of them. We must give better protection to the birds or we shall repent it.

"Having personally eaten some hundreds of species of caterpillars," writes M. Dagin, a French entomologist "raw, broiled, boiled, fried, roasted and hashed, I find most of these pleasant to taste, light and digestable." But the despised cockroach of our kitchen is what M. Dagin waxes most enthusiastic over. "Pounded in a mortor, put through a sieve, and pounded into beer stock, these creatures make a soup preferable to bisque." Nevertheless, a Chinese proverb runs to the effect, "If your stomach is delicate, abstain from the cockroach!"

Redwood forests are practically unharmed by forest fires, and it is common practice for the lumbermen to fell the trees and peel the bark from them and when the dry season is on set fire to the felled timber and burn the branches and bark and other wreckage without practical injury to the saw logs, which procedure would mean disaster to any other wood. Redwood contains no resin or turpentine of any kind, and, owing to its great resistant qualities in severe climatic conditions, is free from cracking or decay, where cinders might lodge and start fires. When burning, it is easily extinguished with a small quantity of water. It has the appearance of burnt cork and is harder to ignite a second time than at first.—*Scientific American.*

A cloud is white because its corpuscles of vapor are large enough to reflect all rays, large and small. But the upper air has infinite numbers of particles so minute that they throw back only the smaller—or blue—waves of light, and not the larger red, yellow and green waves, and thus blue is the predominant but not exclusive color of the sky. This long accepted theory of Tyndall's is now questioned by M. Spring, the Swiss physicist. He has experimented with luminous rays under many conditions getting all colors except blue, which failed to appear until, by the aid of electricity, he secured a pure atmosphere. This was clearly tinged with blue, leading to the conclusion that the blue of the sky is an essential quality of the air, of chemical origin.

The Amateur Naturalist.

A MAGAZINE FOR ALL STUDENTS OF NATURE.

VOLUME III.   ASHLAND MAINE, DECEMBER, 1906.   NUMBER 8.

THE ROMANCE OF A FOSSIL.

BY GEORGE MIDDLETON.

MANY, many moons ago, when the world was young there dwelt on the edge of the Palæozoic sea and dragged its halting shell over the slimy slopes of the ancient beach, along with myriads of its kind,—a Gasteropod. Born like many of its kind, in those early environments when life was of the simplest kind, it crawled its way through a short existence, finding sustenance in the ooze left there by the advancing and receding waters. Babyhood, youth and maturity were here passed amidst the primeval surroundings—"flowerless, fruitless, songless, voiceless, except the occasional chirp of a grasshopper;" while in the distance spread those "dim watery woodlands of Sigillaria, Lepidodendron, Calamites, with underbrush of ferns, inhabited by insects and amphibians.

But our Gasteropod had no eye for the landscape, business and pleasure being combined in the perpetuating of its kind. And so it lived until, as with all things of today, death came.

Tossed here and there by the sluggish waves, being alternately covered and uncovered by the movement of its erstwhile element, it landed in a quiet little hole, undisturbed by the outside world; except that deeper and deeper became the muddy burden. At last it would seem to have been burried beyond the reach of the tides.

But it was not to be thus. Slowly the coast line rose and the waters receding, exposed the erstwhile sea floor again; and the silt being carried away by the torrential rains, our shell was again brought to the light of day, and lay there, a small grain on the muddy wastes.

Once more the sea encroached and renewed deposits covered our shell within its bosom. Heavier and heavier became the burden upon it and its enclosing material, and harder and harder, from mud to rock, along with others of its kind and of other species, and fragments—the flotsam and jetsam of the turbid waters—encompassed with the mighty and resistless power of dynamic force.

And now safely ensconsed and securely bound in the limestone
far down below the level of the changing era, it would appear
that a final resting place had been reached. So time went on:
The Palæozoic era closed by a tremendous revolution. The sedi-
ments which had so long accumulated in the Appalachian region
"at last yielded to the slowly increasing horizontal pressure, and
thickened up into the Appalachian chain, and the rocks metamorphosed."

Slowly our Gasteropod had changed in character with its
primeval form alone to distinguish it from the enclosing rock.
On through the Permian, the transitional period between the
Palæozoic and Mesozoic, the gradual change took place. After
a time great ridges began to appear, the waters receded. On
through the countless years of the Mesozoic the mountains grew,
though the crust had been attacked from birth by winds, the rains
snow, frost and ice, and it seemed like a pigmy hurling grains
of sand against their rugged sides, day by day, year by year, century by century. And yet at the age of maturity, in the late
Cenozoic, the proud and mighty giant had begun to give way, his
crest to crumble and great rents appeared in his sides. Large
masses were split off, and, projected down the slopes with terrific
force making deep gashes in the weakened surface. Stern and
somber as were its lines before the full effects of this titan combat
began to appear, now the lofty towers, crags and minarets,
lent a savage beauty to the scenery. Out of the Pliocene into
the Quaternary the old earth passed with the scars of many a
"conflict on its brow."

But now another revolution, fearful in its character, swept it,
destroying all life, though perpetuating the forms in stone. The
Psychozoic was entered, and at last the ultimate end of all these
preparations, MAN, appeared.

    *   *   *   *   *   *   *   *   *

Near the summit of a limestone mountain, in a small valley
formed by the erosive power of the floods that for ages had been
precipitated upon its devoted head, I walked one afternoon specimen hunting. An interesting boulder attracted my attention and
an attack was made upon it. At the first blow of my hammer it
split as smoothly as if on cleavage line, and, bared to view, against
the white surface, its frosted sides scintillating in the noonday
sun, appeared our Gasteropod of the Palæozoic times, the sinuous
folds of its shell as distinct as in the days of the long ago,—as
beautiful as a dream—a "veritable sermon in stone."

How my thoughts went back through the years, as I gazed upon its glistening purity. In mind's eye I saw it dragging its weary way over the softened trail to the retreating waters, the overcoming and stifling out of its life by the ruthless ooze; its death, burial, and disinterment, and again lost to view down into the hungry maw of the rapacious slimes. Then I saw the changes that came to it and its environment as time swept slowly on, until here, at my very feet lay a record of the immeasurable past, wrest from nature's stony heart, to lay her secret bare to those of her children whose love for her "surpasseth all understanding."

Savannah, Ga.

CORBIN PARK.

BY KATE A. JONES.

THE name Corbin Park is familiar to many in our own land, and to not a few in the countries across the sea. We are justly proud of the fact that this park, which is the largest private park in the world, (containing 25,-000 acres) is in our own America, and among the mountains of New Hampshire, being situated in Cornish, Grantham, and Croyden, and having for its very center Croydon mountain, as it is always the same changeless blue. I have always lived almost under the shadow of this grand old mountain for several years; have studied it in storm and sunshine, in summer and in winter, and have found it always the same deep blue, as if, centuries ago when the earth was young it had been painted with heaven's own fadeless blue. I have seen it when the black clouds piled above it, and the lightning played about its summit. At such times I was able to appreciate the thought of one who has likened living on a mountain-top to "being in a theater horizon wide in which clouds are the actors, electricity the illuminator, and thunder the trumpeter."

Many once fertile farms are inclosed in this park; a few half ruined houses still remain, while cinnamon rose bushes, and tiger lilies, mark the spots where once were peaceful homes.

One finds in Corbin park moose, elk, several varieties of deer, wild boar, and the largest herd of pure blooded buffaloes in the world, at the present time, November, 1906, numbering 175. There are also Rocky Mountain sheep, and Angora goats, the latter, with their long white coats, and quaint looking faces, reminding

one of little women dressed for a ball.   There has never been any
bears placed in the park although some writers have included
them in their list of the animals brought there.   It is the home of
bears, however, and they sometimes climb out over the high wire
fence and wander about the country making sad havoc among
the farmers sheep.   At one time there were Indian ponies, and
they really might have lived there, but Mr. Corbin was so tender
hearted he had them removed lest they suffer from cold and hunger—a lesson in kindness to animals it would be well for all to
remember.

I well remember my first visit to Corbin Park one cloudless
winter day when the sleighing was perfect.   We drove eight miles
over a road which commanded fine views of the snow crowned
hills glistening white against the deep blue sky.   Silence and snow
everywhere, although the tracks of squirrels and rabbits spoke of
the life of the woods.   Coming at length to a great gate we entered the park, and after a short drive along a road bordered with
shapely evergreens, arrived at the Central Station, a long low
building (with a piazza across the front, and dormer windows in
the roof) painted red with white trimmings.   Here we were met
by Mr. Morrison, who came from Scotland several years ago with
the first cattle Mr. Corbin ever imported, and has ever since been
at the Central Station in charge of the dogs, buffaloes and other
animals, which he has studied until he is probably better acquainted with their habits than any other man in the East.   His gentle-
manly manner and smiling face have won him hosts of friends
and every one has a good word for "Billy," as he is familiarly
called.   Everything about the place is perfectly kept, and indicates a busy healthful life.   Some men were drawing birch logs
out into the open with splendid teams of gray horses; others
were bringing in deer in crates, some to be shipped to Germany.
They were such graceful, beautiful creatures, the timid looks
with which they regarded us making them seem almost human.
I thought of their long journey across the sea, and hoped they
might not be homesick in that strange park so far away.   A
short walk through the woods brought us to the winter home of
the buffalo, where (in large yards, with comfortable sheds to
shelter them from the winter storms,) we saw the entire herd.
Some of us ventured into the yard where the young were kept;
they did not appear afraid, and we were able to get very near
them.   In another enclosure were nineteen elk.   Among them was
one old Rocky Mountain goat; a comical fellow without a shad-

ow of bashfulness in his makeup, who gazed at us as much as to say "well, how do you like the looks of *me?*" Turning about we came face to face with twenty wild boar, repulsive creatures, which, as they ran about their pen reminded one of huge rats. We saw the dog kennels where at one time ninety dogs of different varieties were kept. Near one of the large barns was a flock of common sheep, the little lambs frisking about in the sunshine. There are many beautiful drives through the park (and a drive of fifty miles around it) when at every turn, one finds something interesting, and a visit to Corbin Park is never to be forgotten.

Grantham, N. H.

A BOREAL REALITY.

BY NORMAN FOERSTER.

THIS morning dawned cold and foggy. It was one of the coldest mornings of the winter, when the mercury seemed in danger of breaking the thermometer—at the bulb.

The "signs of the season" on the city streets are hard nobby red noses, open steaming mouths, pinched faces, ears as fragile as glass, feet of granite, steps a few inches long, hands that seek the warmth of pockets or shelter purple ears, hard, tight moustaches, ice-coated eyebrows.

If we leave the precincts of town, other evidences of frigidity appear. The trees are bare, as desolately barren as the neutral-colored poles that line the city streets. The ground of the hills is like granite, and well-covered with the snow that crunches under foot like pulverized quartz, while the swamps in sheltered nooks are alternate patches of brittle ice and pasty mud. The sun shines with dazzling brilliance from a sky of steely blueness interspersed here and there with cool, cottony clouds. As we traverse exposed hillsides and the north wind bites sharply, we are prone to think that intense cold is akin to fire, producing as it does a skin as dry and crisp as flames could make it. The familiar creek, where in midsummer we lay on the shady bank and listened to the constant *z-ing* of the ciada and the contented murmur of the water, has now completely dissappeared, its heavy sheet of ice mantled over by a thick cover of soft snow, save where some farmer has broken it for his cattle, exposing the cool blue of a half-foot layer and the dark, rushing water underneath. In the meadow depressions are knee deep drifts, while opener areas are blown almost bare, showing the gray grass, frozen stone hard. The rustle of sere oak leaves hard by the wayside is a characteristic sound. Is their noisy clatter ghostly, as someone has suggested? Nay, it is a pleasant sound, suggestive of approaching June thunder-showers and wind-tossed grain fields, and yet, when we bethink ourselves of the season—stern winter—it seems but a grim reminder of what it used to be but is not now.

Evening approaches. The fluffy clouds give place to yellowish oily looking masses, contrasting sharply with the immaculacy of the snow. The sun sets early now, and it is not long before we retire with a comfortable feeling to the warmth and cheer of the hearth. The merry crackling of the log fire and the yellow light that suffuses a warm glow throughout the room become so fa-miliar that on going to the window, we are almost surprised to find the glass heavily frosted, and draw our hands back in haste if we place them alongside to melt the coating. Outside a green-ish, vitreous sky in the west reflecting a sheen suggestive of ice, indicates the direction of the departed sun. Elsewhere a cold, smoky mist, enveloping all in palapable frigidity, limits the spot-less view.

Pittsburg, Pa.

THE SOUTHERN MOCKING BIRD.
BY GEORGE MIDDLETON.

AMONG the many permanent bird inhabitants of the Sunny Southland, none are more popular and deservedly so, than the mocking bird, whose silvery tones are the first to greet the dawn and the last to speed the departing day.

> "Listen to the mocking bird
> Listen to the mocking bird
> The mocking bird is singing in the trees."

While city life is mildly conducive to the idealic existence of this bird, the sylvan retreats of the rural districts abound in their happy existence.

Slender of build with long tail and wide sweep of wing, he is a graceful bird, if not a beauty. Its gray back, the tail and wings rather blackish, with a white patch on either wing, partly white, this member of *Mannius Pollyglottus* is a remarkable imitator of the notes of the birds. The chirp of the sparrow, the notes of the finch, cat birds, orioles, warblers, etc, with a greater strength and beauty, while he trills with far greater effect than the canary, blending the one into the other with a rapidity that is amazing but yet of charming beauty and cadence that is possible by no other of the feathery kingdom. His imitation of the harsh cry of the catbird and the soft sweet tones of others shows the wide range of his repertoire, and withal gives him a legitimate right to this name.

I have in mind one of this species, belonging to a friend, that though raised in a cage, yet was so devoted to his mistress that after a short excursion into the surrounding trees would invariably come back to the home; and with such a chattering and twittering as though he were trying to tell his experiences. This bird had a particular call for master and mistress and greeted them on coming into the room as though overjoyed at the meeting.

Of course we cannot expect the wilder birds of the fields and woods to greet us in this way, but even in a state of nature they are not wild as other birds are, and while lacking the friendliness of those domesticated, still to my mind the song is more freer, more spontaneous and with a naturalness of expression not found in the caged bird. In his wilder cadences the very air seems to quiver with his melody, the woods seem greener where he sways in the breeze on some slender twig, now rising now falling with the most reckless abandon. It seems almost inconceivable that such a frail looking creature should be able to pour forth such a wealth of melody, morn, noon and even way into the night when the moon is in her glory. To paraphrase Goldsmith's Schoolmaster:

"We listened, and still our wonder grew
That one small throat could let all those sounds come through."

To the farmer the mocking bird is of value in other directions. He is insectivorous and destroys many enemies of the crops.

The eggs are four to six in number, of greenish cast, with drab splotches scattered over them. The nest is built of sticks with straw and grass roots for the lining, and while the outside appears rough the inner nest is smooth and comfortable.

There are other birds belonging to this family, notably the brown thrush which in size and shape resembles the mocking bird closely, but in coloring of body and eggs, and notes, are totally different.

Savannah, Ga.

FACTS ABOUT THE MOON.

BY L. S. METCALF.

WE see the moon first each month as a thin, curved line of light in the western sky. It presents that appearance because in its journey around the Earth from west to east, it approaches our view from the direction of the Sun, and consequently is lighted on the side farthest from us. A few days later it has passed half across the sky, and then we look at it sideways as related to the direction of the Sun's rays, and therefore see half of its illuminated surface. And finally it reaches the eastern heavens, and being then opposite to the Sun, from the Earth, the whole of its lighted half is turned toward us.

When a telescope is pointed at the "new" moon, a view is obtained similar to that which would be presented to an observer who should look from a point in space upon a spot on the Earth just reached by morning sunlight. Every important feature of the surface is seen sharply defined by light and shade, and far beyond the line of full illumination prominent objects stand clearly out. As the bright field widens from day to day, the landscape is found to be very different from that of the Earth. Great tracts are perfectly smooth and of a grayish color, resembling mud flats. These are the portions that by the naked eye are seen to shine less brightly than others, and before the discovery of the telescope were supposed to be oceans. Some of them were bordered by mountains two or three times as high as Mount Washington, rising perpendicularly from the plain and producing a striking effect. When most of the face of the globe has become lighted, bright lines are observed in every direction. Most of them radiate like the spokes of a wheel from mountain centers, but some extend in straight lines across the hills and valleys for hundreds of miles. A few large spots of particular brilliancy also appear. One range of mountains is nearly five miles in height.

But the most peculiar features of the Moon is the circular eminences that are scattered all over its surface. These number no less than 33,000 and are of every size from a barely discernable point to an immense ring over 140 miles in diameter. The interior floor of these circular heights are level and some of them are many thousands of feet lower than the surrounding country. Hundreds of the larger ones contain cones of various sizes. The resemblance of these formations to large volcanoes on the Earth is so great that they are usually spoken of as craters.

The Moon, comparatively speaking, is so near to us, and so clearly exposed to view, that with our modern instruments we ought seemingly to be able to discuss very small objects upon its surface. But here steps in our atmosphere, with all its refractions, vibrations, and impurities, and places a stern limit upon our investigations. A common impression is that a magnifying power of several thousand diameters can be effectively used on our satellite with the largest and best-situated of our present telescopes, but so great are the obstacles presented by our air that only in rare cases can one of more than one thousand be employed with good results, and with that power an object must be 300 feet across to be seen even as a formless speck. A good, small glass, capable of carrying a magnification of 250 diameters, such as is used in many private observatories, will show as a minute spot a figure 1200 feet broad.

No certain indications of air, water, or any kind of vegetation appear on this Moon, hence its habitation by any creatures such as are known to us is not possible. A few observers have thought that they could see evidence that small changes of surface are now going on, but most astronomers are of the opinion that the appearance is due to the greatly different effects that light produces upon irregular objects when striking them at different angles.

Although, generally speaking, the same side of the Moon is always presented to us, in the course of a month we really see, mainly because of the form and inclination of its orbit, nine per cent more than half of its surface. In keeping its face constantly toward us, it rotates once in a month in relation to the Sun, and therefore its days are about thirty times as long as ours. Like all other planetary bodies its course is eliptical and not circular and being in consequence at different distances from the Earth at different times, it appears to our eyes to vary slightly in size.

The moon reflects about one-sixth of the light that it receives from the sun, but only a barely measurable part of the heat that it gets from that source. It is the main cause of our tides, and disturbs our electric currents to some extent, but, common belief nothwithstanding, it has no known influence on our weather. While pursuing its orbit it is attracted by so many other and larger bodies that in computing its longitude mathematicians are obliged to make as many as seventy allowances, and in calculating its latitude, half as many.

The Moon's relative nearness to the Earth can be realized by remembering that while light occupies more than eight minutes in coming to us from the Sun, it can reach us from our satellite in less than a second and a half; and its comparative importance as a heavenly body is illustrated by the fact that if we suppose the Sun to be a globe two feet in diameter and the Earth a small pea, the Moon can be represented by the head of an ordinary pin. —*Lewiston Journal.*

INSECT-EATING PLANTS.

Editor Amateur Naturalist:

I happen to have a little inside information in regard to the article entitled "Plants that Eat Meat" mentioned in the excellent communication of Mr. Addison Ellsworth in your November number and I may say that the author of the article in question made no claims for the diet of *Asclepias;* the editor wanted a thrilling headline and wrote it, whether it fitted or not.

As to *Asclepias* catching flies, bees, etc., there can scarcely be any question that it does so. This fly-catching habit, however, has not the same end in view that the similar habit in the sundew and pitcher plant has. These latter live in soils deficient in nitrogen and find a supply in the bodies of the insects they digest. It is certain that the genus *Asclepias* to which all our milkweeds belong does not catch bees and other insects by intention; nor make use of them when caught. In fact to catch an insect defeats the very end the flower has in view.

It may be explained that the milkweeds have their pollen assembled in little masses, just as many of the orchids do, and that these masses are attached to a sticky gland which clinging to the leg of an insect transports the pollen from one flower to another. Ordinarily the machinery works smoothly, but if an insect too small to drag the pollen mass from its pouch comes in contact with the gland, it is often held fast and may starve to death unless it frees itself by twisting its leg off.

A very similar insect trap, which is also accidental, is found among the dogbanes, is a near relative of the milkweed, catches insects without intending it. It all comes through the structure of the flower which is designed for certain insects and not for others. If the tenderfoot insect will get in, he must look out for himself. The dogbanes and the cruel plant catch insects by their probosces. The way to the nectar is plain enough but when the insect attempts to withdraw its tongue it may slip between the jaw-like projections close to the nectar and then the harder it pulls the tighter does its proboscis become wedged fast.

WILLARD N. CLUTE.

Joliet, Ill.

Notes and Gleanings.

The Chinese Ladybird Beetle.—This variety of Lady bird is the greatest enemy to scale insects of all of its kind. The orange groves of California were suffering great damage from the San Jose Scale. This scale was traced first to Japan, where it was first supposed to have originated, but finding it only on lately planted trees, the investigators traced on to the interior of China where it was found on trees brought down from the mountains. In both countries they found the ladybird in question. In color it is shining black, with two red spots, nearly identical in appearance with our common "twice stabbed" ladybug—*Chilocorus bivulnerus*, a well-known enemy of scale insects, but not of the San Jose Scale to any extent. The Chinese ladybird is classed as *Chilocorus similis*. It feeds freely on the San Jose, and may prove an important factor in controlling the pest. The entomologists of the Department of Agriculture of Washington have lately been trying accurately to determine some of the points with the regard to the appetite of the lately imported Chinese ladybird beetle for San Jose scales. In addition to those fastened in large cages that enclose whole trees covered with these scale, and also others infested with the "white beach" scale, they put three larvæ of the beetle in a small cage, and for three days observed and counted the larvæ of the scale that were eaten. In the three days the three ate 4,500 each, which is 1,500 per day to each insect. When timed by the watch one was noticed to eat from five to six per minute. This is test work, and inasmuch as the young larvæ of the beetles flourish on this diet, which they seem to prefer to all else, it is a very hopeful sign of what may be expected when there are insects enough to turn into some of the scale infested orchards. The appetite of our little friend seems to equal the ability of the San Jose Scale to multiply. The beetle are multiplying so fast in some of the big cages that they have eaten all the scale insects on the trees and are being taken out and put in new cages, where they will have more scale to feed upon, or sent away for experimental purposes. The life of one of these ladybird beetles is estimated by the entomologists at Washington to be from six months to a year, and as they are very active and eat scale of all sizes, especially the young ones, except during their dormant period, which is only in cold weather, even one beetle will devour an immense number of scale insects. At the rate of 1,540 per day, for only six months, it would require 270,000 to satisfy the appetite of a single beetle for that time.—*Journal of the Jamaica Agricultural Society.*

The Yak.—Yaks, which are the beasts of burden in Tibet, are very surefooted and a good one will carry a load of over 200 pounds safely along the steepest hillside. They can exist on the scantiest grass, but grain food suits them for a few days only. Eight miles a day is good average work. Tame yaks are white, black, gray and brown and all intermediate graduations of these colors. The wild yak is invariably black and in the early spring his winter coat almost sweeps the ground. At such times wild and tame are almost indistinguishable.

Mica Mining in India.—Mica mining in India is done by coolies, both men and women, whose wages average three annas (4 cents) a day for the men, and six pice (2 cents) for the women. The former act as miners, and the latter take place of trammers and pumps in a civilized mine, standing or sitting in double line on ladders and in the passages, and passing earthern pitchers full of and baskets containing excavated matter from one to another. In this way it may require as many as seventy women to remove the water from a mine not 35 feet in perpendicular depth, though of course the actual line is considerable longer. The shafts are usually built on an incline, and sometimes have a diameter of 15 to 20 feet; but most are just big enough to allow several pairs of miners to get in and wield their hammers in a cramped position. The tools used consist of a drill, a chisel, and a hammer, the drill and chisel being used alternately, and the miners working in pairs, one to hold and one to drive. As explosives are not used, it does not pay to carry the operation into the hard rock, except where it is very rich, and in this case the ancient fire-breaking method is employed. Some of the larger mines run to a depth of 100 feet, and a few even to 150 feet. In these cases small vertical ventilating shafts, about 2 feet in diameter, are put down to ventilate the inclines, and serve as means for raising the excavated material, for which purpose they are provided with small lifts, called lathes.—*Mineral Collecter.*

Greenland's Glaciers.—Nearly all the Greenland glaciers and tongues from the internal ice cap terminate in vertical faces from 100 to 1,000 feet high. The vertical faces reveal pronounced stratification on the basal ice, even earth materials in the bases carried by the ice being arranged in layers. Fine laminations were seen twelve or twenty to the inch. The layers are sometimes twisted and contorted and even "shoved" over each other. The glacier movement at the ice border is a foot per day to a foot per week.

The Treacherous Lioness.—"Lionesses are far more dangerous than lions," said an animal trainer. "Their tempers are more treacherous. They are more wily. If a lion is in a bad humor, he shows it. He growls and snarls and lashes his sides. You know what is in the wind and prepare accordingly. But a lioness in a bad humor is as affectionate as a girl. She brushes, purring, against your leg, and she minds you with the joyous alacrity of a good fox terrier. Then, as soon as your back is turned, whiz—a yellow streak shoots through the air, and you are on your back, and she is at your throat. With all the cat tribe it is the same. Whenever you hear of a trainer getting mauled or mangled, be sure it was a female, not a male cat that did the deed."

The Ouamiche.—U. S. Senator Albert Beveridge glowingly describes one of Maine's game fish as follows:—The ouamiche is a landlocked salmon, and there is nothing slow about him. He is a surprise party from start to finish. He resists capture, after being hooked, like a scaled tempest, and it is bewildering to watch his antics. He is an aqueous tactician. No fish on earth is gamer than he. He is like a bubble of water on a hot stove. He also acts like a wildcat. He flings himself horizontally some feet out of water: shakes himself as a terrier does a rat; stands on his tail, swims in a circle and executes various acrobatic feats in grand, varied and lofty tumblings. He dashes foward, sidewise, up and down; tugs line; slaps the leader with his tail in an effort to break the line, and does everything a fish can do. Often he succeeds in flinging or tearing the hook out of his tender mouth. He flashes his silvery sides, in three different places, simultaneously, like a submerged meteor; plunges and cavorts in a masterful, protesting manner, with sinuous, athletic, graceful methods, not infrequently leaping clean over the canoe; lashing the water into foam, before the landing net can secure him, and sometimes mocking the angler by a plunge into the depths, to be seen no more.

The Amateur Naturalist

......ISSUED MONTHLY.......

Subscription, 50 Cents per Year.   Single Copies, 5 Cents

ADVERTISING RATES ON APPLICATION.

————————EDITED AND PUBLISHED BY————————

CHARLES D. PENDELL,   -   -   ASHLAND, MAINE.

A HAIR pin and a safety pin were recently found amid the ruins of ancient Rome, both of bronze, and this has led a contemporary to remark that "all" of our modern inventions are but a duplication of arts born, used and lost ages ago. It would indeed be an assumption to claim that some of the highly civilized nations of antiquity were without any of the conveniences essential to modern civilized life but we think the assumption of the editor in question fully as great. Who for instance ever heard of a railroad from Jerusalem to Joppa in the days of Romulus or Cæsar? Aristotle never dreamed of sending a telegram, and surely Mark Antony and Cleopatra never held converse over a long distance 'phone, nor do we read of an electric trolley line running excursions from Babylon out to the old tower of Babel. The sickle did service in the ancient grain fields of Sicily and the ox patiently trod out the grain. Had Rome been lighted with the arc lamp it would not have been necessary for Nero to have set the city on fire to see its glorious illumination and the common incandescent or gas light would have furnished better light than Christains swathed in oiled cloths and impalled on stakes about his gardens. Safety pins and hair pins may have been used in Rome, but they were without the modern cooking stove, and brave as the Roman soldier was his short sword and spear would scarcely prevail against the modern mauser rifle. The condition of the ancient world continued practically unchanged for centuries and though after the "Dark Ages" there were beginnings of improvement it was really not until the dawn of the 18th and 19th centuries that the high civilization of to-day dawned. The year 1907 marks the centennial of the first steamboat and even 20 years after that event there were but 13 miles of railroad in all America.

SOME of us can remember the first telegraph and most of us perhaps can remember the first telephone which dates back about 30 years. The newest accomplishment is, if what is claimed for it is true, one of the greatest scientific wonders yet produced. We refer to the telegraphone. With one of these instruments attached to the telephone, your friend can talk with the 'phone at his end of the line and if you are absent, the message is recorded and on your return you simply take down the receiver, press the button and the conversation will be repeated. And further more a permanent record can be made of any conversation which can be repeated with the original sound and intonation of the voice at any future time or as many times as desired, thus making a telephone contract fully as permanent for evidence as a written one. If there is some public speaker or concert you wish to hear but cannot attend, simply get telephone connection and attach your telegraphone and in the quiet of your own home, listen to it all, while you rock the baby to sleep. This invention is based upon the accidental discovery that a piece of steel can be magnetized in spots, and the discovery like many others of accidental nature has been wrought out into this marvelous instrument which in another decade will be so common as to excite nore m wonder than does the telephone or telegraph now.

OUR offer of THE AMATEUR NATURALIST for three years for $1. has brought us quite a number of long time subscribers lately, and we will state that the offer still holds good. With this number Volume III. is completed and the offer is to furnish the three first volumes for one dollar is hereby withdrawn, except that for the present to all who may begin their subscription with Vol. IV. and wish the back numbers, we will supply them at that rate provided the order comes with their subscription—$1.50 in all.

In reply to inquiries concering an index we take this opportuninity to say that as yet none has been prepared but we anticipate doing so, and when completed, copies will be mailed to all subscribers.

Random Notes.

A year on the planet Neptune is a little longer than 166 earth years—it is 60,-000 days long.

The rotation of a waterspout at the surface of the sea has been estimated as 354 miles an hour, or nearly six miles an hour.

The sun's light is equal to 5,563 wax candles at one foot from the eye. It would take 800,000 full moons to equal cloudless sunshine.

A camel can easily carry a weight of 1,000 pounds on its back, about four times as much as a horse can carry. The camel begins work at the age of four and is useful for half a century. The horse, as a rule, is nearly played out at the age of 15.

Some of the wealthiest sportsmen of Vermont are now engaged in a movement to stock the coverts of Vermont with foreign game birds. Among the birds it is beleived can be introduced into the State are the daleypa, which is native to Norway: the capercailzie, which is found in the highlands of Scotland; black cock and ring-necked pheasants.

It is stated that, in the vast region known as Manitoba and the Northwest Territories there is a total absence of every kind of earthworm, yet the soil is amazingly fertile. The agency which has probably caused the absence of the worms is the praire fires which annualy sweep over enormous portions of the country, totally consuming the grass and converting it into a black ash. This would for months together completely deprive any worms of food and exterminate them.

Thomas A. Edison predicts that the next great advance in the utilization of electricity for power, light and heat, will be the erection of immense electric stations in coal mining regions where fuel is cheap and the cost of transportation from the mines almost nothing. The electric energy, he beleives, will be distrib-uted to industrial centers through wires, instead of carrying coal to distant cities to be converted into electricity there. Edison argues that it is absurd to trans-port the heavy and bulky solid instead of sending the unseen and weightless fluid or wave impulse to do the work for which the fuel is burned.

Up in Cape Breton Island, where there are a great number of collieries digging out coal from under the sea, the submarine area thus undermined now amounts to about sixteen ordinary farms of 160 acres each. The outer end of the hole is something over a mile from shore. Strange as it may seem, the workings have never been invaded by sea-water streams, although fresh-water streams have been encountered flowing out in the strata under the ocean bed. The thickness of the strata over the mines varies from 500 to 1,140 feet. About 5,250,000 tons have thus far been taken from these submarine workings, and there is as yet no indi-cation of failure of these beds.

There are six varieties of asbestos, each of which posesses qualities peculiar to itself. They may be classified as follows: Amianthus, in which the fibres are so exceedingly long, flexible and elastic that they may be woven into cloth. Com-mon asbestos, with the fibres much less flexible; it is heavier than the first va-riety, a dull green in color, sometimes pearly in lustre and oily to the touch. Mountain cork, light enough to float on water. Mountain leather, also very light, but thinner and more flexible than the last. Mountain paper or blue asbes-tos. Mountain wood, which in external appearance resembles dry wood. Nearly all varieties have more or less the appearance of fossilized wood. Asbestos has been found in nearly all parts of the globe.

Lightning Source UK Ltd.
Milton Keynes UK
UKOW07f0604200317

297047UK00009B/472/P